Idaho
Minerals

2nd Edition, Revised and Updated

Idaho Minerals

The Complete Reference and Guide to the Minerals of Idaho

with Special Chapters on
the Coeur d'Alene Mining District,
the Blackbird Mining District,
and the Sawtooth Mountains

2nd Edition, Revised and Updated

by Lanny R. Ream

Museum of North Idaho
PO Box 812
Coeur d'Alene, ID 83816-0812

Copyright © 2004 by Lanny R. Ream

Published by
Museum of North Idaho
PO Box 812
Coeur d'Alene, ID 83816-0812
208-664-3448
www.museumni.org

ISBN: 0-9723356-3-3

Book editing, design and production by Lanny R. Ream using InDesign with Times New Roman and Palatino fonts.

Cover photograph:
Plattnerite, 6.2 cm, Tamarack Mine, Shoshone County.
Photographs in this book are by Lanny R. Ream except where noted.

Printed in Hong Kong
By Mantec Production Co.

To those collectors who are active in the field and
make new information and specimens available to others.

Acknowledgements

A book of this magnitude can only be prepared with the assistance of many others. The first edition of Idaho Minerals was published in 1989. That edition, of which all the information and data are included in this second edition, was completed only with the use of information and data from many authors who have written on the many minerals, ore deposits and geology of Idaho. Their efforts and information are important to this edition as well.

Several individuals, mineral collectors and mineralogists, have provided information in this edition. These include Randy Becker, Gregory C. Ferdock, Norm Radford, Rudy Tschernich and Aaron Wieting. Randy Becker, who has been a friend and field partner for many years, has contributed much information during discussions in the field, including the noting of minerals new to some localities. Conversations with him have also contributed much to my learning and understanding of the mineralogy of the state.

Others have also contributed in a roundabout fashion, sometimes information originally gathered by another has reached me through one of the above. Their indirect assistance is acknowledged, and the efforts of the field collectors who have made discoveries of which the information reached me through my friends or from viewing mineral specimens in other collections, is greatly appreciated.

Other collectors of minerals have provided photographs or allowed the author to photograph their specimens. According to their wishes, individual owners of specimens are or are not acknowledged with the specimen photographs. The author would like to thank all those who contributed in various ways to the extensive collection of color photographs in these pages.

Preface

This reference, the second edition of Idaho Minerals, was written for the purpose of making the information on the mineralogy of Idaho available to all those who are curious about the natural world, study minerals or collect minerals. It is an on going project that will never be complete—new information will continue to be discovered and those who have knowledge that hasn't been published or otherwise passed on to others will become known to the author and others who will pass it on. The author investigates and studies the mineralogy of Idaho and will continue to do so, and expects to publish a third edition of this book.

Although the information in these pages can be useful as a guide to the mineral occurrences of the state for those who are interested in investigating them or collecting mineral specimens, no effort was made to record and explain complete information on ownership and accessibility of the land for each mineral occurrence. The reason being that this book was not prepared to be a field guidebook. Obtaining and maintaining ownership and access information is a time consuming process. Ownership often changes as does access, lands are sold, gates are installed or removed and access roads wash out or deteriorate. Access and ownership information has been included when it was available and believed to be accurate, but no effort was made to ensure this accuracy at the time of publication. It is the responsibility of the individual to determine ownership and right of access before entering any mineral location, mine or other land or property.

Information was obtained from many different sources. All the information that was in the first edition has been included in the second edition. This information has been corrected where needed and updated with new information where available. In addition, much new information has been learned by direct field investigation and laboratory analyses and identification of minerals, the viewing of specimens and by written and verbal communications with others. All entries have a reference of the source, be it a publication, or a listing that it was obtained by the author's personal knowledge as described in the preceding sentence. For the first edition, an extensive literature search provided much information. For the second edition, an extensive search for new publications was not done, this edition is primarily information obtained by the author through personal contact and investigations.

Being that this book is part of an ongoing investigation and study of the mineralogy of the state of Idaho, all comments and information on the minerals of the state are welcome. From various studies and comments, 39 new mineral listings, many for minerals new to the state, and dozens of new listings have been added to this edition over what was in the first edition.

Fig. 1 Map of the state of Idaho showing the counties and a few cities for reference.

Contents

Part 1

Locality Chapters

1

Coeur d'Alene Mining District
Shoshone County

History

The world's largest silver-producing mining district has also been one of the best sources of secondary lead minerals in spectacular specimens. The Coeur d'Alene Mining District, has been producing metals and minerals since its discovery in 1884. For a couple of years, production was low as the outcrops of ore were discovered and slowly put into production. Their discovery led to the production of fantastic specimens of secondary lead minerals, including anglesite, cerussite and pyromorphite, along with native silver and a few other minerals. Unfortunately, few specimens were saved, because interest was primarily in producing ore, and tons of specimens made the short trip to the crusher and smelters, and not to the shelves of mineral cabinets around the world.

The Coeur d'Alene Mining District, as it is now designated, includes an area that was composed of several smaller districts during the early years. When you read histories of the great mines of this area, you will see the names Burke District, Wardner District, Kellogg District, Pine Creek District, and more. These names are primarily long forgotten, along with most of the mines within their boundaries. The Coeur d'Alene District includes all of these and covers an area about 15 miles wide and 25 miles long, extending from Pine Creek, a few miles west of Kellogg, east to the Idaho-Montana border.

Discovery of the district began in 1884 when miners who had left the small gold district to the north (Murray District), in hopes of striking it rich elsewhere, discovered the outcrops of ore that became the Tiger Mine near Burke. That same year, the discoveries of the You-Like, Gold Hunter, Hecla, Polaris mines and several more were made, and in 1885, the deposits of the Bunker Hill, Sullivan, Last Chance and Sierra Nevada mines were made.

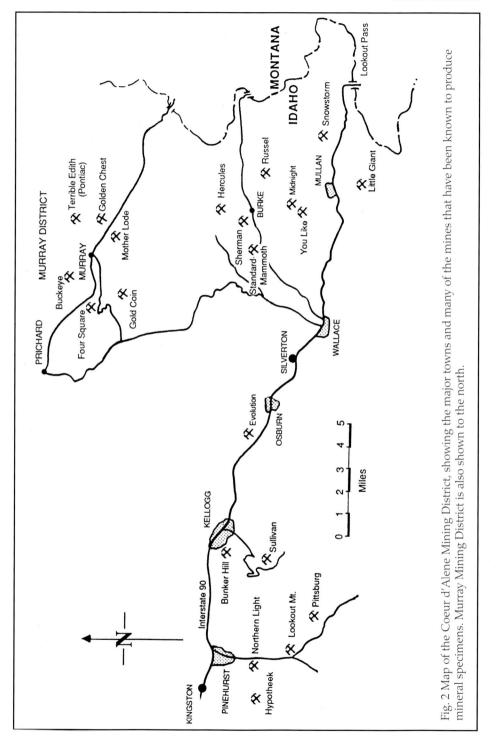

Fig. 2 Map of the Coeur d'Alene Mining District, showing the major towns and many of the mines that have been known to produce mineral specimens. Murray Mining District is also shown to the north.

Development of the district got off to a slow start due to the isolation of the area. Necessity overcame the difficulties and towns began to spring up near the mines including Mace, Gem and Burke in the narrow canyon near the Tiger, You-Like and other mines in that area, Wallace near the mouth of Burke Canyon, Mullan to the east, Osburn and Polaris near the Polaris Mine and Wardner and Kellogg in the area of the mines that would eventually become the Bunker Hill group.

Early production of the rich ores were shipped direct by wagon freight several miles to the Coeur d'Alene River at Cataldo where it was put on a steamer and hauled down the river and across Lake Coeur d'Alene only to be reloaded on another wagon to be hauled many more miles to the nearest railroad across the prairie at Rathdrum. Supplies came to the mines much the same way in reverse. As the years went by, roads were constructed, mills were built, and production from the mines increased.

For several decades the many small towns and mines that grew up, saw tumultuous times. There were fights, in and out of court over ownership of several of the mines, extensions of the veins, and major troubles between mine owners and labor unions. These led to several major gunfights between armed guards on both sides, and the dynamiting of the Frisco mill in 1892, and the Bunker Hill mill in 1899. During the worst times, martial law was declared, federal troops were brought in to restore order, Pinkerton Detectives were used at other times, and a particularly troublesome dispute eventually led to the murder of an ex-Governor of the state.

Through all these difficult times, the area grew and mines were developed, most of them only to be mined out by the 1930s. Fortunately, new deposits were discovered as others were worked out, and despite slow downs, and shut downs from labor troubles and low metals prices, the Coeur d'Alene Mining District has been in continuous production since its discovery.

Since 1884, the district has produced nearly $5,000,000,000 worth of metals, primarily silver, lead, zinc, gold and copper. Production figures for the district are staggering. For example, in 1890 the district (including the Murray gold district to the north) produced 1,499,663 ounces of silver, 8,000 ounces of gold and 27,500 tons of lead (value of $4,132,506). In 1920, the production was 6,639,000 ounces of silver, 9,000 ounces of gold, 128,367 tons of lead, 54 tons of copper and 10,966 tons of zinc (value $30,365,160). In 1950, production was 15,056,131 ounces of silver, 3,416 ounces of gold, 94,197 tons of lead, 1,895 tons of copper and 86,102 tons of zinc (value $64,555,947) (Reid, 1961). In 1984, production was 16,909,356 ounces of silver, 3,762 ounces of gold, 31,336 tons of lead, 3,986 tons of copper and 3,304 tons of zinc (value of $163,862,386) (information from the Coeur d'Alene Mining District Museum, Wallace).

Production from a single mine was often tremendous. In the 1950s, the Bunker Hill Mine was producing 1,750,000 to 2,200,000 ounces of silver, 26,000 to 35,000 tons of lead and 9,500 to 12,500 tons of zinc annually (McConnel, 1961). The Sunshine Mine, alone, has produced more silver than the famed Comstock lode and is still producing.

Metals production from the district has been down during the last twenty three years due to shutdowns because of low metal prices and increased mining costs. Even during these slow times, the Hecla, Coeur and Galena mines have remained in production or intermittent production, producing millions of ounces of silver and thousands of tons of lead and other metals. Recently, the Sunshine Mine has shut down (perhaps permanently), and the Bunker Hill Mine after being shut down continues with limited production.

These production figures may be impressive, but they have little meaning for the mineral collector. During the early years, production was from the oxide ores in the upper few hundred feet of the veins. These oxides contained thousands of large, spectacular crystals

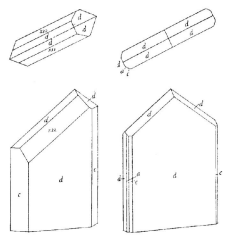

Fig. 3 Acanthite, distorted crystals, Coeur d'Alene District, Shoshone County; crystal drawings from Shannon (1926).

of interest to collectors. Most of the mines had an area underground, often near their portals, where specimens were put on display; spectacular groups and clusters of anglesite, cerussite, pyromorphite and silver graced these special places and the shelves of mining engineers and superintendents. Many miners had them at home sitting on their mantles, but few of these specimens actually made it to museums and the cabinets of interested collectors. Most of them went to the smelter, or from the miner's mantle to become a door stop, then end up tossed in the trash. Rarely, a fortunate collector today finds a good specimen at a neighborhood yard sale.

After about 1930, there was little production from the oxide ores; most of the mines had mined these out, and penetrated lower zones to produce from sulfide ores. Production statistics for most of the 1900s may be impressive, but with the exception of the production of fine specimens from the Bunker Hill Mine in 1980 and 1981, and a few short-term leases for specimen production at other mines, there has been little to speak of from the district since the 1930s. There is occasionally, minor production of pyromorphite or cerussite from one of the few old abandoned mines that still has some low-grade oxide ore remaining. Specimens of siderite, quartz and tetrahedrite are sometimes produced from the limited mining operations.

Geology

The geology of the Coeur d'Alene Mining District has been studied seemingly thousands of times by hundreds of geologists. Many features of the geology are simply explained yet there are many details that those who have tried to understand the mineralization cannot yet explain.

The district is primarily underlain by the Precambrian metasediments of the Belt supergroup; in this area these are the Prichard, Burke, Revett, St. Regis, Wallace and Striped Peak. They are fine-grained quartz-rich rocks that have undergone low grade metamorphism and now consist of sericitic phyllite, sericitic quartzite and some schistose quartzite and sericite schist.

Igneous rocks are restricted to two monzonite stocks of Cretaceous age and related monzonite dikes and a few dikes of lamprophyre and diabase. The major structures in the district are a large anticline and the Osburn fault with strike-slip movement of 17 miles. This fault runs down the valley presently occupied by Intestate 90, along which the cities, as well as most of the mines, are located. Other faults include the Placer Creek and Cate faults and an apparent undefined fault along which the two stocks are intruded, and which may be a major control of ore emplacement. Ore zones are offset by the strike-slip faults, and in most of the mines, local faulting and folding has greatly distorted bedding and ore zones.

The following description of the deposits is from Crowley et al (1982). "The major veins are clustered in two groups: one is centered around the towns of Burke and Mullan,

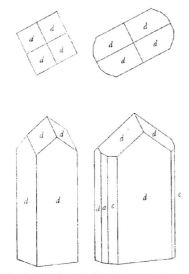

Fig. 4 Acanthite, left—elongated dodecahedral crystal, right—distorted crystal simulating orthorhombic symmetry, Coeur d'Alene District, Shoshone County; crystal drawings from Shannon (1926).

north of the Osburn fault; the other lies south of the Osburn fault and centers around Kellogg, but extends eastward almost to Wallace. The productive veins, with two minor exceptions, lie in belts of slight disturbance or shearing which have been designated as mineral belts. Reconstruction of the major anticline in the district, as it existed before movement on the Osburn, Placer Creek and Dobson Pass faults, brings the two groups of mineral belts together.

The district ore deposits are primarily replacement veins with simple mineralogy. Six periods of mineralization ranging from Precambrian to Tertiary in age are recognized. The main veins formed in stages, though generally not all stages are represented in any one vein. The silicate stages are the oldest and probably formed at the highest temperatures. During a succeeding carbonate stage, siderite and then ankerite were deposited. In some mines a small amount of barite was deposited, probably after the carbonates; in a few veins, barite is a moderately common mineral. Sulfide mineralization followed and some folding and faulting followed the deposition of minerals of particular stages. Sphalerite, tetrahedrite and galena, deposited in that order are present in almost all the productive veins but in widely varying proportions. Veins were formed as replacements with occasional open-space filling. Valuable sulfide minerals have directly replaced quartzose rock or pre-existing quartz or siderite bodies. Some ore sulfides have replaced silicates, carbonates and earlier sulfides."

Mineralogy

There are many minerals in the ores of the district, but those that have been of greatest interest to collectors are the few secondary lead minerals (anglesite, cerussite and pyromorphite) that have been found in large enough quantity that they received at least limited distribution to collectors outside of the area. Other minerals have produced only a few specimens that did not receive widespread distribution. Those minerals that have produced specimens of interest to collectors are described below; those minerals that are common and only occur in massive forms are not described.

Acanthite: In the Orr orebody of the Bunker Hill Mine, acanthite was rarely found as minute, brilliant, black, blade-shaped crystals on cerussite or in tiny vugs in earthy limonite (Figs. 3, 4) (Radford and Crowley, 1981).

In other mines, it is generally massive and finely granular. One specimen, from an undesignated mine, consisted of native silver in curved columns and wires on crystalline acanthite which formed spongy masses of small crystals (Shannon, 1926).

Anglesite: Small crystals of anglesite were rare at the Hercules Mine in Burke Canyon. The crystals were small, tabular, transparent, and up to 2 cm in length on massive anglesite. Some were covered with wire silver, and others were collected as groups of excellent crystals (Shannon, 1926).

The Hypotheek Mine, south of Kingston, has produced crystals over 4 cm in length.

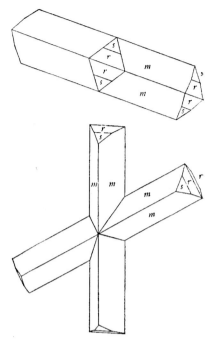

Fig. 5 Arsenopyrite, Hypotheek Mine, Shoshone County; crystal drawings from Shannon (1926).

The mine produced primarily galena and cerussite ore. Anglesite crystals to 9 mm long were abundant in cavities in galena. Some of the crystals were doubly terminated, and most were of a complex habit (Photo. 1). Lead and copper minerals were associated including cerussite, malachite, covellite and bindheimite (massicot?). Shannon (1926) reported that the anglesites were the best found in the U.S.

Prismatic flattened crystals elongated on the b axis, or flattened crystals were found in cavities in galena at the Last Chance Mine. These were up to 5 cm in length and a smoky gray to black color (Photo. 2). Tabular crystals and elongated crystals to about 9 mm long were found in the Tyler Mine (Photo. 3). They occurred in cavities in galena and had a simple habit. Commonly, the crystals were coated with limonite on the prism and pinacoid faces, but the domes were clear (Shannon, 1926).

Anglesite displaying several habits and several colors, including colorless, white, yellowish and smoky (nearly black) were collected in the Bunker Hill Mine from 1979 until it was closed in 1981. Miners, working in upper stopes in the Orr orebody that had not been mined for several decades, recovered numerous specimens. Individual crystals to at least 5 cm were recovered and many excellent matrix specimens were brought out. Most crystals are blocky, but some were tabular (Photos. 4, 5) (Radford and Crowley, 1981; personal).

Ankerite: The carbonate minerals in the ore deposits of the Coeur d'Alene Mining District include ankerite, siderite, dolomite and calcite. Ankerite is generally a minor constituent except in the eastern end of the district (east of Wallace), where it is the most abundant carbonate in many of the mines. Crystals are uncommon; most of the ankerite is a coarsely crystalline, massive vein filling. Small crystals do occur in cavities in some of the veins; most are acute rhombohedrons, sometimes curved. They are nearly white or light brown when fresh, but turn dark brown on exposure (Shannon, 1926).

Arsenopyrite: This mineral is uncommon in the district, but has been found in several of them. In the Standard-Mammoth Mine near Mace, small crystals were found in slaty sericitic rock next to small quartz veins in a stope above the 2,000 foot level. Above Burke, iron-gray crystals were found in slaty rock inclusions in the stibnite-bearing quartz veins of the Stanley antimony mine in Gorge Gulch. Crystals were also reported from the Evolution Mine near Osburn, and in the Pearson, Liberal King and Casey mines and the Corby prospect to the west on Pine Creek. Also on Pine Creek, in the Hypotheek Mine, arsenopyrite occurred as long prismatic crystals with pyrite, chalcopyrite and tetrahedrite (Fig. 5). These were in a carbonate gangue and could be freed by dissolving the carbonate with acid. The crystals displayed twinning, generally with an "X" shape (Shannon, 1926).

Azurite: Secondary copper minerals were not common. In the Caledonia Mine, azurite formed thin crusts and stains, and occasionally, crusts of drusy crystals and some tabular crystals to 2 mm on quartzite. The Standard-Mammoth and the Snowstorm mines contained some azurite as stains and thin coatings (Shannon, 1926; personal).

Barite: Tiny crystals of barite occur in the Little Giant Mine associated with cerussite and pyromorphite (Photos. 117, 118). The tiny crystals are thin tabular and less than 2 mm across (personal).

Bindheimite: Shannon (1926) reports that this mineral was fairly common in many mines of the district, determining that the mineral was bindheimite and not massicot based on the presence of antimony in specimens that were tested with the blowpipe. Radford, et al (1981) reports that most of this was probably massicot, as indicated by recent studies of material from the workings of the Bunker Hill Mine group. Shannon reports bindheimite from the Mammoth, Last Chance, Tyler, Caledonia, Northern Light, Lookout Mountain, Carbonate and Hypotheek mines. Generally bindheimite (and/or massicot) forms yellow, ocherous coatings and masses with secondary lead minerals. At the Caledonia Mine it formed pseudomorphs of tetrahedrite, and at the Northern Light, it formed in cavities in masses of cerussite. It had an acicular habit and was probably pseudomorphous after a sulfide, probably stibnite.

Boulangerite: In the Bunker Hill Mine, boulangerite was found in the Tony sphalerite orebody below the 18 level. Occasionally, small vugs in quartz contained bright black needles, but generally, the boulangerite consisted of films and stringers (Radford and Crowley, 1981). Boulangerite needles filled vugs in quartz in the Gold Hunter Mine, and the needles often impaled rhombic crystals of siderite (Shannon, 1926). In recent years, small amounts of boulangerite have been found in the Gold Hunter vein, now part of the Hecla Mine. Fine thumbnail to miniature size specimens were also found in the Sunshine Mine (personal).

Bournonite: Bournonite was sometimes found in the 5 level of the West Reed area of the Bunker Hill Mine as discrete blebs to 5 cm across. Some minute cogwheel crystals were found in 1975 (Radford and Crowley, 1981).

Brochantite: This mineral was apparently not common in the district. Tom McBride and Art Cooper collected a fine specimen in 1939 from the Smiley lease of the b workings of the Bunker Hill Mine. This specimen, 7.5 cm by 2 cm by 1 cm, has been loaned by the local mineral group to the Kellogg Mining Museum (Radford and Crowley, 1981; personal).

Calcite: Milky scalenohedral crystals to 5 cm were found in the Newgard orebody of the Bunker Hill Mine in an open fissure. Calcite is moderately common in this and the Quill orebodies where it sometimes formed white crystals with a complex rhombic habit, to about 1 cm across, associated with tiny pyrite crystals (Photo. 6) (Radford and Crowley, 1981).

Similar crystals were found in other mines of the district including the Hecla Mine. In the Standard-Mammoth Mine, translucent colorless crystals with the same habit were found in an open fissure on the 2,000 level. Crystals of the same habit were also found in the 800 level of the Hercules Mine, but they had a greenish colored interior and a brownish colored opaque outer layer which was coated with pyrolusite. Drusy coatings were also found in open fractures in the Lombardy Mine on Italian Gulch near Kellogg (Shannon, 1926).

Caledonite: Caledonite was tentatively identified as the pale green coatings occurring with linarite and leadhillite in the Caledonia Mine. It formed blue-green friable masses of tabular microscopic crystals with linarite in the Lookout Mountain Mine (Shannon, 1926). In 1964, Art Cooper found well-formed crystals of caledonite and linarite in the Orr orebody of the Bunker Hill Mine. A few specimens had both minerals on the same specimen (Radford and Crowley, 1981).

Cerussite: Cerussite has been an important ore mineral in many of the mines of the Coeur d'Alene District. Most of it occurs as sand cerussite or other massive forms. Azurite, malachite, linarite, plattnerite, native silver, pyromorphite and anglesite are associated. High quality crystals lining cavities have been found in several mines. These occurrences were in the upper workings which were mostly mined out in the early part of the century. Some specimens of high quality crystals have been produced in recent years from a few of these old workings. Shannon (1926) reported that this district probably had produced the most and best quality cerussite specimens to that time of any place in the world.

Excellent specimens of reticulated crystals, columnar masses, long-fibrous aggregates, honeycomb-like masses of reticulated plates and small crystals of several habits were common. Several mines produced these, including the Bunker Hill and Sullivan, Stemwinder, Tyler, Caledonia, Sierra Nevada, Tiger, Poorman, Hercules (Photo. 11), Morning, You Like and Mammoth. By the 1930s, most of these mines had mined out the surface oxidized ores and crystal production stopped, but some low grade oxidized material remains in a few of the mines.

Most ore production from the district since then has been from deeper unoxidized zones. These ores are of massive argentiferous tetrahedrite and galena, so there are rarely any crystals to be found. Only a few of those mines named are still operating, but occasionally a miner manages to get into the old surface workings and collect a few specimens. These generally are not of the high quality of the early years. The Bunker Hill Mine has extensive upper workings in these oxidized zones. Most of the areas have been mined out, but there are still some crystal-bearing levels. In 1979 to 1982, many fine quality specimens of cerussite, native silver, pyromorphite and anglesite were produced from the Orr orebody on the 9 and 11 levels. During this time, cerussite of many habits, including clear tabular crystals, elongated, twinned, white crystals up to 8 cm long, and V-shaped and reticulated twins, were produced (Photo. 7-10). Some of the cerussite specimens have a light yellow fluorescence under ultra violet light (Radford and Crowley, 1981).

The Sitting Bull Mine, in the northern part of the district has produced some small cerussite crystals. These reticulated crystals on soft gossan have been up to about 1 cm in length. Few good specimens have been produced, most of the crystals are loosely attached to the matrix and easily fall off (Photo. 12).

Crystal production during the early mining period included some of the following finds. The Sierra Nevada Mine in Deadwood Gulch produced some excellent crystals of butterfly twin cerussite. These were colorless and up to 7.5 cm across. Aggregates of tabular twinned crystals were produced from the Mammoth Mine at Mace. Associated minerals included plattnerite and pyromorphite. Some large plates of reticulated twinned crystals were found. Untwinned and twinned crystals occurred in the Last Chance Mine. These were generally in cavities in galena and were mostly colorless or gray.

The Tyler Mine contained cerussite as heavy columnar masses of white material embedded in ocherous impure manganese oxide, reticulated masses of platy crystals, fibrous crystals and crystals with dendritic wires of native silver. A few specimens of six-rayed penetration twins were found. Other mines in the Deadwood Gulch-Wardner area, including the Bunker Hill, Sullivan and Stemwinder produced similar specimens.

The Hypotheek Mine in French Gulch contained an orebody that was oxidized to considerable depth (about 600 feet) and produced excellent specimens of anglesite and cerussite. The cerussite varied from colorless to pink, gray and black. The most common cerussite crystals were globular white masses resembling flattened grapes. They were unlike any other specimens from the district.

Other mines in the Pine Creek-French Gulch area including the Chief, Carbonate,

Northern Light and Lookout Mountain, produced cerussite crystals. The Lookout Mountain Mine produced excellent specimens associated with linarite, leadhillite, caledonite, bindheimite (massicot?) and pyromorphite. The cerussite crystals were up to 5 cm across and colorless, amber, gray and black in color. Several crystal habits were common including prismatic, rayed twins, highly modified crystals and twinned prismatic crystals (Shannon, 1926).

Cervantite: This mineral formed bright yellow ocherous coatings on stibnite in the Coeur d'Alene Mine on Pine Creek and in the Stanley antimony mine in Gorge Gulch where it was associated with stibiconite (Shannon, 1926).

Chalcopyrite: Chalcopyrite is uncommon in the mines of the Coeur d'Alene District, and rare as crystals. A few have been found in the Galena Mine near Wallace (Photo. 13) (personal). It was also reported from the Standard-Mammoth Mine (Shannon, 1926).

Chalcostibite: Gray crystals of chalcostibite were found in the Standard-Mammoth Mine in cavities in the lower levels. Crystals, up to 1 cm across, were rhombic, but highly fractured. Chalcopyrite was associated (Shannon, 1926).

Chrysocolla: The Snowstorm Mine, east of Mullan, is the only mine in the district which contained a notable quantity of chrysocolla, and it was the most important mineral in the oxidized ores of this mine, which was principally a copper producer. It generally formed crusts and seams of white, greenish blue and blue color (Shannon, 1926).

Copper: Copper was locally common, but not found in most of the district. In the Caledonia workings of the Bunker Hill Mine, it was abundant in the oxidized ores. The copper occurred as dendritic moss-like forms embedded in spongy limonite or on cerussite. In the Boyle stope of the Caledonia Mine, nugget-like masses were found intimately mixed with native silver, and in the 700 foot level, it formed crystalline wires with a thin outer coating of silver. Similar wire-like specimens were found in the Tyler Mine (Radford and Crowley, 1981; Shannon, 1926).

At the Snowstorm Mine, east of Mullan, small amounts of copper were found with silver, malachite and bornite; the copper formed small grains and thin coatings. Specimens with crystallized copper were found in the Iron Mask Mine (Shannon, 1926).

Covellite: Oxidized ore above the first level of the Last Chance workings of the Bunker Hill Mine contained streaks of soft, black, sooty covellite. It was indigo in color on the face of freshly broken lumps. In the Caledonia Mine, covellite was argentiferous and appeared to be replacing galena; it contained masses of pyrite and anglesite. Some masses of galena were encrusted with layers of covellite 2 to 10 cm thick (Radford, 1981; Shannon, 1926).

Cuprite: Cuprite occurred in several forms in the Caledonia Mine. Oxidized tetrahedrite in porous quartzite, was surrounded by concentric rings of cuprite, azurite, malachite and chrysocolla. Cavities in spongy cuprite contained grains and filiform wires of native copper. Octahedral crystals of cuprite to 6 mm across, mostly distorted and flattened, deep red in color, occurred in cracks in cellular tetrahedrite. Similar crystals were found in spongy limonite on the 500 foot level (Radford and Crowley, 1981).

Ferro-anthophyllite: Masses of fibers of ferro-anthophyllite occur in the Tamarack and Custer mines in Ninemile Creek, north of Wallace. The fibers are up to 6 cm in length and have a grayish green color. Galena is associated in a quartz vein (Shannon, 1926).

Galena: Although many of the mines of the Coeur d'Alene District have been some of the world's biggest producers of galena, few fine crystal specimens have been found. Much of the galena contains silver, and veins of galena have been found up to 40 feet wide (Hercules Mine). Crystals of galena have been rare and reports of good quality specimens have been essentially unrecorded.

Goethite: Botryoidal goethite is common in the oxidized ores of most of the mines of

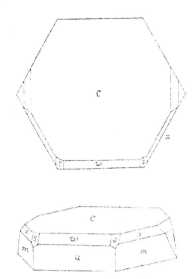

Fig. 6 Leadhillite, Lookout Mtn. Mine, Shoshone County; crystal drawings from Shannon (1926).

the district. It formed fine specimens in a prospect in the basin at the head of the east fork of Milo Creek above Wardner and prospects on Kellogg Peak (Shannon, 1926). It occurs as coatings and small stalactitic masses in a few oxidized zones of country rock along the road west of the Little Giant Mine south of Mullan. Lustrous, black botryoidal masses have also been found along Placer Creek (Photo. 191) (personal).

Brown stalactites of goethite, to several centimeters, have been found in the Bunker Hill Mine on the 11 level, Orr orebody (personal).

Goethite pseudomorphs of pyrite occur in siltite on Hord Gulch south of Wallace. The author found specimens of crystals up to 2 cm across in a freshly bulldozed section of a road at this locality in 1972 (Photo. 192).

Gold: Although native gold was not found in any quantity in the Coeur d'Alene District, it was reported at the Stanley Mine in Gorge Gulch where it formed thin, frost-like films on cracks in stibnite with secondary antimony minerals (Shannon, 1926).

Gypsum: Gypsum forms small, translucent to transparent colorless crystals in the Bunker Hill Mine. Specimens were found in the Barr vein on the 15 level in 1981. These consisted of transparent, elongated crystals on brown iron oxide-coated pieces of breccia. Other specimens from the Bunker Hill Mine collected in 1980 consisted of elongated crystals in sprays and parallel groups. Individual crystals were colorless or white and up to about 3 cm in length (Photo. 15) (personal).

Hemimorphite: The Bunker Hill Mine produced some specimens of hemimorphite in 1972. They were small, white crystal spherulites that were connected together by crystalline hemimorphite and were found in the Newgard orebody above the 9 level. These specimens occurred with milky calcite in a narrow fissure cross-cutting white metasandstone.

Similar spherulites were collected in 1979 above the 11 level of the Quill orebody of the same mine (Photo. 14). These were radiating crystal groups and were moderately abundant in an open fissure along the footwall of a fault. Individual spherules were up to 6 mm in diameter. The white crystals were on brown sphalerite, but hemimorphite was more common on earthy green chlorite overlaying a film of bornite. Crystal groups are mostly thumbnail in size, but were collected up to 7.5 x 10 cm. One specimen had pyromorphite associated with the hemimorphite (Radford and Crowley, 1981).

Hydrocerussite: This mineral was tentatively identified in 1950 in the Orr orebody on the 11 level of the Bunker Hill Mine, and again in 1961 in a different stope in the same orebody. It occurred as a white mineral with silver. In the 1970s, hydrocerussite was identified as the mineral making up the core and base portions of elongated, tapering, rounded crystals of cerussite. It appeared that these were crystals of hydrocerussite that were partially altered to cerussite (Radford and Crowley, 1981).

Jamesonite: Black, lustrous, bladed masses of jamesonite were found in the Coeur Mine in 1985, but specimens have been scarce. Acicular crystals of jamesonite have been projecting into cavities in quartz in the Sunshine Mine. Individual crystals were up to about

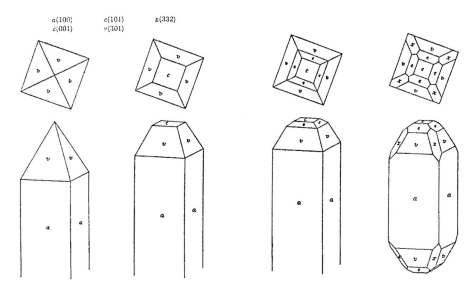

Fig. 7 Plattnerite, You Like Mine, Shoshone County, crystal drawings from Shannon (1926).

1.5 cm in length, and were in "nests" with quartz crystals (Photo. 16) (personal).

Kermesite: Thin coatings of kermesite, with a deep red to brownish red color, occur on cracks in stibnite at the Stanley Mine and may have had the same habit at other antimony occurrences in the district (Shannon, 1926).

Leadhillite: This mineral was collected with cerussite, linarite and possibly caledonite from the Caledonia Mine, as small irregular masses with a greenish to brownish white color. Leadhillite crystals with a pseudohexagonal habit, coated with or replaced by cerussite were found in the Lookout Mountain Mine (Fig. 6). Cerussite, chrysocolla, linarite and caledonite were associated (Shannon, 1926).

Linarite: Linarite and caledonite were found in the Orr orebody of the Bunker Hill Mine in 1964. It occurred in the Caledonia mine with caledonite and leadhillite. These were rosettes up to 1 cm in diameter, of flat bladed crystals with a bright blue color. Linarite was also reported from the Sierra Nevada Mine (Shannon, 1926). Tiny to small elongated crystals of linarite were also found at the Sherman Mine (Photo. 23) (personal).

Massicot: The Last Chance, Caledonia and Bunker Hill ores contain massicot and some bindheimite. Most of the massicot occurs as an earthy, bright yellow coating, primarily on cerussite. The color of the mineral dulls when specimens are brought to the surface, and the mineral is loose and often washes off of specimens (Radford and Crowley, 1981; personal).

Penfieldite: This mineral has been reported as tiny white crystals in the Little Giant Mine. These were found in the back of the adit above the decline shaft. Green pyromorphite crystals and barite were associated (personal).

Plattnerite: The You Like Mine produced some excellent examples of plattnerite in its early days in the late 1800s. These were rounded nodules and botryoidal masses and came from the near-surface workings in the oxide ores. The outsides of the plattnerite nodules were often reddish brown and the interiors were iron-black. They were reported up to 200 pounds in weight, with several up to about 10 x 12 x 20 cm across. Tiny cavities contained minute plattnerite crystals (Fig. 7), and a few crystals of tiny, white, prismatic pyromorphite were associated in some cavities (Shannon, 1926). Similar masses of plattnerite up to about 100 pounds were found in the Mammoth Mine. Botryoidal masses were found in the Hercules Mine (Shannon, 1926).

In 1915, plattnerite was collected in the No. 1 tunnel of the Last Chance Mine, most specimens were recovered from the sorting belt. Similar specimens were found in the Bunker Hill open cut. The Hall lease of the upper Caledonia workings produced some specimens in the 1930s. These were spherical masses of plattnerite with a brown coating of limonite. Spherical masses of plattnerite were also found in the 9 level, Deadwood-Jersey stope (source of fine pyromorphites) of the Bunker Hill Mine. Plattnerite nodules were found in other mines including the Tamarack Mine near Burke (Photo. 20) and the You Like lode of the Morning Mine near Mullan where crystals were also found (Fig. 7). Throughout the district, the rounded masses and nodules of plattnerite had the appearance of iron oxides, and miners called these "heavy iron" (Radford and Crowley, 1981).

Proustite: Flattened and distorted crystals and thin films of proustite were found in the Polaris and Big Creek mines on Big Creek. It was found in fractures in the wall rock (Shannon, 1926).

Pyrargyrite: This mineral was not common in the district, but relatively common as films and minute crystals in the "J" orebody of the Bunker Hill Mine. In 1979, several crystals to 2 mm were collected (Radford and Crowley, 1981). It was reported as thin films coating joints in the 2,000 foot level of the Standard-Mammoth Mine at Mace (Shannon, 1926).

Pyrite: Pyrite is common in many of the ores of the district, but only sparingly as euhedral crystals. In 1980-1981, tiny crystals were found in the Quill orebody of the Bunker Hill Mine with calcite (personal). In the Highland Surprise Mine on Highland Creek south of Pinehurst in the western end of the district, it formed brilliant druses of highly modified minute crystals in cavities in quartz. A few specimens have been found on the dump in recent years (personal). Pyritohedrons to 2 cm were found in sericitic shale, in the Yankee Boy Mine on Big Creek. In the Greenhill-Cleveland Mine at Mace and the Gold Hunter Mine at Mullan, spherical pyrite with an internally radiating structure were found (Shannon, 1926).

Pyrolusite: Lower levels of the Bunker Hill Mine produced steel-gray rosettes of pyrolusite in a rusty brecciated quartz vein. In the Hercules Mine, it formed mossy masses of minute crystals on calcite crystals in cracks in quartzite on the 800 level (Shannon, 1926).

Pyromorphite: The Coeur d'Alene District has produced world class specimens of pyromorphite from several mines. Shannon (1926) said that some of these were equal to those from any other locality in the world. The colors of pyromorphite from the district includes shades of green, colorless, pink, white, gray, orange, yellow and brown. It generally forms drusy crusts of small crystals coating rock fragments, but crystals up to about 3 cm have been found. Most of the crystals only showed the unit prism and basal pinacoid, but the faces of the unit pyramid were common. In some specimens, the terminations formed a bundle of fibers. Excellent groups and aggregates of crystals were found. Some of the crystals were barrel-shaped and some of the larger crystals were hollow (hoppered or cavernous).

Generally it is a solitary mineral, but a few specimens have been found with cerussite and, rarely, minute crystals of wulfenite. Some of the upper oxidized workings of the mines contained extensive oxidized areas with pyromorphite crystals which produced excellent specimens, both on matrix and groups off matrix.

Some of the better finds were at the Hercules Mine at Burke. Some of these were up to

3 cm in length and 1 cm in diameter often with cavernous terminations (Photo. 28). The last reported discovery of pyromorphite in the Hercules Mine was in 1966, including crystals up to 1.7 cm in length and 7 mm in diameter. Cerussite was collected from the same cavity, and some specimens have both minerals (Crowley and Radford, 1982).

At the Sherman Mine, on the south side of Tiger Peak near the Hercules, pyromorphite was produced from the 1500 and 1700 levels and the 1730 raise (Photo. 29). Crystals were yellowish olive-green to light yellow-green and, rarely, a wax-like greenish yellow color. Some crystals were barrel-shaped. Specimens from some pockets were floaters consisting of groups of crystals, with individual crystals up to about 1.2 cm long. The matrix for most specimens from this mine is a red to blackish brown, hard to crumbly limonitic material, with or without quartz fragments. The last production from the Sherman Mine was in 1973. It ended when a minor rock fall injured two experienced lessee-collectors, requiring their evacuation to the hospital. Shortly after that, a major vuggy zone collapsed, and the mine is now inaccessible. Tiny reddish orange crystals of wulfenite, up to about 1 mm across, rarely occurred on the pyromorphite from the Sherman Mine (Crowley and Radford, 1982; personal).

The Russell Mine is south of the Sherman Mine on the other side of the canyon, on the north-facing slope between Sawmill Gulch and O'Neill Gulch. In the 1960s and 1970s, a collector-miner worked this mine for pyromorphite and silver ore. The pyromorphite has a bright olive-yellow-green color, similar to, but somewhat lighter than that of the Sherman Mine. They are also longer than those from the Sherman, often up to 1.2 cm, with a hollow or cup-shaped termination. The matrix is a rusty, oxidized, brecciated quartzite held together by mud, that falls apart when wet (Crowley and Radford, 1982).

Some very fine specimens were collected in the Standard-Mammoth Mine at Mace. It occurred in several of the extensive upper workings of this mine. The Blackbear Mine produced pyromorphite as drusy coatings and massive green pieces.

Pyromorphite crystals were found in the Midnight Mine which was the development on the upper part of the Star vein (Photo. 30). Crystals were a light green or grayish green color. They were often cavernous, tapered and displayed multiple terminations where the crystals separated into numerous smaller parallel crystals, nearly fibrous. They were found on iron oxides and were covered with a thin brown oxide coating (personal).

Pyromorphite is common in the Little Giant prospect on Silver Creek, south of Mullan. Crystals are gray, gray-green and green in color. Most of them are under 1 cm in length, but have been found up to 2 cm. Microscopic crystals occur in many colors (Photos. 31, 32) (Shannon, 1926; personal).

The Little Giant Mine is part of the Atlas Mine properties and is in Sec. 2, T. 47 N., R. 5 E. Gray, grayish green and rarely green pyromorphite occurs in a vein with barite, and in a fractured zone alongside the vein in one portion of the mine. Most crystals are under 1 cm in length and 2 mm in diameter, but a few are larger. Cerussite forms acicular crystals to about 1 cm in length in parts of the vein; penfieldite has been reported in the vein above the decline shaft. A few gemmy bright green microcrystals of pyromorphite have been found at this spot too, as well as elsewhere on white barite in the vein. The mine has been heavily collected in recent years and presently is difficult and dangerous. There is a bad zone of loose rock in the back above the best crystal area at the fracture zone (personal).

Plattnerite was associated with pyromorphite in the You Like Mine, which was developed as part of the Morning Mine. The crystals were up to 1 cm long, white or gray in color and some were stained brown by coatings of plattnerite.

Pyromorphite occurs in the surface working of the Evolution prospect near Osburn. It forms crystals in ocherous limonite, which are unusual because they are colorless and tabular, or stout pale green minute prisms on the hanging wall.

Cup-shaped crystals were found in the Sandow tunnel where it crosses the Caledonia vein. Good specimens were also reported in the Omaha prospect which became part of the Caledonia Mine. Green and pink crystals were found in the Caledonia Mine. The pink crystals were found on the 900 level where they form crusts of minute crystals. The color ranges from colorless, to pink to grayish violet. Most of them are minute but they reached lengths of 1.5 cm. These mines are all part of the Bunker Hill Mine group, and may have labels with that name or the older name of Bunker Hill and Sullivan Mine.

Pyromorphite has been found in the outcrop of the Northern Light Mine south of Pinehurst. Specimens were found in the Lookout Mountain Mine east of the forks of Pine Creek, south of Pinehurst. The mine is located high on the canyon side above the creek. Colorless pyromorphite was found on the outcrop and green prismatic crystals were found underground.

Excellent specimens were found in the Sierra Nevada and Senator-Stewart mines on Deadwood Gulch. Pyromorphite was reported in the Quaker tunnel, but not in the primary workings of the Bunker Hill Mine (Shannon, 1926).

The dumps of the Senator-Stewart mines, including the Omaha tunnel, contained small crystals of yellowish green to green pyromorphite; most crystals are less than 5 mm in length (Photo. 33). These workings were part of the Bunker Hill property. The dumps of the Omaha tunnel and other Senator Stewart workings have been hauled off and the site rehabilitated as part of the Superfund cleanup of the Bunker Hill Mine site. For the mineral potential, it is too bad this was done; the small crystals on these dumps are now lost to mineralogy and mineral collectors (personal).

In late 1980 to early 1982, just before the Bunker Hill Mine was closed, some excellent specimens of pyromorphite were recovered from the 9 and 11 levels (Photo. 18,19, 21-27, 35). Excellent specimens of gray, brown, yellow, orange to red and bright green crystals were collected from various cavities. The gray to brown crystals were generally long prismatic, brilliant, and up to at least 2 cm in length. The green crystals were of several shades from a yellowish green to bright green. These were found as clusters of large size with individual crystals being as much as 2 cm in length. Fortunately a large quantity of these was recovered. The orangish colored specimens occurred as brilliant botryoidal-like groups formed by crusts of numerous small crystals.

Most of the following information is from Crowley (1982) and personal discussions with Norm Radford. Much of the credit for these discoveries can be given to Norm Radford, Senior Mine Geologist at the Bunker Hill Mine at the time, who recognized the economic potential that remained in these upper workings and recommended them for renewed mining, and to his successful convincing of mine managers, and directors of Gulf Resources Inc. (who owned the mine) that specimen recovery would be a worthwhile venture. Also to his skill in training the miners in the stopes in careful and successful mineral collecting techniques. Congratulations also should go to the Bunker Hill Company and Gulf Resources for promoting the collection and preservation of specimens.

These discoveries began in mid-December 1980 on the 9 level in the Deadwood-Jersey vein, 090-23-25 stope, when a series of pockets to 10 by 16 inches were opened. Specimens in these pockets consisted of arsenian pyromorphite in botryoidal masses and plates that were yellow, yellow-orange and deep orange colors. Crystalline groups and drusy coatings on matrix and gray to cream botryoidal pyromorphite were also collected. Crystals were mostly around 6 mm long, but were up to 1.2 cm in length.

As mining progressed, larger cavities were encountered. In mid-January 1981, specimen quality had improved. Exceptional specimens with yellow to yellowish lime-green crystals were being recovered. Crystals were stout prisms terminated by the pinacoid, barrel-shaped crystals and prismatic crystals terminated by a pyramid. Specimens up to 15 x 25 cm coated with crystals from 1 to 2.5 cm in length were recovered. As mining continued upwards, the green color diminished, and the orange arsenian pyromorphite became prominent. By the end of January, it looked like the pyromorphite zone had pinched out.

It was at this same time, that fine cerussite specimens were being produced from the nearby 090-23-21 stope. A few cavities of pyromorphite were also discovered in this stope. Specimens with crystals up to about 8 mm were recovered from cavities up to about 1 meter in length and 15 to 20 cm across. The pyromorphite was a light lime-green color.

By mid-June 1981 minor amounts of pyromorphite was found in the 090-23-25 stope, and some fine cerussite was recovered from the 090-23-21 stope.

Then in early October 1981, a large pyromorphite vug was encountered in the 090-23-25 stope. This cavity was large enough to crawl into and yielded the best of the arsenian pyromorphite yet found, ranging from brownish to multi-color yellows and oranges. Individual grape-like botryoids were up to 2.5 cm across and formed masses up to 46 x 60 cm. Many hundreds of specimens were recovered from this cavity. A few weeks later, another pocket was discovered. From this, specimens of the campylite form of pyromorphite, with a yellow, orange and reddish orange color were collected, and as at the previous pocket, hundreds of fine quality specimens were collected.

The following is from Crowley (1982):

"A week later the upper end of this vug was penetrated and a truly astounding series of pockets opened up. These pockets were lined in part with vitreous, bright, yellow-green, orangish yellow-green to yellowish olive crystals. Individual crystals to nearly 2.5 cm long are common. Composite crystals made up of side-by-side pyromorphite forming crude hexagonal prisms are up to 5 cm long and 2.5 cm in diameter. Several plates up to 35 cm in diameter were found, as well as a multitude of smaller specimens. This series of pockets continued upward, and during the week of November 30 to December 4, 1981, they were again encountered during mining. Crystals this time were slightly smaller and of a slightly darker yellowish lime-green.

Shortly after this find of magnificent crystals, locked steel doors were installed to prevent miners from collecting specimens. The Bunker Hill Company with remarkable foresight began salvaging and collecting these fine specimens. For a period of about a month the company mined and collected pyromorphite from this series of pockets until it became too difficult, without considerable extra expense, to continue to raise even higher in the stope. The specimens mined during this period were dispensed in one large lot to the highest bidder (Roberts Minerals). The Bunker Hill Company and its parent company, Gulf Resources Inc., should be congratulated for their conservation efforts which allowed these fine specimens to be saved and made available to collectors and museums everywhere, instead of sending them to the crusher as so many unenlight-ened companies have done."

At about this same time, a few cavities with pyromorphite were found on the 14 level in the Brown orebody, 140-18-22 stope, which represents the lowest level that oxide minerals have been found in the Bunker Hill Mine. Specimens from this discovery consisted of bright, transparent-colorless to silvery or pinkish brown pyromorphite on a vuggy matrix of corroded, very fine-grained pyrite, sphalerite and galena. The crystals are long prisms terminated by the pyramid or a partial pyramid truncated by the flat pinacoid. A second generation of pyromorphite coated some large crystals with smaller crystals that stick out in all directions, and some of the larger crystals were hollow. Excellent specimens up to small cabinet size were collected. These crystals are very similar to some Bad Ems, Germany pyromorphite.

The Bunker Hill Mine remained closed until late 1988, when production began on a small scale. During 1985 to 1988, the new owners permitted mining and collecting in the pyromorphite zone under a lease. The lessees were attempting to locate more of the high quality green pyromorphite. Collecting had reached the point of drilling and blasting to open specimen areas. In general, the limited amount of pyromorphite collected was not of the quality of the previous finds (personal).

The next new owners of the Bunker Hill Mine (New Bunker Hill Mining Co./Placer Mining, Inc.) reopened the mine for limited production of lead ore in the 1990s. During the mid to late 1990s, mining for pyromorphite in 9 level was conducted periodically. During this time, several significant vugs containing top quality yellow to green and orange pyromorphite, often to large size (crystals over 2 cm with matrix pieces to nearly 1 meter across) were recovered. A few collecting tours were permitted in 1994 and 1995 through Bob Jackson of Geology Adventures. In the late 1990s, specimen mining operations hit barren rock, and after efforts to locate more pyromorphite-bearing vugs failed, specimen mining was halted.

Studies of the various colors of the pyromorphite from the find of the early 1980s indicate that it is all pyromorphite; none of it is mimetite. However, the color is a good indicator of the arsenic content. The yellow and green colored specimens contain no arsenic, and the content increases as the color progresses to yellow-orange to dark red-orange. The darkest orange material contains a maximum of about 6% arsenic by weight (Dunn, 1982).

Quartz: Small crystals of quartz, mostly less than 2 cm in length, are sometimes found with crystals of tetrahedrite and siderite in the lower workings of the Sunshine Mine. Similar specimens have been reported from the Galena Mine and the Silver Summit Mine; a few attractive specimens with quartz crystals to 2 cm in length lying on brown to greenish brown siderite have been found. In the upper Galena Mine, a vug was found, that was big enough to stand up in, with moderately clear quartz crystals. Some groups had crystals to 15 cm in length (personal).

Rutile: Shannon (1926) reported that a specimen of rutile was found as float on the surface at the Lookout Mountain Mine south of Pinehurst. The specimen consisted of red to steel-gray needles in a quartz seam.

Siderite: This mineral is common as gangue in the ore deposits of the district, but is uncommon as subhedral to euhedral crystals. They have been reported, on occasion, from several mines. In the 1970s and 1980s, small crystals were collected in the lower levels of the Sunshine Mine with tetrahedrite and quartz (Photo. 34). Individual crystals were honey-brown in color and up to about 1 cm across. Honey-brown crystals with quartz have also been found in the Silver Summit and Galena mines (Photo. 35) (personal).

Small, translucent, brown rhombohedrons of siderite lined cavities in quartz in the Gold Hunter Mine. Needles of boulangerite filled the vugs and often impaled rhombs of siderite (Shannon, 1926).

Silver: The oxidized ores of the mines of the Coeur d'Alene District contained native silver in several habits associated with cerussite and anglesite. The following description is from Shannon (1926). "It occurs in open cavities in the cerussite ores, sometimes in considerable amount, notably in the Mammoth, Morning, You Like, Hercules, Poorman, Tyler, Bunker Hill, Caledonia, Sierra Nevada and other veins. In the Tyler Mine, coarse aggregates of crystalline wires were attached loosely to cerussite crystals or imbedded in spongy limonite. One small cavity found by the writer in lease workings in 1912 yielded nine ounces of such wire silver and a similar cavity in the Barney stope on this vein was said to have yielded enough loose silver to fill a nail keg. Delicate frost-like silver was common in the Sierra Nevada Mine. In the Bunker Hill ores, silver was not so common, but it occurred near the surface in the Blacksmith stope in white cerussite. The Caledonia Mine probably supplied as much or more native silver as any other mine in the district. Here it occurred in cerussite and limonite and also as strings and wires in large amounts in brecciated and leached white quartzite. Sometimes such quartzite yielded slabs of silver 3 mm in thickness and several centimeters in diameter. Thin foil also occurred in narrow cracks in the ores. In soft clayey gouge, the native silver was intimately mixed with native copper and coarse dendritic wires of copper occasionally had a thin natural outer plating of silver. In the Hercules Mine, native silver was common in the oxidized ores as the usual fine dendritic mossy aggregates and also in places as coarse wires. Some of the mossy silver was deposited on anglesite crystals. In the Yankee Boy Mine on Big Creek, native silver has been found as irregular hackly masses coated with manganese oxide. In the Snowstorm Mine, small grains of native silver occurred disseminated in white quartzite with small amounts of malachite."

During 1979-1981, many excellent specimens of silver were recovered from the Bunker Hill Mine (Photos. 37, 39). Miners collected these from upper workings that were being mined for the first time in several decades; other specimens were collected from old stopes entered by miners for collecting purposes. The silver occurred as arborescent wires, most often in branching groups and masses, coarse single wires and small, thin plates. It was commonly associated with cerussite (personal).

Crystalline wires of silver have also been found in the Sitting Bull Mine with cerussite (Photo. 36). Little is known of the quantity of silver and cerussite crystals this mine may have produced (personal).

Sphalerite: This mineral is a common ore mineral in many of the mines, but rarely occurred as euhedral crystals. In the Amy Matchless Mine, south of Pinehurst, it formed a few minute reddish crystals. In the Greenhill-Cleveland Mine, some ruby-red crystals were found in a fissure in the ore on the 1,600 foot level. Small honey-yellow crystals were reported in the Temby stope of the Bunker Hill Mine (Shannon, 1926). Small dark brown crystals have been found with calcite and quartz crystals in the Bunker Hill Mine, 10 level, Quill orebody (Photo. 38); rarely these are up to 1 cm (personal).

Stephanite: Several dozen well-formed crystals, less than 4 mm in length, were found in the "J" orebody in the Bunker Hill Mine (identification by x-ray). These were associated with a micro-drusy coating of pyrite (personal).

Stibiconite: This mineral coated stibnite in the Stanley Mine. The thin crusts were up to 5 mm thick and had a dirty white color. Valentinite and cervantite were associated (Shannon, 1926)

Stibnite: Stibnite is rare in the district, but in recent years, a few small crystals have been found in the 500 level of the Sunshine Mine. These consist of sprays of acicular crystals to about 2 cm in length (personal).

In the Stanley Mine, it formed coarse blades in quartz. Associated minerals include cervantite, valentinite, stibiconite, pyrite, sphalerite and arsenopyrite. Stibnite was also found in the Gold Hunter Mine where it occurred as acicular crystals that formed nests in cavities in quartz. South of Pinehurst, it occurred in the Star antimony mine. Here it occurred as acicular crystals forming nests in vugs in a brecciated quartz vein (Shannon, 1926).

Tetrahedrite: Euhedral tetrahedrons and other forms of this mineral have been found in the lower workings of the Sunshine Mine (50-K3 stope and 50-O3 stope). Individual crystals are black, dull to brilliant and occur with quartz and siderite (Photo. 34). Lustrous, euhedral, tetrahedrons to about 2.5 cm have been found in the Galena Mine (personal).

Small crystals were found in the Yankee Boy Mine, and in the Hypotheek Mine where crystals occurred in cracks in quartz with pyrite and arsenopyrite. Some of these tetrahedrite crystals were up to 5 mm across, and had shiny faces (Shannon, 1926).

Tyrolite: In the Liberal King Mine next to the Lookout Mountain Mine, tyrolite occurred as an oxidation product in porous quartz on the dump. It formed blue-green films with a vitreous to pearly luster. These films were composed of minute, thin, tabular, hexagonal crystals, associated with pyrite, arsenopyrite and chalcopyrite (Shannon, 1926).

Valentinite: At the Stanley Mine, valentinite occurred as thin crusts and drusy coatings on quartz and stibnite. The color was pale brown when on quartz and olive-green when on stibnite. Kermesite, cervantite, stibnite and stibiconite were associated (Shannon, 1926).

Wulfenite: Tiny crystals have been found on occasion on or associated with pyromorphite in a few of the mines of the district. Art Cooper and Norm Radford recovered many specimens from a lease on the Sherman Mine near Burke in 1970. These form tablet to plate-like crystals of dark orange to reddish orange color, to about 1 mm across. Some are partially translucent and they occur on green pyromorphite (Photos. 40,41) (personal).

A few tiny yellow crystals of wulfenite have been found with yellow pyromorphite crystals in the 9 level, Jersey vein workings of the Bunker Hill Mine. The microscopic crystals are transparent and have the common plate-like habit (Photo. 42) (personal).

2

Blackbird Mining District
Lemhi County

Introduction

The Blackbird Mining District, is the only significant occurrence of cobalt in the United States, and it has produced some excellent specimens of vivianite and ludlamite. Unfortunately, it is not a locality where collectors can go to collect their own, nor is it presently in operation, producing specimens. For an important mining locality, with strategic importance, there is surprisingly little published geologic data on Blackbird, and even less available with descriptions of the minerals. Most of the geologic literature describes the primary ore minerals, but does not describe the secondary minerals and their occurrences. In fact, some references do not even mention the existence of the minerals of most interest to collectors: vivianite, ludlamite and erythrite.

Location and History

The Blackbird Mine (originally the Haynes-Stellite Mine or Cobalt Mine) is the largest mine in the Blackbird Mining District which is near Cobalt, Idaho, about 40 miles southwest of Salmon. The mine is accessible by dirt and gravel roads from Highway 93 via the Williams Creek road 5 miles south of Salmon or the Morgan Creek Road 7.5 miles north of Challis. Cobalt mineralization can be found over a large area, primarily on the upper portions of Blackbird Creek and its tributaries.

The main part of the Blackbird Mining District is located approximately 5 to 7 miles above the mouth of Blackbird Creek. The old mining company town of Cobalt was 2 miles down Panther Creek below the mouth of Blackbird Creek, but it was sold off by Newmont in the 1980s. The Cobalt Ranger Station is 1.3 miles up Panther Creek from the mouth of Blackbird Creek.

This is an area of rugged, steep, forested mountains and narrow canyons. Elevations at the mines are 6,100 to 7,300 feet. The area is generally isolated by deep snowfall in the winter, but roads can be kept open for mining activities.

Development started after the discovery of gold mineralization in 1893. The first development was by the Blackbird Copper and Gold Mining Company on several mineralized zones on Blackbird and Meadow Creeks. The next development was at the Musgrove Mine where gold was produced for a brief period in the early 1900s.

Cobalt was discovered in 1901 (Nash et al, 1986) and the Haynes-Stellite Company

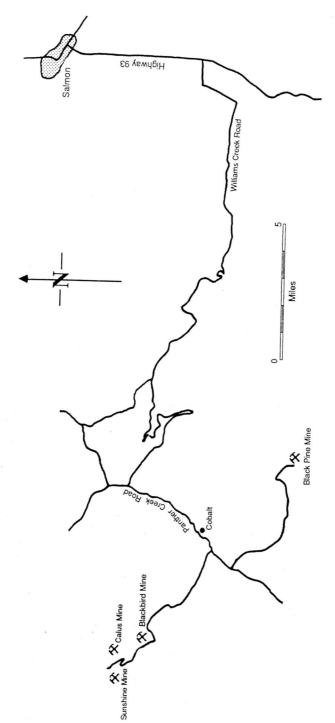

Fig. 8 Map of the Blackbird Mining District and its location from Salmon, Idaho. Several of the major mines are shown; there are many more smaller mines and prospects that are not shown.

operated a mill at the Cobalt Mine from 1918 to 1921. At that time, 4,000 tons of copper ore were mined. Activity was sporadic until the need for cobalt during World War II revived interest in this district.

The first major production of cobalt was by the Uncle Sam Mining Company in the period of 1938 to 1944. This company operated a mill at the Blackbird Mine (formerly the Haynes-Stellite Co. Cobalt Mine) and produced 563 tons of concentrates averaging 2.1% cobalt, 16.5% copper, 0.67 oz. of gold and 0.51 oz. of silver per ton. Operation of the Blackbird Mine and other properties continued sporadically for many years with copper and cobalt being the primary metals produced, with gold providing additional income (Anderson 1947; Purdue 1975). The largest operation in the district was from 1953 to 1958 when the Blackbird Mine was operated by Calera Mining Company. More than 600 men were employed at this time and 6,350 tons of cobalt were produced (Nash et al, 1986; personal).

The Black Pine Mine operated on Copper Creek, across Panther Creek from Blackbird Creek. This mine was operated for its copper ores, which were in a vein separate from the cobalt mineralization. The cobalt vein was not followed due to difficulties with the faulted ore body (personal).

In the 1970s, the price of cobalt sky-rocketed, and interest was renewed in the Blackbird Mine and the district. Being the only significant deposit of cobalt in the United States, it is quite important strategically. Noranda Exploration, Inc., explored the Blackbird Mine, prepared a plan and readied the town of Cobalt, and the mine for mining from 1978 to 1982. After spending many millions of dollars in exploration of the deposit, construction of a mill, environmental studies and rehabilitation, state and federal permits, and other requirements for mining, the price of cobalt fell faster than it had risen, and the project was abandoned. Presently, the property is again being prepared for mining by Formation Chemicals, Inc. which has plans to refine the cobalt concentrates at the Sunshine Mine silver refinery near Kellogg, Idaho.

Cobalt is a strategic metal, that is required for defense and other advanced technical uses. Presently 98% of it is imported from Africa and Canada. This foreign dependence and the strategic need was recognized during the recent congressional designation of the vast River of No Return Wilderness which adjoins the district on the west. The cobalt potential of the area extends into the rugged mountains to the west, the area received a special management designation as a mineral management area, giving the exploration for and mining of cobalt priority, even though such activities would conflict with the bighorn sheep that inhabit the rugged mountains and with other wilderness uses.

A Canadian company bought control of the Blackbird mine and cobalt area and was working on opening the mine in 2003 and 2004. They also purchased the silver refinery of the closed Sunshine Mine near Kellogg in northern Idaho. Their plans are to use the smelter to refine the cobalt concentrates from the Blackbird as well as refine silver concentrates from elsewhere.

Geology

Most of the Blackbird District is underlain by Precambrian metasedimentary rocks of the Yellowjacket formation that are the equivalent of the vast expanse of similar rocks of the Belt supergroup that cover most of Northern Idaho. The metasedimentary rocks include phyllites, micaceous quartzites and schists, with the degree of metamorphism increasing northerly and westerly towards the Idaho batholith.

The southwestern part of the area is underlain by rocks of the Challis volcanic series, including rhyolites, tuffs and fine-grained lake bed sediments.

The intrusive rocks of the Idaho batholith are uncommonly porphyritic in this area. Where they crop out along the road beside Panther Creek, large pink potassium feldspar crystals can be seen frozen in a dark groundmass. The rock composition is variable, but quartz monzonite is dominant. These intrusive rocks are not related to the mineralization.

In the Blackbird District, there are numerous gabbroic bodies and lamprophyre dikes. Mineralization is believed to be related to these igneous rocks.

Mineralization

There are four types of mineralization in the district. These are: 1 — cobalt-tourmaline, 2 — cobalt-biotite, 3 — cobalt-quartz and 4 — gold-copper-cobalt (Anderson, 1947).

The cobalt tourmaline deposits are fine grained and dark colored, similar in appearance to their quartzite host rock. They have formed along fractured and sheared zones. Grains of cobaltite, mostly less than 0.3 mm across and equally fine grained black tourmaline have replaced the quartzite, generally without greatly changing its appearance. In many lodes, a more coarse biotite has also been deposited; this gives the rock a coarse micaceous appearance. The mineralized zones are of moderate size, up to 70 feet across and up to about 300 feet in length.

A second stage of mineralization added muscovite, zoisite, epidote, quartz, arsenopyrite, pyrite and chalcopyrite to the mineral assemblage. All of these are also very fine grained.

The cobalt-biotite deposits are somewhat more coarse, and micaceous because of the increased amount of biotite. However, the finer grained deposits of this type are difficult to distinguish from the tourmaline deposits.

These mineralized zones are smaller than the previously described type, and are rarely more than 100 feet in any direction. The cobaltite is generally scarce, but is more coarse grained than in the cobalt-tourmaline deposits. The grains vary from about 0.5 to 2 mm across. The second stage minerals are also present in these deposits.

The cobalt-quartz deposits are associated with the schistose zones and appear to be replacements of them. The quartz is coarse grained and contains streaks and irregular bunches of cobaltite. The grains of cobaltite are up to about 2 mm or more across. The second stage minerals are mostly absent, and appear to have been replaced by quartz. There is some chalcopyrite, arsenopyrite and native silver.

The gold-copper-cobalt deposits are more complex than the others. They appear to have formed from the addition of gold, copper and cobalt to cobalt-biotite deposits. This stage of mineralization was not as complete as other stages, so that the entire schistose zone has not been changed. The gold-copper-cobalt mineralization is generally restricted to tabular, lenticular or chimney-shaped areas.

Ore zones are irregular and discontinuous, having great length but usually are less than a foot across. In some areas, small stringers and seams produce ore zones that are more than 30 feet across.

Mineralization of these deposits has produced ores that reflect the two-stage mineralization previously mentioned in the other deposits, plus the third stage addition of quartz, gold and electrum.

Mineralogy

The above descriptions of the characteristics and minerals of the ores presents little of interest to collectors. Virtually all of the minerals are of fine grained material in which it is difficult to distinguish individual grains; with one exception, there is no chance of crystals large enough or well formed and of interest to collectors. The exception is that, uncommonly, the cobaltite is somewhat more coarse, and although frozen in fine grained

Photo. 1 Anglesite, 5.8 cm across, Hypotheek Mine, Shoshone County; Rock Currier photograph, E.V Shannon/Brush-Yale specimen.

Photo. 3 Anglesite, 1.6 cm across, Tyler Mine, Shoshone County; Rock Currier photograph, Brush-Yale specimen.

Photo. 4 Anglesite, 3.2 cm high, Bunker Hill Mine, Shoshone County; Norm and Carla Radford specimen.

Photo. 2 Anglesite, 6.4 cm high, Last Chance Mine, Shoshone County; Rock Currier photograph, Brush-Yale specimen.

Photo. 5 Anglesite, specimen 5.2 cm across, Bunker Hill Mine, Shoshone County.

quartz, tourmaline or biotite, does produce euhedral crystals up to five millimeters (or more) across.

The complete list of primary minerals, most of which are fine grained, includes: metallic—pyrrhotite, cobaltite, chalcopyrite, safflorite, arsenopyrite, chalcocite, covellite, silver, gold, sphalerite, galena, enargite, hematite, goethite, erythrite, native copper, cuprite, malachite and jarosite; nonmetallic — quartz, biotite, tourmaline (schorl-dravite), muscovite, zoisite, epidote, siderite, vivianite, ludlamite and apatite.

What makes this mining district of interest to mineral collectors are a few of the secondary minerals, vivianite, ludlamite, copper and erythrite, formed from the weathering and oxidation of the ore minerals. These are occasionally found in very fine to spectacular specimens, especially the vivianite and ludlamite.

Apatite: Tabular crystals of apatite to 9 mm long occur on the Togo claim. The crystals are yellowish, dull and occur with rosettes of chlorite in cavities in schist. Apatite has also been reported in the Haynes-Stellite (Blackbird) Mine as white, prismatic crystals. Cobaltite, biotite and chlorite crystals are associated, disseminated in quartz (Shannon, 1926).

Cobaltoan-arsenopyrite: This mineral occurs in the Blackbird Mine, and probably other mines. It forms silver-white crystals up to 5 mm across that occur in the cobalt-tourmaline ore with cobaltite and quartz. Individual crystals are prismatic with pinacoid and dome modifications. Often, they are short and have a cubic appearance. Shannon (1926) used the (now obsolete) name "danaite" for this mineral.

Chalcocite: Chalcocite is reported to occur in the copper-bearing deposits (Purdue, 1975).

Chrysocolla: Coatings and seams of this mineral occur in oxidized portions of those deposits that contain copper (Purdue, 1975).

Cobaltite: Crystals are reddish gray, and generally have a pyritohedral form with cubic and octahedral modifications, or are cubes or octahedrons. In the various prospects, it has several characteristics. It has been found in pyritohedrons with cubic and octahedral modifications, as cuboctahedral crystals and as micrograins, with malachite, arsenopyrite, pyrite, chalcopyrite and erythrite.

On the Togo claim, cobaltite crystals have been found up to 5 mm across. The cobaltite is associated with apatite. It has been found with chalcopyrite in a 1 cm wide band in schist in the Tom Jefferson claim. In this sulfide band, it forms pyritohedrons with cubic and octahedral modifications. Specimens from the Brooklyn claim contain crystals up to 2 mm across, with chalcopyrite. The cobaltite displays a perfect cubic cleavage. Crystals to 1 mm occur in the Ludwig and Bascom Latest Out claims on the West Fork of Blackbird Creek. It is disseminated in streaks in quartz with schist inclusions. The crystals are cuboctahedrons.

Cobaltite from the Wiley J. Rose claim, 1 mile north of the old Blackbird camp, is partly altered to erythrite. It occurs in veins in quartzose schist. Cobaltite in the Blackbird Mine occurs as micro-reddish gray grains in quartz with tourmaline. Cobaltoan-arsenopyrite is associated. Crystals of cobaltite to 5 mm can be found disseminated in quartz with biotite, chlorite and prismatic apatite. The crystals are cubes or octahedrons.

It has been reported as micrograins with erythrite and chalcopyrite in the Sunshine prospect in Sec. 20, T. 21 N., R. 18 E. The prospect is connected by road to the Calus Mine. A similar occurrence is reported in the Calus Mine on a hillside north of Blackbird Creek in Sec. 21. Here it is in siderite, biotite, quartz and ankerite gangue with safflorite and chalcopyrite. Micrograins are also reported from the Dusty prospect in Sec. 23. The micrograins are associated with malachite in the crests of folds in a quartz-tourmaline rock. The Hawkeye prospect in Sec. 27, contains micrograins of cobaltite with pyrite and erythrite (Shannon, 1926).

Copper: Native copper is uncommon in the district, but locally abundant. Small zones of ore have produced an abundance of native copper as beautiful arborescent groups; copper was reported to be in such quantity in rich zones in the faulted ore of the Black Pine Mine, especially on the 7,400 level, that the ore hung together after being blasted and caused problems in the crusher. Excellent specimens of arborescent groups were found in the Blackbird open pit; it also occurred as thin hackly sheets (Photo. 43) (personal).

Cuprite: Cuprite is reported in the district in the copper-bearing deposits. It was found as a red stain, or thin coating, sometimes surrounding small native copper crystals (personal).

Erythrite: Although, on a worldwide basis, erythrite is a relatively common pink to red secondary cobalt mineral, it is uncommon in fine specimens that would interest most collectors. It is no exception at the Blackbird Mining District, where many fracture surfaces and other cavities in the ore deposits have thin coatings of crudely crystalline and drusy crusts of the mineral, but fine specimens of coarse, euhedral crystals are rare. Some fine quality, coarse crystals were found in the Blackbird Mine open pit and probably occurred in other mines (personal).

In the Blackbird Mine underground, it forms rose-red fibrous coatings along seams and cracks in a black tourmaline-quartz rock (Photo. 44). Thin blades and rosettes of rose-red erythrite occur in a rusty schist in the Bulkley Mine, and it forms similar pink blades and rosettes in the quartzite on the Brooklyn claim. These crystals are tabular to the b axis. In the Sunshine prospect, erythrite occurs with cobaltite and chalcopyrite and it was common in the Sweet Repose Mine (Shannon, 1926; Vhay, 1948).

Ludlamite: In the Blackbird Mine, crystals of ludlamite are about 8 mm to 12 mm across and occur as tablet-shaped crystals with the c(001) face dominant. Sometimes the crystals are more tabular and may occur stacked to about 2 cm high. Crystals vary from pale sea-green to a darker green, and are usually transparent (Photos. 45, 46).

Ludlamite crystals are mostly found on the dark, oxidized wall rock with vivianite, or alone. It is found associated with most of the minerals in the district, including vivianite, pyrite, quartz, calcite, siderite, pyrrhotite, chalcopyrite, cobaltite, safflorite, apatite and tourmaline; although, most of these others do not form euhedral crystals. Much of the oxidized wall rock matrix will disintegrate if placed in water, so clean these carefully (Glass et al, 1949; personal).

Malachite: Thin seams and coatings of this mineral occur on fracture surfaces in the oxidized portions of the copper-bearing deposits. It formed fine, velvety coatings of dark green crystals on botryoidal malachite on the surface oxidized ores of the Black Pine Mine (Purdue, 1975; personal).

Quartz: Few specimens are known, and quartz is uncommon in euhedral crystals, but has been found up to large size, more than 10 cm in length. One vug was reported containing long clear crystals of quartz (up to more than 10 cm) with included brassy pyrite cubes. Sometimes it occurs with ludlamite or vivianite (personal).

Rhodochrosite: Small crystals of rhodochrosite have been reported from the Blackbird District. They are uncommon, but fine quality (Shannon, 1926).

Safflorite: This mineral can be found with cobaltite and chalcopyrite in the Calus Mine in Sec. 21, on the hillside north of Blackbird. Mineralization is in a quartz, pyrite, biotite, ankerite and siderite gangue (Trites et al, 1953).

Vivianite: The Blackbird Mine has produced excellent specimens of this mineral (Photos. 47, 48), some of the world's finest. The color varies from colorless crystals tinged with

Photo. 6 Calcite, crystals are 6 mm across, Bunker Hill Mine, Shoshone County.

Photo. 9 Cerussite, specimen 4.5 cm across, Bunker Hill Mine, Shoshone County; Ben Sheppard specimen.

Photo. 7 Cerussite twins with rods of goethite, 7.3 cm, Bunker Hill Mine, Shoshone County.

Photo. 8 Cerussite, showing the twinning of photo. 7, Bunker Hill Mine, Shoshone County.

Photo. 10 Cerussite, specimen 7 cm across, Bunker Hill Mine, Shoshone County; Norm and Carla Radford specimen.

Photo. 11 Cerussite, 4.9 cm across, Hercules Mine, Shoshone County; Rock Currier photograph, Karl Fair specimen.

Photo. 13 Chalcopyrite, top left crystal 2 cm, Galena Mine, Wallace, Shoshone County; Norm and Carla Radford specimen.

Photo. 12 Cerussite, 2 cm across, Sitting Bull Mine, Shoshone County.

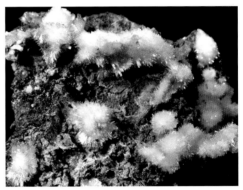

Photo. 14 Hemimorphite, 4 cm across, Quill orebody, Bunker Hill Mine, Shoshone County.

Photo. 15 Gypsum, long crystal is 1.2 cm, 15 level, Barr vein, Bunker Hill Mine, Shoshone County.

pink to grayish blue to purplish black. Specimens are usually colorless, pink or grayish blue and transparent when fresh, but darken to blue and dark blue-black to purplish black on exposure to light. Crystals are typically elongated and blade-like, and are occasionally associated with ludlamite and quartz. They occur as singles and groups on dark altered schist or white quartz. Individual crystals may be coarse and prismatic either solid or parting vertically. Others may form loosely or tightly packed groups; sometimes they are bent and display numerous partings.

Translucent, coarse, single blades have been found up to 11 cm or more in length and 3 cm across. Where they occur in narrow fractures they are shortened or lying parallel to the fracture. Individual crystals typically are 3-4 cm in length. As with the ludlamite specimens, the partially oxidized sulfide-bearing wall rock which forms the matrix is often not stable and will disintegrate when wet, so care should be taken when cleaning and storing these specimens.

In the Chicago vein of the Blackbird Mine, excellent specimens of vivianite occurred on sulfide ore. Ludlamite was associated, but typically did not occur in the same cavities with vivianite. The sulfide disintegrated after a short time of exposure, so few matrix specimens could be collected from this zone (personal).

Small crystals of vivianite also occurred in the Calera Mine. The crystals showing the typical blade-like habit were scattered on matrix (personal).

3

Sawtooth Mountains
Boise, Custer and Elmore Counties

Introduction

Only a few mineral localities offer a wide selection of minerals and the grandeur of rugged glaciated peaks like the Sawtooth Mountains locality of south-central Idaho offered. The granites of the Sawtooth batholith, which are exposed over more than 140 square miles in the Sawtooth Mountains, contain crystal-bearing cavities that attracted mineral collectors for several decades until the Forest Service closed the area to mineral collecting in 1990. Although this locality was known for smoky quartz and limited amounts of topaz and aquamarine for nearly a century, it was not well known by mineral collectors outside of Idaho until the 1970s and 1980s.

The Sawtooth Mountains consist of a rugged area of partially barren mountains centered about 65 miles northeast of Boise, Idaho; their northeastern corner lies just southwest of Stanley. Access is relatively easy to edges of the area on the north, east and south via paved highways and graveled roads, but it is necessary to take to the trails on foot or horseback to enter the main mountainous regions. Most of the range lies within the Sawtooth Wilderness which is surrounded by the Sawtooth National Recreation Area.

The mountains are drained by several main streams and their tributaries including the Salmon River (tributary creeks only), Middle Fork and North Fork of the Boise River and the South Fork of the Payette River.

This rugged mountain range has a relief of nearly 6,000 feet. Barren peaks, surrounded by glacial lakes, with rugged sawtooth ridges, arêtes and horns that reach a maximum elevation of 10,830 feet (Thompson Peak), and are typically over 9,000 feet dominate the range. Knife-edge ridges and cliffs with vertical or overhanging faces are the rule for the upper elevations, whereas the lower elevations consist of broad, steep-walled glaciated valleys. The upper elevations are nearly barren of vegetation, but the lower elevations are covered by pine forests.

Mining claims cannot be located in the Wilderness Area, but there were a few claims remaining of those that were located prior to the Wilderness and Recreation Area designations. The first claims were located by those rugged prospectors who extended their searches for gold from the Atlanta, Hailey and Ketchum districts in the 1870s to 1880s. Mineralized areas on the ridges with rusty iron oxides or black manganese oxides showing attracted these early prospectors, but gold, silver and other metallic minerals were not

Photo. 16 Jamesonite, area of crystals is 1 cm across, Sunshine Mine, Shoshone County; Norm and Carla Radford specimen.

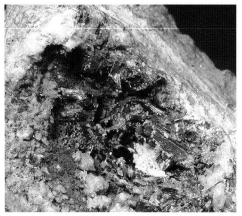

Photo. 18 Pyromorphite, 5.5 cm across, 9 level, Jersey vein, Bunker Hill Mine, Shoshone County; Norm and Carla Radford specimen.

Photo. 17 Linarite, cavity is 2 cm across, longest crystal is 6 mm, 1700 level, Sherman Mine, Burke, Shoshone County; Norm and Carla Radford specimen.

Photo. 19 Pyromorphite, 1 cm high, 14 level, Brown vein, Bunker Hill Mine, Shoshone County.

Photo. 20 Plattnerite, 6.2 cm across, #3 level, Tamarack Mine, Burke, Shoshone County; Norm and Carla Radford specimen.

Photo. 21 Arsenian pyromorphite, 9.4 cm, 9 level, Bunker Hill Mine, Shoshone County; Norm and Carla Radford specimen.

Photo. 22 Arsenian pyromorphite, 6 cm across, Bunker Hill Mine, Shoshone County.

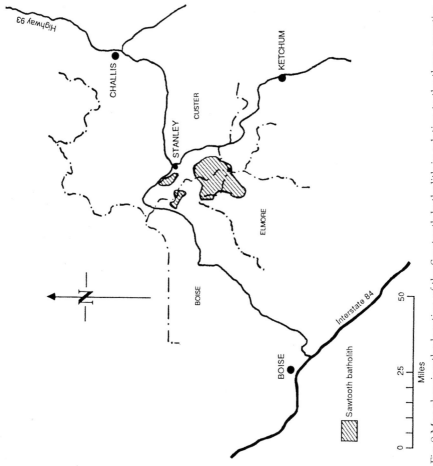

Fig. 9 Map showing the location of the Sawtooth batholith in relation to the three counties it lies in.

discovered in quantities greater than trace amounts.

After the turn of the century, the blue masses, veins and joint coatings of aquamarine attracted those interested in beryllium and the possibility of aquamarine gems. In spite of the effort of many prospectors and would-be miners, there has been no commercial production of beryllium from the Sawtooth Mountains, and only small amounts of gem and specimen quality aquamarine.

In the 1980s there was increased interest in the area by active field collectors attracted by smoky quartz, aquamarine, topaz and other minerals. Prior to this, collectors who had ventured to these mountains apparently spent much of their time looking for aquamarine in an area around Camp Lake southeast of Glens Peak where there is a concentration of aquamarine. Other areas have also proven to be good localities to collect smoky quartz, topaz and aquamarine, as well as other minerals. A few local residents regularly ventured into the northeastern and other parts of the range collecting smoky quartz.

The topography of the Sawtooth Range is highly corrugated, rendering much of the rock exposures difficult, if not impossible, to collect in for most individuals. Various glacial features, such as roche moutonnées and glacial benches, are steep-sided and their surfaces are polished. The arêtes (typical sawtooth ridges) are near vertical and unstable. In places, post-glacial ice weathering has caused the development of large talus slopes composed of granite blocks from fist to house size. The resulting terrain is not easily explored or collected in; anything off the trails can become unexpectedly treacherous.

Collecting in most parts of the Sawtooth Mountains required backpacking from about 6-15 miles, generally over one or two mountain passes to get into the desired area. The weather can be quite nice and sunny during the summer months; but winter snows don't leave the slopes until June or July and return for winter season as early as October (even September). Many collectors have been unexpectedly caught in snowstorms that have dumped as much as six inches in July, August or September. Thunderstorms, some quite intense, are common in July and August and it is not unusual to wake up to a heavy coating of frost any morning.

All visitors should be prepared for wet and cold weather (or sunburn!). The change from a warm sunny day to a cold rainy day (or snow), can occur in a matter of hours. The snowfall from a summer storm may only last for a day or two, but the temperatures may remain low for days.

Even though mineral collectors and rockhounds were told many times during the creation of the Wilderness Act and during the designation of individual Wilderness Areas that mineral collecting and rockhounding activities would not be stopped because of the designation of areas as Wilderness, the Sawtooth Wilderness, like most other Wilderness areas, was closed to collecting by the Forest Service in 1991. The Wilderness Act does not prohibit mineral collecting, and it is an accepted recreational activity on National Forest lands. The Forest Service has expressed an opinion that mineral collecting in Wilderness Areas is an acceptable recreational activity as long as such activities do not interfere with or damage the wilderness values. In the Sawtooth Wilderness, mineral collecting was done by removing specimens from exposed cavities on cliffs and in boulders in talus, hardly a significant impact to the Wilderness values.

The loss of this unique location to the wonderful hobby of mineral collecting reaches beyond the loss of the recreational value of mineral collecting, a popular family hobby. Not only did it remove one of the most interesting mineral locations and one of the most wonderful areas to hike and backpack in from those ever diminishing number of available mineral localities, it also brought to a halt the ongoing mineralogic studies of this unusual mineralized granite batholith. Without the fresh finds by mineral collectors, studies of the

Photo. 23 Pyromorphite, 5 cm across, 9 level, Jersey vein, Bunker Hill Mine, Shoshone County; Norm and Carla Radford specimen.

Photo. 26 Arsenian pyromorphite, 8.2 cm across, Bunker Hill Mine, Shoshone County.

Photo. 24 Pyromorphite, 12 cm across, 9 level, Jersey vein, Bunker Hill Mine, Shoshone County; Norm and Carla Radford specimen.

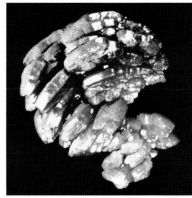

Photo. 27 Pyromorphite, 3.8 cm high, 9 level, Jersey vein, Bunker Hill Mine, Shoshone County; Norm and Carla Radford specimen.

Photo. 25 Pyromorphite, 5.3 cm across, Bunker Hill Mine, Shoshone County.

Photo. 28 Pyromorphite, cavity 3.8 cm across, Hercules Mine, Shoshone County, Norm and Carla Radford specimen.

Photo. 29 Pyromorphite, specimen 17.1 cm across, Sherman Mine, Shoshone County; Norm and Carla Radford specimen.

Photo. 30 Pyromorphite, green crystals with a brown limonite coating, specimen is 15 cm across, Midnight Mine, Shoshone County; Joan and Bryant Harris specimen.

Photo. 31 Stout, translucent pyromorphite microcrystals to 0.7 mm long, Little Giant Mine, Shoshone County.

Photo. 32 Pyromorphite on iridescent goethite, crystals to 0.6 mm long, Little Giant Mine, Shoshone County.

mineralogy of the Sawtooth Mountains has essentially ended.

There are other granite bodies in Idaho with miarolitic cavities that contain some of these minerals; all of the Tertiary granite intrusives are miarolitic and have feldspars, smoky quartz and other minerals in the cavities. A few of them are known to also contain beryl and topaz. It is unknown how complex the mineralogy of most of the other granite bodies may be.

The Sawtooth Mountains were also unique in one other main factor, its high altitude and thus the amount of exposed rock. The other Tertiary age granite intrusives are mostly of lower relief, with few outcrops, and typically, very little is projecting above timberline. In these, outcrops are mostly rounded and weathered.

Investigations of the mineralogy of these has shown the presence of beryl (mostly aquamarine) in a few, and similarly, topaz has been found in a few. The presence or absence of more unusual minerals is not known, except for the few single occurrences that have been found. Not enough cavities have been found with their contents intact to prove or disprove the presence of these uncommon and rare minerals. This part of the study of the mineralogy of Idaho will remain unstudied.

Geology of the Sawtooth Range

The Idaho batholith is the largest batholith in the western United States, and covers most of the mountainous parts of central and south-central Idaho. Gray granodiorite and quartz monzonite (which will be referred to as granodiorite) of this Cretaceous age batholith underlies this region and forms the outer parts of the Sawtooth Range. Tertiary age granite of the Sawtooth batholith intrudes this granodiorite forming an elongated mass in the central part of the Sawtooth Mountains, underlying less than half of the range. Two satellite stocks are exposed in the northern part of the range.

The Cretaceous age granodiorites are not uniform in composition or texture, but are generally medium-grained, light gray, leucocratic granodiorite. Rocks of the Tertiary Sawtooth batholith are leucocratic granite with a medium grain size and light pink color, although the color is light gray in many areas. Dikes and segregations of alaskite, aplite, pegmatite or diabase are common too. Some of these (especially the diabase dikes) are quite long and may extend for hundreds of feet.

There are few notable structures in the range; generally, joints are widely spaced and are dominated by northwesterly and northeasterly trending, steeply dipping fractures. Locally, they may be closely spaced with both steeply dipping and gently dipping joints shattering a peak or ridge which is also altered and oxidized so as to present a rusty-brown color.

Faults are not major features of significance to mineral occurrences, but one northwest-southeast trending structure forms most of the northeastern contact of the Sawtooth batholith with the Idaho batholith. Smaller, often short, faults, mostly north-south trending, are common in the granites. Some of these are mineralized with manganese oxides and may be the structural influences in the rusty, highly fractured areas described above.

Pegmatites are of interest, because they offer the possibility of crystal-bearing cavities. In the Sawtooth Range, pegmatite bodies may have any of several shapes including dikes, pods and lenses. They may be as small as less than an inch in one dimension or up to several tens of feet in one or more dimensions. There are numerous exposures which have been called sheet pegmatites in the literature. These are dikes which are parallel to a joint, or glaciated surface, and are exposed as a sheet on the outcrop. Cavities may or may not occur in any of the pegmatites, and there is no correlation between the size of a pegmatite and the size of the cavity it contains.

The pegmatite bodies generally consist of pink potassium feldspar and quartz. Either mineral may be dominant with the other forming a lesser percent of the total volume; minor minerals include zinnwaldite and fayalite.

Locally common are pegmatite pods, irregular in outline, that are dominantly coarse pink feldspar with a zone of quartz. If present, a single cavity is usually within the quartz or at the quartz-feldspar contact. These pegmatite bodies are typically from about one foot to about three feet across. The minerals in the cavities are generally smoky quartz and feldspar with lesser amounts of other minerals, including topaz.

Another type of pegmatite is uncommon, but has been found in several areas. Pegmatites of this type are fairly large tabular bodies, that may be exposed on a large area of an outcrop. They are quite coarse and consist of quartz and feldspar with an unusual texture of coarse milky quartz crystals (large, often up to about a foot across and two feet in length) surrounded by a medium- to coarse-grained matrix of feldspar and quartz. The exposure typically displays the milky crystals in cross section and the molds in the matrix where the large crystals have been pulled out as the pegmatite has been weathered and split open. Interestingly, although the hollows where the quartz crystals had been pulled out of the enclosing feldspar matrix are often seen, the part of the pegmatites containing the quartz crystals are rarely seen. These pegmatite bodies may be up to about 60 feet or more across, and only rarely contain cavities.

The sheet pegmatites are usually only about an inch thick and may have vuggy zones with small crystals rarely more than 1 cm in length. Some of them display fine specimens of microcline and smoky quartz, sometimes with spessartine, or an interesting and attractive combination of aquamarine and spessartine. Rarely can specimens be safely collected from these, due to the difficulty of removing specimens from a broad flat surface exposure on solid rock.

Only one zoned, complex pegmatite has been found. It appears to be steeply dipping, varies from less than three feet across to about six feet across, and is about 35-40 feet in length. It is dominantly quartz with lesser amounts of pink microcline; most of the central portion is coarse-grained quartz with aquamarine and hematite, with much of the outer portion being fine to medium-grained quartz, microcline and aquamarine. A line rock (consisting of lines or layers of feldspar and aquamarine) is developed on one end. This pegmatite was worked for aquamarine many years ago when there were mining claims located in the area, but is now partially slumped and buried.

Other minerals consist of bertrandite up to 6 mm, hematite to about 10 cm, spessartine, zinnwaldite and a pink to purplish mica forming rims on zinnwaldite and small fine-grained masses. One crystal of topaz, one fragment of a crystal of purple fluorapatite, and a small amount of fluorite were also found on the dump in recent years.

In the central part of the pegmatite, intergrown with the quartz are subhedral blades of hematite up to about 10 cm in maximum dimension and opaque aquamarine crystals (often altered and granular) to about 12 cm long and 3 cm across. Angular cavities in coarse crystalline quartz rarely contain small fine quality crystals of aquamarine (sometimes gem quality), micro-bertrandite coating quartz or aquamarine, hematite and smoky quartz.

Cavities in the outer zone and the line rock are similar. They are generally small, mostly one half to two and a half inches across, and contain small crystals of quartz, secondary aquamarine and microcline. Bertrandite crystals line the cavities and coat surfaces of quartz, microcline, albite and aquamarine.

Mineralogy of the Sawtooth Batholith

Mineralogy of the granite has been studied by several individuals, but detailed work has only begun on the cavity mineralogy. The essential rock forming minerals include: quartz,

Photo. 33 Cavernous pyromorphite, 1 cm across, Omaha tunnel, Bunker Hill Mine, Shoshone County.

Photo. 35 Siderite with quartz, specimen is 7.6 cm across, Galena Mine, Wallace, Shoshone County; Norm and Carla Radford specimen.

Photo. 34 Tetrahedrite on siderite, tetrahedrite is 9 mm across, specimen 6 cm across, 500 level, Sunshine Mine, Shoshone County; Norm and Carla Radford specimen.

Photo. 36 Silver and cerussite, the area of silver on the right is 1.2 cm across, Sitting Bull Mine, Shoshone County; Norm and Carla Radford specimen.

Photo. 37 Silver on cerussite, 3.5 cm across, Bunker Hill Mine, Shoshone County.

Photo. 39 Silver on cerussite, 5.6 cm across, Bunker Hill Mine, Shoshone County.

Photo. 38 Sphalerite on quartz, sphalerite is 1 cm across, 10 level, Quill orebody, Bunker Hill Mine, Shoshone County; collected February 1989 from the muck pile after a blast, the only sphalerite crystal collected at the time; Larry Hansen specimen.

Photo. 41 Wulfenite on pyromorphite, largest wulfenite is 1 mm across, Sherman Mine, Shoshone County.

Photo. 40 Wulfenite on pyromorphite, wulfenite is 0.5 mm across, Sherman Mine, Shoshone County.

Photo. 42 Wulfenite on pyromorphite, wulfenite is 2 mm across, Bunker Hill Mine, Shoshone County.

mesoperthitic orthoclase and plagioclase (albite in the southern part, grading to oligoclase in the north), with hornblende, biotite and muscovite. Accessory minerals include: fluorapatite, allanite, ilmenite, fluorite, magnetite, titanite, zircon and aquamarine. Alteration has produced sericite, leucoxene, clay and pennine. Composition of the pegmatites is essentially the same (Pattee et al, 1968; Reid, 1963).

Good, euhedral crystals are obtained only from cavities; these are primarily gas pockets (miarolitic cavities) in the granite. Some cavities have been found in pegmatite dikes, lenses and pods. Glacial ice and post-glacial weathering has plucked 90% or more of the cavities clean, so intact cavities with crystals in any acceptable condition are very difficult to find. Small miarolitic cavities, measuring little more than a few sixty-fourths of an inch across, are quite common in some areas; some rock is literally a gaseous froth of thousands of tiny openings. Size varies from less than a sixty-fourth of an inch to about six inches in two dimensions and a foot in the third for most cavities. Larger cavities, up to about two feet in two or more directions are uncommon, and very large cavities, up to about 10-15 feet in two directions and 30 feet in the third have been seen with the largest cavity being about 65-75 feet in length. Apparently, all really large cavities have been naturally weathered out and emptied of crystals. Only a few cavities three to six feet across have been found with contents intact.

These miarolitic cavities are mostly ovoid in cross section and often tube-like. They can be surrounded by a layer of graphic granite, coarse to pegmatitic granite, or show no change in texture from the granite wall rock to the crystal lining. Some cavities are irregular, but most are relatively smooth with curving walls. They may occur sparsely or densely in any given area. Sometimes they are lined up along a thin pegmatite or fracture. For the most part, there appears to be no control over their orientation, and if longer in one dimension, or tube-like, the long dimension may point in any direction (down, horizontal or up). Interestingly, a cavity dipping down into the rock is no assurance that the crystal contents will be found intact, just as the cavity running up into the rock is no sure indication that the crystals have all been weathered out and dumped.

Most of the cavities display features of crystal growth after collapse of the cavity. The collapse may have been minor, with only a few crystals broken loose and some slabs separating a little from the walls, or complete collapse with all crystals broken loose either as individual crystals or with some as slabs of feldspar with smoky quartz and other crystals attached.

Crystal growth often continued after the collapse, so that a secondary growth of quartz, with or without albite, was deposited. This commonly partially healed the broken bases of the quartz crystals, so that the broken surface developed a myriad of small quartz faces or terminations. Sometimes, the secondary quartz growth forms a normal termination on the broken end, creating a doubly terminated crystal. The feldspar plates developed a coating of small quartz crystals on the broken side. This late stage growth most often has the same appearance as the primary smoky quartz or it may be colorless or milky. In some areas, it is commonly milky and may coat the termination and three sides of each crystal.

The mineralogy of the Sawtooth batholith miarolitic cavities appears to be deceptively simple: quartz, microcline and albite are the main constituents of cavities in both the massive granite and the later pegmatitic phases. But a close examination indicates the presence of other minerals containing beryllium, fluorine, hydroxyl, lithium and rare earth elements, indicating a more complex mineralogy associated with the concentration of the lighter elements and volatiles associated with pocket mineralization.

The cavities occasionally contain secondary and alteration minerals such as clays, goethite or manganese oxides. Albite crystals may encrust earlier primary minerals (smoky quartz and microcline) or replace microcline; manganese minerals, like spessartine and helvite are in turn planted on the secondary albite, indicating an even later origin. In some areas, the late stage quartz forms a shell or outer layer on the smoky crystals. This often somewhat milky or grayish quartz layer may not completely cover the primary crystal, forming a slightly sceptered crystal. In other cavities, a late stage quartz growth consists of tiny misshapen quartz crystals accompanied by clay or very fine-grained muscovite which are packed in all crevices between larger crystals. Bertrandite or topaz form fine-grained coatings on the quartz and feldspar crystals in many cavities. A smooth, sometimes shiny, gray silicate coating, of undetermined composition, coats crystals in most cavities that are open and many that are filled with clays and dirt. This coating is difficult to impossible to remove from specimens without damaging the crystals.

There are many other characteristics about the zoning, habits and associations of the individual minerals and their associations that may be interesting to many readers. It probably is accurate to say that information gathering in the Sawtooth batholith was just beginning, so some of the observations may be open to a better explanation in the future if more data is available. The zoning, paragenesis and associations of the cavity minerals is difficult to accurately determine. Much information on zoning (individual occurrences and concentrations across the batholith) is not available to any one individual, because there are many collectors in the batholith, and not all information reaches those who have an interest in the geology, mineralogy and chemistry of this locality. Now that the area is closed to specimen removal, the scientific studies are not being done.

The associations can be reasonably determined from the specimens available from the author's and others' collections. Comments on what minerals are associated with each described mineral are given throughout the listings that follow this section. They are not complete, but are only generalities of what minerals are most commonly found with a given mineral and don't always include the rare and uncommon minerals.

Not enough information is available to determine the zoning for many minerals, especially those that are uncommon and rare. Microcline, albite, quartz, masutomilite, zinnwaldite, topaz and beryl occur throughout the batholith. There are areas where each one is more abundant than in others, and there are areas where any one of them may be missing. In some areas, the quality of specimens (translucency, color and brilliance) may be much greater than the average or much lower. The habits and characteristics are subject to local differences. For instance, aquamarine is typically moderately to severely etched, yet in some areas, much of it is etched little or not at all. Topaz is generally not etched (or is etched very little), but in some areas it has suffered severe etching in many cavities. In the area from Ardeth Lake southerly to the south side of Glens Peak, topaz commonly has a white layer at the termination. This is uncommon throughout the rest of the batholith. Spessartine is a local mineral; there are many places where it is common, or even abundant, but it cannot be found in much of the batholith. Topaz and aquamarine have not been found together in the same cavity (with the exception of microcrystals of beryl and helvite in the topaz crystals from a single cavity), but may be found in cavities that are close to each other, and have been reported in the same pegmatite. Helvite and beryl likely do not occur in the same cavity (with the exception of the micro-inclusions in topaz mentioned above), but helvite has been found in cavities close to a beryl inclusion in the granite. Carpholite and a potassium-bearing carpholite is known from only a few cavities widely scattered in one large area.

The minerals that are listed in these pages as uncommon or rare have been found in only one or a few cavities. This is partly due to the fact that most of them are small to microscopic, and may go unrecognized; specimens may be left behind with the pocket debris

Photo. 46 Ludlamite, large crystal at the top is 1.2 cm long, Blackbird Mine, Lemhi County.

Photo. 43 Thin sheets of native copper in fractures in quartz, specimen 2.7 cm across, Blackbird Mine, Lemhi County.

Photo. 47 Vivianite, 6 cm across, Blackbird Mine, Lemhi County; Norm and Carla Radford specimen.

Photo. 44 Erythrite, crystals mostly around 2 mm in length, Blackbird Mine, Lemhi County.

Photo. 45 Ludlamite on quartz with vivianite, specimen is 6 cm across, Blackbird Mine, Lemhi County; Ben Sheppard specimen.

Photo. 49 Bastnaesite-(Ce) with fluorite, bastnaesite is 1.2 mm across, Baron Lakes area, Sawtooth Mountains, Boise County.

Photo. 48 Vivianite, 11 cm high; an unusually large crystal, apparently the large crystal formed around a quartz crystal as indicated by the hexagonal shape of the notch at the top, Blackbird Mine, Lemhi County; Joan and Bryant Harris specimen.

Photo. 51 Tiny bertrandite crystals on aquamarine (1 cm high) on quartz, Ardeth Lake area, Sawtooth Mountains, Boise County.

Photo. 50 Aquamarine and spessartine on albite, the largest aquamarine is 2 cm long, Ardeth Lake area, Sawtooth Mountains, Boise County.

or are presently sitting, unrecognized, on specimens in collections. It is also due to the fact that approximately 90% of the exposed cavities in the Sawtooth batholith are weathered out and empty; thus a lot of material is missing and unavailable. Thus some of these uncommon and rare minerals may actually be much more common than is presently known. Similarly, the habits and occurrences known for them may well enough typify them, or for some, may actually be only one of many, or may be an unusual habit for them.

Mica Group Minerals

There are several species of mica group minerals that have been identified in the cavities of the granite, and possibly one or more species of chlorite group minerals. The primary mica minerals are zinnwaldite and masutomilite. The masutomilite is of great interest because this is only the third locality known for it (first in the U.S.), and at this locality it is apparently common. The secondary or late stage mica is muscovite; it is mostly very fine- to fine-grained. A more intense study may indicate the presence of lepidolite. Fine scaly micaceous coatings and rims on coarse micas are sometimes pink, the presence of lithium and the results of x-ray diffraction studies (which are not definitive for separating the micas) suggest lepidolite may be present.

The primary mica minerals are determined by the presence or absence of Fe, Mn and Li. If Fe was dominant (with Li), then zinnwaldite formed and if Mn and Li were present then masutomilite formed. Studies of the micas showed that the golden to brown micas contained Mn and Li and little or no Fe, and are masutomilite, whereas, the green to black micas contain Fe and Li and sometimes Mn, and are zinnwaldite. Some of the pink micas (mostly tiny to small flakes) contain only Li, little or no Fe or Mn, which, suggests lepidolite, but these have not been studied by X-ray to make this determination.

Masutomilite appears to be the dominant mica in cavities with topaz, especially those in which topaz is abundant. In aquamarine cavities, zinnwaldite is most common.

Fine-grained to small colorless to light green micaceous minerals have not been intensely studied, but have been identified in three specimens as muscovite, by X-ray diffraction. Some fine-grained, light green to grayish green micaceous material has tested (flame test) positive for Li, with little or no Fe or Mn, which suggests cookeite, but the X-ray analysis mentioned above on this type of material suggests muscovite. This material is most often a late stage coating on feldspars, or the surfaces of quartz, where, if it is scraped off, the underlying quartz often has an etched or frosted surface. Other specimens, with a more coarse habit, green color and sometimes in books and worm-like elongated books contain Fe and may be a chlorite group mineral or zinnwaldite. Much work needs to be done on the micas and other fine-grained minerals in the cavities of the Sawtooth batholith.

Cavity Minerals

Minerals identified (primarily from cavities), include albite, anatase, bastnaesite-Ce, bertrandite, beryl (mostly blue, variety aquamarine), biotite, calcite, carpholite (and a potassium-bearing carpholite), cassiterite, chabazite, unidentified clays, epidote, fayalite, ferrimolybdite, ferrocolumbite, fluorite, fluorapatite, goethite-limonite, gypsum, helvite, magnetite, masutomilite, microcline, molybdenite, montmorillonite, monazite, muscovite, orthoclase, phenakite, pyrite, pyrophanite, quartz, rutile, siderite, spessartine, stilbite, topaz, uranophane, wodginite, zinnwaldite, zircon and several unidentified minerals.

Mineral Descriptions

Albite: Albite is found in almost every cavity, usually as subparallel and curved groups of small crystals. Colorless, white and sometimes purplish albite often forms attractive groups or coatings of crystals associated with quartz, microcline, topaz and spessartine. Often, it is rounded, pitted and altered-looking when associated with the less common to rare late-stage minerals, including helvite, carpholite, topaz, spessartine, ferrocolumbite and zircon.

Albite may be a primary pocket-lining mineral, but it is most often a late-stage mineral and commonly coats microcline or other minerals. It may replace microcline partially to completely, both in the wall rock and in the cavities. Individual crystals are typically 2 to 6 mm high; occasionally they may be stacked forming groups having the appearance of individual crystals to about 1.5 cm high. It rarely has the bladed habit commonly referred to as cleavelandite.

Anatase: Anatase has been seen as clusters of lustrous, black crystals in a few cavities. They have been found in cavities in the feldspar matrix or near the bases of feldspar crystals. Crystals have a steep dipyramidal habit and are up to 0.5 mm in length.

Bastnaesite-(Ce): Micro crystals that have been identified as bastnaesite-(Ce), were found in a few cavities in the Sawtooth Mountains. The micro crystals are white to cream color and hexagonal (Photo. 49). In one microprobe analysis the results of Ce 20%, La 10%, Y 0.2% and Ca 0.5% were obtained, and similar results were obtained from another specimen from a different cavity that was analyzed in a different test. Positive identification was made by x-ray analysis.

Bertrandite: This mineral is relatively common, sometimes associated with aquamarine, forming crusts of small crystals on the sides or terminations of corroded aquamarine, or coating albite or quartz (Photos. 51, 56). It is also found surrounding or inside of hexagonal cavities in quartz, apparently formerly occupied by aquamarine. It is believed that bertrandite forms as a secondary mineral when beryllium is released during the etching and dissolving of aquamarine (at the same time kaolin, montmorillonite and other secondary minerals formed), but may also form where aquamarine never has been present or is present, but is seemingly unetched. Sometimes, a bertrandite-bearing cavity contains small fragments or larger pieces of etched and dissolved aquamarine, but in other cavities, no indications of aquamarine remain. Bertrandite may form a thin, white crust of micro crystals coating quartz or other minerals. Sometimes, this crust consists of a base of very tiny crystals, that are indistinguishable under magnification of about 70 diameters or less, covered with a layer of larger crystals, commonly up to about 1 mm each.

In the zoned, complex pegmatite, bertrandite occurs in cavities with several associations. It can be found in the outer part of the central zone in the angular cavities in quartz in which no other mineral is present or in which hematite is present. In the outer zone and line rock, it occurs in small cavities with fresh, brilliant, unetched aquamarine with quartz and microcline. The bertrandite crystals are deposited on all of the other minerals in these cavities.

Crystals are flattened square to rectangular prisms with modifying faces beveling some edges. It may be twinned, either forming a "V" or "T" shape in cross section. The mineral is colorless and has a vitreous luster; discrete, euhedral crystals uncommonly exceed 1 mm across and about 2 to 4 mm in length. Associated minerals include aquamarine, albite, smoky quartz, microcline, hematite and zinnwaldite.

Beryl: The occurrence of beryl in the Sawtooth batholith is unusual: virtually all of the material, both massive and euhedral, is colored some shade of blue (Photos. 50-56). The massive segregations of aquamarine in the granite are an unusual geologic phenomenon, known in only a few localities, including two locations other than the Sawtooth Mountains in Idaho, where the segregations are scarce (van Laer and Ream, 1986).

Aquamarine is found as anhedral to subhedral crystals in the granite and in veins,

Photo. 55 Aquamarine, etched so that the terminations and prism faces are reduced to a series of tiny needles, 3.5 cm long, Ardeth Lake area, Sawtooth Mountains, Boise County.

Photo. 52 Aquamarine, 5.2 cm long, Ardeth Lake area, Sawtooth Mountains, Boise County.

Photo. 56 Bertrandite on aquamarine in quartz, longest aquamarine is 2.2 cm long, Ardeth Lake area, Sawtooth Mountains, Boise County.

Photo. 53 Aquamarine, 5.5 cm long, white to yellow patches are areas of alteration to clay or other minerals under the surface, Upper Cramer Lake area, Sawtooth Mountains, Custer County.

Photo. 54 Aquamarine, unusually dark blue, the longest is 3 cm, Upper Cramer Lake area, Sawtooth Mountains, Custer County.

Photo. 59 Potassium-bearing carpholite, radial groups are 3 mm across, with pink montmorillonite, Ardeth Lake area, Sawtooth Mountains, Boise County.

Photo. 57 Carpholite on microcline with black manganese oxide staining, carpholite groups are 3 mm across, Bowknot Lake area, Sawtooth Mountains, Custer County.

Photo. 60 Goethite pseudomorph of siderite, 6 cm across, Imogene Lake area, Sawtooth Mountains, Custer County.

Photo. 58 Helvite on smoky quartz with topaz, large twinned helvite crystal is 1.5 cm high, Benedict Creek, Sawtooth Mountains, Boise County.

pods, lenses and sunbursts coating joints. Euhedral crystals occur in miarolitic cavities, or rarely, frozen in pegmatite. The massive occurrences are found in areas with concentrations of beryllium, so that locally, much of the granite is covered with deep blue, massive aquamarine or replaced by it; most of this material is both difficult to collect and relatively worthless to the collector, but is particularly striking to see, especially when associated with spessartine.

Fine crystals of aquamarine have been found in miarolitic cavities in the granite and pegmatites. They are usually small, measuring from less than 5 mm to 7 cm in length, but have been found much larger. Pocket material is often severely corroded, with the prism faces deeply etched. Typically the faces are etched so that numerous needle-like projections are common, oriented parallel to the prism (Photo. 55). A collector must beware not to run a finger down the sides of such crystals! Also they are a threat to the fingers while the collector is hand digging the crystals, dirt and debris from the cavity. Etching may occur on either the prism or termination faces or on both.

Portions of some crystals display a type of etching in which the prism faces are reduced to numerous scallops and dimples that remain brilliant. In one cavity, this was the only type of etching. The terminations of the small crystals from this cavity are pointed so that they resemble a sharpened pencil or needle.

Color ranges from pale sky blue to fine medium to dark blue; massive material sometimes approaches deep cobalt blue. Crystals are typically prismatic; terminations are usually the simple pinacoid, sometimes with the first and the second order pyramids. Common for aquamarine, the crystals are often zoned, so that when seen in cross section, they display a few layers of varying intensities of blue. When etched, the dissolving action is typically selective (Photo. 55), favoring one layer over another. This creates a crystal in which either an outer or inner layer(s) is etched much more than other layers. This may produce hollow or cavernous areas in some crystals, stepped growths or pagoda-like shapes.

Associated species include albite, bertrandite, hematite, smoky quartz, microcline, zinnwaldite, pyrophanite and goethite pseudomorphs of siderite and of pyrite. Matrix specimens are rare, and the few known have aquamarine crystals less than 2 cm in length; single crystals, detached from the wall rock or doubly terminated, are the general rule. Often aquamarine has been partially to completely dissolved and bertrandite has formed; on etched aquamarine crystals, small bertrandites may be found along fractures and at etched crystal terminations, or on other minerals in the cavity.

Aquamarine cavities are often packed with crystals. It is uncommon for a cavity to contain only a few small crystals, and the aquamarine may nearly pack the cavity full, with only room for a little clay between crystals. Smoky quartz in aquamarine cavities is most often of poor quality, being somewhat gray or milky and often having milky overgrowths. Microcline is usually a minor mineral, occurring in small crystals only and typically etched.

Beryl is not expected to occur in the same cavity with helvite and has not been reported in the same cavity with topaz. However, one cavity was found which contained topaz with tiny inclusions of helvite and what appears to be beryl. The beryl inclusions are hexagonal prisms with pinacoid terminations and pyramid modifications. Inclusions of beryl are completely enclosed in the topaz, about 2 mm below the surface, and there are also several cavities with hexagonal outlines that extend from the surface to about 2 mm into the topaz; these appear to represent beryl that has been dissolved.

There is apparently no correlation between aquamarine masses, pods and sunbursts on joint surfaces or frozen in the granite and the occurrence of crystals in nearby cavities.

Biotite: Biotite is rare in the cavities, but does occur as one of the alteration products of fayalite in some pegmatites. It has been found in cavities; in one, it formed unusual lath-like crystals upon which microcline crystals formed (Boggs and Menzies, 1993).

Calcite: This mineral has been found as coatings in a few cavities. Subhedral or better crystals are not known to occur.

Carpholite: Carpholite is rare in the miarolitic cavities of the Sawtooth batholith. This is apparently the first reported occurrence of this mineral in the U.S. (Ream, 1989b). A probable new species, with potassium substituting for manganese and containing lithium, was reported previously (see below). Only a few cavities in the Sawtooth Mountains are known to have produced a carpholite group mineral. Samples from two of them have been analyzed and are known to be the new species, and specimens from one cavity found by the author, has been determined to contain no potassium (microprobe analysis) and is identified as carpholite. No work has been done on material from other cavities, but their characteristics are closer to those of the new species, and they were found in the same area.

The carpholite occurs as tiny acicular crystals in radiating tufts. These are coating small microcline crystals, generally perched on the tops of the microcline (Photo. 57). Quartz, zinnwaldite and albite are associated. The crystals are up to about 1.5 mm in length and are less than 0.2 mm across. They have a light yellowish brown color (personal).

Potassium-bearing carpholite: Specimens of a carpholite group mineral with potassium substituting for manganese, and containing lithium have been identified from the Sawtooth Mountains. Work was not completed to have this apparent new mineral characterized and accepted as a new mineral. It consists of acicular crystals as radiating spherules and compact groups. They vary from less than 2 mm in length to about 1.2 cm in length. The color is colorless to white or light yellowish brown.

This possible new species was identified from two cavities, and tentatively identified from two others. In one cavity, it forms a thin crust of tiny spherules (Photo. 59) and as tiny tufts and hemispheres on and embedded in the surface of smoky quartz. The longest crystals are about 4 mm, and they are around 0.2-0.5 mm across. Montmorillonite, microcline, albite, quartz, zinnwaldite-masutomilite and topaz are associated.

In other cavities, it forms late and occurs as acicular or needle-like crystals in a compact radiating habit, forming spheres or hemispheres on secondary albite. Crystals are known up to about 1.2 cm in length and hemispheres up to 1.7 cm across; they have only been found in weathered cavities where the crystal groups have been broken and separated. The four cavities occur in one basin, about 0.75 miles apart.

(Specimens of the potassium-bearing carpholite have also been found in an aquamarine-bearing pegmatite, probably Tertiary age, near Centerville, Idaho, about 45 miles west of the Sawtooth Mountains.)

Cassiterite: Microcrystals of cassiterite were identified in one cavity. These occurred as brilliant, black tetragonal prisms with pyramidal terminations and are less than 1 mm in length. Similar crystals have been found in a second cavity, associated with ferrocolumbite.

Chabazite: Tiny crystals, with a cubic or nearly cubic habit, were found in cavities in one diabase dike. The habit and association suggests that these are chabazite, but no identification work was done.

Clay Group: Several minerals fill cavities and coat other minerals in most cavities; montmorillonite was positively identified from two cavities by x-ray diffraction. These clay minerals vary in physical texture from very fine to somewhat sandy, and in color from nearly pure white to gray, brown and pink. There have been few studies of these minerals, and their identification is generally unknown.

Clinozoisite: This mineral was identified from small crystals found in cavities west of

Photo. 61 Masutomilite on quartz, masutomilite is 4.5 cm across, Upper Cramer Lake area, Sawtooth Mountains, Custer County.

Photo. 62 Hematite, 3.5 cm across, Sawtooth Mountains, Boise or Custer County.

Photo. 63 Tiny laumontite crystals on smoky quartz, specimen 5.3 cm across, Upper Cramer Lake area, Sawtooth Mountains, Custer County.

Photo. 64 Microcline with smoky quartz, the large microcline is 6.5 cm high, Hell Roaring Lake area, Sawtooth Mountains, Custer County.

Photo. 66 Manebach twin of microcline, 6.2 cm across, Upper Cramer Lake area, Sawtooth Mountains, Custer County.

Photo. 65 Microcline with etched surfaces and minor coating of tiny green chlorite crystals, 5 cm across, Baron Lakes area, Sawtooth Mountains, Boise County.

Mount Everly. The tiny crystals had a grayish brown color and were found in a talus slope that also contained similar appearing green crystals of epidote. The long prismatic crystals were under about 8 mm in length.

Dravite: This tourmaline group mineral has been identified from one cavity in the granite of the Sawtooth batholith. It formed felted masses of tiny dark gray to black crystals. Identification was by x-ray diffraction (personal).

Epidote: Small crystals of epidote (identification by physical means only) have been found in several cavities in the southwestern part of the batholith. Individual crystals are typically less than 6 mm long and green in color, most are translucent to transparent. Generally, crystals occur in abundance coating microcline and smoky quartz in small cavities. Around some cavities, it forms a green rim, and occasionally coats fracture surfaces on the granite.

Fayalite: This iron silicate is relatively common in the Sawtooth Mountains, but not as euhedral crystals. It forms veins and masses in the granite and lath-like crystals to large size (up to at least 14 cm) frozen in the pegmatite bodies. Generally it appears to be dark brown to black in color, but may have a somewhat yellowish color on thin edges. Often, it is altered to hematite, limonite and other iron oxides.

Ferrimolybdite: Ferrimolybdite has been reported as a yellow, powdery coating on molybdenite from one occurrence.

Ferrocolumbite: Small to microcrystals have been identified in several cavities, and appear to be common in a few areas. These black, bladed crystals are 1 to 3 mm in length, less than 1 mm across and less than 1 mm thick. Individual crystals are vertically striated and commonly occur in groups radiating from a common point. Microprobe analysis done on one specimen yielded the results of Fe 12.5%, Mn 2%, Nb 40% and Ta 20%. Similar results were obtained in another analysis, but more Mn was present.

Crystals are commonly embedded in and projecting from the surfaces of albite crystals, or included in the outer portion of smoky quartz crystals. They may be more common in cavities in which the albite is altered and crumbly. Ferrocolumbite has been found with quartz, albite, microcline, zinnwaldite-masutomilite, topaz, zircon and other minerals.

Fluorapatite: Fluorapatite has been found in at least three pegmatites. A fragment of purple fluorapatite was found on the dump of the zoned, complex pegmatite described previously. The fluorapatite was positively identified by X-ray techniques. Only one small gemmy fragment was found; a search of the debris failed to locate more specimens.

In a simple pegmatite, a thin, weathered, exposure of white quartz and white microcline, an opaque, purple, prismatic crystal was found intergrown with the quartz. This specimen is zoned with the center having a light purple color and the outer portion being medium purple. The crystal is broken, about 8 mm across and 12 mm in length.

In another white pegmatite in pieces of a white granite boulder scattered down a talus slope, several subhedral crystals of fluorapatite with pink to purple color, with some yellowish zones, were found. These varied from opaque to somewhat translucent. They were up to about 1.5 cm in length and 1 cm across. Pieces of this white granite contained cavities with stilbite, aquamarine, microcline, albite and smoky quartz.

Fluorite: Although relatively common in the Sawtooth batholith in some areas, it is rarely found in fine quality crystals. Most often fluorite forms anhedral crystals in the pocket lining. It does form small crystals in cavities, but even when a euhedral crystal is exposed in a cavity, it is usually only a corner poking out between the feldspar matrix crystals.

Crystal size varies from about 2 mm to 2 cm across, although larger specimens have been found. The color varies from colorless to bright medium green or rarely pink. The darker shades of green are scarce in euhedral crystals in cavities, but are more common in the anhedral masses in the cavity linings. Euhedral pocket crystals are usually cubes or octahedrons, light green in color, with a frosted or etched surface or are highly corroded.

Pink fluorite was found on one matrix specimen as a crude, stepped-growth octahedron 1.25 cm across. The crystal has some cleaved surfaces, but is translucent and fair quality. Another specimen has been found that has a 4 mm octahedron included in the base of a faded quartz crystal. This pink crystal appears to be fluorite (indicated by shape, color and apparent cleavage fractures), but there is a dark halo around the inclusion, which generally suggests a radioactive influence, not common with fluorite. It may be that the dark halo is a remnant of the original smoky color which remains due to the stress on the quartz caused by the fluorite inclusion.

Goethite: Studies have not been done to determine the identity of the iron oxides and hydroxides in the cavities, but goethite has been identified and is probably the most common. It can be found as small hemispherical masses associated with smoky quartz, microcline and albite. A few highly weathered cavities contain large spongy masses of brown iron oxides or thin coatings and crusts. These masses and coatings are generally unattractive and not desirable for collections.

Several iron oxide/hydroxide pseudomorphs of siderite have been found; these are either acute rhombohedrons or intergrown acute rhombohedrons with a flattened, rounded habit (Photo. 60). Individual pseudomorphs have been found up to about 7 cm across. Some of the smaller crystals are only partially altered; the centers remaining as yellowish colored siderite.

Occasionally goethite also forms pseudomorphs of pyrite crystals. Generally the sharpness of the cubic crystals is faithfully maintained (Photo. 70). These are widespread, but are uncommon.

Not all of the dark oxides are goethite. One dark brown botryoidal mass was proven to be a Mn oxide by microprobe analysis. No X-ray or other work was done to determine the species.

Gypsum: A crust of gypsum was found in one cavity and may be the mineral forming small granular coatings and masses in other cavities.

Halloysite: This mineral has been identified as one of the minerals, along with albite, replacing an unknown prismatic mineral in a white granite north of Ardeth Lake. The broken pieces of the pseudomorph were thought to be apatite and display a subhedral hexagonal cross section. The color is cream to purplish-pink (personal).

Helvite: Helvite is a manganese-beryllium neso-silicate. It belongs to a series with iron (danalite) and zinc (genthelvite) end members. A continuous series exists between helvite and danalite and between danalite and genthelvite. These three minerals occur in several geologic environments, generally associated with granitic intrusions. Helvite is the most common of the three minerals (Dunn, 1976).

The helvite identification has been confirmed by X-ray diffraction. A detailed analysis of Sawtooth helvite using an Atomic Absorption Spectrophotometer on material from one cavity gave the following results: $MnO = 36.16\%$, $FeO = 8.49\%$, $ZnO = 8.22\%$. Microprobe analysis done on a specimen from another area of the Sawtooth Mountains, yielded the results of 17.82% Mn and 14.3% Fe.

Helvite is found as a late-forming mineral in miarolitic cavities. The crystal habit is tetrahedral, with some octahedrons occurring; typical crystals display both the positive and negative tetrahedrons in which the negative tetrahedrons are minor, only flattening the corners (Photo. 58). Spinel twins, consisting of the positive and negative tetrahedrons interpenetrating, have been found. One of these is approximately 1 cm across. The color is usually clove to reddish brown with some thin areas being yellowish brown; broken frag-

Photo. 67 Microcline or orthoclase, 5 cm high, Baveno twin, from Profile Lake, Sawtooth Mountains, Custer County.

Photo. 68 Microcline or orthoclase, 3 cm high, Carlsbad twin, from Profile Lake, Sawtooth Mountains, Custer County.

Photo. 69 Phenakite, crystals are 1-2 mm in length, Decker Creek area, Sawtooth Mountains, Custer County.

Photo. 70 Pyrite partially replaced by goethite, 6 mm across, on microcline and albite, Baron Lakes area, Sawtooth Mountains, Boise County.

ments are vitreous to resinous. The luster on euhedral crystal faces is mostly dull, but may be vitreous.

Some specimens are found with a black coating of manganese oxides, sometimes staining the surrounding matrix minerals. Individual crystals rarely exceed 1 cm, but one crystal is a simple tetrahedron of helvite measuring 3.6 cm on edge. Massive material, apparently replacing cavity wall rock, was observed at one site. Helvite is found associated with albite, microcline, topaz, zinnwaldite-masutomilite and smoky quartz. In one cavity, it occurs as micro-inclusions in topaz.

Generally, helvite forms in areas where aquamarine does not form, and would not be expected in the same cavity with aquamarine, but they may occur in close proximity. Unexpectedly, both micro-size helvite and beryl were found included in topaz crystals from one cavity. Both minerals were included in the outer 2 mm of the topaz with both beryl and topaz being present in two crystals.

In one small area, approximately 10 cavities were found containing helvite. In addition, it formed more than 50% of the mass of a nearby small pegmatite pod.

Helvite is uncommon in the Sawtooth Mountains, but may be locally abundant and occur in a few cavities in a small area. Fine specimens of helvite on smoky quartz, albite or microcline are scarce, but have been found. Typically, the late-forming helvite crystals are perched on the quartz and other minerals of the cavity, but when found, they have already been detached and only single crystals can be obtained.

Hematite: Small, brilliant hexagonal plates of hematite occur in cavities, occasionally associated with aquamarine. These may be incomplete and broken, and are generally less than 8 mm across and 2 mm thick. It may also form small crystals on feldspar in zones of spongy wall rock. Rarely found, are roses up to 3 cm across which may be associated with albite and smoky quartz (Photo. 62).

Microprobe analysis has shown that some of the hematite crystals have a core of pyrophanite. Much of the hematite does not yield a red streak and is slightly magnetic. This needs to be studied, and may be due to alteration to magnetite.

Laumontite: Laumontite is rare in the cavities. It has been collected in only a few as white prismatic crystals of the typical habit. In one cavity, it was abundant as crystals up to about 1 cm in length, most of them loose. A few remained attached to the base of quartz crystals on micro-albite (Photo. 63).

Magnetite: Magnetite is rare as small octahedral crystals, with striated surfaces, dull to bright luster, less than 7 mm across. These occur with quartz, microcline and albite. They have been found in only a few cavities. It may be common as a partial replacement of hematite and fayalite crystals.

Masutomilite: This rare mica group mineral was identified in the Sawtooth batholith in the 1980s; the first occurrence of it in the U. S. (Ream 1985c), and apparently only the fifth occurrence in the world. It forms yellow to golden-brown zones intergrown with zinnwaldite in coarse, zoned, pseudohexagonal books. Apparently all the yellowish to golden brown colored mica zones are Mn- and Li-bearing, which indicates that the micas in the Sawtooth Mountains with this color are masutomilite. Thus it is common in the Sawtooth batholith.

In the type specimen, an elongated book lying on edge, the innermost zone is missing, dark brown zinnwaldite forms the next zone with the outer part of the zone grading into yellow-brown masutomilite. Outside of this zone is a dark green zone of zinnwaldite. The Li content is about the same across the crystal, but the Mn content of the inner zones increases outward and replaces part of the Fe so the crystal is two thirds Mn-bearing in the masutomilite zone. The outer green zone is rich in iron, and tiny spessartine crystals are present. This indicates a fluid chemistry in which there was an increasing Mn content as the mica formed, changing from zinnwaldite to masutomilite, but during the growth of the last stage, spessartine formed, consuming the Mn, so the last zone of the mica was rich in iron again.

Similar appearing mica crystals, with a golden colored zone and dark zone of zinnwaldite, or crystals that are dominantly golden color have been found throughout the Sawtooth batholith. It is abundant in an occasional topaz pocket, and has been found in intergrown specimens with topaz, consisting of a cluster of small masutomilite books (individually 0.5 to 1.5 cm across) sprinkled with topaz crystals from 5-8 mm long. Often, the zoning cannot be seen except on a freshly cleaved surface. Associated minerals include microcline, albite, quartz and topaz.

Fine specimens of unweathered books on albite, microcline or smoky quartz have been collected (Photo. 61), but are uncommon. Typically, the micas have suffered the effects of exposure and weathering in the open cavities, and express this with rounded edges and broken, cleaved crystals. Books typically readily separate into many layers, so that a broken section of a masutomilite crystal is the most common specimen.

Microcline: Generally orthoclase is a constituent part of the massive granite, and microcline is found lining cavities. Microcline has often undergone considerable corrosion and dissolution, so that few sharp euhedral crystals are recovered. Many specimens (especially larger crystals) have rough surfaces and numerous holes from alteration and weathering (Photo. 65).

Individual crystals rarely exceed 8 cm in any dimension; clusters and matrix specimens are usually composed of smaller crystals, averaging less than 3 cm in length. Large crystals on matrix are rare. Color ranges from white to tan and pink and rarely light green, but light pink is most common. Truly white crystals are uncommon. Baveno (Photo. 67) and Manebach twins are common and Carlsbad twins can be found (Photo. 68); variations and combinations also occur, including chevron twins (Manebach law) (Photo. 66) and multiple Baveno twins and combined Manebach and Baveno twins. Microcline crystals may be encrusted by albite or partially to completely replaced by it. Some microcline displays curved faces which may indicate partial replacement by albite. A secondary, bright pink feldspar, possibly microcline, has been found as small crystals in small vugs in altered matrix in one cavity with fine-grained, green micaceous material.

Microcline does form spectacular specimens and matrix pieces with smoky quartz, albite, zinnwaldite-masutomilite, and topaz (Photos. 64, 71, 73, 82), but because of the weathering, really fine microcline specimens are rare. Most any of the other minerals may be intergrown with or perched on microcline.

Molybdenite: A rare mineral in the Sawtooth Mountains, molybdenite has been found in at least three small mineralized areas, not in cavities. It generally forms small flakes, and has the typical gray color, with crystals up to about 1 cm across. At one occurrence, the molybdenite was coated with a yellow alteration of ferrimolybdite.

Monazite: This mineral has been reported from one cavity only, where it formed tabular crystal aggregates with a yellow color. Individual aggregates were up to 2 mm across.

Montmorillonite: Many of the cavities contain clay, and some cavities are nearly filled with it. An intensive study of the clay mineralogy has not been done, and it is likely that there are several minerals in these cavities that are called "clay" because of their grain size and other characteristics but are not actually a clay mineral. Montmorillonite has been identified as the clay in two cavities. It was very light gray and contained little or no impurities in one cavity, and packed the cavity full. Associated was topaz (unetched), smoky quartz (frosted surfaces), microcline and masutomilite. In another cavity, it was pink and occurred in sparse amounts in the open cavity. The potassium-bearing carpholite, masutomilite, topaz, quartz, microcline and albite were associated.

Muscovite: This mica mineral is common as tiny scales, larger flakes and small books. It has been identified as gray to light greenish gray coatings on quartz, microcline and albite. Larger, silvery to colorless flakes and books up to about 1 cm across are apparently muscovite; although some may be weathered zinnwaldite-masutomilite.

Orthoclase: One known occurrence of pocket orthoclase has been verified. The orthoclase identified in the one pocket consisted of cream colored crystals to about 2.2 cm in length. Most faces were clean, but somewhat rough. Smoky quartz, some albite and an unidentified mineral, possibly microlite or pyrochlore, were associated.

The adularia variety of orthoclase is also rare in the cavities. In a few, it has been found as an overgrowth on the earlier formed orthoclase as colorless coatings and single crystals. In one cavity, a few doubly terminated blocky, twinned crystals up to 1.5 cm in length were found; these appear to be multiple Baveno twins. The crystals were colorless to white, and most were sharp and brilliant.

Phenakite: This species was positively identified by x-ray diffraction of crystals from two cavities. Phenakite is associated with topaz, microcline and smoky quartz. Crystals are simple, elongated prisms terminated by third order pyramids or are rhombic. They are tiny crystals, generally around 1 mm across for crystals with the rhombic habit and about 1 mm in length, up to 2 mm, for those with the prismatic habit (Photo. 69).

Pyrite: This mineral is uncommon in the cavities in the Sawtooth batholith where it occurs as cubes up to at least 6 cm in maximum dimension, but most crystals are under 1 cm across. It has a sharp cubic habit, but most often is partially to completely replaced by goethite (Photo. 70). It is found associated with smoky quartz, aquamarine, microcline and albite. Through much of the area, it is quite scarce or does not exist, but is locally fairly common. Pyrite is a late stage mineral planted on the surfaces of albite, microcline and quartz.

Pyrophanite: Pyrophanite has been found in a single pocket as a central zone in hematite crystals. There has been no testing of other hematite specimens to determine how common pyrophanite may be. The identification was made by microprobe and x-ray. Associated minerals include aquamarine, bertrandite, albite, zinnwaldite and minor smoky quartz. It is possible that small crystals, identified as hematite in other pockets, are actually pyrophanite.

Quartz: Smoky quartz is the most common cavity mineral that can be found in fine quality specimens (Photo. 64, 71-73, 82). Although colorless quartz is found, it is apparent that for most colorless quartz here the original smoky color has been driven off by exposure to sunlight; with the exception of a few cavities in quartz segregations in which the quartz may have always been colorless. Quartz crystals found lining pocket walls are invariably some shade of brown to black. The presence of euhedral smoky quartz and microcline is a characteristic of the Tertiary age of the granite; similar plutons in Idaho and western Montana of the same age also contain such cavities.

In pockets where quartz, microcline and albite are the only contents, it is often the quartz that is the only undamaged mineral; the feldspar minerals are either corroded, cleaved or generally unattractive.

Smoky quartz occurs in prismatic crystals, from equant to elongate; sizes range from less than one millimeter to as much as 40 cm. Flattened crystals are relatively common, especially those formed from the healing and regrowth of fragments as described below.

Some crystal faces are often bright and lustrous, affording handsome specimens; some are clear and gemmy. In most pockets, smoky quartz crystals may be frosted or pitted and coated with muscovite, clay or bertrandite on all faces or on one side of each crystal (three adjoining faces).

Most quartz crystals have a simple habit with the r, z and m faces the only ones present. The faces x and s, are relatively common, and on some crystals are as large or larger than the rhombohedral faces. Typically the x or s faces are frosted. Other faces may be present on some crystals, but they are not easy to distinguish. There is often minor distortions, and cyclical-alternating intergrowths of m, r, x and/or s, faces creating large "faces" or skeletal features, making it difficult to determine which are less common faces and which are combinations of common faces. Individual crystals are generally elongate, that is about 50% or more longer than wide, but stubby crystals are common.

Cavities with small to micro-size, late stage or secondary, quartz crystals on the feldspar crystals or around the base of the feldspar and large quartz crystals are common. Often, many of these microcrystals are flattened or otherwise distorted, and they usually have frosted faces. Because of the distorted shapes, it is typically difficult to determine that some of these are actually quartz and not some exotic unknown mineral.

Many crystals exhibit twisting or rotation around the c axis. This twisting is common throughout the batholith, and generally gives individual crystals only a slight twist which is only noticeable when looking down the c axis so the curving of the edges is obvious, or by reflecting the light off the prism faces so the slight curving can be detected. An occasional pocket produces a few crystals in which the curving is much more prominent, with the measured rotation being as much as 15 degrees, possibly more, so that the edges and prism faces have developed a pronounced curve. Measuring this rotation is often difficult because overgrowths and stepping of the prism faces make it difficult to determine how much of the curving is actually due to twisting and how much is caused by the surface features of the stepping and overgrowths. In one broken specimen in the author's collection, one side of the crystal displays a twist measured at eight degrees, yet the other side clearly shows a twist of 17 degrees.

It is common for the pockets to have collapsed or burst before crystal growth was completed, so that multiple terminations formed on the broken bases disguising the broken end. The collector finds what appear to be doubly terminated crystals in which one end consists of numerous small terminations. Some crystals heal with one normal-looking termination creating a doubly terminated crystal (Photo. 75); this can usually be detected by a milky zone delineating the healed break.

In other pockets, the collapse has filled the pocket with quartz shards of all sizes; usually the pieces have healed and regrown forming flattened crystals, often odd-shaped, or the broken sides have been healed and display multiple faces. In others, healing did not occur so there are numerous sharp edges that present a hazard to the collector's fingers probing the pocket filling.

Smoky quartz is found associated with nearly all the minerals reported from the Sawtooth batholith; both single crystals and matrix specimens have been found. Some crystals are composed of several smaller individuals in parallel to subparallel growth. Matrix specimens of quartz, microcline and albite are fairly common in small sizes. Inclusions observed in quartz include beryl (aquamarine), a dark blue-green acicular mineral, zinnwaldite and/or masutomilite, a pinkish octahedral mineral (appears to be fluorite), ferrocolumbite, elongated reddish needle-like crystals (probably rutile), helvite, potassium-bearing carpholite and spessartine.

Chalcedonic quartz rarely occurs as small nodules in cavities in a few of the diabasic (basaltic?) dikes scattered through the Sawtooth batholith. The nodules are generally less than 1 cm across.

Rutile: Rutile is another mineral that is uncommon at this locality. It has been identified as the twinned aggregates of black, platy crystals, up to about 1 cm across in one cavity. It is suspected to be the identity of bladed and acicular crystals included in quartz from other cavities.

Siderite: Siderite is uncommon in the cavities of the batholith, and is always partially or completely altered to goethite. It occurs as small rhombs or flat acute rhombs with nearly circular form, either as singles or groups. They can occur on the feldspar matrix or on smoky quartz. Most crystals are less than 6-7 mm across, but a few large crystals to 7 cm across have been found (Photo. 60).

Generally, these altered crystals have a brown to black color. When broken, some of them display a cream to tan-colored center that appears to be unaltered siderite. Apparently, no completely unaltered siderite crystals have been found. Associated minerals include quartz, microcline, albite, topaz, zinnwaldite, aquamarine and bertrandite.

Spessartine: Garnets from the Sawtooth batholith are dominant in manganese content; this, plus the similarity of other pegmatitic or granitic occurrences, indicates spessartine. Spessartine occurs most commonly in trapezohedral crystals, but some dodecahedral forms have been observed. Size generally ranges from 1 to 6 mm across, but crystals have been found up to about 2.5 cm across. The color is yellow to light golden, orange and deep orange-red to dark reddish black in the larger size crystals. Faces are often brilliant and lustrous. Matrix specimens with spessartine perched upon smoky quartz, microcline and topaz are quite striking (Photo. 76). Sometimes spessartine is found included in smoky quartz or topaz.

Good quality spessartine specimens are scarce; most crystals exposed in pockets or on rock surfaces are fractured and broken. Massive to subhedral spessartine is sometimes found in close association with aquamarine concentrations.

Some sheet pegmatites display subhedral to euhedral, medium to dark blue, transparent to opaque aquamarine sprinkled with 2 to 6 mm orange-red spessartine crystals. A striking combination in the field, but nearly impossible to collect in acceptable quality specimens.

Spessartine is scattered through the batholith, primarily in local concentrations, missing in many areas. It is a late stage mineral that is perched on albite, quartz or microcline. Most often these are scattered single crystals, but may form a crust of small crystals.

Stilbite: Micro to small crystals of stilbite are uncommon but have been found in several cavities. They were found at one location, lining thin, irregular cavities along joint surfaces. Individual crystals are less than 3 mm in length, have an amber to pinkish orange color, typical stilbite habit, and are translucent. They are common in this zone, high on the eastern side of the small peak north of Payette Peak (between Payette Peak and The Arrowhead).

At another location in the upper portion of Hell Roaring Creek, stilbite was found in several cavities in a zone of white granite. Tiny white crystals and brownish crystals (caused by feathery brown inclusions in colorless stilbite) form crusts coating quartz and microcline, or lining the cavities (Photo. 77). In one cavity the stilbite was associated with and intergrown with aquamarine, and in another, white crystals to about 4 mm were sprinkled on microcline associated with smoky quartz. Similar crystals were found in two cavities near Baron Lakes where the stilbite crystals were associated with smoky quartz and microcline, primarily on the smoky quartz (Photo. 74).

Topaz: Topaz is sparsely scattered through much of the Sawtooth batholith and is locally abundant. Crystals are stubby to elongate prismatic, as individuals and in parallel to subparallel groups. It is also rarely in roughly hemispherical masses consisting of crystals radiating from a central point. Sometimes, crystals are found perched on smoky quartz crystals, but are usually growing on albite and microcline.

Forms include the prisms m and l, often with prism face b; terminations are primarily the two brachydomes f. Other forms represented are the pinacoid c, pyramid o and the macrodome d.

Crystals generally have sharp, brilliant prism faces, but the terminations are most often lightly etched or rough. All faces of the crystals from a cavity are sometimes etched and corroded; these crystals range from rough and pitted to brilliant and jagged reducing crystals to a few irregular pieces with needle-like projections or irregular pieces with pits and scallops. Often, the etching follows one zone only and is obvious by the color variation between the etched and unetched zones. In one cavity it may be an inner zone on the crystals which is etched (Photo. 84), but in another cavity, it is the outer zone.

Sometimes, not all crystals in a cavity will be etched. One cavity produced hundreds of small (3 to 6 mm in length), brilliant, colorless to dark sherry colored topaz crystals attached to the lower portions of quartz and sides of microcline crystals, five larger (1 to 2 cm), brilliant, light sherry colored crystals and one 2 cm, very light sherry colored, deeply etched crystal. In this cavity, masutomilite was abundant in books to 6 cm across (mostly cleaved and weathered), the quartz was grayish brown and frosted and microcline was in large, pitted and cleaved crystals.

Colors range from colorless, to pale yellow to yellow, to light sherry brown to medium sherry brown and rarely pale blue. Coloring is sometimes distinctly zoned. A number of specimens exhibit a translucent white overgrowth on the terminations, probably finely crystalline topaz. Exposure to light bleaches the topaz crystals; apparently an original sherry color will become light yellow or colorless. Very few cavities have been found in which the topaz crystals have never been exposed to light, so the range of the original coloration is unknown. Most of the topaz is somewhat milky, especially towards the centers of crystals, and small fractures are common (Photos. 80, 82). Transparent crystals are rare (Photo. 78). Some crystals with an inner zone that is somewhat milky show a fluorescence in ultra violet light in this milky layer. Fluorescence in topaz is uncommon; the fluorescence is typically a light yellowish color.

Euhedral topaz crystals range from less than a millimeter to as much as 12 cm in length; the average specimen is in the 0.5 to 2 cm range. It is found associated with smoky quartz, microcline, albite, masutomilite, muscovite, spessartine, ferrocolumbite, zircon and potassium-bearing carpholite. Matrix specimens with the larger crystals are uncommon but often attractive (Photo. 82). These are difficult to obtain because of the basal cleavage which has permitted the crystals to break off during pocket collapse and the weathering processes. Matrix specimens with crystals 1 cm or less in length are fairly common.

In one cavity, the elongated topaz crystals were mostly attached in pairs forming a "V" that appear to have consistent angles. This may be a form of twinning, which is rare in topaz. These specimens have not been studied to determine if the angles are indeed the same between specimens and thus indicate they are twins.

One unusual pocket contained fine specimens of topaz pseudomorphs of microcline (Photo. 79). The topaz occurred as small crystals, 1-5 mm in length, with similar size quartz crystals that formed a cast of the microcline or, more commonly, replaced the microcline with a spongy mixture of the topaz and quartz.

In some areas, topaz is common as crystals from about 0.5 to 1 cm in length in small cavities. Several crystals may be seen on the surface of the granite in shallow cavities, but typically, many of these are broken. Sometimes, a topaz pocket contains an abundance of large topaz crystals, anywhere from 10 to 30 or more crystals from about 1 cm to 4 cm in length. Rarely, some of these are still attached to the microcline and albite matrix. Topaz may also be secondary occurring as tiny, microscopic crystals coating quartz. These generally coat two or three faces of each quartz crystal and consist of tiny, colorless crystals projecting from the surface. Individual crystals are usually 1 to 2 mm, up to about 3 mm in length.

The smoky quartz in topaz cavities is often of fine quality, with a light to medium color, brilliant surfaces and gemmy interior. Fluorite is fairly common with topaz, but is typically in small corroded crystals.

Unknown Minerals: There are many micro- and small-size minerals that have not yet been studied to determine their identification and are uncommon to rare in their occurrence in the Sawtooth batholith. Many of these have been found in only one cavity each, and for some, only one crystal is known. Most of them are found in cavities in which the albite appears to be corroded and is often coated with a very fine grained micaceous or clay-like material.

Other minerals, generally massive, that sometimes attract attention and do not occur in the cavities, include black manganese oxides which coat joint surfaces and replace wall rock. Some of the joint coatings appear to be micro-crystalline.

There are presently more than 35 unknown-unidentified specimens, associated with most of the common minerals, and many of the uncommon to rare minerals described on these pages. It is hoped that studies will done, and these will be identified in coming years to fill in the missing data on the Sawtooth mineralogy.

Uranophane: Uranophane has been identified in one small cavity and is probable in another in the Sawtooth batholith. In the one cavity, it formed a cluster of radiating acicular crystals to about 1.5 mm in length, the specimen about 3 mm across. Individual crystals have a light yellow color and waxy luster. Identification was by x-ray diffraction. In another cavity, it forms a yellow lining on a tiny cavity, about 2 mm across.

Wodginite: This mineral was identified from one specimen (Ream, 1989a). It forms two black, prismatic crystals, approximately 2 mm high perched on albite (Photo. 81). A third crystal is exposed on an apparent cleaved surface of a microcline crystal. The surfaces vary from dull, slightly pitted, to smooth and brilliant. Corroded and crumbly albite, microcline, smoky quartz, small green books of zinnwaldite, and tiny, corroded topaz crystals are associated. The entire specimen is coated with a white to cream colored clayey to micaceous material.

Zinnwaldite: Zinnwaldite appears to be the most common mica mineral in the cavities in the Sawtooth batholith. Generally it forms pseudohexagonal books, usually lying on edge, up to about 5 cm across and up to 6 cm or more in length. It has a dark greenish brown to dark green, nearly black, color and is commonly zoned with individual zones showing the green color variations and golden zones being masutomilite.

It is found throughout the batholith and is associated with nearly every mineral. It is most commonly seen as books intergrown with microcline, albite and smoky quartz, but fine specimens of zinnwaldite are rare. Typically, it has weathered surfaces and may be separated into many layers.

Zircon: This mineral has been found in several cavities where it forms prismatic crystals up to 4 mm, with a green, reddish brown or brown color. These have been found partially enclosed in or entirely enclosed in albite, exposed only where the albite is broken. Individual crystals are sometimes sharp and euhedral, but are typically slightly rounded, and may be distorted. Some of them are elongated, being less than 0.5 mm across and about 2-3 mm in length. Often there is a reddish brown halo in the albite surrounding the zircon crystal. Associated minerals include quartz, albite, microcline, aquamarine, ferrocolumbite, zinnwaldite-masutomilite and topaz.

Part 2

Mineral Descriptions

ACANTHITE

Ag_2S, monoclinic

Dimorphous with argentite. Often occurs as pseudomorphs of argentite. Argentite is only stable above 177° C, thus acanthite is the mineral found in the surface environment. Sectile, iron-black; found as pseudomorphs with the cubic forms (cubic, octahedral, rarely dodecahedral, reticulated, arborescent) of argentite. A primary silver mineral associated with other silver minerals and sulfides in veins. Many of the following occurrences were described in the literature as argentite, but have been changed to their proper identification of acanthite (acanthite pseudomorphs of argentite).

Boise County: Acanthite was one of the main ore minerals of the Banner District. It formed rich streaks in the quartz veins in the granites of the district. Stephanite, native silver, pyrargyrite, sphalerite and pyrite were associated (Shannon, 1926).

In the Quartzburg District, acanthite occurred in the veins on Clear Creek. Other silver minerals and iron arsenates were associated (Shannon, 1926).

Elmore County: Acanthite was apparently uncommon in the mines of the Atlanta District where it was found with other silver minerals. It occurred in the Buffalo-Monarch vein with pyrargyrite, silver and quartz. Crystals are not mentioned in the literature but did occur; at least one spectacular, large crystal was preserved from the Buffalo Mine (Photo. 83). Acanthite formed mossy grains in the Atlanta lode with stephanite, stromeyerite, polybasite, miargyrite, gold, galena and tetrahedrite (Anderson, 1939; Shannon 1926).

Owyhee County: Numerous mines in the Silver City and DeLamar Districts produced acanthite. It was generally in veins, masses, small crystals, crusts or films in quartz veins in the Poorman, War Eagle, Pauper, Trade Dollar and Rising Star mines. Crystals were found in a raise 1,300 feet from the portal of the Blaine tunnel in the Silver City District. These were small dull crystals on drusy quartz in cavities. Associated minerals in the various mines include pyrargyrite, miargyrite, polybasite, stephanite, stibnite, chalcopyrite, quartz and orthoclase (Piper and Laney, 1926; Shannon, 1926).

Acanthite occurred as tiny crystals (to 2 mm) in the silver-bearing ores of the DeLamar pit. The mine is now closed and is being rehabilitated, so there will be no more minerals produced from this mine. The tiny acanthite crystals were found with naumannite crystals on fractures (personal).

Shoshone County: Acanthite has been reported from several mines in the Coeur d'Alene District. It is generally massive and finely granular. Shannon (1926) reported one specimen, from an undesignated mine, that consists of native silver in curved columns and wires on crystalline acanthite. The acanthite forms spongy masses of small crystals with various habits.

Minute crystals of acanthite were rare in the Orr orebody of the Bunker Hill Mine. These were brilliant black, blade-shaped crystals on cerussite or in tiny cavities in earthy limonite (Radford et al, 1981).

Washington County: Acanthite was reported in the ores of the Ruthberg District, 18 miles north of Salubria. It was associated with cerussite, native silver and chlorargyrite (Shannon, 1926). Salubria is now an abandoned town site a couple miles southeast of Cambridge. The Ruthberg District is not known. It may be the district now called the Cuddy Mountain District with mines and prospects in the northeastern part of T. 16 N., R. 4 W. or the Hornet District to the northeast with several mines and prospects in the northwestern part of T. 17 N., R. 3 W. Shannon listed the county as Adams, but the boundary with that county is a short distance to the north.

ACTINOLITE

$Ca_2(Mg,Fe)_5Si_8O_{22}(OH)_2$, monoclinic
Actinolite is a member of the amphibole group, and forms a complete series with tremolite and with ferro-actinolite. It is white to brownish white, transparent or translucent, and forms radiating groups, coarse blades or felted masses. Actinolite is most common in impure, crystalline, dolomitic limestones, talc schists and contact rocks.

Custer County: Actinolite occurs in the contact silicate rocks in the Mackay (Alder Creek) District. It forms finely divided crystals in white marble and veins up to two inches wide consisting of fibrous and acicular crystals in blue limestone (Shannon, 1926).

Shoshone County: Large pieces of fibrous actinolite have been found in the southern part of the county in the St. Joe River area. Specimens have been found at a copper prospect in an unreported locality. Actinolite consists of radiating olive green fibers up to 25 cm in length that form masses of large size. Some of them enclose large cubes of pyrite (Shannon, 1926).

AESCHYNITE-(Ce)

$(Ce,Ca,Fe,Th)(Ti,Nb)_2(O,OH)_6$, orthorhombic
As prismatic or tabular crystals or massive. Black, brown, yellow; transparent to translucent. Found in nepheline syenites, alkali syenites, granite pegmatites and carbonatites in alkalic rocks.

Elmore County: Tiny crystals of what has tentatively been identified as aeschynite-(Ce) are rare in miarolitic cavities in the granite of the Steel Mountain stock. The thin, lath-like, red-brown crystals occur with small crystals of albite, chlorite, smoky quartz and microcline (Photo. 85). Identification was by electron microprobe analysis; they have not been X-rayed. The chemistry and physical characteristics are consistent with aeschynite-(Ce). This is the first discovery of this mineral in Idaho (personal).

AGUILARITE

Ag_4SeS, orthorhombic
Intergrown crude dodecahedral crystals; massive. Iron-gray to iron-black; opaque with brilliant metallic luster if fresh. Uncommon with other sulfides and silver minerals.

Custer County: Fine-grained to massive aguilarite occurs in the Yankee Fork District in T. 12-13 N., R. 15 E. on the Yankee Fork of the Salmon River. It is reported to occur with pyrite, sphalerite, tetrahedrite, arsenopyrite, enargite, pyrargyrite and miargyrite (Anderson, 1949).

AIKINITE

$PbCuBiS_3$, orthorhombic
Massive or prismatic to acicular; striated; metallic, blackish lead-gray, tarnishes brown or copper-red. Uncommon with sulfides, galena and gold.

Adams County: What was tentatively identified as aikinite, was found in the Seven Devils District in the "North Drift in R.R. Tunnel." It occurred as light gray indistinct, striated, flattened plates intergrown with calcite, quartz and cubes of pyrite. An analysis done by Shannon (1926) was inconclusive because of the small sample.

Blaine County: Aikinite occurs in the Peace of Mine on Pole Creek in the upper part of the Salmon River Valley, east of Alturas Lake. The tiny gray crystals occur in cavities in masses of gladite-aikinite. Identification of the gladite was by X-ray diffraction; microprobe analysis indicates that the crystals in cavities are aikinite (personal).

Butte County: Aikinite has been found in the St. Louis Mine on a branch of Champagne Creek in Sec. 15, T. 3 N., R. 24 E. The portal of the Main adit is at 6,310 feet elevation. The aikinite forms microcrystals of a blackish lead-gray color which are tabular or acicular, but not free standing, in cavities. It also forms crusts. Chalcopyrite, dolomite, melanterite and pyrite are associated (Anderson, 1929).

ALBITE

$NaAlSi_3O_8$, triclinic
Forms a solid-solution series with anorthite, the CaAl end member. As the percentage of Ca increases and the Na decreases, the species changes from albite to oligoclase to andesine to labradorite to bytownite to anorthite, forming the plagioclase feldspar group. As grains or prismatic or tabular crystals; polysynthetic twinning on albite or pericline laws; sometimes twinned by Carlsbad, Baveno or Manebach laws. Colorless, white and gray; transparent. In granite, syenite, rhyolite and trachyte as a rock-forming mineral, and in other igneous rocks. Common in miarolitic cavities in granitic rocks.

Adams County: Small crystals of albite line scarce cavities in an altered, greenish gray granodiorite near its contact with limestone on the Helena claim at the head of Copper Creek in the Seven Devils District. The granodiorite reportedly had a pinkish coloration due to the formation of zoisite in the feldspar. Albite specimens had been found on the mine dump of the upper adit (Livingston et al, 1920; Shannon, 1926). In later years, mining was done by open pit methods, and evidence of the adits has been eliminated. The albite is not now evident, except for the rare specimen on the dump (personal).

Boise, Custer and Elmore Counties: Albite is common in miarolitic cavities in the granites of the Sawtooth Mountains. Generally it forms white euhedral crystals, less than 1 cm in length and mostly less than 6 mm. It is common lining the cavities of the rocks in many areas of this Tertiary age batholith.

Smoky quartz, topaz, aquamarine, hematite, zinnwaldite-masutomilite and spessartine are associated. Albite may be a primary pocket-lining mineral, but it is often a late-stage mineral and commonly coats microcline or other minerals; it also replaces microcline in some cavities. Most of the albite is white, but it may have a bluish, purplish or greenish cast. Rarely it has the bladed habit of the variety cleavelandite (personal).

Camas County: Tiny crystals of albite occur on potassium feldspar in the small cavities of the Soldier Mountain stock of Smoky Dome northwest of Fairfield. Albite crystals are colorless to white and less than 4 mm across. They are associated with calcite, epidote, magnetite and smoky quartz. The granites of the stock are exposed only on Smoky Dome and cavities are small and uncommon (personal).

Elmore County: Small crystals of albite are common in the miarolitic cavities in the granite of the Steel Mountain stock, northwest of Rocky Bar. It occurs with microcline, smoky quartz, epidote and rarely prehnite. Typical albite crystals are white, although it sometimes has a bluish color and is in the bladed habit called cleavelandite. Crystals are generally small, less than 5 mm across, and are usually planted on, and intergrown with microcline (personal).

Steel Mountain forms a high peak north of the intersection of the Trinity Mountain road and the road to Rocky Bar. Small miarolitic cavities are uncommon. Most cavities are only a few centimeters across, but a few larger cavities have been found. The granite of the Steel Mountain stock is light colored.

Lemhi County: In the Yellowjacket Mountains from Yellowjacket Lake to Golden Trout Lake and northwesterly into the Bighorn Crags, albite occurs in habit and associations similar to the Sawtooth Mountains occurrence. The host rocks are the quartz monzonites and granites of the Tertiary age Crags batholith. In much of the area they are porphyritic. Albite occurs in miarolitic cavities and generally appears to be a primary mineral. Crystals are mostly less than 1 cm across, but may form combinations that are more than 3 cm across. The color is generally white although many of the larger crystals have a bluish tint or rarely a greenish tint. Microcline, smoky quartz, muscovite, topaz, anatase, hematite, zircon and aquamarine are associated. In the eastern portion of the area, outcrops are scarce and rounded, and in the more rugged western portion, in the Bighorn Crags, cavities are uncommon (personal).

ALLANITE

$(Ce,Ca,Y)_2(Al,Fe)_3(SiO_4)_3(OH)$, monoclinic

Now allanite-(Ce) and allanite-(Y). Yellow, brown to black, opaque to subtranslucent. Massive or granular; crystals tabular or long prismatic, bladed. Accessory mineral in igneous rocks, often with epidote; also in metamorphic rocks.

Idaho County: Black crystals of allanite occur in the placer deposits of the Florence District. The crystals are up to 1.3 cm in length. Gold, titanite, zircon and other minerals are associated (Reed, 1939).

Lemhi County: Allanite occurs in radioactive deposits in a 1.5 mile wide belt that extends from the canyon across from the mouth of Dump Creek, 4 miles below the town of North Fork, northwesterly across the drainages of Sage, Indian, Papoose, Squaw and Spring Creeks to the state line and into Montana. The crystals are generally a dull grayish black color and resemble hornblende. Rutile and monazite are associated in most deposits. Exploration has been done in this area in the past, but most cuts and dumps are slumped and overgrown.

In the pegmatites across the gulch from the Last Chance Mine on the upper slope of the Salmon River drainage across from the mouth of Dump Creek, the crystals are abundant. One pegmatite that is one to two feet in width is about 50% allanite. The crystals are mostly 2.5 cm in length and over, with some of them being up to 5 cm. Some exploration has been done on these claims (Anderson, 1958).

ALLOPHANE

An amorphous hydrous aluminum silicate

Member of the kaolinite group. Has no cleavage, a conchoidal to earthy fracture and is very brittle. Mostly massive, commonly as crusts, as stalactites or powdery aggregates. Colorless, white, yellow, brown, green or bluish; transparent to translucent. Luster is vitreous or resinous to waxy. Most common in fissures and cavities in metallic mineral veins.

Lemhi County: Allophane is common as a filling in fractures and cavities in the lead-silver veins of the Little Eightmile District. It forms incrustations that show a mammillary structure, and varies from colorless to sky blue. These vein and cavity fillings are most common in the Buckhorn Mine (Thune, 1941).

ALMANDINE

$Fe_3Al_2(SiO_4)_3$, cubic

Member of the garnet group, forms a series with pyrope and spessartine. Red, brownish red or purplish red; generally in subhedral to euhedral crystals, mostly dodecahedrons or trapezohedrons. Common in metamorphic rocks, especially schists.

Benewah County: Almandine crystals occur on the lower reaches of Emerald Creek. Many of these deposits are being mined to produce the small garnet crystals for industrial uses. For a description of the occurrence see Latah County in which most of the deposits occur.

Boise County: Small garnet crystals are common in many of the placer deposits of the Boise Basin. Most of the crystals are less than a few millimeters across, but anhedral crystals to about 2 cm have been found. The crystals are red or brownish red in color and trapezohedral in shape; the source is unknown (personal).

Clearwater County: Many localities in the county produce garnets. They are mostly almandine or intermediate with spessartine, and vary from sand size to at least 3 cm across. Fine purplish red crystals have been found in the placer deposits of Cow Creek and Rhodes Creek, near Pierce. Excellent crystals have been found in the placer deposits and schists along the Clearwater River. These are often of large size, but most of the large crystals are anhedral (Shannon, 1926; personal).

Latah County: Excellent crystals of almandine can be found on several tributaries of Emerald Creek, south of Fernwood (Photos. 86-91). The locality is very popular for the gem quality crystals that commonly produce asterated cabochons (Emerald Creek star garnets). Collecting is permitted during the summer months on National Forest land by permit only. Collecting is done by digging in the stream deposits of the creeks of Trail 281, Pee Wee, Garnet and No Name gulches. The gravels can be washed and screened to collect the garnets. Collecting has sometimes been permitted for a fee on leased land down stream.

Most of garnets occur as sand size crystals or larger crystals and fragments up to more than 2 cm across. Euhedral crystals are common, and have been collected up to more than 7 cm across. These are mostly modified dodecahedrons with intensely striated faces, many of them with a rounded form, and trapezohedrons are common. Their color is reddish purple to dark purplish black. They show little rounding and abrasion from stream transport.

Rarely, the garnets are encountered in the host rock. Matrix specimens containing crystals more than 6 mm across have been collected. There are several areas along the Emerald Creek road and other roads in the surrounding area where small crystals are plentiful in the rock.

The host rock is a schist formed from metamorphism of the siltites and phyllites of the Precambrian age Belt supergroup. They occur in a large area around Clarkia, and along the Clearwater River to the east (see Clearwater County). Small garnets can be found in the gravels of many of the tributary streams. Larger crystals, anhedral to euhedral, have been found in isolated areas in the schist. Good specimens displaying euhedral crystals of large size are uncommon (personal).

Garnet crystals, generally almandine, are uncommon in the pegmatites in the Avon area. Crystals up to at least 1.2 cm across occur in the pegmatite of the Luella Mine; smaller crystals have been found in the Muscovite Mine. The crystals are purplish red and friable due to numerous cracks. Most are imperfect trapezohedrons and are frozen in quartz or muscovite. There are several mines and prospects in the area that have produced muscovite, and some beryl, quartz and schorl are also associated. Garnet is generally uncommon (Shannon, 1926; personal).

Lemhi County: Almandine crystals occur in the metamorphic rocks in numerous areas in the county. They are up to 2 cm in diameter (Shannon, 1926).

Shoshone County: Large crystals, up to at least 10 cm, have been found in a small drainage on Cats Spur Creek, a few miles southeast of Clarkia. The crystals occur in the soil and alluvium in this normally dry grassy swale. The occurrence is apparently restricted to a small area only about 20 feet across and about 100 feet in length. This is National Forest acquired land, collecting is not permitted.

Crystals are not solid, but generally largely fractured, subhedral to euhedral, but rough (Photo. 92). The color is dark purplish black; they are similar to the crystals of Emerald Creek. Large star gems (mostly 6-ray) can be cut from these, but fractures are numerous. Fracture-free material is normally small pieces only (personal).

Almandine crystals are common in the metamorphic rocks south of the St. Joe River from about Marble Creek upstream to the headwaters. Garnets occur in many areas but not everywhere. Gem quality fragments occur with poor quality crystals and fragments in the soil and alluvial material alongside a small creek on the west side of the road, 6 miles from the St. Joe River road up Marble Creek. This locality, and many of the other deposits along Marble Creek, is on National Forest acquired land, thus collecting is not allowed. Crystals and fragments of colorless and blue kyanite, up to about 3 cm in length, are associated in many of the deposits (personal).

Garnets are abundant as sand size to crystals about 6 mm in the gravels of the St. Joe River from Red Ives upstream to Broken Leg Creek. In some areas they can be seen on the surface of the gravel bars. On the upper end of the bar opposite Scat Creek, crystals are abundant in concentrates panned from the gravel at water level. They are similarly abundant downstream on the bar at the Spruce Tree Campground. Fine placer gold is associated (personal).

Crystals to 3 mm across occur with staurolite in micaceous quartzite on Lookout Mountain near Avery. The almandine crystals are up to nearly 3 mm across and flattened.

The staurolite forms crystals up to 6 mm long (Shannon, 1926).

On Bathtub Mountain, tiny almandine crystals occur in schist along the road on the south side of the mountain, and along Trail 100 which heads easterly off the road on the southeast corner of the mountain. Along the trail, the tiny garnets occur with staurolite (personal).

Large crystals have been removed from the gneissic country rock north of the former site of the lookout on the ridge top of Freezeout Mountain in Sec. 12, T. 42 N., R. 3 E. The gneiss forms a small outcrop on the west side of the road and displays a small worked area. The crystals are up to at least 15 cm in diameter and have a subhedral to euhedral dodecahedral shape (Photo. 93). They are difficult to remove from the matrix and commonly contain biotite inclusions (personal).

Almandine crystals occur in the gneiss along Goat Mountain. Several areas are located along the road where small reddish crystals can be found; typically, these are easiest to find in the road. Some have good form, but others are granular and not sharp, many are rounded (Photo. 94). Most crystals are less than 2 cm across, but some are larger (personal).

A few miles to the east, on the south side of Moses Butte, larger crystals can be found in the rock and as float scattered across a ridge above the road. These crystals are anhedral to subhedral and up to at least 25 cm across. They have a rough surface and inclusions of kyanite and biotite. Individual crystals can be found exposed on outcrops of the gray anorthosite and possibly the gneissic country rock. The largest crystals were noted on the surface of the ground on the side of the ridge. Large boulders along the road contain pink and blue kyanite crystals to at least 5 cm in length (personal).

Also on Moses Butte, small reddish pink or rose pink crystals occur in white anorthosite north of the summit on the ridge that runs to South Butte. These are fine dodecahedral crystals and generally occur with several crystals in a small area (Photo. 95). Most crystals are less than 1 cm across, but have been found to more than 2.5 cm across. Kyanite occurs in nearby zones, and large, crude almandine crystals can be found to the south and below the red almandine area (personal).

ANALCIME

$NaAlSi_2O_6 \cdot H_2O$, cubic

Member of the zeolite group. Generally trapezohedrons, sometimes modified cubes; colorless to white. A common secondary mineral in volcanic rocks associated with other zeolites, calcite and quartz.

Adams County: Analcime occurs with other zeolites, calcite, apophyllite, gyrolite and quartz in small cavities in basalts south of Pinehurst. There are good exposures in roadcuts along Highway 95 from about one half mile north of mile post 176 to mile post 178 (Photo. 96). Most crystals are tiny and occur as colorless drusy coatings, but some crystals are up to about 8 mm across. The highway in this area was reconstructed in 2000 with the outcrops and roadcuts blasted and the highway widened and straightened. During construction, there were good collecting opportunities, but most roadcuts are now large and massive with few areas accessible for rock to be broken. The rock from these cuts has been dumped along the river throughout this area and does provide some opportunities for collecting (personal).

Blaine County: Colorless crystals to nearly 3 mm coat fractures in granitic rock at the Golden Bell Mine near Bellevue, Wood River District (Shannon, 1926).

Custer County: Crystals occur with mordenite, heulandite, calcite, quartz and other minerals southeast of Challis. This is in volcanic rocks interbedded with Miocene lake sediments. The analcime forms single crystals and groups embedded near the centers of large masses of "cottony" mordenite in vesicles, and druses along fractures in the enclosing rocks. Individual crystals reach a diameter of 1.4 cm and are generally colorless or milky due to included fibers of mordenite and grains of quartz. Most crystals are trapezohedrons q(112), and a few show cube a(100) or trisoctahedral faces w(233). Flattened crystals or hemispheres that formed between plates of calcite are reported at this locality. The flattened crystals may be as much as 10 mm across and only 1.5 mm thick (Shannon, 1926).

Analcime is uncommon on quartz pseudomorphs of apophyllite in an undisclosed area near Antelope Flats, SE of Challis. The small crystals, are under 8 mm across and of the typical habit. Only a few crystals have been found on specimens of the pseudomorphs (personal).

Idaho County: Analcime forms crystals up to about 1.5 cm across in basalt in the roadcut on the north side of Skookumchuck Creek along Highway 95. Most cavities are small and contain tiny crystals of analcime, apophyllite, chabazite, heulandite, mesolite, phillipsite, levyne, offretite, cowlesite, tacharanite or tobermorite and okenite. An uncommon vesicle is larger, up to 6 inches across, and contains analcime crystals to 2.5 cm and larger than average apophyllite (personal).

Analcime can also be found in the cavities in the roadcut 2 miles east of Highway 95 on Forest Service road 354 up Slate Creek. The analcime crystals are up to 2 cm across and occur in small cavities with natrolite. Chabazite also lines the cavities that contain analcime, and small amounts of natrolite may occur in these also. Most cavities are small and the analcime often fills or nearly fills the cavity. Small veins contain tiny chabazite as phacolite twins on natrolite needles (personal).

Washington County: Tiny to small crystals of analcime occur in small cavities in Columbia River basalts in a roadcut 3.9 miles downstream on the Wildhorse River road from the road to Cuprum. There probably are other zeolites in the area, but access is limited. The lands along the valley floor are private, making access to the public lands along the valley walls difficult. At this location, the zeolites occur in a small roadcut (personal).

ANATASE

TiO_2, tetragonal

Trimorphous with rutile and brookite. Acute pyramidal, uncommonly obtuse pyramidal, also tabular, rarely prismatic. Luster adamantine or metallic adamantine. Color brown, yellowish and reddish brown, indigo-blue, black, greenish, blue-green, pale lilac, slate-gray and rarely, nearly colorless. Transparent to translucent. In vein deposits of the Alpine type in gneiss or schist; widespread in igneous and metamorphic rocks. Associated with rutile, quartz, adularia, hematite, chlorite and brookite.

Boise, Custer and Elmore Counties: Lustrous, black crystals of anatase occur singly or form clusters in a few cavities in the granite of the Sawtooth Mountains. Individual crystals have a steep dipyramidal habit and are up to 0.5 mm in length. They can be found perched on albite or in small cavities between albite crystals (personal).

Elmore County: Tiny crystals of anatase are rare on albite and microcline in miarolitic cavities in the Steel Mountain granite stock northwest of Rocky Bar. The tiny black crystals occur in groups on the feldspar crystals. Anatase crystals are mostly less than 1 mm in length and 0.25 mm across (personal). See the albite listing for more information on the Steel Mountain stock.

Lemhi County: Tiny crystals of anatase are rare in miarolitic cavities in the quartz monzonite of the Crags batholith in the Yellowjacket Mountains (Photo. 98). They have been found up to about 1 mm in length and 0.5 mm across. The dark bluish black crystals have an elongated, dipyramidal habit, with somewhat curved faces. They can be relatively abundant in a cavity. Anatase appears to be a late stage, secondary, mineral, perched on the walls of tiny cavities in albite and microcline, and mixed with clay filling in the cavities. Tiny flakes of hematite, an unknown, black, blocky mineral, albite and microcline are associated (personal).

ANDALUSITE

Al_2SiO_5, orthorhombic

Trimorphic with kyanite and sillimanite. Forms coarse, nearly square prismatic crystals, that are red, reddish brown or olive-green; massive or compact. Transparent to nearly opaque. Common in some metamorphic rocks, especially slates, argillaceous rocks and schists.

Blaine County: Small grains and crystals of andalusite occur in metamorphosed shales at the contact of the granitic pluton west of Hailey in the Wood River District (Shannon, 1926).

Shoshone County: Andalusite crystals occur in schists in several areas along the St. Joe-Clearwater River Divide. Translucent, light gray to pinkish crystals can be found along the road to Blackdome Peak and Goat Mountain in schist. Most crystals are subhedral and average about 5 cm in length but have been found up to 15 cm (Abbott et al, 1954; personal).

Valley County: Schists in the Yellow Pine District contain andalusite. Specimens have been collected on the ridge southwest of the Smith camp in a thick layer of schist. The crystals may be tiny (Shannon, 1926).

ANDESINE

$(Ca,Na)AlSi_3O_8$, triclinic

Middle member of the plagioclase group of feldspars. Colorless, white or yellowish, in prismatic or tabular crystals or grains. Carlsbad, albite or pericline twinning. Common rock forming mineral in igneous rocks with intermediate silica content, especially andesite.

Fremont County: Crystal Butte about 18 miles north of St. Anthony produces andesine crystals to 7 cm long. They are colorless to yellow and tabular to (010) with some of them twinned on the albite law. A few are of gem quality. The butte is composed of volcanic rock, probably basalt or andesite. Andesine crystals occur as phenocrysts in the rock and lying on the surface of the ground where they have weathered free (Shannon, 1926).

ANDRADITE

$Ca_3Fe_2(SiO_4)_3$, cubic

Member of the garnet group. Common as subhedral to euhedral crystals, dodecahedrons or trapezohedrons, also massive and granular. Yellow, green, brown, reddish brown or black. Common in metamorphosed limestones and contact zones.

Adams County: Andradite crystals can be found in several areas and mines in the Seven Devils District. Light to dark brown crystals occur in the Peacock Mine (at the portal to the eastern-most adit of the South Peacock Mine) in glassy copper-stained quartz in masses of garnet (Photo. 97). The crystals can be easily separated to display excellent lustrous specimens, although most crystals are less than 1 cm across. Many of them have a porous center, with the pores filled with chrysocolla.

The crystals are dark-brown and are trapezohedron and dodecahedron combinations with forms (101), (211) and sometimes (321). They are up to at least 2 cm in diameter, but most are under 1 cm.

Other crystals have rough surfaces and a dodecahedral form. These have a core of garnet and a shell of quartz displaying the garnet morphology. The quartz layer is about 0.5 mm thick. Iridescent epidote coats the quartz layer, and in some specimens, a layer of specular hematite occurs between the quartz and epidote. Unbroken specimens look like epidote and quartz pseudomorphs of andradite (Shannon, 1926; personal).

Andradite crystals from the Copper Key Mine are deeply rounded by etching (originally forms (101) and (211)). The etching has greatly modified the crystals; from Shannon 1926: "The crystals have been rounded by deep corrosion of all edges, the solvent action having been greatest at the ends of the trigonal axes where uneven faces have been produced. Shallow rounding of the angles at the ends of the axes gives, in some cases, an approximation to a cubic face. The etch facets would give no measurable reflections, but their position show that they are in part trisoctahedrons and in part hexoctahedrons. The faces of both (101) and (211) still retain a brilliant luster, but the former are marked by beautifully symmetrical and sharp etch pits of rhombohedral outline, their edges parallel to the dodecahedral edges of the crystals. The faces of (211) are grooved quite deeply parallel to the same edges." Some of the crystals reach large size; one portion of a well-formed crystal was 17.5 cm across (Livingston et al, 1920; Shannon 1926).

Some excellent crystals can be found in the Queen Mine. Most garnets from this occurrence are anhedral and form masses of crude crystals. The euhedral crystals are dodecahedrons and trapezohedrons or combinations of the two forms, up to 3 mm across. Some of them are composed of several layers, each one having a perfect shape but varying in color from brownish red to greenish gray to brown. This may indicate a change from andradite to grossular and back to andradite (Shannon, 1926).

Specimens from the Arkansas Mine are masses of red-brown garnet that contain some epidote. Vugs contain dodecahedral crystals to 1 cm. Similar masses of grossular are associated (Shannon, 1926).

Reddish black crystals of andradite can be found in the Copper Boy Mine. These are dodecahedrons modified by trapezohedrons and are up to 2 cm in diameter. Brown crystals up to 5 cm across are associated; these are also dodecahedrons modified by the trapezohedron. They are interstitial to columnar epidote (Shannon, 1926).

Boundary County: Andradite crystals to about 6 mm have been reported from the Tungsten Hill Mine in Sec. 13, T. 64 N., R. 1 E. These are brown to reddish colored single crystals and massive garnet. Some calcite crystals are associated, as are masses of tremolite (Navratil, 1961).

Custer County: Dodecahedral crystals up to 2 cm occur in massive garnet in a prospect at 8,560 feet elevation across the canyon from the Phi Kappa Mine in Phi Kappa Canyon east of Trail Creek summit. The crystals are light brown in color and are associated with chalcopyrite, galena, sphalerite and pyrite. They occur in calcareous beds in Ordovician age shale (Shannon, 1926).

Good specimens of dodecahedrons of andradite up to 6 mm across have been reported from the tunnel of the Basin claims at an elevation of 8,050 feet, northeast of Trail Creek summit. These are from a metamorphosed calcareous lens of shale showing skarn-type mineralization. The garnet occurs with vesuvianite, epidote, prehnite and some sulfides (Shannon, 1926).

ANGLESITE

$PbSO_4$, orthorhombic
Colorless, white, gray or yellow, granular or massive; often as euhedral crystals. In oxidized lead veins with other secondary or primary metallic minerals.

Bonner County: Anglesite occurs in the oxidized surface ores of the Glasscock Mine north of Lakeview in the $SE^1/_4$ Sec. 35, T. 54 N., R. 1 W. Anglesite and cerussite replace galena in gossan (Kun, 1974).

Butte County: Grape-like masses of anglesite occur in the mines of the Lava Creek District northwest of Craters of the Moon National Monument in T. 2-3 N., R. 24 E. It also forms large crystals on galena (Anderson, 1929).

Boundary County: Anglesite occurs in the vein of the Continental Mine east of Priest Lake. The ores of this vein were mined in the early part of the 20th century, but there was some exploration at the mine in the late 1980s. One area of the vein exposed during some of that exploration contains small cavities with tiny anglesite crystals of several habits, including sharp rhombic crystals, associated with small masses of galena. The anglesite crystals are white or nearly colorless (Photos. 99,100) (personal).

Elmore County: Small white crystals of anglesite have been found in cavities in galena in the Atlanta Mine, Atlanta District. These occur with pyrargyrite and stephanite (Shannon, 1926).

Shoshone County: Crystals of anglesite were rare at the Hercules Mine in Burke Canyon. The small crystals were tabular, transparent and rarely up to 2 cm in length on massive anglesite, sometimes with wire silver. Prismatic flattened crystals, up to 5 cm in length, elongated on the b axis were found in cavities in galena at the Last Chance Mine. In the Tyler Mine, crystals, up to about 9 mm long, occurred in cavities in galena and had a simple habit (Shannon, 1926).

The Hypotheek Mine, south of Kingston, has produced crystals over 4 cm in length; crystals to 9 mm long were abundant in cavities in galena. Some of the anglesites were doubly terminated, and most were of a complex habit.

Anglesite displaying several habits and several colors, including colorless, white, yellowish and smoky (nearly black) were collected in the Bunker Hill Mine in 1979 to 1981 when the mine closed. Individual crystals to at least 5 cm were collected and many excellent matrix specimens were brought out (Radford and Crowley, 1981; personal).

ANKERITE

$Ca(Fe,Mg,Mn)(CO_3)_2$, hexagonal
Forms a series with dolomite and another with kutnohorite; member of the dolomite group. Crystals are usually rhombohedrons, often curved. Most commonly in coarse, granular, cleavable masses or fine and compact. A vein mineral in many lead and zinc deposits.

Shoshone County: Iron carbonate is one of the most common gangue minerals in the silver, lead and zinc veins in the mining districts of Northern Idaho. Throughout most of the Coeur d'Alene Mining District, siderite is the most common of the carbonates, but in the eastern end (east of Wallace), ankerite is prominent in many of the mines. Crystals are uncommon, most of the ankerite is a coarsely crystalline, massive vein filling, but small crystals have been found in cavities of the veins. These are usually small, acute rhombohedrons, some may be curved. They are nearly white or light brown when fresh, but are dark brown after exposure (Shannon, 1926).

ANTHOPHYLLITE

$(Mg, Fe)_7Si_8O_{22}(OH)_2$, orthorhombic

Member of the amphibole group. Rare in euhedral prismatic crystals, commonly fibrous or lamellar, massive. White, gray, green or brown. Only in metamorphic rocks; schists, gneisses or metasomatic rocks.

Idaho County: Several lenses of anthophyllite occur about 14 miles southeast of Kamiah. It forms as masses with an asbestos-like habit in which the fibers are 6 to 18 mm in length. Some are in radial groups to 12 cm across. Individual fibers are white and flexible.

The deposits have had some production. There are several lenses to 200 feet long and 40 feet wide in mica schist in an area of a few square miles (Shannon, 1926).

ANTIGORITE

$(Mg,Fe)_3Si_2O_5(OH)_4$, monoclinic

Crystals flaky or lath-like, minute; usually massive, very fine-grained. White, yellowish, shades of green, brownish green or bluish. Widespread, often mixed with chrysotile, as the principal constituent of serpentines.

Adams County: Antigorite has been reported from the Seven Devils Mining District (Shannon, 1926).

ANTIMONY

Sb, hexagonal

In thick tabular pseudocubic crystals; more commonly massive or lamellar. Twinning common forming complex groups, fourlings and sixlings. Metallic luster and tin-white color. Most common in veins with antimony, arsenic and silver minerals.

Elmore County: Native antimony occurs in the vein deposits of the Hermada Mine on the East Fork of Swanholm Creek. The mine is in the center of the $W^{1}/_2$ Sec. 13, T. 6 N., R. 9 E., 10 miles west of Atlanta. Mineralization is in quartz veins in a wide shear zone in quartz monzonite and granodiorite of the Idaho batholith. Some mineralization is along dikes that intrude the batholith.

The antimony forms fissure-fillings, pods of coarse crystals, or scattered small grains in the hanging wall of the most productive veins. Stibnite is the most common ore mineral, it forms fine grains disseminated in the quartz veins. Secondary antimony minerals are common in the oxidized surface zones. Cherry-red kermesite and pale greenish yellow stibiconite are the most common. Some white cervantite and valentinite are associated. There is some pyrite, but no other sulfide minerals are known.

The mine has been developed as a small open pit and adit. There are other mineralized zones which have been prospected in a two square mile area around the Hermada, but none of them have had significant production (Popoff, 1953).

APOPHYLLITE

$KCa_4Si_8O_{20}(OH,F) \cdot 8H_2O$, tetragonal

Two minerals—fluorapophyllite and hydroxylapophyllite that form a series. They cannot be distinguished by normal physical means in hand specimens. Ditretragonal or dipyramidal crystals, sometimes have the appearance of an isometric combination of a cube and octahedron. Colorless, white, grayish or greenish; transparent to translucent. A secondary mineral that lines cavities in basalt and other volcanic rocks, associated with the zeolite group, calcite and quartz.

Adams County: Apophyllite occurs with zeolites, gyrolite, calcite and quartz in small cavities in basalts south of Pinehurst. There are exposures in roadcuts along Highway 95 from about one half mile north of mile post 176 to mile post 178. It forms small, nearly cubic crystals in small cavities, often on drusy coatings of chabazite or heulandite. Most crystals are white, but many are nearly colorless. In the roadcut about 0.2 miles north of mile post 177, apophyllite forms blocky crystals to 2 cm. Other small crystals (to 3 mm length) are elongated, with a slight tapering form. Apophyllite is associated with gyrolite and chabazite (Photos. 101, 102). See the analcime section for more information on this area where the road was recently reconstructed (personal).

Custer County: See the quartz section for an interesting description of an occurrence of quartz pseudomorphs of apophyllite. Although these specimens are now quartz, they display the apophyllite morphology well, and some were very large apophyllite crystals at one time—up to 8.2 cm. Apophyllite has not been reported to occur in the county at this time (personal).

Idaho County: Apophyllite, with a radial structure, lines cavities in Columbia River basalt on the east side of the Little Salmon River just south of Boulder Creek, south of Riggins. Prehnite, heulandite and natrolite are associated. The basalt layers are exposed in numerous outcrops above the river (Hamilton, 1963).

In the roadcut along Highway 95, on the north side of Skookumchuck Creek, apophyllite forms small colorless to white crystals lining cavities in basalt. Associated minerals include analcime, chabazite, heulandite and an acicular zeolite (personal).

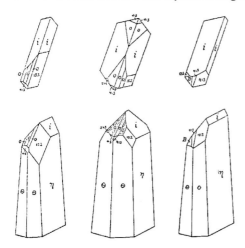

ARAGONITE

$CaCO_3$, orthorhombic

Acicular, tabular or pseudohexagonal twinned crystals; polymorphous with calcite. Colorless, white, yellow or other colors; transparent or translucent. Unstable at normal surface conditions, tends to invert to calcite; much less common than calcite. Lacks the rhombic cleavage of calcite.

Blaine County: Aragonite crystals can be found in a prospect on the west bank of Wood River between Bellevue and Hailey just north of the mouth of Mammoth Gulch. The crystals occur in cavities in limonite, average about 2 mm to 3 mm in

Fig. 10 Aragonite, near Mammoth Gulch, Wood River District, Blaine County; crystal drawings from Shannon (1926).

length and are colorless (Fig. 10). They are unusual in the fact that the terminal faces are not symmetrical. Terminations may have modifying domes and other faces on one side of a termination but not the other. Shannon (1926) noted that the measured angles are consistently slightly different from the theoretical angles of aragonite. Chemical tests prove that the mineral is aragonite and not another carbonate species.

Custer County: Oxidized ores of the Beardsley Mine in the Bayhorse District contain acicular crystals of aragonite. These form sheaves and "fibers" with calcite. Psilomelane is associated and replaces some of the aragonite, forming rosettes of psilomelane pseudomorphs of aragonite (Shannon, 1926).

Crystals of aragonite have been reported from the Aragonite Crystal Mine at Sullivan Rock on the Salmon River above Clayton (Shoup, 1953).

Lemhi County: Aragonite forms branching plant-like forms (flos ferri) in the Pittsburg-Idaho Mine in the Texas District (Shannon, 1926).

ARGENTOPYRITE

$AgFe_2S_3$, orthorhombic

Most common as grains; sometimes pseudohexagonal crystals, sometimes interpenetration twins forming six-sided stars. It has a metallic luster and steel-gray to tin white color; tarnishes bronze brown, green, blue, yellow and purple. Dimorphous with sternbergite. Associated with arsenic, proustite and pyrite.

Custer County: Small blebs of argentopyrite occur in the ores of the mines in the Slate Creek area. It occurs with sphalerite, jamesonite and geocronite. Other minerals in the area include cubanite, digenite, libethenite and pentlandite. Most of these minerals occur as irregular grains, typical of many ore veins (Kern, 1972).

ARSENIC

As, hexagonal

Grains, masses or pseudocubic crystals. Tin-white on fresh surface; tarnishes to dark gray. Rare in veins with silver, cobalt or nickel.

Bonner County: Arsenic occurs in a narrow vein in diorite of the Kaniksu batholith near the contact with Cambrian rocks of the Prichard formation at the Vulcan Mine. A small adit has been driven on a galena-bearing vein which is parallel to the arsenic vein. Pyrite, calcite and epidote are associated (Shannon, 1926).

The prospect is located alongside the road about 2 miles north of the town of Lakeview on the east site of Lake Pend Oreille. There has been some exploration and drilling at the prospect, but the adit is caved (personal).

ARSENOPYRITE

FeAsS, monoclinic

Silver-white crystals common; prismatic, often striated. The most common arsenic-bearing mineral. Common in veins with sulfides and gold. Cobaltoan arsenopyrite was at one time considered a separate species with the name danaite, and has a similar occurrence to that of arsenopyrite, occurring where cobalt is also present.

Blaine County: Arsenopyrite can be found in several mines in the Hailey Gold Belt.

Crystals in the Red Cloud Mine are prismatic and occur with galena and pyrite (Shannon, 1926).

In the Wood River area, arsenopyrite occurs in the lead-silver mines including the Minnie Moore, Independence and North Star. In the North Star, it is associated with galena, sphalerite and boulangerite in quartz, and commonly has a pale yellow color similar to pyrite. Some crystals are very slender and are embedded in sphalerite. Others occur in ankerite and can be freed by etching away the associated ankerite with acid. The crystals are often doubly terminated. They have a prismatic habit with the dominant form being the prism m(110); terminations include the faces l(011), s(012) and q(013), either individually or combined (Shannon, 1926).

In the Rosetta and Warm Spring Districts west of Hailey, it occurs in mines near Carrietown. Small prisms occur in quartz associated with galena and sphalerite in the No. 3 level of the Dollarhide Mine. In the Silver Star Mine arsenopyrite forms small prisms with pyrite and galena in quartz and siderite. The Stormy Galore Mine contains small gray prismatic crystals in wall rock inclusions in siderite (Shannon, 1926).

Boise County: Arsenopyrite crystals occur in vugs in the Mountain Chief Mine in the Quartzburg District. Chalcopyrite and pyrite are associated. A few crystals occur on comb quartz in the Gem of the Mountains Mine in the Pioneerville District with galena and pyrite (Shannon, 1926).

Boise and Gem Counties: In the Pearl (now part of the Westview) District, between Emmett and Horseshoe Bend, arsenopyrite forms small crystals in vugs with dolomite and quartz in the I.X.L. Mine. Small tin-white crystals occur in the Checkmate Mine disseminated in granite. Gold-bearing sulfides are associated in quartz seams (Shannon, 1926).

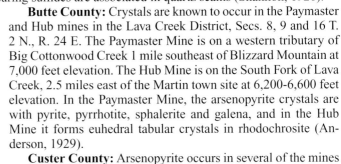

Butte County: Crystals are known to occur in the Paymaster and Hub mines in the Lava Creek District, Secs. 8, 9 and 16 T. 2 N., R. 24 E. The Paymaster Mine is on a western tributary of Big Cottonwood Creek 1 mile southeast of Blizzard Mountain at 7,000 feet elevation. The Hub Mine is on the South Fork of Lava Creek, 2.5 miles east of the Martin town site at 6,200-6,600 feet elevation. In the Paymaster Mine, the arsenopyrite crystals are with pyrite, pyrrhotite, sphalerite and galena, and in the Hub Mine it forms euhedral tabular crystals in rhodochrosite (Anderson, 1929).

Custer County: Arsenopyrite occurs in several of the mines in the Bayhorse District. In the Ramshorn Mine, it forms slender doubly terminated prismatic crystals in siderite. The crystals can be exposed by dissolving the siderite in acid. In the No. 5 tunnel of the Utah Boy claim, stout prismatic crystals occur in vugs in siderite and tetrahedrite. Mossy chalcopyrite coats crystals of siderite and tetrahedrite (Shannon, 1926).

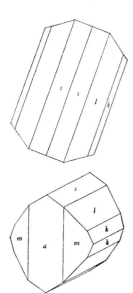

Arsenopyrite occurs about 650 feet south of the north end of the Empire ledge in the Washington Basin District. It forms gray crystals to 1 cm long in quartz (Fig. 11). The crystals may be doubly terminated and twinned; elongation on the a axis causes a prismatic habit (Shannon, 1926).

Fig. 11 Arsenopyrite, Washington Basin District, Custer County; crystal drawings from Shannon (1926).

Elmore County: Arsenopyrite occurs in the Vishnu Mine in the Rocky Bar District. It forms masses and imperfect crystals in quartz. It has also been reported from the Neal District (Shannon, 1926).

Idaho County: Gray crystals were found in the South Fork Mine, 7 Miles southwest of Elk City. They are sharp euhedral crystals and occur in quartz. Arsenopyrite is also reported from a few mines in the Warren District (Shannon, 1926).

Lemhi County: Cobaltoan arsenopyrite occurs in the Blackbird District, in the Haynes-Stellite Co. Mine on Blackbird Creek 2 miles above the mouth of the creek. It forms silver-white crystals up to 5 mm across. They are disseminated in a quartz-tourmaline rock with cobaltite. Although the crystals are frozen in quartz, crystals were exposed by carefully chipping away the quartz. Crystals are prismatic with pinacoid and dome modifications. Most are short and stout and some almost look cubic; they may occur in several of the mines in the district (Shannon, 1926).

Owyhee County: Arsenopyrite occurs with black sphalerite, galena and chalcopyrite in the South Mountain District. It forms euhedral crystals of simple habit up to 1 cm long in the Bay State Mine. Similar material has been reported in the Laxey Mine where the arsenopyrite occurs with quartz and sphalerite (Shannon, 1926; personal).

Shoshone County: Arsenopyrite has been found in a few of the mines in the Coeur d'Alene District, including the Standard-Mammoth Mine near Mace where small crystals were found above the 2,000 level. Iron-gray crystals occur in the slaty rock inclusions in the stibnite-bearing quartz veins of the Stanley antimony mine in Gorge Gulch. Similar crystals were rare in the Evolution Mine near Osburn, and in the Pearson antimony, Liberal King and Casey mines on Pine Creek.

Crystals replacing wall rock in the O.K. Mine in Government Gulch and in the Corby prospect on Pine Creek are brilliant silver white and are similar in the Hypotheek Mine south of Kingston. Here the long prismatic crystals occur in a quartz-carbonate gangue associated with pyrite, chalcopyrite and tetrahedrite (Shannon, 1926).

Valley County: Arsenopyrite occurs with stibnite in veins in the Yellow Pine District. The occurrence is in high-grade lenticular fissure filling quartz-stibnite veins, and in large low grade disseminated deposits of stibnite in shears in monzonite.

The arsenopyrite forms subhedral crystals of small size. Gold, silver, stibnite and kermesite are associated. Most of the minerals are of small size, generally less than 1 mm across (White, 1940).

AURICHALCITE

$(Zn,Cu)_5(CO_3)_2(OH)_6$, orthorhombic

Generally acicular or lath-like crystals, grains or masses. Pale green to blue; transparent. A secondary mineral in copper and zinc deposits.

Blaine County: Tiny crystals of aurichalcite occur in prospects northwest of the saddle north of Blizzard Mountain. The tiny radial groups of aurichalcite crystals are associated with hemimorphite. Other cavities in the same gossan contain chrysocolla pseudomorphs of aurichalcite (personal).

Custer County: Aurichalcite occurs in the Empire Mine in the Mackay District. It forms minutely bladed crusts, with a blue color, coating cavities in a garnet-bearing contact rock. The aurichalcite is composed of very thin transparent laths. The rock contains some fluorite, and very small blades of hemimorphite are associated (Shannon, 1926; personal).

Fine coatings and groups of micro crystals are rare in a prospect on the south side of the Salmon River about 1 mile east of Spud Creek, downstream from Clayton. The adit is about 250 feet above the river on a grassy slope at the bottom of a rocky ridge. The aurichalcite occurs with malachite in chalcopyrite-bearing oxidized vein material. The tiny crystals occur as compact fillings or as groups of pale blue crystals with the typical very thin habit (personal).

Lemhi County: Tiny crystals of aurichalcite occur with in the Ima Mine near Patterson (Photo. 103). These are associated with azurite, malachite and other minerals in the oxidized ores of the mine. Aurichalcite is rare at this location where they form small groups of the typical very thin light blue crystals (personal).

Owyhee County: Aurichalcite has been found in the oxidized ores of the Laxey Mine on South Mountain. It is associated with azurite, calcite, cerussite, chrysocolla, malachite and quartz (Photo. 104). It forms microcrystalline crusts and hemispheres of the typical very thin scaly to lath-like crystals of white to blue color (personal).

Shoshone County: In the eastern part of the county, near the Montana border, aurichalcite is uncommon in the oxidized portion of the ores of the Monitor Mine. Radiating groups of the tiny elongated crystals have been found associated with azurite, chrysocolla, malachite and zalesiite (personal).

AUTUNITE

$Ca(UO_2)_2(PO_4)_2 \cdot 10\text{-}12H_2O$, tetragonal

A secondary mineral; tabular crystals or foliated or scaly masses. Yellow to dark green, fluoresces yellow-green. Easily loses water to form meta-autunite I; most crystals collected are this latter form.

Lemhi County: Autunite forms small crystals to 5 mm in prospects in the Salmon and Gibbonsville areas. They have been found in the Garm-Lamoreaux, Surprise and Dot claims near Gibbonsville. The Garm-Lamoreaux Mine is 5 miles west of Gibbonsville in Sec. 31, T. 26 N., R. 21 E. on Allen Creek, a tributary of Hughes Creek. It is a gold property in phyllites, argillites and quartzites. The Surprise Mine is in Friedorf Gulch several thousand feet northwest of the Moon claim (which is in Sec. 21, T. 26 N., R. 21 E. in Doolittle Gulch). There is a 700 foot adit with several drifts. Strong mineralization is noted at 200 feet and 500-600 feet in from the portal. The uranium minerals occur in the fractured quartzite above the band of footwall gouge. They also occur in the stripped outcrops several hundred feet above the adit and below it.

The Dot claims are west of Gibbonsville about 0.5 mile northwest of the Surprise Mine. It consists of bulldozer cuts and exposures on a ridge crest. All three of the uranium minerals (autunite, torbernite and uranophane) of the area occur here.

The E-Dah-How claims are 6-8 miles south of Salmon along Highway 93. Autunite forms small crystals that are scattered on fractures in volcanic rocks with torbernite and uranophane (Photo. 105). Both the autunite and torbernite crystals are platy and fluoresce, the autunite a brilliant yellow to green and the torbernite a faint green.

The mineralization is in welded tuffs with hematite bands. Autunite and uranophane, with some torbernite, as small crystals can be found in fractures and vugs in the volcanic rocks (Anderson, 1958).

AZURITE

$Cu_3(CO_3)_2(OH)_2$, monoclinic

Azure-blue prismatic crystals, masses or thin coatings. Often replaced by malachite; a very common secondary mineral in the oxidized portions of copper-bearing ore deposits. Is found with malachite, chalcopyrite, pyrite, iron oxides and other ore and gangue minerals.

Adams County: Azurite occurs in the secondary mineralized zones of several of the mines in the Seven Devils District. At the Arkansaw-Decorah-Marguerite Mine, it occurs with chrysocolla, caledonite, covellite, bornite, chalcopyrite, malachite and cuprite. The contact metamorphic host rock contains epidote, garnet, pyroxenes, quartz, calcite, tremolite, zoisite, hornblende and other minerals. The occurrence is similar at several of the other mines in the district, but azurite is uncommon, and generally only forms coatings and thin crusts (Livingston et al, 1920; Shannon, 1926; personal).

Clark County: Small bladed crystals of azurite occasionally form hemispheres in the mineralized limestones of the Weimer Mine in Skull Canyon, thin coatings on fracture surfaces and as single crystals and groups on quartz in small cavities (Photo. 106). Malachite is associated, and is much more common. Azurite sometimes forms small groups of crystals on quartz crystals in small cavities in limestone. The largest azurite crystals are about 5 mm in length and are the common dark blue blades. They are sometimes associated with malachite (Photo. 107). Chrysocolla pseudomorphs of azurite also occur, but are rare (Anderson et al, personal, 1944; personal; Shannon, 1926; Umpleby, 1917).

Custer County: In the Mackay (Alder Creek) Mining district, azurite forms small tabular crystals. It is not abundant, but has been found throughout many mines in the district (personal; Shannon, 1926).

Small crystals can be found in several mines in the Bayhorse District where it forms small crystals in cavities in oxidized tetrahedrite ore. In the Bull of the Woods Mine, it forms small crystals encrusting tetrahedrite and chalcopyrite. It occurs with malachite and bindheimite in oxidized galena-tetrahedrite ore in the Ramshorn Mine, forming thin coatings and possibly euhedral crystals. At the Silver Bell Mine, it forms botryoidal coatings and drusy crusts in oxidized tetrahedrite (Photo. 108). Spongy limonite containing cavities with small azurite crystals occur in the Skylark Mine, and thin crusts and coatings can be found in several other mines and prospects in the district. At the Turtle Mine in the southern part of the district, small drusy crystals and microcrystalline masses of azurite occur with malachite (personal; Pontius, 1982; Shannon, 1926).

Lemhi County: The Blue Jay Mine, high on a ridge on the south side of Big Eightmile Creek, west of Leadore, contains azurite with malachite and chrysocolla. The mine is developed as an open pit and several cuts that expose a copper-mineralized breccia in diorite. This same type of mineralization is exposed in two other areas down the ridge along the access road. There appears to be more chrysocolla in the lower zones.

The azurite occurs as very thin crusts of microcrystals or spheres. Malachite forms thin coatings, as does chrysocolla. The chrysocolla is sometimes in thicker layers and nodules to about 1 cm, and some of it is slightly botryoidal. Large surfaces of malachite and chrysocolla can be found, but most of the azurite occurs as patches only 1-2 cm across. In the Blue Jay Mine, a black coating (tenorite or melaconite?) covers much of the other minerals (personal).

Azurite occurs as microscopic crystals in groups and singles in cavities in the vein quartz of the Ima Mine on Patterson Creek. The tiny crystals are equant or bladed. They occur on microcrystalline crusts of jarosite and segnitite with mimetite, malachite and wulfenite (Photos. 109, 110) (personal).

At the Junction Mining District at Leadore, azurite occurs in gossan with brochantite, cyanotrichite and malachite at the Iron Dike Mine on the east side of Stroud Gulch. It occurs as light blue to dark blue coatings and tiny to small crystals as singles or scattered on matrix and as rose-like or spherical groups. Some of the thin coatings are light blue, but the crystals are the typical "azure" blue; these are often altered to malachite (Photo. 111). Azurite occurs on soft powdery gossan, spongy gossan and on fractures in hard brown jasperoid. See cyanotrichite for further information on this locality and on the reported occurrence at the Peacock Mine (personal).

Owyhee County: Crusts and well-developed crystals of azurite have been found in the Laxey Mine on South Mountain, and it is reported at other mines. It is in the oxidized hedenbergite-ilvaite rock of the contact metamorphic zone, with aurichalcite, bindheimite, malachite, minium, galena, caledonite, cerussite and linarite (personal, Sorenson, 1927).

Shoshone County: Azurite was common as thin crusts and stains in the Caledonia Mine. It also formed crusts of drusy crystals and some tabular crystals to 2 mm in length.

Several other mines in the Coeur d'Alene Mining District, including the Snowstorm and Standard-Mammoth also contained azurite, but it was generally only stains and thin coatings (Shannon, 1926; personal).

Tiny azurite crystals and crystalline crusts are uncommon in the Monitor Mine. Associated minerals include chrysocolla, malachite and zalesiite (personal).

BARITE

$BaSO_4$, orthorhombic

Crystals are usually tabular or diamond-shaped, also prismatic; colorless, white, yellow, red or blue. Transparent to translucent, specific gravity 4.5 (high for a nonmetallic mineral, thus a distinctive physical property). Common as a gangue mineral in metallic ore deposits, with calcite in limestone.

Blaine County: Barite occurs near Hailey and may be present in several of the mines in the area (Palache et al, 1951; personal).

Butte County: Large barite crystals have been found in the Last Chance Mine on Champagne Creek in Sec. 15, T. 3 N., R. 24 E. Pyrite, melanterite and other sulfides have also been reported (Anderson, 1929).

Cassia County: Euhedral crystals occur in the Black Pine District. The Valantine Mine has been reported as one of the best localities. The mine is in Sec. 35, T. 15 S., R. 29 E. at 6,000 feet elevation. Barite forms porous aggregates of tabular white crystals up to 3 cm in diameter. The crystals have a simple habit with only the base and simple prisms displayed. Scorodite, sooty cinnabar and possibly realgar are associated (Anderson 1931; Shannon, 1926).

Custer County: Barite forms rhombic blocky crystals to large size in fractures in dolomite in Spar Canyon east of the East Fork of the Salmon River southwest of Challis (Photo. 113). Three fractures on a rocky knob on the north side of the canyon are lined with clear, gray or white crystals. They form small clusters and clusters of large crystals that are up to at least 20 cm on an edge.

One vein has been exposed in a cut; the other two are exposed in outcrops that have received some hand work. The upper portions of the fractures are partially collapsed and filled with barite and rock debris which is partially cemented by caliche (calcium carbonate) and a white opaline material. Where coated, the barite crystals may be pitted and frosted. Crystals occur as singles and plates; few of them are lustrous, most are dull with a frosted appearance.

Drusy quartz coats some surfaces and may have barite crystals perched on the coating or may coat some barite crystals. Some small barite crystals are tabular and a few are prismatic (personal).

On the next knob to the north, another barite vein has been exposed in a small cut. This vein also has a few cavities. The barite crystals are smaller; they are mostly less than 3 cm across, but have the same blocky form. Crystals are white to grayish and most have a white coating of a fine-grained, scaly, talc-like material (personal).

About 0.5 mile to the west, another cut has been made on a barite vein. This deposit is brecciated along the open barite-bearing fracture. Barite crystals are mostly blocky and are similar to those at the first deposit described above, although smaller. Most of these are, however, coated with a druse of quartz crystals with a thin iron oxide stain (Photo. 112), and are much less common in the vein (personal).

In the Alta Mining District, on Little Fall Creek, barite is rare with fluorite on the Purple Spar claims. Mineralization is on the northeast side of the creek around 9,000 feet elevation. Barite was found in one cavity where it occurred as small crystals, 1 mm thick and up to 6 mm across, of a thin plate-like habit. The crystals formed a few small groups with fluorite, and are zoned alternating white and colorless. The fluorite is found as octahedral crystals on drusy quartz (personal).

On Keystone Mountain, 10 miles southwest of Challis, barite occurs with fluorite in a silica box work in breccia zones in the Ramshorn dolomite. Fluorite is found in many areas where the dolomite has been brecciated and silicified. There are several cuts, trenches and other prospects on the northwest face of the mountain. Other cuts can be found on spur roads that take off to the west from the access road lower on the mountain.

In a long cut at about 9,200 feet elevation on the west side near the top of the mountain, small, colorless barite crystals occur with colorless fluorite. This zone is near the southern end of the cut. The fluorite occurs as tiny pseudocubes, up to about 4 mm across lining the cavities of the box work. In parts of the zone, barite occurs as a few blocky crystals with the fluorite, or as crystals lining the cavities with little or no fluorite present. Barite crystals are mostly blocky, although they are sometimes prismatic, and are colorless. Occasionally, they are coated with tiny drusy quartz crystals. Most crystals are less than 5 mm across, but some are up to about 8 mm (personal).

In the Empire Mine in Washington Basin, small barite crystals occur on pyrite lining cavities in massive pyrite and bismuthinite (Shannon, 1926).

Tabular crystals of barite have been collected on a ridge on a fork of Willow Creek, about one mile east of Freighter Spring. The barite occurs in cavities in limestone. Most crystals are blocky to tabular, colorless to white or yellowish, sometimes with an outer gray zone (Photos. 114,116). Most are up to about 1 cm across, but locally, they are tabular and up to about 3 cm, or more, across. One tabular crystal has been found that is 2 x 5.2 x 9.2 cm, and a creamy yellow color, on matrix with smaller crystals (Photo. 116). In one cavity, some of the crystals were thin tabular, colorless to white with a dark gray zone around the outer edge (Photo. 115). Crystals occur on a matrix of fine-grained gray barite, apparently replacing limestone. Cavities are scarce, and occur at the soil level on a ridge top in weathered limestone. Small barite crystals have been reported in the limestone outcrops on a ridge to the east, but are apparently uncommon (personal).

Lemhi County: Excellent barite crystals have been found in the mines of the Gravel Range District in T. 18 N., R. 16-17 E. The mines are about 1 mile from Meyers Cove and about 38 miles southwest of Salmon. Tabular white crystals to 10 cm, which average about 2.5 cm in length, have been found. They occur as a vein filling or crustification on fluorite, some covered by fluorite; crystals are uncommon. Barite is most common in the stibnite-bearing deposits (Anderson, 1943c, 1954b).

Shoshone County: Barite crystals are uncommon in the Coeur d'Alene Mining District. In the Little Giant Mine, south of Mullan, it forms micro crystals associated with pyromorphite. The tiny crystals are typically thin plates, less than 2 mm across and under 0.3 mm thick. They are colorless to white and often have color zoning showing distinct phantom shapes (Photos. 117,118) (personal).

Owyhee County: Barite was rare as minute crystals in cavities, some in naumannite in the DeLamar Mine in the DeLamar District. It also occurred in kaolin in the same mine, but probably not as euhedral crystals (Piper and Laney, 1926; Shannon, 1926).

Valley County: Small crystals of barite have been reported to occur in veins on the ridge east of the landing strip between Mile Flat and Hard Boil Bar on Big Creek; this is in the River of No Return Wilderness. The crystals are tabular and up to about 1.2 cm in length (personal).

BASTNAESITE-(Ce)

$(Ce,La)(CO_3)F$, hexagonal
Usually tabular, sometimes short prismatic, often massive or granular. Color wax-yellow, tan, light brown to reddish brown; transparent to translucent. With other rare earth minerals in intrusive and contact metamorphic rocks.

Boise, Custer and Elmore Counties: Microcrystals of bastnaesite-(Ce) have been found in a few cavities in the Sawtooth Mountains (Photo. 49). One specimen has three microcrystals on the back side of a smoky quartz and albite specimen. The crystals are white to cream color and have a pseudohexagonal shape (personal).

BAYLDONITE

$PbCu_3(AsO_4)_2(OH)_2 \cdot H_2O$, monoclinic
Forms crusts, granular masses, drusy surfaces and mammillary concretions with a fibrous structure. Green or yellow-green; subtranslucent. It is a secondary mineral that occurs with other arsenates, mimetite and copper minerals.

Custer County: An olive green to yellow-green mineral coats acicular, yellow mimetite on cerussite crystals at the Ramshorn Mine, Bayhorse District. This mineral combination occurs in small cavities in galena-tetrahedrite ore. The green mineral forms minute grains and prismatic crystals. Shannon (1926) tentatively identified it as bayldonite.

Lemhi County: Microcrystalline crusts of bayldonite are rare at the Ima Mine (Photo. 119). The bright green crusts are associated with other secondary minerals including mimetite and vanadinite. It has been found in very few samples from the uncommon areas of secondary minerals on the mine dumps. It has been identified by X-ray analysis (personal).

BERTRANDITE

$Be_4Si_2O_7(OH)_2$, orthorhombic
Crystals thin tabular or prismatic; often pseudomorphic after beryl. Colorless or pale yellow; transparent. Found in granite pegmatites, greisens, aplites and pneumatolytic hydrothermal veins; with beryl, feldspar, quartz, phenakite and tourmaline.

Boise, Custer and Elmore Counties: Bertrandite is common in cavities in the Sawtooth batholith (Photos. 51, 56). It occurs as colorless microcrystals with a tabular habit, sometimes twinned or complex. Most crystals are less than 3 mm long. They usually occur as groups coating feldspar, quartz or rarely etched aquamarine. Their occurrence appears to be secondary, formed from redeposition of the beryllium released from the etching or complete dissolving of the aquamarine in cavities, although it has been found on or associated with brilliant and sharp, apparently fresh, crystals of aquamarine. Associated minerals include aquamarine, microcline, albite, zinnwaldite, masutomilite and smoky quartz (personal).

Valley County: Bertrandite occurs at the Independence Mine, west of Big Creek in T. 21 N., R. 9 E. It is accessible by the Warren Road from the Yellow Pine Road. The McCrae adit is at the edge of the road, and the Goldman adit is below the road on the south side of Smith Creek valley.

Bertrandite occurs with fluorite in quartz that has replaced argillites and quartzites of the Yellowjacket formation. The fluorite and bertrandite occur with calcite, sericite and very small amounts of scheelite in small flat-lying seams that are up to 20 inches wide. Fluorite and presumably bertrandite, occur near the portal of the McCrae adit and in the inner 128 feet of the Goldman adit. Various sulfides including pyrite, sphalerite, tetrahedrite and galena also occur in the silicified zones (Pattee et al, 1968).

BERYL

$Be_3Al_2Si_6O_{18}$, hexagonal

Prismatic, hexagonal crystals, translucent or transparent; colorless, yellow, light green, bluish green, emerald-green, blue, yellow or pink. Mostly in granitic rocks, commonly in pegmatites. Includes the gem varieties emerald, aquamarine, morganite, red beryl and golden beryl.

Boise, Custer and Elmore Counties: Beryl, primarily the blue variety aquamarine, is common in the granites of the Sawtooth batholith in the Sawtooth Mountains in south central Idaho. Most of the beryl is blue, although the color may be white, light-green or greenish blue.

It forms masses, veins, sunbursts of crystals and single grains on fractures and frozen in the rock. Rarely, it forms euhedral crystals in miarolitic cavities in granite or granite pegmatites. Most of the aquamarine crystals are less than 3 cm long, but some have been found up to and over 18 cm long and 3.5 cm in diameter. In some cavities, they are gem quality, but these are rare (Photos. 53, 54, 56).

Individual crystals are commonly etched or partially altered to clay (Photos. 52, 55). The alteration may be so intense that the pocket is filled with clay and only small shards and needle-like remnants of the aquamarine crystals remain, or no indications of aquamarine remain at all, only a coating of bertrandite. Crystals from other pockets are altered only to the extent that there are deep vertical striations or pits in the prism faces; the terminations are much less altered or etched.

The color of the crystals varies from nearly colorless to medium blue to inky blue for those frozen in rock, and generally light to medium blue for euhedral crystals in cavities. Rarely, specimens from cavities may also be dark blue.

Some high quality specimens have been collected in recent years, but good quality and better specimens are uncommon. While excellent single crystal specimens (and occasionally two or three intergrown crystals) have been found, there have been very few matrix specimens collected with aquamarine crystals greater than a centimeter in length.

Several minerals, most as euhedral crystals, are associated in the same cavities or nearby cavities. These include smoky quartz, microcline, albite, spessartine, hematite, ilmenite, fluorite, zinnwaldite, masutomilite and topaz (not in the same cavity with beryl) (personal).

Boise County: There is another occurrence of aquamarine that has been reported in Boise County, in the Centerville area. Excellent specimens were occasionally found in this area in the past. Most of these were recovered by chance from the gravels of a few of the many gold placers. In the 1980s, there was a small production of excellent quality specimens from a pegmatite dike that was originally exposed in one of the gold placers.

These specimens vary from less than 2 cm long to more than 17 cm long and 2 cm across. They have about the same characteristics as the material from the Sawtooth Mountains, but are less etched. At least one pocket produced a few specimens that were of excellent medium blue color with brilliant faces and gem quality throughout (Photo. 120), possibly the best aquamarine from a U.S. locality. Most of the crystals have been of light to medium color with inclusions, fractures and some etched faces like the Sawtooth material. Topaz, smoky quartz, microcline, albite and at least two unidentified species of mica are associated. Apparently this pegmatite has been mined out (personal).

Boundary County: Beryl occurs in a small pegmatite in the Lake View Mine on Wabaningo Mountain in Sec. 26, T. 61 N., R. 5 W., east of Priest Lake. Access is gained by taking Highway 57 south from Nordman for 0.5 mile, then southeast for 2.4 miles on a logging road, then south for 500 feet on a bulldozed trail to a pit. The pegmatite was exposed in a pit excavated in granodiorite of the Kaniksu batholith. The pegmatite dike is only three to four and a half inches wide. Beryl crystals are small and light green (Pattee et al, 1968).

Clearwater County: Beryl occurs in a pegmatite at the Allgood prospect. The dike is along the road to Browns Mill, 6.2 miles east of Weippe in the $NW^1/_4NW^1/_4$ Sec. 16, T. 35 N., R. 5 E. The pegmatite is exposed in a small pit and cuts quartz diorite. The beryl is aquamarine. It replaces albite and forms crystals up to 6 mm by 22 mm. Garnet, tourmaline, albite and quartz are associated (Pattee et al, 1968).

Beryl occurs at the Heywood Creek prospect in the $NE^1/_4SE^1/_4$ Sec. 32, T. 36 N., R 5 E. It is accessible by taking Highway 11 northeast from Weippe for 3.9 miles, then 2.1 miles southeast on the Space Creek road, then 0.5 mile north on a logging road to a pegmatite exposed in a roadcut. Pegmatite float can be found a few feet to the north, and may indicate another dike. Associated minerals include garnet and tourmaline (probably schorl) (Pattee et al, 1968).

Beryl occurs in small pegmatites at the Pierce Divide in a roadcut on Highway 11, 3.6 miles southwest of Pierce. The pegmatite stringers cut altered quartz diorite. Crystals to 6 mm in diameter have been found. Tourmaline occurs in the edges of the stringers (Pattee et al, 1968).

Beryl, variety aquamarine, has been found with elbaite, smoky quartz and colored tourmaline crystals, probably elbaite, west of the Fohl Picnic area at Pierce Divide. Small crystals and pieces have been reported. The occurrence is in pegmatites and a colluvial(?) deposit. Collectors have dug into the occurrence to recover pieces of beryl, smoky quartz, topaz and tourmaline (personal).

Elmore County: Three occurrences of beryl are known in the Trinity Mountain area about 45 miles east of Boise, One occurrence is the Blue Cloud prospect on Sheep Creek in Sec. 14-15, T. 4 N., R. 7 E. It is accessible by going east from Boise for 18 miles on Highway 21, then northeast on the Atlanta road for 24.5 miles to a bridge near Sheep Creek, then east on a trail for 4 miles, then south up Devils Creek for 0.5 mile. Bluish green beryl occurs in quartz veins in granodiorite in a pit. Crystals are up to 5 mm in diameter and 19 mm in length (Pattee et al, 1968).

The second occurrence is at North Star Lake in Secs. 4, 9-10, T. 3 N., R. 8 E. The lake is about 4 miles west of the Trinity Lakes Road by trail. Beryl occurs in an area that extends about 0.8 mile east and 0.5 mile north of North Star Lake, on a glaciated ridge between the headwaters of Smith and Sheep Creeks. The beryl is in granitic rock similar to that of the Sawtooth batholith. It occurs as aquamarine that forms grains and subhedral crystalline masses up to 2.5 cm across. Some of it may be filling miarolitic cavities. The pegmatites that contain aquamarine are mostly irregular masses that are several centimeters across, but the barren pegmatites are dikes up to 7 cm wide and several meters in length. It is possible that some of the latter contain aquamarine.

This occurrence is similar to the Sawtooth Mountains, except the host rocks are more highly weathered and rounded. There are few cavities, and most cavities are weathered and empty of any crystals. Rock outcrops generally are on ridge tops only, although there are a few lower glacial benches. Ridges and hill sides are covered with grass and sage brush that have grown on a shallow soil cover (Pattee et al, 1968; personal).

Beryl (aquamarine) has also been reported at Dismal Swamp. The author has received one report of a small cavity of aquamarine being reported in an outcrop near the swamp. There are few outcrops of the granite in the Dismal Swamp area and most are weathered and rounded, so the potential for finding crystal cavities in the area is low (personal).

Gem County: Beryl occurs in one or more pegmatites a few miles northeast of Ola. Access is by way of the High Valley-Squaw Creek road. The pegmatite area is at 5,300 feet elevation on Ola Ridge.

 The pegmatites are in contact rock and granodiorite of the Idaho batholith. Schist is common in the area. Garnet and muscovite are associated with the beryl; some schorl also occurs in the pegmatite (see schorl for information on a pegmatite that contains excellent specimens of that mineral). Beryl crystals are pale bluish green and occur in the feldspar zone near the quartz cores of the pegmatites (Pattee et al, 1968, personal).

Kootenai County: Beryl has been found with smoky quartz, albite and microcline in pegmatites on Red Hog, a forested ridge 10 miles southwest of Coeur d'Alene. The occurrence is in Precambrian age gneiss (and migmatite) which is locally deeply weathered and forms few, rounded outcrops. Vegetation cover and deep soil development hampers collecting, and the area is private land.

Small pegmatites less than two inches across are most common, but others are more than 12 inches across. They are exposed in roadcuts, or may be located by tracing float. Cavities occur in only a few of the dikes and are generally small. Beryl is scarce but at least one crystal, about 10 cm in length, has been found (personal).

Latah County: Beryl has been found in several pegmatites in an area about 5 miles north of Avon. The pegmatites were mined for beryl and muscovite; they intrude schist that has formed from metamorphism of rocks of the Belt supergroup. The zone of dikes is within 1 mile of the contact of the schist with the Thatuna batholith.

The Muscovite Mine, in Sec. 22, T. 41 N., R. 2 W., is on the crest of a ridge that extends southerly from Mica Mountain. It contains the largest pegmatite and has received the most intensive mining, by both underground and surface operations. Muscovite and beryl have been produced during several periods of operation. Beryl crystals are light green or yellowish green (Photo. 121). Most of them are less than 5 cm in diameter, but have been found up to at least 20 cm in diameter and more than 30 cm in length. They can be found in the pegmatite in the walls of the pit or in the material on the dump (Pattee et al, 1968; personal).

The Steelsmith Mine is in the $N^1/_2$ Sec. 27, T. 41 N., R. 2 W. on the ridge crest 0.5 mile south of the Muscovite Mine. Several pegmatites were worked, primarily west of the road. Beryl crystals up to 15 cm across and 20 cm in length were found during mining operations. The crystals were yellowish or green in color (Pattee et al, 1968; personal).

The Last Chance Mine is near the center of the district in the $SW^1/_4$ Sec. 22, T. 41 N., R. 2 W. Beryl crystals up to 2 cm across occur in two pegmatites that have been mined by surface and underground operations. Beryl has been reported in several other pegmatites in the area. Many of these have received some prospecting or production (Pattee et al, 1968).

Photo. 71 Smoky quartz, microcline and albite, longest quartz crystal is 5.6 cm and longest microcline is 3 cm, Hell Roaring Lake area, Sawtooth Mountains, Custer County.

Photo. 72 Smoky quartz, 8 cm long, note the transparent gem quality, Upper Cramer Lake area, Sawtooth Mountains, Custer County.

Photo. 73 Smoky quartz and microcline, specimen is 7 cm across, Ardeth Lake area, Sawtooth Mountains, Boise County.

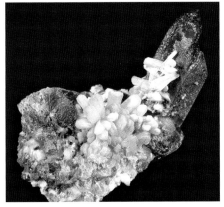

Photo. 74, Stilbite on smoky quartz, stilbite crystals are 5 mm, Baron Lakes area, Sawtooth Mountains, Boise County.

Lemhi County: Beryl crystals have been found in pegmatites and miarolitic cavities in the Yellowjacket Mountains. The occurrences are on National Forest lands along the Crags and Cathedral Rocks roads north of Yellowjacket Lake to Golden Trout Lake; and northwesterly into the Bighorn Crags. The area is accessible by taking the Panther Creek road south from Cobalt for 8 miles, then going west on the Porphyry Creek road for 7 miles, then north on the Crags (Hoodoo Meadows) road for 7 miles.

Most crystals are less than 2 cm in length, are frozen in porphyritic granite or quartz monzonite, frozen in pegmatites or rarely in miarolitic cavities. The host rock is the porphyritic Crags batholith of Tertiary age. Beryl is mostly of the aquamarine variety, but some is green. Most of it is opaque and highly fractured. The occurrence is similar to that of the Sawtooth Mountains.

One small zone was seen in which aquamarine is common associated with some green beryl. It occurs as fibrous to coarse crystals to at least 3 cm in length and in masses up to 10 cm across. This occurrence is below the road about 1.3 miles west of the intersection with the Hoodoo Road. Crystals are in thin pegmatite dikes that cut porphyritic granite. Some of the dikes occur on fractures, exposing an abundance of beryl. Even though the pegmatites are vuggy (cavities up to 2 cm across and 1 cm thick), the beryl tends to occur around but rarely projecting into the cavities. Aquamarine pseudomorphs of microcline occur in some of the cavities. These crystals are typically about 6 mm in length and project into the small cavities associated with small quartz crystals.

Miarolitic cavities larger than 2.5 cm across are uncommon in the area. Pegmatite dikes are uncommon and are rarely vuggy. Most of the miarolitic cavities are weathered out, but a few contain small smoky quartz and feldspar crystals. Rarely, these cavities contain aquamarine, and topaz has been reported. The color is light to medium blue. In some cavities, aquamarine is etched much like that of the Sawtooth Mountains.

Although elevations are about the same as those of the Sawtooth Mountains, there are fewer outcrops in the roaded area which has a moderately steep rolling surface with a pine forest cover. Rock outcrops are mostly glaciated benches and monoliths that protrude above the trees. Weathering is intense and there is a shallow to deep grussic soil cover. Most rock outcrops are weathered and cavities tend to be weathered out (Pattee et al, 1968; Reid and Choate, 1960; personal).

BINDHEIMITE

$Pb_2Sb_2O_6(O,OH)$, cubic

In masses, often nodular or reniform with concentric layering, earthy; yellow, brown, reddish brown, gray or greenish. Occurs in oxidized lead-antimony ores, often replacing lead-antimony minerals.

Blaine County: Bindheimite occurs in the oxidized ores of the Wood River area. It has been reported from the No. 2 tunnel of the Golden Glow Mine in Boulder Basin where it is an alteration product of boulangerite. It may occur elsewhere in the area (Shannon, 1926).

Custer County: Bindheimite occurs with malachite and azurite in the Ramshorn Mine in the Bayhorse District. It forms yellow-green waxy coatings as an alteration product of tetrahedrite and galena (Shannon, 1926).

A similar occurrence is reported from the River View Mine where it is yellow in color and occurs with cerussite and galena. It has also been reported from the Cave Mine, and occurs with malachite and anglesite on the Hoosier claims. Compact waxy yellow bindheimite occurs with linarite in the Pacific claim. At the Skylark Mine, it forms compact masses stained green by copper, and is associated with azurite (Shannon, 1926).

Lemhi County: Bindheimite occurs in the areas of secondary mineralization at the Ima Mine. It has been found as medium olive green, cryptocrystalline to glassy, masses with other secondary minerals. Locally it forms a significant portion of the rock, often replacing tetrahedrite (Photo. 122). It often is as thin layers, around 1 mm thick, and small irregular masses. The surfaces of the thin layers often show microcrystalline faces (personal).

Owyhee County: At the South Mountain District, bindheimite forms an ocherous yellow powder. It occurs in cavities in galena with anglesite and linarite in the Monkey Mine. At the Rocksyfellow Mine, it is found with cerussite and anglesite coating coarse galena. Yellow stains of bindheimite occur with cerussite and minium at the Golconda Mine (Shannon, 1926).

It has also been found in the Laxey Mine where it forms a yellowish dusty alteration product of galena. It is associated with minium, azurite, hedenbergite, ilvaite, caledonite, cerussite and linarite (Sorenson, 1927).

Shoshone County: Shannon (1926) reported that bindheimite was common in the Coeur d'Alene Mining District, but studies done in recent years on material from the Bunker Hill Mine indicate that most of the material is massicot (Radford and Crowley, 1981). Shannon reported it as being common in the Hercules Mine with cerussite, and as concentric layers of yellow and greenish yellow surrounding cores of tetrahedrite at the Mammoth Mine.

A very light coating of bindheimite dusted cerussite at the Last Chance Mine, and has been reported at the Tyler Mine. At the Caledonia Mine, it formed pseudomorphs of tetrahedrite. In this form, it is nearly pure friable masses, some of them several feet across. A few specimens that appeared to be pseudomorphs after galena were also found. At the Northern Light Mine, it occurred in vugs in masses of cerussite. The habit is acicular and may be pseudomorphous after a fibrous sulfide, possibly stibnite. It has also been reported from the Lookout Mountain, Carbonate and Hypotheek mines (Palache, 1951; Shannon, 1926).

BIOTITE

$K(Mg,Fe)_3(Al,Fe)Si_3O_{10}(OH,F)_2$, monoclinic

Tabular or short prismatic crystals or foliated masses; perfect cleavage so that it may be separated into thin sheets. Dark green, brown to black. A common accessory mineral in igneous rocks and some gneisses and schists.

Boise, Custer and Elmore Counties: Biotite appears to be rare in the granite of the Sawtooth Mountains. Most of the dark mica group minerals are masutomilite or zinnwaldite. The dark mica in one cavity apparently has proven to be biotite, and may be present in others. In this cavity, it forms small books and flakes with microcline, albite and smoky quartz.

Lemhi County: Biotite forms well-developed rosettes in the cobalt mines in the Blackbird District. It is a common rock-forming mineral in the host rocks of the ore deposits. Fine specimens have been found in the Togo Mine (Shannon, 1926).

BISMUTH

Bi, hexagonal (trigonal)

Laminated or granular. Silver-white with reddish tone; metallic luster. Rare, generally

Photo. 75 Smoky quartz, 11.2 cm long, from a collapsed pocket in a pegmatite, the grayish termination on the right is the healed surface of the base of the crystal where it was broken from the matrix when the pocket burst, Ardeth Lake area, Sawtooth Mountains, Boise County.

Photo. 76 Spessartine on albite with quartz, 7 cm across, the quartz has faded to nearly colorless because of exposure to sunlight in the exposed cavity. Benedict Creek area, Sawtooth Mountains, Boise County.

Photo. 77 Stilbite on microcline, specimen 3.7 cm across, upper Hell Roaring Creek area, Sawtooth Mountains, Custer County.

Photo. 78 Topaz, 3.7 cm high, Ardeth Lake area, Sawtooth Mountains, Boise County.

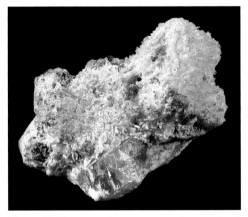

Photo. 80 Topaz, 4.5 cm high, not visible in the photograph are tiny reddish tetrahedral inclusions that appear to be helvite, Upper Cramer Lake area, Sawtooth Mountains, Custer County.

Photo. 79 Topaz and quartz pseudomorph of microcline, 5 cm across, Imogene Lake area, Sawtooth Mountains, Custer County.

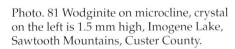

Photo. 81 Wodginite on microcline, crystal on the left is 1.5 mm high, Imogene Lake, Sawtooth Mountains, Custer County.

associated with silver, cobalt, nickel, lead and tin.

Custer County: Bismuth forms silver-white to reddish grains disseminated in quartz veins in the Empire claims of the Idaho-Montgomery Mining Company in Washington Basin at the head of the East Fork of the Salmon River. Some of the bismuth is altered to bismutite, and it is associated with bismuthinite, barite, pyrrhotite and pyrite (Shannon, 1926).

Kootenai County: Grains of native bismuth occur in quartz veins in the Caribou Mine on Beauty Bay Creek southeast of Coeur d'Alene. The veins are in argillites of the Belt supergroup and in diorite at the contact of the argillites with a Tertiary diorite stock. Bismuth is said to occur in all of the quartz in the surface workings with bismuthinite and pyrite (Shannon, 1926).

Lemhi County: Native bismuth has been reported from one of the cobalt mines of the Blackbird District (Shannon, 1926).

BISMUTHINITE

Bi_2S_3, orthorhombic

Generally massive foliated or fibrous, flexible and sectile; crystals prismatic, stout to acicular, vertically striated. Lead-gray to tin-white color. A rare mineral, occurs mostly in low temperature hydrothermal veins and granite pegmatites.

Boise County: In the No. 4 tunnel of the Mountain Chief Mine in the Quartzburg District in Boise Basin, bismuthinite occurs as small prismatic and acicular crystals (Fig. 12) and grains in quartz with pyrite crystals. Small prismatic crystals occur in cavities between quartz crystals. Some of these bismuthinite crystals are curved and bent. Matildite and lillianite are associated. Columnar and fibrous crystals of steel-gray bismuthinite occur in the Gold Hill Mine near Quartzburg. This occurrence is in gold-quartz ore and the bismuthinite contains native gold (Ballard, 1924; Shannon, 1926).

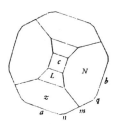

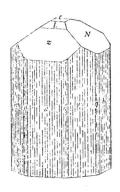

Fig. 12 Bismuthinite, Mountain Chief Mine, Boise County; crystal drawings from Shannon (1926).

Custer County: Acicular crystals of bismuthinite occur in massive pyrite and fibrous masses in quartz and altered granite in the Empire claims of the Idaho-Montgomery Mining Company in Washington Basin at the head of the Salmon River. Associated minerals include native bismuth, bismutite, jamesonite, jarosite, pyrite and sphalerite. Mining was primarily for gold and silver; gold tellurides have been reported (Shannon, 1926, Van Noy, et al, 1986).

BISMUTITE

$Bi_2(CO_3)O_2$, tetragonal

Occurs as earthy masses, opaline crusts and radially fibrous crusts or as scaly to lamellar aggregates. Straw-yellow to brownish yellow or other colors including green, black and bluish; small grains are transparent. A common secondary mineral formed from the alteration of bismuth minerals. Associates are malachite, cerussite, beyerite and ilmenite.

Boise County: What was tentatively identified as bismutite occurred as small grains in the placer deposits of the Leary and Brogan claims north of Placerville. The grains were gray and appeared to be fibrous (Shannon, 1926).

Custer County: Earthy bismutite partially fills cavities in bismuthinite in drusy quartz in the Empire Mine, Washington Basin District. It is dirty white in color (Shannon, 1926).

Kootenai County: Dirty white bismutite occurs in the near-surface portions of the veins of the Carver and Varnam claims in the Beauty Bay District. It is earthy and partially fills cavities in quartz (Shannon, 1926).

BORNITE

Cu_5FeS_4, cubic

Brownish bronze when fresh; readily tarnishes to purple and blue. Cubic or dodecahedral or octahedral crystals, more commonly massive. Widespread in mesothermal or magmatic hypogene deposits; associated with chalcopyrite, pyrite and chalcocite.

Adams County: The primary copper mineral in the epidote-garnet contact rock in the Seven Devils District was bornite. It is generally argentiferous and contains up to 20 ounces of silver per ton. Most of it forms brilliant masses in quartz veins, such as in the Great Eastern vein. It is the most abundant metallic mineral in the pegmatitic textured orthoclase and quartz vein in the Panama Pacific prospect. Most of the bornite in the district is replaced by chrysocolla, malachite or brochantite where weathered (Shannon, 1926).

Lemhi County: Bornite forms masses in the Copper Queen Mine on the South Fork of Agency Creek, in Sec. 15, T. 19 N., R. 25 E. The mine is developed on a brecciated fault zone nine to 22 feet wide that cuts light-gray to tan micaceous Precambrian quartzite. Bornite is the most abundant copper mineral of the vein, it fills the spaces between fragments. Gold forms nuggets up to 1 cm across in the bornite, and is more common where the vein cuts a diorite dike. Other copper minerals include chalcopyrite, covellite and malachite. The nearby Blue Lupine vein is parallel to the Copper Queen vein, and contains similar mineralization (Shannon 1926; Sharp and Cavender, 1962).

The Blue Bird Mine in Sec. 14, T. 19 N., R. 25 E. contains similar copper mineralization with copper carbonates, hydrous copper oxides and chrysocolla. The mine is 1 mile west of Lemhi Pass on the flat overlooking the valley of Agency Creek. Shallow pits and shafts have been developed on the vein. Gold and silver also occur (Sharp and Cavender, 1962).

A similar occurrence of bornite is at the Idaho Pride, Azurite and Stage Coach claims on Horseshoe Bend Creek. Mineralization is in a shear zone of the Lemhi Pass fault zone. Bornite is the most abundant copper mineral and is associated with chrysocolla, copper carbonates and green chalcedony. These minerals fill fractures in quartz veins on the east side of the creek. Several short adits, open cuts and pits have been developed on the veins (Sharp and Cavender, 1962).

BOULANGERITE

$Pb_5Sb_4S_{11}$, monoclinic

Plumose, fibrous, acicular or in masses. Bluish lead-gray, oxidizes to yellow. In vein deposits with other lead sulfosalts, stibnite, galena and sphalerite.

Blaine County: The North Star, Independence and Minnie Moore mines in the Hailey District contain boulangerite. Associated minerals are galena, pyrite, sphalerite, chalcopyrite, stibnite, pyrrhotite and arsenopyrite, all in quartz. The boulangerite forms compact

Photo. 82 Topaz with smoky quartz, microcline, albite and zinnwaldite-masutomilite, specimen is 22 cm across, Hell Roaring Lake area, Sawtooth Mountains, Custer County.

Photo. 83 Acanthite, 4.8 cm high, Buffalo Mine, Atlanta District, Elmore County; collected about 1888; Norm Radford photograph.

Photo. 84 Topaz, 8.3 cm high, etched termination and prism faces, Hell Roaring Lake area, Sawtooth Mountains, Custer County.

Photo. 85 Aeschynite-(Ce), 0.5 mm long, Steel Mountain, Elmore County.

Photo. 88 Two intergrown almandine crystals, specimen 3.5 cm across, Garnet Gulch, Emerald Creek, Latah County.

Photo. 86 Almandine, rounded trapezohedron, 3.5 cm across, Emerald Creek, Latah County.

Photo. 89 Almandine, dodecahedron, 3.2 cm across, Emerald Creek.

Photo. 87 Almandine, dodecahedron, 2.2 cm across, Emerald Creek.

Photo. 90 Almandine, dodecahedron, 7 cm across, Emerald Creek.

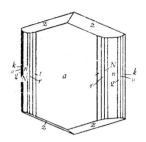

Fig. 13 Boulangerite, Independence Mine, Blaine County; crystal drawing from Shannon (1926).

parallel fibrous masses, slender acicular crystals lining cavities, wool-like aggregates in cavities, and massive forms with the other sulfides. It lines cavities or occurs between quartz crystals in comb quartz.

Some specimens from the Independence Mine have a felted or curved-fibrous structure. Fractures in the massive ore of this mine contain rosettes of boulangerite crystals up to 1 mm across. The crystals are tabular, have a lead-gray color and a "polished" metallic luster (Fig. 13). Similar rosettes occur in the Minnie Moore Mine with brown hisingerite. Stibnite occurs as radiating aggregates of needle-like crystals on fracture surfaces in the Independence Mine.

The North Star Mine is in North Star Gulch, a tributary of the East Fork of Big Wood River, in Sec. 23, T. 4 N., R. 18 E. Mineralization is in veins in the argillites and sandstones of the Milligen formation. The Independence Mine is nearby on Independence Creek, about 4 miles east of Ketchum, in the same section (Shannon, 1926; Umpleby, 1930).

Fibrous massive boulangerite occurs with arsenopyrite in the Ontario claims on Boyle Mountain in the Warm Springs Creek District (Shannon, 1926).

Lemhi County: Boulangerite is uncommon in the stibnite veins in the Buckhorn Mine in the Little Eightmile (Junction) District. The mine is located southeast of Cedar Gulch. The veins are in a 55 foot wide altered dike about 450 feet from the portal of the adit. The boulangerite forms small radiating groups of acicular crystals. Stibnite and jamesonite are associated (Thune, 1941).

Shoshone County: Steel-gray boulangerite forms acicular crystals or felted wool-like masses in small cavities in quartz or fibrous masses in quartz and siderite in the Gold Hunter Mine at Mullan. The elongated boulangerite crystals often penetrate the quartz crystals in the cavities and microscopic rhombs of siderite are entirely penetrated by the crystals (Shannon, 1926).

Crystals of boulangerite were found in the Bunker Hill Mine in the Tony sphalerite orebody, mostly as films and stringers but occasionally as black needles in small vugs. The Standard-Mammoth Mine contained a fibrous lead-antimony mineral, probably boulangerite, in the ores between the 1,800 and 2,000 foot levels and as subcolumnar and granular masses in galena in the Greenhill-Cleveland ore shoot (Radford and Crowley, 1981; Shannon, 1926).

BOURNONITE

$PbCuSbS_3$, orthorhombic

Stubby, prismatic, sometimes tabular; twinned on prism plane m[110] as fourling forming a "cogwheel." Brittle, fracture subconchoidal to uneven. Opaque; steel-gray to black; metallic. Widespread, but euhedral crystals uncommon. In hydrothermal veins with other sulfides, including galena, tetrahedrite, chalcopyrite, sphalerite and pyrite.

Shoshone County: Bournonite was found in the 5 level of the West Reed area of the Bunker Hill Mine as discreet blebs to 5 cm across, and rarely as minute cogwheel crystals (Radford and Crowley, 1981).

BRANNERITE

(U,Ca,Y,Ce)(Ti,Fe)$_2$O$_6$, monoclinic

Black, but may be brownish yellow on the surface from alteration. Mostly indistinct crystals; grains and masses. Occurs in pegmatites; generally found in placer deposits as pebbles or prismatic crystals.

Custer County: Brannerite occurs in the placer deposits near the head of Kelly (Kelley) Creek in the western part of the county. This is the type locality for this mineral. It forms small prismatic crystals and grains which are a brownish yellow color on the outside. This light color may be due to weathering as they are black inside. Most of the specimens are broken fragments and irregular, but many of them show prism faces. Terminations are rare. The bedrock of the area is granite(?) cut by pegmatite dikes; the crystals may be weathering out of the dikes. The placer deposits along Kelly Creek also contain tiny crystals of cinnabar, monazite, ilmenite, rutile, xenotime and euxenite, and these placers have been studied for their potential to produce the heavy mineral concentrates. Brannerite has also been reported on nearby creeks (Choate, 1962); Shannon, 1926).

BRAUNITE

MnMn$_6$SiO$_{12}$, tetragonal

Pyramidal crystals or granular masses. Dark brownish black to steel-gray; weakly magnetic. Commonly associated with other manganese minerals in veins and lenses formed from the metamorphism of manganese oxides and silicates, or as a secondary mineral formed by the oxidation of manganese minerals.

Lemhi County: Brownish black granular masses and scattered minute pyramidal crystals of braunite have been found in the Kittie Burton Mine in the Indian Creek District. It occurs in a vein of bluish quartz with gold, pyrite, chalcopyrite, pyrrhotite and rhodochrosite, which coats fractures in the ore (Shannon, 1926).

BROCHANTITE

Cu$_4$(SO$_4$)(OH)$_6$, monoclinic

Prismatic to acicular, rarely tabular, drusy crusts and massive. Emerald green to blackish green, sometimes light green; transparent to translucent. A secondary mineral in oxidized copper ores, most common in arid regions.

Adams County: Brochantite occurs in several mines in the Seven Devils District. Small green prismatic crystals have been found in the South Peacock Mine in cavities in quartz and specular hematite. Specimens of prismatic and radiating fibrous crystals forming small groups, masses and thin coatings on fractures have been found in other mines (Shannon, 1926).

Bannock County: Small crystals have been found at an unreported locality near Pocatello. Brochantite replaces chalcocite and occurs massive and as small crystals. Crystals display the prism m(110), the pinacoid b(010) and the base c(001) (Shannon, 1926). This may be in the Fort Hall District where it occurs with chalcocite and chalcopyrite (Palache et al, 1951).

Custer County: Malachite and azurite occur with brochantite in the Mackay District. Most brochantite is massive, but some small vertically striated rhombic prisms have been

Photo. 91 Almandine, rounded
trapezohedron, 4 cm across,
Emerald Creek, Latah County.

Photo. 94 Almandine, from boulder of gneiss
along Goat Mountain road, 3.2 cm across,
Shoshone County.

Photo. 92 Almandine,
dodecahedron, 7 cm across, Cat's
Spur Creek, Shoshone County.

Photo. 95 Almandine in anorthosite, 9 mm
across, Moses Butte, Shoshone County.

Photo. 93 Almandine, 2.6 cm across,
Freezeout Mountain, Shoshone County.

Photo. 98 Anatase, 0.7 mm long, in small cavity in matrix of microcline and albite specimen, Crags batholith, Lemhi County.

Photo. 96 Colorless, complex analcime crystals enclosing gyrolite spheres, with larger apophyllite, analcime crystals 1-3 mm across, near Pinehurst, Adams County.

Photo. 100 Anglesite, 6 mm wide complex crystal with smaller crystals, Continental Mine, Boundary County.

Photo. 97 Andradite crystals from the Peacock Mine, largest crystal 1.6 cm across, Adams County.

Photo. 101 Apophyllite and gyrolite, the large apophyllite is 1 cm across, Pinehurst area, Adams County.

Photo. 99 Anglesite, 2 mm, Continental Mine, Boundary County.

found. It forms in the centers of narrow veins of azurite in limestone in the 300 foot long Empire tunnel (Shannon, 1926).

Crusts of small green crystals line cracks in iron-stained rock in the Parallel tunnel of the Reed and Davidson Mine in the Copper Basin District at the head of the East Fork of Big Lost River (Shannon, 1926).

Lemhi County: Tiny crystals of brochantite occur with cyanotrichite, malachite and azurite in gossan in the Iron Dike Mine on the east side of Stroud Gulch in the Junction District near Leadore. The crystals are in groups and consist of elongated and lath-like, transparent green crystals less than 2 mm long (Photo. 123) or more equant crystals around 1 mm across. They were most common in one small area of gossan in the "iron dike" just west of the adit, associated with cyanotrichite with some azurite (personal).

Brochantite forms excellent tiny crystals in the Ima Mine associated with azurite, malachite, wulfenite and other minerals. The tiny crystals are fibrous to prismatic and blocky (Photos. 124, 125) (personal).

Shoshone County: Brochantite has been found in the Sierra Nevada workings of the Bunker Hill Mine, and sparingly in other mines in the district (Radford and Crowley, 1981).

In the Hansy Mine workings, tiny blocky crystals of brochantite occurred with malachite in the oxidized ores (Photo. 126). The adits of this mine are located on the west side of Olentange Creek, a tributary of Loop Creek (personal).

BROOKITE

TiO_2, orthorhombic

Usually as crystals, mostly tabular, often elongated and striated; sometimes pseudohexagonal or pyramidal. Luster is metallic adamantine to submetallic and the color brown, yellowish brown, reddish brown or dark brown to black. Transparent in small fragments. Usually in veins in gneiss and schist of the Alpine type with anatase, titanite, adularia, quartz and rutile. Also in gneiss, schist and igneous rocks as an accessory mineral or rarely in contact deposits.

Boise County: Brookite is rare in the placer deposits of the Boise Basin. The crystals have a variable habit and an adamantine to submetallic luster. They are mostly iron-black and commonly translucent. They probably are derived from the weathering of the many igneous rocks in the area (Sidler, 1957).

CALCITE

$CaCO_3$, hexagonal (trigonal)

Extremely varied in habit, often very complex. Over 300 forms have been described; more than any other mineral. Three forms are most common: 1: prismatic, 2: rhombohedral, 3: scalenohedral; these forms and others are often combined forming highly complex crystals, often twinned. Perfect rhombic cleavage. Colorless, white, yellowish most common, also shades of most other colors; transparent to translucent. Common in sedimentary rocks, and as a gangue in mineral deposits.

Ada County: Scalenohedral crystals of calcite occur at the picnic area on the south side of Lucky Peak Dam, 10 miles east of Boise (Photo. 127). Crystals are up to about 3 cm in length, but most are less than 1 cm. They are colorless to yellowish, and fluoresce reddish or an orangish cream color; sometimes both fluorescent colors occur on one matrix specimen. Calcite is most common in roadcuts, where it occurs with chabazite; below the road in outcrops along the reservoir, calcite is less common, but chabazite, levyne with offretite-erionite and phillipsite can be found (personal).

Adams County: In the White Mountain Mine in the Seven Devils District, calcite forms large cleavage rhombohedrons that are surrounded by a spherical layer of radial-fibrous calcite which terminates in a drusy surface that is coated with quartz crystals. Melaconite, green chrysocolla and malachite fill the spaces between the spheroidal masses (Shannon, 1926).

Calcite occurs with zeolites, gyrolite, apophyllite and quartz in small cavities in basalts south of Pinehurst. There are good exposures in roadcuts along Highway 95 from about one half mile north of mile post 176 to mile post 178. Calcite varies from coarse subhedral crystals and masses filling cavities to rhombic crystals, and sometimes it forms prismatic-like crystals with a triangular cross section up to about 4 mm or as similar tiny spindle-shaped crystals. More information on the occurrence can be found in the analcime and gyrolite sections. Calcite also occurs a little further north in the roadcuts around Fall Creek where it occurs as small rhombic or scalenohedral crystals (personal).

Bannock County: Calcite crystals occur with hematite in garnet-calcite rock on Lanes Creek in the NW$^1/_4$ Sec. 9, T. 6 S., R. 43 E. The crystals often display zoned layers of transparent and buff calcite colored by iron oxide. Most crystal faces are dull; garnet and hematite are associated (Shannon, 1926).

Blaine County: Large rhombs of calcite have been found in the Lead Belt District. Some of the crystals have a pinkish color and are associated with rhodochrosite and sulfides (Anderson, 1929).

Photo. 102 Apophyllite, 3 to 6 mm across, on chabazite with minor gyrolite, Pinehurst area, Adams County.

Photo. 103 Aurichalcite and azurite, cavity 1.3 mm across, Ima Mine, Lemhi County.

Photo. 104 Aurichalcite, micro crystals, Laxey Mine, Owyhee County.

Photo. 105 Autunite, view is 2.6 cm across, Salmon area, possibly the E-Da-How claim, Lemhi County.

Photo. 106 Azurite on quartz, field of view is 1.1 cm, Weimer Mine, Clark County.

Photo. 107 Azurite and malachite on quartz, field of view is 9 mm, Weimer Mine, Clark County.

Photo. 108 Azurite, 12.2 cm across, Silver Bell Mine, Bayhorse, Custer County; Norm and Carla Radford specimen.

Photo. 109 Azurite (0.2-0.4 mm), bluish green malachite spheres to 0.9 mm, tiny green segnitite crystal groups, and gray radial group of mimetite (left), Ima Mine, Lemhi County.

It is also reported as combs of scalenohedral crystals associated with the ore minerals in the mines of the Hailey Mining District (Shannon, 1926).

Boise County: Crystals of calcite have been found in the Overlook Mine in the Pioneerville District. The colorless crystals are up to 1 cm in length and are prismatic. These are associated with quartz, galena and pyrite in a gold-bearing ore (Shannon, 1926).

In a roadcut on Highway 55 and a nearby small pit on private land about 1 mile north of Gardena, small calcite crystals occur with chabazite, mesolite, stilbite and thomsonite (personal).

Boise, Custer and Elmore Counties: Calcite is rare as a coating, filling, and tiny crystals, in a few cavities in the Sawtooth Mountains (personal).

Boise and Gem Counties: In the Willow Creek (now part of the Westview) District, calcite is abundant in the veins of many of the mines including the Friday Mine. In the Black Crook vein, it is reportedly colored pink by manganese, and is associated with quartz (Shannon, 1926).

Bonneville County: The mines on the east slopes of Caribou Mountain in Secs. 4 and 9, T. 4 S., R. 44 E., contain calcite, pyrite, chalcopyrite and bornite. The primary workings are the Robinson and Pittsburgh mines. Crystals may be found where mineralization has occurred in cavities that formed where limestone xenoliths were leached out (Hamilton, 1961).

Camas County: Calcite is rare in uncommon miarolitic cavities in the granitic rocks of the Smoky Dome stock, north of Fairfield. Corroded cleavage fragments and possibly corroded scalenohedral crystals have been found. The fragments are transparent and amber in color. Associated are small crystals of microcline, albite, smoky quartz and epidote (personal).

Custer County: Calcite occurs in cavities in altered andesite with quartz pseudomorphs of apophyllite in an undisclosed area near Antelope Flats southeast of Challis. The crystals are rhombs and plates or rarely prismatic, sometimes coated with tiny quartz crystals. In one cavity in the rocks, the rhombic crystals formed clusters with corners touching (Photo. 130). Parallel groups of plates sitting on drusy quartz were also found in that cavity (Photo. 128) (personal).

Plates of calcite up to 6 inches or more across occur with zeolites in cavities in volcanic rocks southeast of Challis. Reticulated quartz crystals coat the surfaces of the plates. Needle-like crystals of mordenite and small crystals of analcime are included in, or rest on the calcite (Ross and Shannon, 1926).

A similar occurrence is at the Rat's Nest claim where calcite crystals of several habits occur in the cavities with heulandite and mordenite (Photos. 129, 131). Calcite crystal habits include: dogtooth, prismatic, blocky, rhombic, pseudohexagonal tabular and thin plates (argentine habit). The plates are mostly colorless to white, and the crystals are colorless to light yellow. Some thick layers and fillings of the cavities are cream colored or brown (root beer) colored. Most crystals are etched, sometimes rounded, and only a few good specimens have been collected (personal).

In the volcanic rocks up Malm Gulch, there are a few veins of calcite running vertically up the canyon walls in one area. In one of these, a cavity 1 foot wide and 2 feet high and deep was found. It contained white crystals of calcite of a low rhombohedral form. Clusters of these occurred (often as floaters) with individual crystals to 7 cm across and 1.5 cm thick (Photo. 133). This area has been known to produce petrified wood (personal).

Along Road Creek, a tributary of the East Fork of the Salmon River, thin plates of calcite are uncommon in quartz-lined geodes in the volcanic rocks of the area. The thin plates are white, very thin and up to about 6 inches across, often spanning the cavity or forming clusters (Photo. 132). They occur with quartz and agate, rarely the quartz is pale amethyst, and the geodes are up to at least a foot across (personal).

Calcite occurs in brecciated limestone at two small prospects above the Chilly Cemetery, off the Mackay to Ketchum Road. The calcite does not form crystals, but forms irregular masses. It varies from colorless transparent to slightly yellow to gray, nearly opaque. Some pieces are large enough and of fine enough quality to be cleaved into clear rhombs 3-4 cm across. This material can be found on the dumps (personal).

Elmore County: Calcite occurs as rhombohedral crystals in basalt vesicles 5 miles below Glenns Ferry. The amber colored crystals are up to 5 mm in length and line the cavities and are in turn coated with chabazite and thomsonite (Shannon, 1926).

Idaho County: On the White Bird grade, north of White Bird, at mile post 227, calcite forms micro crystals of a cream color. The crystals partially line cavities with chabazite and phillipsite and sometimes coat the phillipsite.

In a roadcut 0.3 miles south of mile post 227 on the grade, calcite is uncommon in veinlets that sometimes form pockets that are lined with colorless to dark amber crystals. The crystals are sharp rhombic shape and are up to nearly 1 cm across (Photo. 134).

Small crystals of calcite occur with analcime, heulandite and mordenite in small cavities in Columbia River basalt in roadcuts along Highway 95 from mile post 218 for about 0.3 miles south. All cavities are small, mostly less than 1 cm across, and oval-shaped. Calcite occurs as small crystals less than 6 mm long, as rhombs or scalenohedrons (personal).

In a roadcut along the old highway which is accessible from Highway 95 a short distance north of Skookumchuck Creek, calcite occurs in cavities in the Columbia River basalt with heulandite. Singles and groups of dogtooth crystals with a white to light yellow color occur (Photo. 135) (personal).

Calcite crystals occur in cavities in limestone in the Slate Creek area. The rhombic crystals are translucent to transparent, and have a dark golden yellow to amber color (Photo. 136). They have been found in compact groups (personal).

Fine quality crystals of calcite occur in the greenish Columbia River basalts in high cliffs in an oxbow of the Salmon River. The area is 0.6 mile up the McKinzie (or McKenzie) Creek road off Highway 95. Crystals are scarce in the water-laid, greenish breccia. The calcite varies from colorless to yellow and forms rhombs or pointed rhombs (Photo. 137, 138). Crystals are scarce, but have been found up to about 3 cm associated with a druse of tiny heulandite crystals on celadonite (personal).

Lemhi County: Calcite crystals have been found in the Pittsburg-Idaho Mine in the Texas District (Shannon, 1926)

Small crystals of calcite are associated with aragonite in the Parker Mountain Mine, Parker Mountain District. The two minerals are in cavities in psilomelane (Shannon, 1926).

Calcite occurs in all mines in the Little Eightmile District, mostly as interstitial fillings between sulfide grains in the primary ore zones and as veinlets and crystalline coatings in small cavities in the oxidized ore zones. In the cavities, calcite forms microscopic to larger crystals up to about 6 mm. They are scalenohedrons, with some rhombohedrons (Thune, 1941).

In the Excelsior Mine in the Spring Mountain District, tiny, thin, complex rhombic crystals of calcite are associated with hemimorphite and rosasite. The white crystals are uncommon, and thin and nearly plate-like (Photo. 139) (personal).

Owyhee County: Calcite is undoubtedly the mineral that platy quartz is pseudomorphous after in the mines of the Silver City District. Only a very few specimens of this platy calcite have been found. One specimen consisted of thick plates of calcite,

Photo. 110 Azurite, 0.9 mm long, Ima
Mine, Patterson, Lemhi County

Photo. 111 Azurite and malachite ps.
azurite, largest crystals are 2.2 mm, Iron
Dike Mine, Junction District, Lemhi
County.

Photo. 112 Barite with tiny brown
stained quartz crystals, these are from
the prospect west of the saddle but are
similar in color and habit to those from
south of the saddle, specimen is 14.1 cm
across, Spar Canyon, Custer County.

Photo. 113 Barite, somewhat translucent; blocky barite crystals are on a
thin (5 mm) layer of drusy quartz crystals; large crystal on the right is
4.8 cm wide, from south of the saddle, Spar Canyon, Custer County.

Photo. 115 Barite, colorless to slightly yellowish; partially translucent; thin, dark gray outer zone; large crystal is 2.8 cm across, Willow Creek, Custer County.

Photo. 114 Barite, creamy yellow on top darkening to gray on the bottom; large crystal in the back is 4.7 cm across; Willow Creek, Custer County.

Photo. 116 Barite, large crystal is 9.2 cm across, Willow Creek, Custer County.

tabular to the basal pinacoid. These were arranged in a cellular aggregate.

Another specimen, this one from the tunnel below the Blaine tunnel on Long Gulch, consisted of brecciated basalt fragments surrounded by massive yellow-green epidote. Quartz crystals lined the cavities, and thin white plates of calcite were deposited on these (Shannon, 1926).

Shoshone County: Complex rhombic crystals of calcite have been found in many of the mines of the Coeur d'Alene Mining District. Crystals to 1 cm were found in the Bunker Hill Mine. Some scalenohedral crystals have also been found in this mine, and in the Hecla Mine. In the Standard-Mammoth Mine, crystals were up to 2 cm across. Crystals of the same habit were found in the 800 level of the Hercules Mine. These were translucent, had a greenish colored interior and a brownish colored opaque outer layer which was coated with a crystalline aggregate of pyrolusite. Small druses of a similar flattened rhombic habit have been found in open fractures in basic dikes in the Lombardy Mine in Italian Gulch near Kellogg, in a large altered dike intersected by the Kellogg (No. 9) level of the Bunker Hill mine, and in other basic dikes of the district (Shannon, 1926).

Milky scalenohedral crystals to 5 cm have been found in the Newgard orebody of the Bunker Hill Mine. Calcite is moderately common in Newgard orebody and in the Quill orebody, where complex rhombic crystals were up to about 1 cm across (Photo. 6). On the 10 level, they were associated with sphalerite and quartz crystals (Radford and Crowley, 1981; personal).

Teton County: Large calcite crystals (up to a foot in length) have been reported from the Red Mountain area. This is an old gold mining area with gold occurring in quartz veins in quartzite. Red Mountain is several miles northwest of Victor, a little north of the Teton County line (personal).

CALEDONITE

$Pb_5Cu_2(CO_3)(SO_4)_3(OH)_6$, orthorhombic

Crystals small, elongated prismatic, divergent groups, also massive; green or bluish green. Secondary mineral scattered widely, but not abundant. Associated with other secondary copper, lead and zinc minerals.

Butte County: Microscopic blue-green crystals that were tentatively identified as caledonite were found in the Wilbert Mine in the Dome District, south of the Dome town site. They were associated with linarite (Shannon, 1926).

Owyhee County: Caledonite has been found in the Laxey Mine on South Mountain. It forms minute waxy globules associated with linarite and cerussite in oxidized lead ore (Sorenson, 1927).

Shoshone County: What was tentatively identified as caledonite occurred as pale green coatings with linarite and leadhillite in the Caledonia Mine, and as blue-green friable masses of microscopic crystals with linarite in the Lookout Mountain Mine on Pine Creek. The microscopic crystals were tabular and rectangular. Caledonite crystals were found with linarite in the Orr orebody of the Bunker Hill Mine (Radford and Crowley, 1981; Shannon, 1926).

CARPHOLITE

$MnAl_2Si_2O_6(OH)_4$, orthorhombic

Forms a series with ferrocarpholite and one with magnesiocarpholite. Fibrous as radiating tufts; straw yellow to wax yellow. Known in only a few localities. In the Sawtooth Mountains, several specimens of carpholite were found which have potassium substituting for manganese and containing lithium. Although analyses indicated that this is a new mineral species, work has not been completed for it to be approved as a new mineral.

Boise, Custer and Elmore Counties: Carpholite is rare in the miarolitic cavities of the Sawtooth batholith. This is apparently the first reported occurrence of this mineral in the U.S. (Ream, 1989b). Perhaps only five cavities in the Sawtooth Mountains are known to have produced a carpholite group mineral. Samples from two of them have been analyzed and are potassium-bearing, apparently a new species, and specimens from one cavity found by the author, has been determined to contain no potassium and are identified as carpholite. Specimens from the other two cavities appear to be the new species.

The carpholite occurs as tiny acicular or fibrous crystals in radiating tufts. These are coating small microcline crystals, generally perched on the tops of the microcline (Photo. 57). Quartz, zinnwaldite and albite is associated. The carpholite crystals are up to about 1.5 mm in length and are less than 0.2 mm across. They have a dark yellow color (personal).

The apparent new species from one cavity forms a thin crust of tiny spherules, and tiny tufts and hemispheres, on and embedded in the surface of smoky quartz (Photo. 59). The longest crystals are bout 4 mm, and they are around 0.1-0.3 mm across.

In the other cavities, the mineral was weathered and was found primarily as individual acicular crystals and radiating groups or compact spherical groups to about 1 cm in length with microcline, albite and quartz (personal).

Boise County: A pegmatite near Centerville is the reported source of specimens of the apparent new potassium-bearing carpholite mineral, which was associated with aquamarine, smoky quartz, microcline and albite. Specimens from this discovery were the first ones studied, but the investigation of the mineral was continued with specimens found in the Sawtooth Mountains. At the Centerville locality, the mineral occurs as hemispheres of white needles. Individual crystals are up to about 6 mm in length and form hemispheres about 9 mm across. These occur on microcline, and only a few specimens were recovered from one cavity (personal).

CASSITERITE

SnO_2, tetragonal

Mostly massive granular in reniform shapes; crystal forms are prisms and dipyramids. Brown or black, sometimes yellow-white; translucent, rarely transparent. Most common in veins with quartz and fluorine- and boron-bearing minerals.

Boise, Custer and Elmore Counties: Microcrystals of cassiterite were identified in one cavity, and tentatively identified in two others, in the granite of the Sawtooth Mountains. They form brilliant, black, tetragonal prisms with pyramidal terminations, and are less than 1 mm in length (personal).

Lemhi County: Cassiterite, in the nodular form known as stream tin, occurs on Panther Creek near its junction with Moyer Creek and in Silver Creek. It forms small rounded grains and pebbles up to about 1.2 cm across. In Panther Creek, the pebbles are uncommon in the lower beds of gravels which vary from four to 20 feet in thickness. The color of the pebbles varies from pale to dark brown, reddish brown and black. The source of the cassiterite is unknown, and it is not known in any of the lode deposits of the area (Shannon, 1926).

Owyhee County: The stream tin variety of cassiterite occurs in the gravels of Jordan

Photo. 117 Barite, 0.5-0.8 mm, Little
Giant Mine, Mullan, Shoshone County.

Photo. 118 Microcrystals of barite showing
phantoms, 1-1.5 mm, with pyromorphite,
Little Giant Mine, Mullan, Shoshone County.

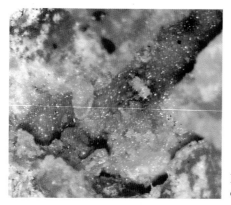

Photo. 119 Bayldonite, microcrystalline
crust, Ima Mine, Lemhi County.

Photo. 120 Aquamarine; light to medium blue color; translucent at
the base grading to transparent at the termination; 7 cm in length;
Centerville, Boise County; Joan and Bryant Harris specimen.

Photo. 122 Bindheimite as thin green layers and masses replacing tetrahedrite, field of view is 1.9 cm across, Ima Mine, Lemhi County.

Photo. 121 Beryl crystal with a quartz cap, 3.8 cm high, Muscovite Mine, Latah County.

Photo. 124 Brochantite, blocky crystals are 0.3-0.4 mm across, prismatic crystals are 0.4-0.6 mm long, with azurite, Ima Mine, Lemhi County.

Photo. 123 Brochantite, to 0.6 mm, Iron Dike Mine, Lemhi County.

Photo. 125 Brochantite, crystals are 0.6-0.9 mm long, Ima Mine, Lemhi County.

Creek in the Silver City District. It forms concentric banded and rounded masses to 1.2 cm in diameter. The source of these nodules are unknown as cassiterite has never been found in any of the mines or the rocks of the area (Piper and Laney, 1926; Shannon, 1926).

CERUSSITE

$PbCO_3$, orthorhombic
Crystals of varied habit, often tabular and twinned or in elongated crystals which often form jackstraw or reticulated groups. Colorless, white or gray, transparent to subtranslucent. An important supergene lead ore mineral associated with primary and secondary lead and silver minerals.

Blaine County: Groups of reticulated crystals were found in the Hailey District, and in the Era District it occurred with smithsonite, chlorargyrite and proustite. Smithsonite, galena, anglesite and wulfenite were associated with cerussite in the Birch Creek Mine in the Birch Creek District (now Scott Mine in Clark County). Specimens from the Golden Glow Mine contained small colorless crystals. Twinned prismatic crystals were found in an unreported locality, probably the Independence Mine. The crystals were elongated and twinned on the unit prism. Some of them resembled quartz crystals. They occurred in cavities in galena (Shannon, 1926).

Boise County: Small twinned crystals occurred on limonite-stained rock in the Hall Brothers claims in the Deadwood District. Other specimens from the same locality were of small gray to black crystals on iron oxide-stained quartz with pyromorphite (Shannon, 1926).

Butte County: Cerussite is reported in the Wilbert Mine, Dome District with caledonite, smithsonite and linarite (Palache, 1951).

Clark County: Small twinned crystals associated with wulfenite and anglesite were found in the Weimer Mine in the Skull Canyon District. These were on kidneys of galena in platy barite (Shannon, 1926).

Custer County: Cerussite was reportedly the most important lead mineral in Custer County. It was very prominent in the Bayhorse District, generally as friable sandy masses. In the Red Bird Mine, glassy masses of white cerussite in limonite contained cavities lined with calcite and prismatic cerussite crystals.

The Ramshorn Mine contains cerussite in vugs. It forms colorless and white crystals with mimetite and bayldonite in vugs in galena-tetrahedrite ore. The crystals are short and prismatic to the a axis or thin and tabular to the b axis (Shannon, 1926).

Tiny crystals of cerussite occur in gossan at the Confidence Mine (formerly Lucky Strike Mine) on the north side of upper Fourth of July Creek. The tiny prismatic crystals occur in vuggy iron oxide and quartz on the dump of a small adit alongside the road (Photo. 140). Similar rock on nearby dumps may also contain cerussite (personal).

Crystals of cerussite and smithsonite have been found near the head of Little Fall Creek at 9,100 feet elevation, west of Mackay. Vuggy quartz veins can be found on the Alto Silver claims near the head of the south tributary of the creek. The small crystals line cavities in the iron stained honeycombed quartz. Pyrite as striated cubes (some with galena cores), galena and sphalerite are associated. The veins occur in argillite and interbedded slate (Tuchek and Ridenour, 1981; Umpleby, 1913b; Umpleby et al, 1930).

Lemhi County: Cerussite was the most important lead ore in the Nicholia, Spring Mountain and Texas Districts. The Lena Delta Mine in the Nicholia District produced some cerussite as gray crusts and druses coating cavities in limonite (Shannon, 1926).

Prismatic twinned and untwinned crystals occurred in vugs in massive cerussite in the Pittsburg-Idaho Mine in the Texas District. Most crystals were elongated on the a axis. Unusual specimens of compact gray massive cerussite containing abundant pyrite crystals were found in the bottom of a stope between the 300 and 400 levels of the east vein of the mine.

Cerussite was found in the Silverton prospect in the Eureka District 3 miles northwest of Salmon in Sec. 35, T. 22 N., R. 21 E. It occurs with malachite, azurite, copper and cuprite in gouge along faults (Ross, 1925).

Cerussite was the important ore mineral in the lead-silver veins in the mines of the Little Eightmile (Junction) District. It generally occurs in sandy masses, but crystals have been found. Well-developed crystals were rare in the Buckhorn Mine. These were found about 45 feet within the west 650 foot crosscut. Orthorhombic crystals were uncommon in the Maryland Mine where they occurred as crystal fillings in cavities in high-grade ore. Galena and anglesite are common associates in the ores (Thune, 1941).

In the Iron Mask Mine in the Spring Mountain District, cerussite is uncommon as micro to small crystals associated with vanadinite and descloizite. The nearly colorless to white crystals were commonly twinned (Photos. 141, 142) (personal).

Tiny to small crystals of cerussite occur in the quartz veins of the Ima Mine on Patterson Creek. The colorless to white crystals are bladed or platy, commonly twinned and are often coated with an unidentified, pale blue microcrystalline mineral. They are associated with azurite and pyromorphite (personal).

Owyhee County: Small crystals occur in cavities in massive white cerussite in the Golconda Mine in the South Mountain District. Minium and bindheimite occur with the cerussite crystals (Shannon, 1926).

White prismatic crystals have been reported from the Bay State shaft on South Mountain. The cerussite crystals are found on smithsonite which forms thin botryoidal crystals of a grayish green to brownish color in oxidized ore (Sorenson, 1927).

At the Laxey Mine, tiny crystals of cerussite are associated with aurichalcite, azurite, calcite, malachite and quartz (personal).

Shoshone County: Cerussite has been an important ore mineral in many of the mines of the Coeur d'Alene District. Most of it occurs as sand cerussite or other massive forms. Azurite, malachite, linarite, plattnerite, native silver, pyromorphite and anglesite are associated. High quality crystals lining cavities have been found in several mines. These occurrences were in the upper workings which were mostly mined out in the early part of the century. Some specimens of high quality crystals have been produced in recent years from a few of these old workings. Shannon (1926) reported that this district probably had produced the most and best quality cerussite specimens to that time of any place in the world.

Excellent specimens of reticulated crystals, columnar masses, long-fibrous aggregates, honeycomb-like masses of reticulated plates and small crystals of several habits were common. Several mines produced these, including the Bunker Hill and Sullivan, Stemwinder, Tyler, Caledonia, Sierra Nevada, Tiger, Poorman, Hercules, Morning, You Like and Mammoth. By the 1930s, most of these mines had mined out the surface oxidized ores and crystal production stopped.

Most ore production from the district since then has been from deeper unoxidized zones. These ores are of massive argentiferous tetrahedrite and galena, so there are rarely any crystals to be found. The Bunker Hill Mine has extensive upper workings in these oxidized zones. Most of the areas have been mined out, but there are still some crystal-bearing levels. In 1979 to 1981, and again in the 1990s, a few fine quality specimens of cerussite,

Photo. 126 Brochantite, 0.3-0.5 mm, Hansy Mine, Olentange Creek, Shoshone County.

Photo. 127 Calcite on chabazite, calcite is 1.5 cm long, Lucky Peak Dam, Ada County.

Photo. 128 Parallel group of thin plates of calcite with a thin quartz druse, specimen 10.5 cm across, near Antelope Flats, Custer County.

Photo. 129 Calcite, mordenite and heulandite, fresh from a cavity, calcite crystals are 4.5 to 6 cm across, Rat's Nest claim, Custer County; John Cornish specimen.

Photo. 130 Parallel groups of rhombic crystals of calcite with a thin quartz druse, specimen 16.5 cm across, near Antelope Flats, Custer County.

Photo. 132 Thin hexagonal plates of calcite (large plate 1.8 cm across) from a quartz lined geode, Road Creek, Custer County.

Photo. 131 Calcite (argentine habit) with minor mordenite on surface, 6.6 cm across, Rat's Nest claim, Custer County.

native silver, pyromorphite and anglesite were produced from the 9 and 11 levels (Photo. 143) (see Coeur d'Alene Mining District Chapter).

Crystal production during the early mining period included some of the following finds. The Sierra Nevada Mine in Deadwood Gulch produced some excellent crystals of butterfly twin cerussite. These were colorless and up to 7.5 cm across. Aggregates of tabular twinned crystals were produced from the Mammoth Mine at Mace. Associated minerals included plattnerite and pyromorphite. Some large plates of reticulated twinned crystals were found (Shannon, 1926).

Untwinned and twinned crystals occurred in the Last Chance Mine. These were generally in cavities in galena. The crystals were mostly colorless or gray (Shannon, 1926).

The Tyler Mine contained cerussite as heavy columnar masses of white material embedded in ocherous impure manganese oxide, reticulated masses of platy crystals, fibrous crystals and crystals with dendritic wires of native silver. A few specimens of six-rayed penetration twins were found. Other mines in the Deadwood Gulch-Wardner area, including the Bunker Hill, Sullivan and Stemwinder produced similar specimens (Shannon, 1926).

Microcrystals of cerussite occur in the vein of the Little Giant Mine south of Mullan. The tiny crystals are generally elongated and striated (Photo. 144) (personal).

The Hypotheek Mine in French Gulch contained an orebody that was oxidized to considerable depth and produced excellent specimens of anglesite and cerussite. The cerussite varied from colorless to pink, gray and black. The most common cerussite crystals were globular white masses resembling flattened grapes. They were unlike any other specimens from the district.

Other mines in the Pine Creek-French Gulch area including the Chief, Carbonate, Northern Light and Lookout Mountain, produced cerussite crystals. The Lookout Mountain Mine produced excellent specimens associated with linarite, leadhillite, caledonite, bindheimite and pyromorphite. The cerussite crystals were up to 5 cm across and colorless, amber, gray and black in color. Several crystal habits were common including prismatic, rayed twins, highly modified crystals and twinned prismatic crystals (Shannon, 1926).

Cerussite occurred in the Monarch Mine in the Murray District. Crystals were up to more than 1 cm, in clusters to several centimeters. Individual crystals are colorless to white, plate-like or tabular and only 0.5-3 mm in thickness. They commonly formed groups and clusters on an iron oxide-stained matrix (Photos. 145,146). Twinned crystals are common (personal).

CERVANTITE

$SbSbO_4$, orthorhombic

Small acicular crystals; more commonly as a fibrous crust, powder or massive. White or yellow; transparent. Formed from the oxidation of other antimony minerals; with stibiconite, valentinite and bindheimite.

Blaine County: Cervantite has been reported in the mines on the Wood River (Shannon, 1926).

Elmore County: Cervantite occurs with stibiconite, kermesite and valentinite in the Hermada antimony mine on the East Fork of Swanholm Creek, 10 miles west of Atlanta. It occurs as white powder in the oxidized surface zones. Mineralization is primarily stibnite in quartz veins. Native antimony is common in some areas. An open pit and an adit have been developed on the veins (Popoff, 1953).

Shoshone County: Bright yellow ocherous coatings of cervantite occur on the stibnite from the Coeur d'Alene Mine on Pine Creek and the Stanley Mine in Gorge Gulch above Burke. It generally forms a thin crust and is associated with stibiconite (Shannon, 1926).

CHABAZITE

$CaAl_2Si_4O_{12} \cdot 6H_2O$, hexagonal (trigonal)

Member of the zeolite group; rhombohedrons with nearly cubic angles most common. Penetration twins common. White, yellow, pink or red; transparent to translucent. A secondary mineral associated with other zeolites in volcanic rocks.

Ada County: Tiny crystals of chabazite can be found at the picnic area on the south side of Lucky Peak Dam, 10 miles east of Boise. Crystals are colorless and form a druse lining small cavities in the gray to black and brownish red volcanic rock. Chabazite is most common above the road in the roadcuts, with calcite. Below the road in outcrops along the reservoir, chabazite is less common, but levyne with offretite-erionite and phillipsite can be found (personal).

Adams County: Small chabazite crystals occur with stilbite and heulandite in massive garnet rock on the Blue Jacket claim in the Seven Devils District. The crystals coat cracks and joint surfaces. They average 2 mm across and have an amber color (Shannon, 1926).

Chabazite occurs with analcime, cowlesite, levyne, offretite, heulandite, stilbite, tacharanite or tobermorite, apophyllite, calcite and gyrolite in small cavities in basalts south of Pinehurst. There are exposures in roadcuts along Highway 95 from about one half mile north of mile post 176 to mile post 178. Most of the chabazite occurs as tiny crystals and crystal coating, but some crystals are up to about 10 mm across. They are generally white, although some, especially the tiny drusy coatings, are colorless. Cavities are commonly lined with a druse of chabazite crystals and the other zeolites are on the chabazite. Most crystals are singles or simple twins, but the phacolite twins also occur. The highway in this area was rebuilt in 2000, and many of the zeolite-bearing roadcuts are now large massive rock faces (personal).

Small crystals of chabazite and other zeolites occur in several areas 6-9 miles up the Middle Fork of the Weiser River, southeast of Council. Mesolite and phillipsite are associated in cavities in volcanic rocks exposed in roadcuts and up small canyons. Most specimens are small and cavities are generally under 3 cm across (personal)

Boise County: Vesicular basalts along Warm Springs Creek, east of Boise, contain chabazite. It forms crusts and intergrown crystals, sometimes nearly filling the vesicles, which are up to 2 cm across. The crystals are colorless to white and generally not well formed. White radiating crystals of thomsonite occur in the same vesicles (Shannon, 1926). Warm Springs Creek is a tributary of the Payette River.

In a roadcut and a small pit on private land about 1 mile north of Gardena, along Highway 55, small chabazite crystals occur with calcite, mesolite, stilbite and thomsonite (personal).

Boise, Custer and Elmore Counties: Chabazite has been tentatively identified as rare microcrystals in diabase dikes in the Sawtooth Mountains. The nearly cubic-appearing crystals were identified by their habit and occurrence (personal).

Elmore County: White crystals of what may be chabazite (or possibly phillipsite or both) occur in vesicular basalt on the Snake River 5 miles below Glenns Ferry. The crystals coat amber calcite in the vesicles with thomsonite. They are up to 5 mm across, are intimately intergrown, twinned and poorly formed (Shannon, 1926).

Photo. 133 Calcite, specimen 20.5 cm across, Malm Gulch, Custer County.

Photo. 136 Calcite, dark golden yellow color, translucent to transparent; specimen 4.3 cm across, Slate Creek, Idaho County; Norm and Carla Radford specimen.

Photo. 134 Calcite, large crystal in the center is 1.5 cm high, note the darker root beer colored rod in the center of each crystal, White Bird grade, Idaho County.

Photo. 135 Calcite, specimen 4.6 cm across, from roadcut on old highway 95, north of Skookumchuck Creek, Idaho County.

Idaho County: Tiny crystals of chabazite form drusy coatings in small vesicles in Columbia River basalt in a roadcut on Highway 95 north of White Bird. Specimens have been collected in the outcrop at mile post 227. Tiny crystals of phillipsite and calcite are associated.

The outcrops that are 0.2 and 0.3 miles to the south have numerous small vesicles with small chabazite crystals and some small phillipsite crystals. Veins of chabazite rarely form pockets with partially transparent to white crystals of chabazite that are up to 1 cm or more across (personal).

North of Skookumchuck Creek, about 0.2 miles north of mile post 220, along Highway 95, chabazite forms tiny transparent crystals in small vesicles in Columbia River basalt with mesolite and stilbite (personal).

Chabazite can also be found in the roadcut on the north side of Skookumchuck Creek, a little north of mile post 219. Here it is in mostly small cavities in Columbia River basalt. The crystals are transparent or white and tiny. Associated minerals include apophyllite, analcime, mesolite, heulandite, quartz and calcite. Most crystals are small, but a few larger cavities did contain analcime to 2.5 cm (personal).

Chabazite is uncommon in a similar occurrence south of Skookumchuck Creek, near Russell Bar, about 0.2-0.3 miles south of mile post 218. The tiny crystals are associated with analcime, heulandite and mordenite. In one zone of the roadcut, the small chabazite crystals are pink (Photo. 147) and associated with heulandite on black clay. The zeolites occur in several small areas in two large roadcuts (personal).

Latah County: In the Nirk basalt quarry, tiny chabazite crystals have been reported with labradorite and pyrite. Reportedly cavities are small, crystals are tiny and the minerals are not common. The quarry is on the west side of Highway 95 near Deep Creek road 6-7 miles north of the junction with Highway 6 to Potlatch (personal).

CHALCANTHITE

$CuSO_4 \cdot 5H_2O$, triclinic
Short prismatic, tabular crystals or massive, stalactitic or reniform. Pale blue to deep azure-blue; transparent to translucent. Widespread; in oxidation zone of copper-bearing deposits.

Adams County: Chalcanthite occurs with sulfur and other copper minerals at the Red Ledge Mine in the Seven Devils District. The minerals form layers several centimeters thick in caves at the foot of the cliff at the mine (Shannon, 1926).

Custer County: Thin crusts of fibrous crystals of chalcanthite occur in the Copper Bullion Mine in the Mackay (Alder Creek) District (Shannon, 1926).

CHALCOCITE

Cu_2S, monoclinic
Short prismatic or thick tabular crystals or massive; commonly twinned. Blackish lead-gray. A supergene mineral common in the enriched zones of sulfide copper deposits or in veins. Associated with bornite, covellite, cuprite, malachite and azurite.

Adams County: Chalcocite occurs as a secondary mineral in the skarn deposits of many of the mines of the Seven Devils District. It replaces chalcopyrite and galena in the Red Ledge Mine, and is partially altered to chrysocolla and malachite in the ore of the Fidelity claims. Tetrahedrite and bornite are associated in a 15 cm wide quartz vein at the

Badger Mine. It replaces bornite and chalcopyrite in the Panama Pacific and Garden mines and occurs in fractures in chalcopyrite with bornite in the Lucky Strike (Walter James) prospect (Shannon, 1926).

Bannock County: Gray masses of chalcocite have been found in the Moonlight Mine on Rabbit Creek in the Fort Hall District, 9 miles east of Pocatello. The occurrence is in white quartz and much of the chalcocite is altered to brochantite. Mineralization is in small kidney-shaped masses and seams on fractures in conglomerate (Shannon, 1926).

CHALCOPYRITE

$CuFeS_2$, tetragonal
Usually massive; crystals pseudotetrahedral. Brass-yellow; metallic. The most common copper mineral. Associated with pyrite, pyrrhotite and many copper, lead and zinc minerals. Chalcopyrite is common in many of the mining districts of the state, but only a few localities have produced crystals.

Adams County: Chalcopyrite has been found in most of the mines of the Seven Devils District where it occurs with malachite and chrysocolla. Some small crystals have been reported, but it generally forms small masses and grains (Palache, 1944; personal).

Microcrystals of chalcopyrite have been found in prospects at the mica mine west of Mica Hill, about 12 miles southeast of Council in Sec. 8, T. 15 N., R. 2 E. Muscovite forms books to 20 cm across, and chalcopyrite crystals are reported to occur in a dark mica schist. Beryl is reported to occur in the schist too, but the area has a dense vegetation cover and the old workings are slumped and overgrown (personal).

Boise County: Chalcopyrite is a common mineral in the mines of the county, but rarely occurs as euhedral crystals. In small cavities in the Carroll-Driscoll Mine in the Quartzburg District, chalcopyrite forms minute, blue, sphenoidal crystals coated with covellite. It also occurs as masses with pyrite, sphalerite and tetrahedrite (Shannon, 1926).

Bonner County: Small crystals of chalcopyrite occur in the ores of the Talache Mine. It forms small, well-shaped crystals coating fractures. Polybasite, quartz, siderite, pyrite and other sulfides are associated (Humphreys and Leatham, 1936).

Custer County: Crusts of drusy chalcopyrite crystals occur in the Utah Boy No. 5 tunnel of the Ramshorn Mine in the Bayhorse District. These are in cavities in siderite-tetrahedrite ore with galena (Shannon, 1926). Tetrahedral crystals were found in other mines of the Bayhorse District. These were most common in small vugs in tetrahedrite with sphalerite, sometimes on small galena cubes. Other sulfides were associated, and various secondary minerals also occur in these mines (Umpleby, 1913b).

Elmore County: Small chalcopyrite crystals have been found in the Atlanta District. They occur as coarse poorly formed sphenoids modified by other forms, grains and granules. These occur in or on quartz crystals in comb quartz and druses. The crystals are associated with sulfides and generally contain gold (Anderson, 1939).

Shoshone County: Chalcopyrite is uncommon in the mines of the Coeur d'Alene District, and is rare as crystals. A few large crystals have been found in the Galena Mine near Wallace in recent years (Photo. 13) (personal).

CHALCOSTIBITE

$CuSbS_2$, orthorhombic
Massive and granular; crystals prismatic or bladed and striated. Dark lead-gray; opaque.

metallic. Occurs with tin and antimony minerals, pyrite, quartz, sulfosalts and sulfides.

Shoshone County: This uncommon mineral has been found in the Greenhill-Cleveland and Standard-Mammoth mines. It occurs in narrow quartz veins that cut the main ore veins in the lower levels. Vugs contained gray crystals up to 1 cm across. They are rhombic, but are so highly fractured as to be impossible to remove intact. Chalcopyrite and possibly nontronite are associated (Shannon, 1926).

CHEVKINITE

$(Ca,Ce,Th)_4(Fe,Mg)_2(Ti,Fe_3)_3Si_4O_{22}$, monoclinic

Dimorphous with perrierite. Slender pencil-shaped prisms or short stubby prisms of micro size, but usually irregular masses to 10 cm. Dark reddish brown to velvety black, nearly opaque and resinous. Occurs in pumice fragments and air fall ash in Cenozoic volcanic rocks of the western U.S., and as an accessory mineral in granite and syenite.

Unknown County: Chevkinite forms microscopic crystals and inclusions in rhyolitic ash from Idaho. The color is dark brown to nearly black translucent to opaque (Young, 1960).

Valley County: Chevkinite occurs as dark brown, opaque grains in syenite in the Big Creek quadrangle, northeast of McCall (Leonard, 1963).

CHLORARGYRITE

AgCl, cubic

Crystals rare, usually massive, often resembling wax. Pearl-gray to colorless, darkens to violet-brown on exposure to light. An important supergene silver ore mineral. Chlorargyrite occurs in several mining districts of the state, but mostly as thin films and masses, few occurrences are noteworthy. It has also been reported in the silver mines of Blaine, Boise, Custer, Elmore, Idaho, Lemhi and Shoshone Counties, where it apparently only forms thin films, crusts and small masses.

Lemhi County: Crystalline masses of chlorargyrite occur in the Silver Moon Mine in Silver Moon Gulch south of Gilmore. The small masses form crystalline groups and coatings. Small masses have also been reported from the Democrat Mine (personal).

Owyhee County: Most of the mines in the Silver City District contained chlorargyrite in the upper workings. It generally formed films and sheets, as in the Poorman Mine where sheets up to a foot square and 2 mm thick occurred in some veins. It often formed euhedral crystals in these same veins. The crystals were up to 1.2 cm across and were mostly cubes and cuboctahedrons. Twins of interpenetrating cubes were uncommon (Piper and Laney, 1926; Shannon, 1926).

In recent years, chlorargyrite was found in the pit of the DeLamar Mine and at the associated Stone Cabin Mine on Florida Mountain. In the latter, chlorargyrite formed thin sheets between quartz crystals and masses and cubic crystals in cavities with quartz crystals. Grains and sheets of silver and rounded grains and poorly formed crystals of naumannite were also associated. The chlorargyrite was colorless, but turned lavender, to purplish brown after exposure to light. Perfect lustrous cubic crystals, translucent and micro size were rare (Photo. 149) (personal). In the DeLamar Mine, it occurred as sheets and coatings, but also as tiny dodecahedral crystals (Perry, 1971).

CHLORITE

general formula: $A_{4-6}Z_4O_{10}(OH)_8$, A=Al,Fe,Li,Mg,Mn,Ni, Z=Al, B, Fe, Si
monoclinic or triclinic

A group of minerals: chamosite, clinochlore, cookeite, gonyerite, manandonite, nimite orthochamosite, pennantite and sudaite. Colors: colorless, white, yellow, green, greenish gray, black and red. Commonly tabular with hexagonal cross section, in masses, finely foliated or scaly; widespread in many geologic environments and rock types; often a product of hydrothermal alteration in ore deposits.

Elmore County: What is probably a chlorite group mineral forms thin scales and tiny crystals that occur in masses and thin coatings on other minerals in the miarolitic cavities of the Steel Mountain stock. The tiny crystals are silvery, light to dark green or greenish black in color. They coat microcline, albite and smoky quartz and are sometimes included in the quartz (personal).

Washington County: Small chlorite crystals occur in the pit on Iron Mountain. Very good quality books of green chlorite (species not determined) occur in the skarn (Photo. 148). It forms masses, often mixed with dark powdery oxides, associated with grossular and quartz. Occasionally, with unknown fine grained oxides, it forms pseudomorphs of an unknown mineral or minerals (Photos. 150, 151). These crystals are rough surfaced, have a tetrahedral shape and have been found up to 4 cm across, or have a shape similar to some titanite crystals.

In the some areas, chlorite forms small crystals associated with magnetite crystals in cavities in magnetite. It also occurs as fine crystals with grossular crystals. Chlorite books are often thin and stand on edge, a few have a rose-like development (personal).

CHLORITOID

$(Fe,Mg,Mn)_2Al_4Si_2O_{10}(OH)_4$, monoclinic and triclinic

One of the brittle micas. Foliated masses with micaceous habit; rarely tabular or pseudohexagonal crystals. Gray or greenish gray to dark green. Most common in metamorphosed sedimentary rocks, mica schists and phyllites. Also a hydrothermal alteration product in lavas and other rocks.

Lemhi County: Coarse granular chloritoid of a dark grayish green color occurs in the Nickel Plate and adjoining property in the Blackbird District. It is in a contact metamorphic rock alongside a dike that is about 10 feet wide. Specimens consist of interlocking crystals that average about 1 cm across. Green chlorite and muscovite fill fractures in the chloritoid (Shannon, 1926).

CHONDRODITE

$(Mg,Fe)_5(SiO_4)_2(F,OH)_2$, monoclinic

Massive; crystals prismatic, often complex. Light yellow to red; translucent. Common in metamorphosed dolomitic limestone with phlogopite, spinel, pyrrhotite and graphite.

Custer County: Small grains of chondrodite are common in a limestone near a small tarn in a cirque at the head of Wildhorse Canyon on the east side of Mount Hyndman. It has a resin-brown color, and forms irregular grains up to 2 mm across that make up about 50% of the rock. Small grains of green spinel and colorless clinochlore are associated, but none of these minerals are reported to occur in large euhedral crystals or occur in cavities (Shannon, 1926).

CHROMITE

$FeCr_2O_4$, cubic

Crystals small and uncommon, generally octahedral. Also massive, granular to compact. Iron-black to brownish black color; subtranslucent with submetallic luster. Common in peridotite rocks and serpentinites; also a secondary mineral in other igneous rocks. The only ore of chromium.

Boise County: Chromite occurs as minute octahedral crystals in the placer deposits in Boise Basin. The small crystals have a metallic luster and iron-black color (Sidler, 1957).

CHRYSOBERYL

$BeAl_2O_4$, orthorhombic

Usually in tabular crystals, vertically striated. Common as multiple twinned crystals with a pseudohexagonal appearance. Green, brown or yellow in color; vitreous luster. The gem variety alexandrite is emerald-green, but red by transmitted light and artificial light. Cat's-eye is a variety that displays a strong single ray when cut as a cabochon. A rare mineral that can be found in granitic rocks and mica schists.

Shoshone County: Chrysoberyl has been found as small tabular crystals in the corundum-bearing rock at the corundum deposit on Trail Creek, south of Goat Mountain (personal).

CHRYSOCOLLA

$(Cu,Al)_2H_2Si_2O_5(OH)_4 \cdot nH_2O$, monoclinic

Cryptocrystalline or massive; green to greenish blue. Forms grains, thin veins and masses. Secondary copper mineral associated with copper, malachite and azurite.

Adams County: In the Arkansas Mine in the Seven Devils District, chrysocolla is an important ore mineral. It is generally various shades of green and forms massive or botryoidal crusts. Most of the chrysocolla has an opaline texture and is associated with malachite. It consists of thin waxy crusts where it forms from the alteration of bornite. At the Peacock Mine, chrysocolla is waxy and translucent, and is various shades of blue and blue-green. Similar material occurs at the Helena Mine.

Chrysocolla is common at many of the mines in the district, generally as small masses, grains and nodules. It is associated with epidote, quartz, garnet, chalcopyrite and other minerals. Occasionally small blebs of native copper are disseminated in the chrysocolla (personal; Shannon, 1926).

Blaine County: Chrysocolla occurs as pseudomorphs of small, radial groups of aurichalcite associated with aurichalcite and hemimorphite in prospects near Blizzard Mountain (Photo. 152). The prospects are a short distance northwest of the saddle north of the mountain (personal).

Clark County: Chrysocolla occurs in the Weimer Mine in Skull Canyon. It forms small masses and also replaces small rosette-like groups of azurite (Photo. 153). These are up to about 7 mm across (personal).

Custer County: Chrysocolla occurs in many of the districts in Custer County. Only a few of the more interesting occurrences are given below. Scaly masses of chrysocolla occur in fluorite in the Empire Mine. It is associated with an unidentified yellow-green mineral which forms microscopic radial fibrous spherulites (Shannon, 1926).

Chrysocolla with an acicular structure, or as mammillary crusts or irregular grains occurs in the mines of the Mackay District. It has a green color (Shannon, 1926); microcrystals have been reported (Hurlbut, 1966).

At the Tiger claim, chrysocolla is emerald-green to blue-green or blue and is associated with fluorite. It occurs in a massive garnet rock with fluorite. Sky-blue chrysocolla forms masses up to 2 cm in diameter at the Peterson claim. Blue chrysocolla forms large masses in the Copper Bullion Mine. Where it lines small cavities, it has a botryoidal surface (Shannon, 1926).

Chrysocolla occurs as small masses between quartz crystals and as pseudomorphs of an acicular to needlelike mineral, probably malachite (Photo. 154) and as pseudomorphs of an elongated blade-like mineral, probably azurite, at the old silver mines on the north side of Keystone Mountain southwest of Challis. The area is on the northern edge of the Bayhorse District, and are in the area of the Garden Creek to Daugherty Gulch fluorite mines. Associated minerals include calcite, conichalcite, plumbojarosite, quartz and willemite (personal).

Lemhi County: Chrysocolla can be found at the Blue Jay Mine, west of Leadore, on Big Eightmile Creek, with azurite and malachite. The mine is developed as an open pit and several cuts that expose a copper-mineralized breccia in diorite. This same type of mineralization is exposed in two areas down the ridge along the access road. There appears to be more chrysocolla in the lower zones.

Chrysocolla forms in layers and nodules to about 1 cm, and some of it is slightly botryoidal. Large surfaces of malachite and chrysocolla can be found, but most of the azurite occurs as patches only 1-2 cm across. In the Blue Jay Mine, a black coating (tenorite or melaconite?) covers much of the other minerals. The mine is accessible by a good mine road from the Big Eightmile Creek Road a couple of miles before the campground at the end of the road (personal).

Shoshone County: Small amounts of chrysocolla may have occurred in several of the mines of the Coeur d'Alene District, but it was common only in the Snowstorm Mine. Here, it was the most important copper mineral in the oxide ores. It occurred as crusts and seams with a white, greenish blue and blue color; malachite and native silver were associated (Shannon, 1926; personal).

At the Monitor Mine in the eastern part of the county near the Montana border, chrysocolla occurs as small masses and pseudomorphs of a needle-like mineral, probably malachite. Associated with chrysocolla in the oxide zone of the mine are aurichalcite, azurite, malachite, zalesiite and a light green unknown (personal).

CHRYSOTILE

$Mg_3Si_2O_5(OH)_4$, monoclinic and orthorhombic

Common or field name for the three paramorphs with the above formula; clinochrysotile (monoclinic), orthochrysotile (orthorhombic) and parachrysotile (orthorhombic); cannot be distinguished in hand specimens. Members of the kaolinite-serpentinite group. Fibrous; white, yellow or greenish. Associated with chromite and magnetite. The principal asbestos minerals.

Blaine County: This fibrous mineral can be found at the Queen of the Hills Mine which is 1.5 miles west of Bellevue. Chrysotile is associated with calcite in a black slate. It is buff colored and consists of parallel fibrous masses with fibers up to 11 cm in length (Shannon, 1926).

CINNABAR

HgS, hexagonal (trigonal)

Crystals usually rhombohedral; penetration twins common; but mostly fine granular masses. Vermilion-red when pure to brownish red when impure. Transparent to translucent. The most important ore of mercury. Commonly occurs as deposits in Tertiary age volcanic rocks associated with pyrite, marcasite, stibnite, copper sulfides, gold, opal, chalcedony, quartz, barite and other low temperature minerals.

Cassia County: Cinnabar occurs 4.5 miles west of Black Pine. The occurrence is in a prospect at the top of a limestone bed below shale. Barite, quartz and cinnabar replace the limestone. Cinnabar is primarily a very thin, sooty or dust-like, red coating. Barite forms small tabular crystals that line cavities. Some arsenic is present and may indicate a mixture of realgar and cinnabar (Shannon, 1926).

Valley County: Cinnabar forms grains in quartz and chert-like silica veins and irregular bodies in marble in the Yellow Pine Mining District. Some pyrite and stibnite is associated in some of the deposits. Most of the cinnabar is coarsely crystalline but not known as euhedral crystals (Shannon, 1926).

Washington County: Small anhedral to subhedral crystals of cinnabar occur as grains in opalite rock on the east side of the Weiser River on the western edge of T. 11 N., R. 4 W. Mineralization is in sandstone, siltstone and shale. Locally, these rocks have been altered to opalite and clay. The grains of cinnabar are mostly quite small, but individual grains and crystal faces can be seen associated with pyrite and clay. A small amount of gold is reported to occur associated with the pyrite, and the opal forms rounded to irregular banded aggregates, which may be up to several inches across. The clays include beidellite, nontronite and kaolinite (Ross, 1956).

CLINOHUMITE

$(Mg,Fe)_9(SiO_4)_4(F,OH)_2$, monoclinic

Humite group mineral. Crystals are varied in habit, typically highly modified. Transparent to translucent; white, yellow or brown. Found in serpentine and talc schist, in contact zones in dolomite and in veins.

Lemhi County: Clinohumite occurs as light colored grains in the carbonate matrix with ludwigite in the skarn on Quartzite Canyon in the Spring Mountain District. These have been reported in only a few samples studied and the extent of their occurrence is not known (personal).

CLINOZOISITE

$Ca_2Al_3(SiO_4)_3(OH)$, monoclinic

Colorless, yellow, gray, green, pink and reddish pink; translucent to transparent. Member of epidote group. Crystals short to long prismatic or acicular, often massive or granular.

Found in regionally metamorphosed rocks, igneous rocks at contacts at contact zones with carbonate rocks, also an alteration of plagioclase feldspars.

Boise, Custer and Elmore Counties: Clinozoisite has been identified (x-ray diffraction) as the greenish-brown prismatic crystals on microcline and albite near the western edge of the Sawtooth batholith west of Mt. Everly. Individual crystals are up to about 8 mm in length. They have a habit and appearance similar to the epidote from the same area, differing only in color (personal).

Shoshone County: Small crystals of clinozoisite have been identified from a small simple pegmatite in a roadcut on Trail Creek. Several brownish olive green and pinkish crystals have been found in a few cavities and a few small, zoned gray to blue corundum crystals also were found in the pegmatite. A few tiny crystals that appeared to be zeolites were noted as was a greenish black, elongated wedge-shaped mineral. This was in a roadcut a short distance west of where the road crosses Trail Creek (personal).

CLINTONITE

$Ca(Mg,Al)_3(Al_3Si)O_{10}(OH)_2$, monoclinic

A mica group mineral. Colorless, yellowish, green, reddish brown and copper red; transparent to translucent. Pseudohexagonal tabular crystals; scaly masses or foliated. Found in crystalline limestones, in contact zones and chloritic schists.

Lemhi County: Clintonite occurs in the skarn on Quartzite Canyon in the Spring Mountain District. It forms small green micaceous books associated with diopside and forsterite in several areas. Most often the clintonite is in small cavities in massive diopside. Other minerals in the area include spinel, ludwigite, magnetite and forsterite (personal).

COBALTITE

$CoAsS$, orthorhombic (pseudocubic)

Generally cubes, octahedrons or pyritohedrons, massive or granular. Silver-white somewhat reddish. In high temperature hydrothermal vein deposits with nickel and cobalt minerals or as disseminations in metamorphic rocks.

Lemhi County: The only important occurrence of cobalt in the state is in the Blackbird District. Cobaltite occurs as reddish gray grains, crystals and granular masses. The crystals and grains are mostly less than 1 mm across. It has been found with chalcopyrite in a 1 cm wide band in schist in the Tom Jefferson claim. In this sulfide band, it forms pyritohedrons with cubic and octahedral modifications. Specimens from the Brooklyn claim contain crystals up to 2 mm across, with chalcopyrite. The cobaltite displays a perfect cubic cleavage. Crystals to 1 mm occur in the Ludwig and Bascom Latest Out claim on the West Fork of Blackbird Creek. It is disseminated in streaks in quartz with schist inclusions. The crystals are cuboctahedrons (Shannon, 1926).

Cobaltite from the Wiley J. Rose claim 1 mile north of the old Blackbird camp is partly altered to erythrite. It occurs in veins in quartzose schist. Cobaltite on the Haynes-Stellite Co. Mine on Blackbird Creek, occurs as micro reddish gray grains in quartz with schorl. Cobaltoan arsenopyrite (old name: danaite) is associated. Crystals of cobaltite to 5 mm can be found disseminated in quartz with biotite, chlorite and prismatic apatite. The crystals are cubes or octahedrons (Shannon, 1926).

It has been reported with erythrite and chalcopyrite in the Sunshine prospect in Sec. 20, T. 21 N., R. 18 E. The prospect is connected by road to the Calus Mine., The cobaltite forms micro grains. A similar occurrence is reported in the Calus Mine on a hillside north of Blackbird Creek in Sec. 21. It is in a siderite biotite, quartz and ankerite gangue with safflorite and chalcopyrite. Micro grains are also reported from the Dusty prospect in Sec. 23, and are associated with malachite in the crests of folds in a quartz-tourmaline rock. The Hawkeye prospect, in Sec. 27, contains micro grains of cobaltite with pyrite and erythrite (Anderson, 1947b; Trites and Tooker, 1953).

CONICHALCITE

$CuCa(AsO_4)(OH)$, orthorhombic

Member of the adelite group. Equant to short prismatic crystals, botryoidal to reniform crusts and masses with radial fibrous structure. Yellowish green to emerald green; subtranslucent. A secondary mineral in oxidized copper-bearing ore deposits.

Custer County: Conichalcite has been found on Keystone Mountain. On the north side of the mountain, in the zone where there are several prospects and small workings for fluorite are a few small mines and prospects for silver. These were developed in the late 1800s (Anderson, 1954a). There are several mine dumps and a few cuts and adits. Most of the workings are caved and inaccessible. The mines are developed in quartzite and dolomite.

Mineralization on the dumps includes chrysocolla, chrysocolla pseudomorphs of malachite, jarosite and plumbojarosite, conichalcite, willemite and other unidentified arsenates. The conichalcite occurs as tiny green hemispheres or tiny single crystals scattered on cavity surfaces or on other minerals or as microcrystalline crusts coating areas of the cavities (Photo. 155). Occasionally the conichalcite forms small crystals, usually complex. This is the first occurrence of conichalcite in Idaho known to the author (personal).

COPPER

Cu, cubic

Cube, dodecahedron and octahedrons, often complex; most crystals distorted. In arborescent and branching groups, scales and masses. Copper-red color; malleable and ductile. In copper veins, especially in oxidized zones of copper deposits. Usually associated with malachite, azurite and cuprite.

Adams County: The South Peacock Mine and Helena Mine in the Seven Devils District, contain some native copper in the oxidized ores. Grains of copper are sometimes found in masses of chrysocolla and malachite; most grains are only 1 to 3 mm across. It has been reported from some of the other contact metamorphic deposits in the district (Shannon, 1926; personal).

Tiny crystals of copper, forming wires, occur in microcrystalline coatings of analcime from the roadcut along Highway 95 at mile post 177.8, about 7 miles south of Pinehurst. Only a few specimens have been found in cavities that often contain chabazite, gyrolite, apophyllite and mesolite (personal).

Boise County: Native copper has been found in small amounts in the Coon Dog Mine in the Summit Flat District. The mine is on the divide between Grimes Creek and the Payette River. The copper forms fine sheets scattered through thin seams in rhyolite near the surface (Jones, 1917; Shannon, 1926).

Custer County: In the Mackay (Alder Creek) District, native copper forms thin films along fractures on the 300 foot level of the Empire Mine. It also forms small grains in nodules of cuprite (Shannon, 1926).

Latah County: The oxidized ores of the Mizpah Mine in the Hoodoo District contain some native copper. It is associated with cuprite, chalcopyrite and malachite, and occurs as small grains and thin seams (Shannon, 1926; personal).

Lemhi County: Thin films of copper were uncommon on fractures in the mines of the Indian Creek and Beaver Creek Districts (Shannon, 1926).

Native copper is uncommon in the Blackbird District, but locally abundant. Small zones of ore have produced an abundance of native copper in the faulted ore of the Black Pine Mine on the east side of the district. Excellent specimens of arborescent groups were found in the Blackbird open pit, and it also has been found as thin hackly sheets to a few millimeters across in fractures in shattered quartz (Photo. 43) (personal).

Shoshone County: Native copper occurred with chrysocolla, native silver, malachite and bornite in the Snowstorm Mine east of Mullan. Crystallized specimens were found in the Iron Mask Mine, and dendritic copper occurred in the Caledonia Mine. These dendritic crystals were on cerussite in limonite. In the Boyle stope of the Caledonia Mine, nugget-like masses of copper were mixed with native silver, and in the 700 foot level, it formed crystalline wires with a thin outer coating of silver. Similar wire-like specimens were found in the Tyler Mine (Shannon, 1926; personal).

CORUNDUM

Al_2O_3, hexagonal (trigonal)

Crystals are prismatic or hexagonal pyramids, often barrel-shaped. Transparent to translucent; brown, pink, blue or, less commonly, white, gray, green or red. A common accessory mineral in metamorphic rocks, especially crystalline limestone, mica-schist or gneiss.

Adams County: Gray, pink and light purple colored corundum crystals have been found in the gold placers in Rock Flat near New Meadows along the Brundage Mountain recreation area road. Some of them are gem quality. Pink stones to 1 carat and blue stones to one half carat have been cut from these. Rubies of poor quality have been reported; these have a silky sheen and may produce some asterism. Most of the corundum is of poor quality, but many colors can be found. Crystals and fragments of quartz crystals, topaz, tourmaline and spinel have also been collected here; surprisingly, many of these show little damage from transport. Diamonds have been reported in this popular gem collecting area (Beckwith, 1972; Shannon, 1926; personal).

Boise County: Crystals have been found in the gravels of the gold placers of several tributaries of the Payette River, including Gold Fork (Shannon, 1926).

Clearwater County: Corundum pebbles up to 2 cm have been found in the gold placers around Pierce. They have been reported from Rhodes and Orofino Creeks as having various shades of blue and green, some of them have a blue core with a gray or green outer layer. Most of the crystals are gray and are water worn, rough and imperfect. Their habit is mostly hexagonal prisms with basal pinacoid terminations, but a few are double hexagonal pyramids. Some specimens have small muscovite flakes coating them (Shannon, 1926). It has been reported that a few have small areas that are faceting quality (Beckwith, 1972).

Idaho County: Corundum has been found in the gold placer deposits near Burgdorf (originally called Resort). The crystals are mostly under 1 cm but are up to 2.5 cm in diameter and have a typical hexagonal tapering pyramidal shape. The colors include pinkish gray and bronze (Shannon, 1926; personal).

Corundum crystals can be found in the placer deposits along Ruby Creek, southeast of

Burgdorf and along Lake Creek to Burgdorf. The crystals are mostly rough, with the typical barrel shape. Most have mica inclusions, and the colors are mostly gray with reddish purple and bluish. Some have a bronze color and can be cut into low quality star gems. Red garnet crystals and fragments also occur in these deposits (personal).

Corundum, as small sapphires of various colors, has been reported from a few of the creeks that are tributaries of the Lochsa River in the area of Lowell. The small, rounded crystals are reported to be scarce (personal).

Latah County: Large corundum crystals, up to 7.5 cm across have been found with zircon and quartz crystals alongside a gravel road near Joel, east of Moscow. The location is now reported to be overgrown with grass and vegetation (personal).

Shoshone County: Corundum crystals are abundant in schist on Trail Creek, a fork of Floodwood Creek. The crystals are up to about 2 cm in length, although most are less than 1 cm, and dipyramidal in habit. They are mostly white or gray with some blue zones and rarely pink terminations, and are fractured. Chrysoberyl and vesuvianite are associated but rare. One cavity in a pegmatite was found with large blue corundum crystals projecting into a cavity. The large corundum crystals displayed a few faces, are opaque and up to about 4 cm across. In another pegmatite in a roadcut, corundum occurred with small crystals of clinozoisite (personal).

Valley County: Crystals of corundum with zircon and garnet can be found in the placer deposits on Boulder Creek, southeast of McCall in Secs. 19, 20, 29 and 30, T. 18 N., R. 4 E. Crystals are similar to those in the other areas to the north, as described above in Idaho County (personal).

Corundum crystals occur in schist 5 miles east of Smiths Ferry in Sec. 22, T. 11 N., R. 4 E. The corundum forms metacrysts in the pods and lenses of the schist which are included in the border zone of the granodiorite of the Idaho batholith. The schist inclusions are up to about 30 feet across and consist of biotite, oligoclase and corundum.

Most corundum crystals are less than 3 mm in length, but occur up to at least 3 cm in length and 2 cm in width. They are subhedral, and some are tabular. The crystals have a light gray to buff color, but appear pale blue, lavender and pink on thin edges (Fryklund, 1951).

COVELLITE

CuS, hexagonal

Thin hexagonal plates with pyramidal faces; most commonly massive. Euhedral crystals are rare. Indigo-blue to darker blue. Occurs in secondary enriched zone of copper deposits with enargite, bornite and chalcocite.

Custer County: In the Empire Mine in the Mackay District, covellite occurs as films on other sulfides. It is mixed with chalcopyrite in the Hearst tunnel which is west of the Empire Mine. The habit is intergrown plates which probably are replacing the chalcopyrite (Shannon, 1926).

Grains, masses and fracture coatings of covellite occur in the mines and prospects of the Slate Creek area. Associated minerals include cubanite, digenite, libethenite and pentlandite (Kern, 1972).

Idaho County: Coarse grained covellite has been collected in the Homestake Mine 4 miles southeast of Orogrande near the crest of the high divide which separates the Salmon and Clearwater River basins. There is a road to the mine and to the Badger Mine which has a similar occurrence. The covellite is on fractures in oxidized ore with pyrite, galena, chalcopyrite, sphalerite, tetrahedrite, malachite and pyromorphite (Shenon and Reed, 1934).

Lemhi County: Covellite occurs as spongy microcrystalline masses replacing tetrahedrite in quartz veins in the Ima Mine, at Patterson (Photo. 156). The masses are small, mostly under 1 cm across. Associated minerals include remnant grains of galena and tetrahedrite and microcrystals of pyromorphite, cerussite, azurite, malachite and other minerals (personal).

Owyhee County: Microcrystalline crusts of covellite form coatings on fractures in oxidized chalcopyrite in the oxidized portions of the ore bodies of the Laxey Mine on South Mountain. Individual covellite crystals are under 0.2 mm across and coatings and groups can be more than 1.5 cm across. The covellite is associated with microcrystals of azurite, aurichalcite, cerussite, chrysocolla, malachite, quartz and other secondary minerals (personal).

Shoshone County: Covellite occurred in the Last Chance workings of the Bunker Hill Mine in the Coeur d'Alene District. It formed soft, black, sooty streaks. It also occurred in the Caledonia Mine where masses of galena were encrusted with layers of covellite up to 10 cm in thickness (Radford and Crowley, 1981; Shannon, 1926).

COWLESITE

$Ca[Al_2Si_3O_{10}] \cdot 5\text{-}6H_2O$, orthorhombic

Forms tiny to small pointed blades or laths; mostly under 2 mm long and 0.1 mm thick; often in spherical groups. Colorless, white, gray or yellow; transparent to translucent. Occurs in volcanic rocks, especially olivine basalts. Typically associated with levyne and other zeolites.

Adams County: Cowlesite occurs as tiny crystals that form spheres lining cavities in Columbia River basalt with other zeolites in the zone south of Pinehurst. It is rare at one location, 0.8 mile north of mile post 177, where it occurs with levyne and phillipsite. All crystals are tiny and are found in small vesicles; the cowlesite spheres are about 1-1.5 mm across and are translucent (Photo. 157). This is the first occurrence of cowlesite in Idaho, and was originally identified by Rudy W. Tschernich on a specimen found by the author (personal).

CUBANITE

$CuFe_2S_3$, orthorhombic

Brass to bronze-yellow; magnetic. Forms twins as pairs of fourlings; no cleavage. Found in high temperature deposits with pyrrhotite and pentlandite, in contact metamorphic deposits, and in gold-quartz veins. Chalcopyrite, sphalerite and pyrite are also associated.

Custer County: Cubanite occurs with pentlandite, chalcopyrite, covellite, sphalerite and digenite in the mines of the Slate Creek area. It is known to occur in the Last Chance Number Five Mine 1 mile up Last Chance Creek, and is accessible by road from Slate Creek. Mineralization can be found in several adits (all but one caved) adjacent to a north-south fault.

Mineralization is in large calcite crystals in the Milligen formation and is most abundant in a marble outcrop above the open adit. Associated minerals include jamesonite, sphalerite, pyrite, anglesite, covellite and tetrahedrite. It may occur in other mines in the area (Kern, 1972).

CUPRITE

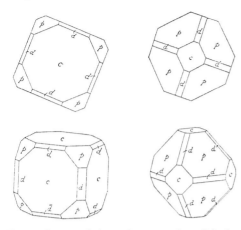

Fig.14 Cuprite; left—cubic crystal modified by octahedron and dodecahedron, Mackay District, Custer County; right—octahedral crystal modified by dodecahedron and cube, Caledonia Mine, Shoshone County; crystal drawings from Shannon (1926).

Cu_2O, cubic

Most crystals octahedral, sometimes highly modified. Also in cubes that are elongated forming reticulated or capillary groups, known as chalcotrichite. Red to almost black. Common in the oxidized zone of copper deposits, associated with many of the secondary copper minerals.

Adams County: Cuprite is uncommon in the Seven Devils District but has been found in the Blue Jacket Mine and in the Peacock Mine (Shannon, 1926).

Custer County: Cuprite occurs as nodular bunches in chrysocolla in the 300 foot level of the Alberta Mine in the Mackay (Alder Creek) District. The nodules are up to 2.5 cm across and are coated with a thin layer of tenorite. Specimens from an unreported locality in the district, have crystals of a deep red color on limonite crusts on massive garnet. The crystals are combinations of the cube, octahedron and rhombic dodecahedron (Fig. 14). Reticulated elongate crystals of chalcotrichite are associated (Shannon, 1926).

In the Skylark Mine in the Bayhorse District, cuprite crystals coat cracks in iron-stained rock. They are red in color and are believed to be an oxidation product of tetrahedrite. The habit is octahedral with modifying cube and rhombic dodecahedron faces (Shannon, 1926).

Latah County: Cuprite is associated with other copper minerals (malachite, azurite, chrysocolla and chalcopyrite), quartz and pyrite in the Mizpah Mine (Shannon, 1926; personal).

Cuprite has also been found in the Gold Hill Mine in the Gold Hill District, north of Harvard. It occurs with malachite and other copper minerals (Faich, 1937).

Lemhi County: Cuprite occurs in an adit which is 390 feet east of the Cobalt triangulation station, and is 2,000 feet east of the Calus Mine in Sec. 21, T. 21 N., R. 18 E. The characteristics are unknown, but it is associated with malachite and chalcopyrite (Trites and Tooker, 1953).

It has also been reported from the Lemhi Pass District on Agency Creek. Here it occurs with bornite, chalcopyrite, chalcocite, malachite, azurite and gold and silver minerals (Trites and Tooker, 1953).

Cuprite of unreported size and habit was found in the Silverton prospect 3 miles northwest of Salmon in Sec. 35, T. 22 N., R. 21 E. It occurs in fault gouge with malachite, azurite, copper and cerussite (Ross, 1925).

Tiny crystals of cuprite occur with cyanotrichite, malachite and azurite in gossan in the Iron Dike Mine on the east side of Stroud Gulch in the Junction District near Leadore. The small crystals (mostly under 3 mm, but up to 6 mm across) are coated with malachite and sometimes replaced by malachite (Photo. 158) (personal).

Shoshone County: Cuprite occurred in several forms in the Caledonia Mine. Oxidized tetrahedrite in porous quartzite, was surrounded by concentric rings of cuprite, azurite, malachite and chrysocolla. Cellular tetrahedrite contained minute cuprite crystals. Grains and filiform wires of native copper occurred in cavities in granular and spongy cuprite. Octahedral crystals to 6 mm across occurred in cracks in the ore. These crystals were deep red and transparent. Rusty limonite-stained quartzite on the 500 foot level contained small transparent deep red cuprite crystals that were associated with cerussite crystals. The cuprite crystals were octahedrons, some of them had cube and dodecahedron modifications (Fig. 14) (Shannon, 1926).

Washington County: Chalcotrichite occurs in cavities in granular cuprite from Little Bar on the Snake River. Chrysocolla and a brown copper silicate are associated (Shannon, 1926).

CUPROTUNGSTITE

$Cu_2(WO_4)(OH)_2$, system unknown
Massive, microcrystalline, friable to compact, as crusts. Color is brownish green or yellowish green to emerald-green. Uncommon; in contact metamorphic deposits.

Adams County: Cuprotungstite occurs as an alteration product of scheelite in the South Peacock Mine, in the Seven Devils District. The cuprotungstite is similar in appearance to the lindgrenite which forms veinlets, crusts and drusy crusts of micro tabular crystals at the Helena Mine. Mineralization is in a tactite along the contact of a diorite and marble; molybdenite, chrysocolla, brochantite, lindgrenite and powellite are associated. Specimens were noted during mining operations, but all of these minerals are scarce in the district now. The tactite is mostly massive garnet and epidote with some crystals in uncommon cavities (Cannon and Grimaldi, 1953; Cook, 1954, personal).

CUSPIDINE

$Ca_4Si_2O_7(F,OH)_2$, monoclinic
Crystals are spear-shaped and very small; commonly massive, fine granular, lamellar. Colorless, white, greenish gray, pale rose red. Transparent to translucent, vitreous luster. Occurs in metamorphic rocks and in limestone near contacts with intrusive rocks.

Custer County: Custerite was named for Custer County from specimens collected in the Mackay (Alder Creek) District in 1912 (Umpleby, 1923). This material was later proven to be the same as the mineral cuspidine, and the name custerite was dropped. It occurs as finely granular masses mixed with magnetite in a group of prospects a short distance beyond the crest of the high ridge northwest of the Copper Bullion Mine tunnel. It was found only along the inner edge of a garnet-diopside rock which surrounds a large limestone inclusion in granite porphyry. This cuspidine is greenish gray to white, and was reported as common to abundant at this locality (Shannon, 1926).

CYANOTRICHITE

$Cu_4Al_2(SO_4)(OH)_{12} \cdot 2H_2O$, orthorhombic
Usually in very fine acicular or hair-like crystals forming plush coatings, radial-fibrous or tufted. Sky-blue or azure-blue. Uncommon as a secondary mineral in copper deposits.

Lemhi County: Copper secondary minerals have been known from the Junction Mining District near Leadore since active mining in the district (1950s), but few specimens have been found by mineral collectors. Literature is sparse on the district or on the Peacock Mine, reported to be the source of some very fine azurite and cyanotrichite specimens in the 1950s. The Peacock Mine is apparently the main workings west of Stroud Gulch in the western part of the district on Mineral Hill. The author noted in two visits to the Peacock Mine that no copper secondary minerals could be seen on the dumps and in the small workings; this is typical of nearly all the mines in the district.

Small amounts of cyanotrichite have been found in the Iron Dike Mine immediately east of Stroud Gulch. A few specimens of compact fibrous coatings, blue tufts and radiating fibrous groups have been found in the "iron dike" gossan associated with azurite, brochantite, cuprite, malachite and an unidentified hydrated sulfate (Photos. 159, 160). Small layers of tiny fibers of cyanotrichite were found in a small zone above the portal of the adit associated with malachite and black manganese(?) oxides. In colluvium, in the western side of the pit, thin layers of cyanotrichite were seen in two small areas.

Pieces of gossan on the dump are scarce, but a few were found that contained fine coatings of cyanotrichite as well as tiny azurite, cuprite and malachite crystals. Although Small bits and pieces of these minerals are common on the dumps, only a few specimen quality pieces have been found.

Even though mineralized scraps are common at the Iron Dike Mine, they are rare on the dumps of the other mines of the district (personal). The author has communicated with other collectors who also noted the lack of any mineralization at the Peacock Mine and the other mines. It is the author's belief that with this type of surface mineralization in this part of the mining district, it is unlikely that the Peacock Mine produced the fine quality azurite and cyanotrichite specimens attributed to it without leaving any traces on the dumps. It is more likely that the source of these minerals was the Iron Dike Mine a half mile to the east.

DELAFOSSITE

$CuFeO_2$, hexagonal (trigonal)

Generally as botryoidal crusts; tabular crystals are rare. Opaque; color is black; metallic luster. Weakly magnetic. Occurs with secondary copper minerals, including cuprite, native copper and tenorite; also magnetite and quartz.

Lemhi County: The rare mineral, delafossite, occurs in the Pope-Shenon Mine about 8 miles southwest of Salmon. The mine is located in Sec. 9, T. 20 N., R. 22 E, midway up a mountain ridge overlooking the Salmon River Valley. Delafossite has been reported as a primary mineral that forms banded or layered masses along the walls of ore shoots that contain chalcopyrite, but Ross (1925) reports that it is a minor constituent of this rock. Much of it has a concentric ellipsoid or shell-like structure. It is black, quite hard and resembles magnetite. Mineralization is along shear zones in a dark green quartzite. Biotite, chlorite, sericite, muscovite and epidote also occur in the shear zones.

Various secondary minerals can be found associated with the delafossite, which occurs in all levels of the mine. Most common of the secondary minerals are malachite, azurite, chrysocolla, cuprite, chalcocite and native copper (Anderson, 1943, 1956; Ross, 1925).

DESCLOIZITE

$Pb(Zn,Cu)(VO_4)(OH)$, orthorhombic

A member of the descloizite group. Crystals commonly pyramidal, prismatic or tabular, but variable in form, also plumose aggregates, crusts and botryoidal. Orange-red to reddish brown to blackish brown and dark green; transparent to nearly opaque. Occurs as a secondary mineral in vanadium-bearing lead-zinc-copper deposits, widespread.

Lemhi County: No mention of descloizite in the state was found in any of the geologic literature researched by the author. Apparently, the recent discovery of it in the Iron Mask Mine in the Spring Mountain District, and nearby in the Gilmore District are the first for Idaho. In the Iron Mask Mine, descloizite is uncommon associated with vanadinite. It was found on the dumps of the caved mines of the Iron Mask group of workings. It forms yellowish to brown or black crystals, generally very tiny, less than a mm across. A few specimens have been found with orange to red descloizite crystals. These were on cream colored vanadinite or on darker larger descloizite crystals found in a section of the vein on the cirque wall (Photo. 161, 162). Generally, descloizite occurs as druses on the iron oxide or dolomite matrix or as scattered crystals on the matrix or rarely on drusy quartz. See the vanadinite listing for a more thorough description of the occurrence (personal).

In the Gilmore District, descloizite was found as small crystalline coatings in the Democrat Mine which is northwest of Gilmore. Chlorargyrite and smithsonite have also been reported from here. It was also reported in the Silver Moon Mine south of town (personal).

DIAMOND

C, cubic

Crystals are octahedral, often modified, with curved faces. Color is pale yellow or colorless, gray, black or other colors. Has a greasy appearance and adamantine luster. Occurs in kimberlite or, rarely, other ultramafic rocks.

Adams County: The only known occurrence of diamonds in Idaho is in the Rock Flat gold and corundum placers at the head of Little Goose Creek Canyon 5 miles east of New Meadows. Three small crystals were found in several cubic yards of gravel during a testing operation. The largest crystal was one third carat, it was grayish in color and octahedral in shape. Gold, ilmenite, magnetite, chromite, zircon, corundum, garnet and monazite were associated in the concentrates; these minerals can be found extensively in the gravels in this area (Shannon, 1926).

DIGENITE

Cu_9S_5, cubic

Mostly massive, does occur as octahedral crystals; most common as grains and blebs in other minerals. Blue to black. Chalcopyrite, chalcocite, bornite and other copper minerals are associated.

Custer County: In the Slate Creek area, digenite occurs with several copper minerals in a few of the mines and prospects. It mostly occurs as grains or blebs with chalcopyrite, sphalerite, cubanite and galena. It may occur in the Last Chance Number Five mine as well as other mines (Kern, 1972).

DIOPSIDE

$CaMgSi_2O_6$, monoclinic

Crystals square or eight sided prisms; also granular or massive. White to light green; transparent to translucent. Most common in contact metamorphic rocks, especially carbonates. Associated with garnet, tremolite, scapolite, quartz and titanite.

Adams County: Diopside is common in the contact metamorphic copper deposits of the Seven Devils District. It is mostly granular or as coarse, interlocking, subhedral crystals and dark green in color. Small euhedral crystals may project into small cavities. Calcite, garnet, epidote, quartz, secondary copper minerals and minor quartz are associated (personal).

Blaine County: Diopside forms large masses in the crystalline rocks that form the crest of the mountain range of the Hailey quadrangle. There are good exposures at the cirques on the west side of Mount Hyndman at the head of the East Fork of Wood River. At this locality, the diopside varies from white to blue-gray (Shannon, 1926).

Bonner County: Tiny crystals of diopside occur with scheelite and garnet in the skarn at the Vulcan Mine northeast of Lakeview on the east side of Lake Pend Oreille. See the scheelite section for complete description of the occurrence and access. The skarn contains massive diopside and garnet with many small vugs that contain euhedral crystals of both minerals and tiny scheelite crystals. The diopside crystals are generally 2-6 mm long, green and often translucent; they often have a thin iron staining and many are fractured (personal).

Custer County: Diopside is common in the metamorphic and contact metamorphic rocks and ore deposits of the county. Generally it is green and granular massive. It is associated with garnet, augite, hedenbergite and fluorite in the Mackay (Alder Creek) District. Near Challis, massive diopside contains disseminated molybdenite. Garnet-diopside rock can be found in the Copper Basin District at the head of the East Fork of Big Lost River. The Reed and Davidson Mine, in this district, contains diopside with magnetite and copper silicates (Shannon, 1926).

Lemhi County: Diopside is common in the skarn along Quartzite Canyon, Spring Mountain District. It forms green masses of subhedral to euhedral crystals in cavities in massive diopside, calcite and forsterite. Most crystals are under 1 cm, but a few to 2 cm have been found. Diopside crystals are generally green when larger, but the small crystals vary from white to light green. Generally the crystals occur alone, but rarely may have other minerals including clintonite, magnetite or spinel associated (personal).

It also occurs in the skarn a few miles to the northwest on the Colorado claims on Lemhi Union Gulch. At this locality, it can be found in the small bulldozer cut on the top of the ridge above the adit by the road. The diopside is green and forms masses with crystal-lined cavities. Diopside crystals are mostly about 2-6 mm long, but were seen up to about 1.5 cm in length (Photo. 163). Tiny crystals of spinel are associated (personal).

Owyhee County: Diopside occurs in lime-silicate contact rock along the road on Williams Creek 2 miles below the Golconda and other mines in the South Mountain District. Large pale gray-green rough crystals up to 1 by 3 cm have been found here. Some diopside occurs with other metamorphic minerals in the contact rocks in the mines of the district (Shannon, 1926).

DOLOMITE

$CaMg(CO_3)_2$, hexagonal (trigonal)

Rhombohedrons, often curved forming saddle-shaped crystals; massive or granular. Transparent or translucent; colorless, white, pink, gray or other colors. Forms dolomitic limestone, or occurs as a vein mineral.

Blaine County: Small cavities in a cream colored carbonate from the North Star Mine in the Wood River District contain curved rhombohedral crystals of iron-bearing dolomite. Dolomite may occur in other mines of the district (Shannon, 1926).

Boise and Gem Counties : Dolomite is associated with quartz crystals and arsenopyrite in the I.X.L. Mine in the Pearl (now part of the Westview) District. The dolomite forms saddle-shaped crystals with an opaque pale gray color (Shannon, 1926).

Butte County: Rhombohedral crystals of dolomite can be found in vugs in the host rock of the ores of the St. Louis Mine in Sec. 15, T. 3 N., R. 24 E. on a branch of Champagne Creek. The main adit of the mine is at 6,300 feet elevation. Most of the dolomite crystals are of tiny to small size. Calcite, aikinite, melanterite and other minerals are associated (Anderson, 1929).

DRAVITE

$NaMg_3Al_6(BO_3)_3Si_6O_{18}(OH,F)_4$, trigonal

Tourmaline group member. Crystals mostly short to long prismatic, but sometimes nearly equant; usually 3- 6- or 9-sided; as single crystals, groups or radial groups. Brown, brownish black to black, dark red or pale bluish green to emerald green. Most common in metamorphic and metasomatic rocks, also in pegmatites and in some basic igneous rocks.

Boise, Custer or Elmore Counties: Dravite has been identified from one cavity in the granite of the Sawtooth batholith. The identified material formed felted masses of tiny dark gray to black crystals, and similar material was reported from another cavity but was not analyzed. Identification was by x-ray diffraction (personal).

Washington County: Black acicular tourmaline crystals, forming small parallel groups in the pit on Iron Mountain have been identified as dravite by X-ray. These occur in a skarn with grossular, phlogopite and chlorite. They form small parallel groups of long crystals in vuggy quartz masses. Individual crystals are 1-2 mm across and up to 3-4 cm in length (personal).

DUFRENOYSITE

$Pb_2As_2S_5$, monoclinic

Forms tabular crystals, elongated and striated; perfect cleavage; metallic luster. Color is lead-gray to steel-gray; subtranslucent; dark red-brown in transmitted light.

Blaine County: Dufrenoysite is reported to occur in the Wood River District (Palache, 1944).

Boise County: Dufrenoysite is reported to occur in the Banner District (Palache, 1944).

DUFTITE

$PbCu(AsO_4)(OH)$, orthorhombic

As rough, rounded minute crystals, crusts and aggregates. Apple-green to olive green and grayish green; translucent. A secondary mineral found in the oxidized portions of lead- and copper-bearing ore deposits.

Clark County: Tiny, platy duftite crystals forming groups are rare at the Weimer Mine (Photo. 164). The tiny crystals form spherical or disk-like groups and were found on only one specimen associated with fornacite, mimetite and wulfenite. This is the first identification of this mineral in Idaho (personal).

Custer County: Tiny crystals of duftite, or possibly beta duftite, have been found with other secondary minerals on one of the dumps of the old silver prospects on the north side of Keystone Mountain. The mineral is uncommon at this locality, but does form good microscopic crystals which occur as green coatings and groups. Identification was by electron microprobe analysis. This is the second discovery of this mineral in Idaho (personal).

ELBAITE

$Na(Li,Al)_3Al_6(BO_3)_3Si_6O_{18}(OH)_4$, hexagonal (trigonal)

Member of the tourmaline group. Pink, green, colorless or blue; transparent to translucent. Most commonly found in lithium-bearing pegmatites with quartz, beryl and lepidolite.

Adams County or Idaho County: Small crystals of pale green tourmaline crystals, probably elbaite, have been found in the Seven Devils Mountains (Photos. 165, 167). The crystals are about 1.2 to 2 cm in length and 6-7 mm across. The translucent, somewhat gemmy crystals were collected as singles with no matrix. The northern part of the range is in Idaho County and the southern part in Adams County, but the location has not been revealed (personal).

Boise County: Flat blades of bluish gray elbaite were found in rusty limonite-stained sericite from the Boise Basin (Shannon, 1926).

Clearwater County: Colored tourmaline crystals, probably elbaite, have been reported from pegmatites and a colluvial(?) deposit a short distance west of the Fohl Picnic area at Pierce Divide. Small crystals and pieces have been reported. The possible colluvial deposit is an unusual occurrence of unknown origin with angular and rounded rock fragments and angular and rounded crystals fragments mixed with clay. It is on the west side of the saddle at the end of a ridge. Collectors have dug into the occurrence to recover pieces of beryl, smoky quartz, topaz and black tourmaline (personal).

Idaho County: Small crystals of pinkish to greenish tourmaline crystals, probably elbaite, were found by an elk hunter in the Orogrande area. These were found loose on the surface in a talus slope and were 1-2 cm in length (personal).

ENARGITE

Cu_3AsS_4, orthorhombic

Elongated crystals, vertically striated, tabular, bladed or massive. Grayish black to iron-black. An uncommon mineral; occurs in vein and replacement deposits with covellite, chalcocite, bornite and pyrite.

Custer County: Massive enargite occurs in the Dickens Hill Mine in the Yankee Fork District. Euhedral crystals have been found in vugs in the ore veins of the mine and in other mines of the district. In the Dickens Hill Mine, veins are around 2.5 cm across. Vein fillings display cockade structure with some minerals nicely crystallized. Chalcopyrite, sphalerite, galena, tetrahedrite, arsenopyrite, stephanite, miargyrite, pyrargyrite, gold, silver, acanthite, chlorargyrite, covellite, malachite, azurite and chalcocite occur in the district. The district is located on the Yankee Fork of the Salmon River in the northwestern part of the county in T. 12-13 N., R. 15 E. (Anderson, 1949; Cass, 1973; Shannon, 1926).

EPIDOTE

$Ca_2(Al,Fe)_3(Si,O_4)_3(OH)$, monoclinic
Prismatic crystals, often elongated parallel to the b axis; also granular or fibrous. Sometimes twinned. Pistachio-green or yellowish to blackish green; transparent to translucent. Occurs in crystalline metamorphic rocks; especially the contact metamorphic rocks and skarn zones.

Adams County: Epidote is common in many of the copper mines of the Seven Devils District. In the Peacock Mine, it forms green crystals in cavities in massive epidote (Photo. 166). Excellent crystals to 30 cm in length were found when the mines were active. Crystals are often flattened parallel to the base and are elongated parallel to the b axis. Most crystals have simple terminations. Twinning is common with a(100) as the twin plane. Often, the crystals are formed with several shells. Each layer being well-formed and lustrous.

Specimens from the Fidelity claims are pale green, poorly-formed prisms, and fibrous masses with quartz and calcite and radiating green prisms in quartz. Similar crystals have been found in the Helena Mine with brown garnet, dark green diopside and quartz. Epidote from the Copper Boy Mine forms masses of green crystals. Some terminations project into chrysocolla-filled cavities. Some specimens from the Peacock Mine form radiating columnar masses in brown garnet or prismatic crystals to 5 cm long (Shannon, 1926; personal).

Boundary County: Masses of parallel to radiating groups of grayish green crystals can be found in the Golden Scepter Mine on Hall Mountain. They are most prominent in quartz at the mouth of a short adit below the road at the cabin. Crystals can be found frozen in the quartz around the portal of the adit and in several areas of the rock outcrops near the adit.

Specimens can be collected that contain crystals to 20 cm length. The quartz matrix is generally not easily removed from the epidote so that the crystals can only be exposed in section, often broken. Erythrite and tourmaline have been reported.

The mine is on the west face of the mountain overlooking the Kootenai River valley floor in Sec. 14, T. 65 N., R. 1 W. It is accessible by a steep switchback dirt road (Le Moine, 1959; personal).

Camas County: Small crystals of epidote occur in miarolitic cavities in the Tertiary granite of the Soldier Mountain stock. This granite body is primarily exposed as Smoky Dome peak, northwest of Fairfield. Epidote crystals (not analyzed, may be clinozoisite) have the common green color and prismatic form of epidote. They occur in small miarolitic cavities with albite, calcite, potassium feldspar and quartz (personal).

Clearwater County: Fragments of well-formed crystals have been found in the placer deposits in the county. The fragments have been up to 3 cm long and associated with corundum, rutile and garnet (Shannon, 1926).

Custer County: Epidote occurs on the Basin prospect on the mountain across Park Creek from the point where the Ketchum to Mackay Road crosses the Trail Creek divide. It coats small cavities which have been filled with prehnite. Perfect doubly terminated crystals occur, associated with garnet, hedenbergite, vesuvianite, wollastonite and galena.

They are lath-shaped and elongated on the b axis. Most are under 2 mm in length and are transparent yellow-green in color (Shannon, 1926).

Epidote occurs in the Wildhorse Mine on Wildhorse Creek northeast of Ketchum, in T. 5 N., R. 20 E. The mine is 9 miles up the Wildhorse Creek road which forks off the East Fork of Big Lost River road. There are several tactite zones that have been explored for tungsten. The largest zone is at the Hard to Find claim which is on the left fork of Wildhorse Creek, about 1,000 feet above the main fork. The Steep Climb claim is above the mill on the west side of the Creek and the Beaver outcrop is about 0.9 mile north of the mill on the east side of the creek. The Pine Mouse claims are in a cirque on the west slope of Wildhorse Creek valley about 1.4 miles north of the mill. There are several tactite bodies in the walls of the cirque.

Epidote occurs as short, perfect crystals, and scheelite occurs as large white crystals. Garnet, diopside, vesuvianite, quartz, calcite, pyrite and molybdenite are associated. Some of the vesuvianite and diopside contains beryllium. Exposures are poor, open cuts have slumped and are overgrown and the tactite is mostly fine grained and massive. Cavities are uncommon and most of the epidote is fibrous or forms crystals less than 6 mm in length (Heungwon, 1955; Pattee et al, 1968; personal).

Elmore County: Small crystals of epidote occur with smoky quartz, microcline, albite and, rarely, prehnite in miarolitic cavities in the Tertiary granite of the Steel Mountain stock northwest of Rocky Bar. Epidote forms groups and single crystals that are perched on the other minerals; most crystals are less than 6 mm in length and 1 mm in width. They are transparent to translucent and typical "epidote green." The mineral also forms granular coatings on some joint surfaces. Epidote is uncommon, but is locally abundant (personal).

Latah County: Epidote crystals to 10 cm (or more) in length have been collected in a wheat field about 7 miles northeast of Genesee. The crystals are found in a clay soil and decomposed granitic rock by digging to depths of six feet or more. Individual crystals are dark greenish black and translucent. Many of them are twinned (Photo. 169). They occur only as single crystals, often several in a small area in the clay, probably the remains of de-composed crystal pockets. Fragments of quartz crystals are sometimes found; one report-edly had the appearance of being part of a Japan-law twin (personal).

Lemhi County: Epidote forms small green prismatic crystals in the Copper King Mine and the Carmer Creek property. The crystals are in fragments of schist that are enclosed in the ore veins (Umpleby, 1913a).

The Porterfield prospect, on the west side of Milkey Creek, contains small epidote crystals. These are found most easily by searching the mine dump where they form clusters associated with the ore minerals. The prospect is in T. 20 N., R. 22 E., apparently in Sec. 22 (Ross, 1925).

Tiny epidote crystals are uncommon in cavities in the contact rock at the Bruce Estate magnetite deposit at the head of Bruce Canyon (Photo. 170). The tiny crystals occur in small cavities in the igneous rock at the contact zone on the north side of the magnetite body where it is exposed in a cut (personal).

Owyhee County: Epidote is common in many of the ore zones in the Silver City area, especially in the mines of Florida and War Eagle Mountains. It occurs as pistachio green and yellowish green crystals in the quartz-feldspar gangue (Piper and Laney, 1926). Tiny crystals of epidote occur in cavities at the Dewey Mine on the north side of Florida Moun-tain (personal).

Valley County: Near Granite Lake (north of McCall in Sec. 3, T. 20 N., R. 3 E.), epidote occurs with garnet in skarn zones cutting granitic rock on a ridge that runs south of the lake. Epidote can be found as small, euhedral crystals in cavities. The occurrence is similar to the Deep Creek occurrence which lies 1.5 miles to the east and is described below (personal).

Epidote forms long prismatic crystals, in small parallel clusters, mostly not terminated, in a skarn zone in a roadcut below the mouth of Deep Creek north of McCall. These have been found with titanite, microcrystals of spinel and tiny crystals of an unidentified light orangish micaceous mineral. Dark reddish orange garnet crystals are uncommon. Some epidote crystals are of large size, up to about 8 cm, but extend from wall-to-wall across cavities. Pink calcite may fill the epidote-bearing vug but can be removed with acid. Occasionally, a few smaller terminated epidote crystals may occur in a cavity. Small crystals of white adularia can also be found on many of these cavities (personal).

Very fine quality small epidote crystals have been reported east of Donnelly. The epidote occurs with quartz crystals, sometimes rutilated, in a deposit that was prospected for quartz of radio crystal quality during WW II. Epidote crystals, often brilliant and translucent, were up to 2.5 cm in length, and have been reported to 10 cm.

Three pits were dug in a small area on a hillside where prospecting was done along a rusty white quartz vein(s?). The small pits are slumped and overgrown, there are no rock outcrops. Most of the quartz and epidote was discarded on the dumps and may have been found by digging and screening the debris. Nice crystals of either mineral are rare (personal).

Large quartz crystals and some epidote and garnet crystals have been reported from Green Mountain, in Secs. 6 and 7, T. 17 N., R. 5 E. The epidote is found with garnet in much of the rock of the area; euhedral crystals may occur in cavities (personal).

Epidote occurs as small crystals with orange to red garnets and quartz crystals in a skarn exposed in a roadcut about .25 miles east of the Sloans Peak Lookout jeep trail, east of Donnelly. Access is gained by taking the Paddy Flat Road (#388) to road number 389 for about 11 miles. Turn south on road number 401 towards the lookout turnoff at the top of a ridge then east to the roadcut.

Epidote is mostly small to about 1 cm, garnet crystals (probably grossular) are tiny to about 2 cm, but mostly less than 6 mm. Small crystals are generally orange (often translucent to transparent), and the color darkens as the size increases. Quartz crystals are uncommon, but massive gray to smoky quartz is common in the western part of the deposit. Quartz crystals occur in cavities in the quartz and in the fine-grained massive diopside with the quartz. Some coarse garnet crystals also occur frozen in the quartz and may be exposed in matrix by carefully chipping away the quartz.

EPSOMITE

$MgSO_4 \cdot 7H_2O$, orthorhombic
Crystals are rare; generally forms botryoidal masses or fibrous crusts. Transparent to translucent; colorless to white. Has a very bitter taste. Occurs in lake deposits or as an efflorescence on rocks in caves or mine workings.

Lemhi County: Epsomite is common associated with the stibnite veins in the Buckhorn Mine in the Little Eightmile (Junction) District. It forms delicate fibers lining cavities in the veins and as a capillary efflorescence coating some of the mine workings. It is most common as the efflorescence on a carbonaceous limestone near the dacite dike about 450 feet inside the adit. At this location, the individual capillary crystals are up to 5 cm in length (Thune, 1941).

Owyhee County: On the Claytonia claim on Jump Creek, epsomite occurs in a bed of coarsely crystalline salts 10 inches thick (Shannon, 1926).

ERIONITE

$(K_2,Ca,Na_2)_2Al_4Si_{14}O_{36} \cdot 15H_2O$, hexagonal

Long prismatic, fine fibrous, minute, wool-like. Colorless, white, gray, green or orange; translucent. Occurs with offretite and other zeolites in volcanic rocks. Closely related to offretite and is probably always intergrown with it; extremely difficult to distinguish from offretite.

Ada County: Erionite is probably at least a minor component of the offretite that occurs as submicroscopic fibers on the surfaces of levyne crystals at the Lucky Peak Dam about 10 miles east of Boise. This occurrence is described under offretite (personal).

Adams County: Erionite is probably at least a minor component of the offretite that occurs as submicroscopic fibers on the surfaces of levyne near Pinehurst. See the offretite description for more information (personal).

ERYTHRITE

$Co_3(AsO_4)_2 \cdot 8H_2O$, monoclinic

Most commonly as thin crusts or coatings; crystals prismatic and vertically striated. Pink to reddish; translucent. A secondary mineral in the oxidized portions of cobalt deposits.

Lemhi County: Erythrite occurs in several of the mines in the Blackbird District. In the Blackbird Mine, it forms rose-red fibrous and crystalline coatings along seams and cracks in a black tourmaline-quartz rock (Photo. 44). It has been found both in the pit and upper portions of the underground workings. Thin blades and rosettes of rose-red erythrite occur in a rusty schist in the Bulkley Mine, and it forms similar pink blades and rosettes in the quartzite on the Brooklyn claim. The crystals are tabular to the b axis (Shannon, 1926, personal).

In the Sunshine prospect, erythrite occurs with cobaltite and chalcopyrite. The mine is in Sec. 20, T. 21 N., R. 18 E. and is connected by road to the Calus Mine (Trites and Tooker, 1953).

Shoshone County: Erythrite has been found with cobaltiferous gersdorffite on a prospect 1 mile above the mouth of Slate Creek, a tributary of the St. Joe River. It forms crusts and druses of rose-pink microcrystals (Shannon, 1926)

EVANSITE

$Al_3(PO_4)(OH)_6 \cdot 6H_2O$, amorphous

Massive, botryoidal or reniform coatings. Colorless to milky-white sometimes yellowish, greenish, bluish, brownish or reddish. Transparent to translucent. A secondary mineral that occurs with limonite and allophane.

Custer County: Evansite occurs at Goldburg as masses and crusts in seams. It is white, yellow, brown and dark red in color and is brittle with a conchoidal fracture (Shannon, 1926).

FAYALITE

Fe_2SiO_4, orthorhombic
Member of olivine group; brittle, fracture conchoidal. Crystals usually thick tabular, wedge-shaped terminations; small. Mostly massive or granular. Common in small amounts n acid and alkaline igneous rocks, in quartz syenites and in lithophysae in obsidian.

Boise, Custer and Elmore Counties: Fayalite can be found in the granite of the Sawooth Mountains, where it forms anhedral to subhedral crystals in pegmatites or veins. Generally, it occurs as elongated blades, up to 15 cm in length in quartz segregations in pegmatite, or as irregular masses or tabular masses in the granite. It is dark brown to almost black. Much of it has been altered to magnetite and other iron oxides, but occasionally it is unaltered (personal).

FELSÖBANYAITE

$Al_4SO_4(OH)_{10} \cdot 5H_2O$, orthorhombic(?)
Occurs mostly as spherulitic aggregates or concentrically arranged thin tabular crystals. Colorless, white or yellow; vitreous, pearly on cleavage surfaces. An uncommon mineral; occurs in mineral deposits with stibnite, marcasite, barite and quartz.

Lemhi County: Felsöbanyaite was tentatively identified as fine grains in the Buckhorn Mine in the Little Eightmile (Junction) District. The grains are white and form thin crusts along one fracture near the lead-silver vein in the east crosscut (Thune, 1941).

FERBERITE

$FeWO_4$, monoclinic
Crystals elongated, striated, and commonly flattened; often twinned. Black; forms a series with huebnerite. The intermediate forms are known as wolframite. Occurs in quartz-rich veins, pegmatitic veins associated with granitic intrusive rocks, hydrothermal veins and in contact metamorphic deposits.

Camas County: Three narrow quartz veins, 0.5 to 4 inches wide and 20 inches apart, on Corral Creek near the Soldier Mountains (Secs. 5 and 8, T. 1 N., R. 13 E.), produced ferberite. The rock is a trachyte or syenite porphyry, and the phenocrysts are kaolinized around the mine. The ferberite fills fractures in the rock where it is brecciated. It is scarce as drusy crystals lining cavities and the sharp crystals are up to about 8 mm in length and

3-4 mm wide. They have sharp chisel-shaped terminations (Photo. 168). The large crystals are striated and rounded, and small crystals are combinations of the base, dome and pinacoid. Some crystals have notched ends and appear to be twinned. They are all black in color but are coated with limonite. Both ferberite and huebnerite fill frac tures in breccia in the veins; apparently the mineralized sections of these veins were com pletely mined out prior to 1916. At least a few specimens were recovered, but these may be labeled as being from Blaine County. Camas County was part of Blaine County until about 1919 (Kerr, 1946; Livingston, 1919, personal, Shannon, 1926, Smith, 2001).

FERGUSONITE-(Y)

$YNbO_4$, tetragonal
Crystals short to long prismatic or pyramidal, massive or granular. Brownish black to black, gray, yellow or brown. Brittle, fracture conchoidal. Occurs in granite pegmatite with other rare earth minerals.

Boise County: Grains and small crystals of fergusonite occur in some of the place gravels at Idaho City. The crystals are pyramidal and brown in color. They were found in concentrates from the dredge and were rare (Shannon, 1926).

FERRIMOLYBDITE

$Fe_2(MoO_4)_3 \cdot 8H_2O(?)$, orthorhombic
Generally massive, as powdery coatings or as fibrous crusts; also as tufts or radial fibrous aggregates. Yellow to greenish yellow and very soft. Widespread as an oxidation product of molybdenum sulfide ores; often associated with limonite.

Blaine County: Yellow coatings and crusts of ferrimolybdite occur at the Happy Day Mine on a tributary of Camp Creek, southwest of Hailey. It has not been reported if micro or larger crystals have been found (personal).

Boise, Custer and Elmore Counties: A yellow, powdery coating of ferrimolybdite was found on the molybdenite at one location in the Sawtooth Mountains. Molybdenite has only been reported at three isolated locations in the Sawtooth batholith, so it is expected that ferrimolybdite is rare at this locality (personal).

Lemhi County: Ferrimolybdite occurs as yellow to slightly greenish yellow acicular crystals and tufts of crystals at the Missouri Belle Mine (Photo. 171), northwest of North Fork in Lemhi County. The mine is about a mile south of the Idaho-Montana border, and is accessible by road. Mineralization is in quartz veins in a gneiss; pyrite, tetrahedrite and molybdenite was noted in the quartz. The tetrahedrite and pyrite typically are oxidized, of ten with only the hollow cavities remaining, sometimes with remnant grains and fragment of the original minerals. The molybdenite typically is unaltered, next to fresh, lustrous hexagonal plates of molybdenite frozen in the quartz often are cavities containing the yel low fibers of ferrimolybdite. The cavities and fracture surfaces in the quartz are commonly coated with iron oxides.

Veins of epidote and reddish orange garnet also occur adjoining and in the quartz, sometimes with associated mineralization of undetermined composition. Small cavities lined with colorless to purple fluorite cubes are uncommon, and fluorite crystals coat some fractures. Secondary minerals include wulfenite, which occurs in the cavities in the quartz, most often on the iron oxides. Tiny blocky barite crystals also occur (personal).

FERRO-ANTHOPHYLLITE

$(Fe,Mg)_7Si_8O_{22}(OH)_2$, orthorhombic

Forms a series with magnesio-anthophyllite and anthophyllite. Member of amphibole group. Crystals prismatic; usually massive, fibrous or lamellar. Color is white, gray, greenish, brownish green, clove brown, yellowish brown or dark brown. Transparent to nearly opaque. Found in metamorphic rocks; widespread.

Shoshone County: Ferro-anthophyllite, occurs in the Tamarack and Custer mines in Ninemile Creek north of Wallace. It forms masses of fibers to 6 cm in length with a grayish green color. The occurrence is with galena in a quartz vein. The mine is located near quartz monzonite intrusions (the Gem stocks) in the metasediments of the Belt supergroup. Ferro-anthophyllite was first described from these deposits (Shannon, 1926).

FERROCOLUMBITE

$FeNb_2O_6$, orthorhombic

Forms a series with ferrotantalite and one with manganocolumbite. Usually not pure, contains Mn, Mg and Ta. Commonly in crystals; short prismatic or thin tabular. Iron-black; often iridescent. Occurs in granitic rocks, sometimes in pegmatites with common pegmatite minerals.

Boise County: Columbite has been reported to occur with samarskite in the heavy minerals in the gold placers of the Boise Basin around Idaho City; it is probable that this is ferrocolumbite. The crystals are tabular or square prismatic in habit and are black. They have been found up to 1 cm in length in the placer deposits in the Centerville area where they are grayish black (Shannon, 1926).

Columbite (probably ferrocolumbite) has been mined from pegmatites in several mines in the Garden Valley District. One of these occurrences is the Vaught columbite mine 3 miles south of the South Fork of the Payette River at the crest of the ridge between Wash Creek and Horn Creek in Sec. 24, T. 8 N., R. 4 E. and Sec. 19, T. 8 N., R. 5 E. It forms fine grains to coarse crystals with samarskite. One 309 pound crystal was found near the west portal of the tunnel through the ridge. It had a core of ferrocolumbite with an outer layer of samarskite. A 100 pound samarskite crystal was also reported to have been recovered from the mine. Ferrocolumbite and samarskite crystals occur frozen in the pegmatite with plagioclase, muscovite and quartz in a zone just east of the center of the tunnel (Fryklund, 1951; Id. Bur. of Mines, 1964).

Ferrocolumbite occurs with samarskite in the Mirandeborde prospects on the west side of Wash Creek opposite the Bowman prospect in Sec. 12(?), T. 8 N., R. 4 E. There is an adit and pits developed on the largest pegmatite of the group. The characteristics of the large grains or crystals of these minerals are not reported (Fryklund, 1951).

Boise, Custer and Elmore Counties: Ferrocolumbite is locally common in the cavities of the Sawtooth Mountains in many areas. It forms small, black, bladed crystals up to about 6 mm in length that are perched on albite, often intergrown with the surface of the albite crystals. Most crystals are under 3 mm in length and only about 0.5-0.7 mm across. Occasionally, ferrocolumbite crystals are embedded in the outer portion of quartz crystals. The crystals are typically vertically striated, and occur in groups that radiate from a common point. Microprobe analysis of one specimen yielded the results of Nb 40%, Fe 12.5%, Ta 20% and Mn 2% (personal).

FLUORAPATITE

$Ca_5(PO_4)_3F$, hexagonal

Apatite group; fluorapatite is the most common species and is generally the mineral referred to when the name apatite is used. Crystals long prismatic or tabular. Green, brown, blue, white or colorless; transparent or translucent. A common mineral in all classes of rocks. It is probable that fluorapatite is the species present at the localities below, although the references were all to apatite (except in the Sawtooth Mountains where fluorapatite was confirmed).

Boise County: Small terminated crystals of apatite occur in the placer deposits of the Boise Basin. They are generally colorless and have a vitreous luster (Sidler, 1957). Larger crystals, up to 10 cm in length and over 7.5 cm across have also been found. These are green with a colorless overgrowth. It is reported that these were found in pegmatites exposed during gold mining operations. Other crystals have been reported to be green and bluish in color (personal).

Boise, Custer and Elmore Counties: Fluorapatite has been found in three pegmatites in the Sawtooth Mountains. A gemmy fragment of a crystal was found in the prospector's debris at one heavily worked pegmatite. This fragment was identified by X-ray studies. An opaque, purple, prismatic crystal was found intergrown with quartz in another pegmatite. This crystal is 1.2 cm in length, and is color zoned. In pieces of another pegmatite, found in float, three broken crystals, yellowish to light purple in color, one of them partially translucent, were found (personal).

Idaho County: Subhedral to euhedral crystals occur in the placer deposits of the Florence District. They are almost colorless to black and up to 6 mm in length. Allanite, zircon, and gold are associated (Reed, 1929).

Lemhi County: Tabular crystals of apatite to 9 mm long occur on the Togo claim in the Blackbird District. The crystals are yellowish, dull and occur with rosettes of chlorite in cavities in schist. Apatite has also been reported in the Blackbird Mine as white, prismatic crystals. Cobaltite, biotite and chlorite crystals are associated, disseminated in quartz (Shannon, 1926).

White fluorapatite crystals are rare in the border zone of the magnetite skarn at the head of Bruce Canyon in the Mountain Spring District. The white prismatic crystals have been found up to 5 mm across and 1.6 cm in length in massive diopside. The identification as fluorapatite and not hydroxylapatite is tentative but most probable. Magnetite and ludwigite are associated (personal).

FLUORITE

CaF_2, cubic

Cubes or octahedrons; cubes often have penetration twinning. Also in crusts or masses. Colorless, green, yellow, bluish, pink or purple. Commonly in veins with lead and silver minerals and many other deposits. Associated with calcite, barite, quartz, sphalerite and galena.

Boise, Custer and Elmore Counties: Fluorite is relatively common in the Sawtooth Mountains in some areas, but only rarely as fine crystals. It generally forms euhedral crystals in the pocket lining, and occasionally as small crystals projecting into the cavity from the feldspar matrix. Crystals are mostly about 2-10 mm across but may be up to about 2 cm. The color is mostly light green, sometimes dark green in the pocket lining, however, occasionally the color is colorless or light pink.

Custer County: Pale green octahedral crystals of fluorite, up to 1 cm across, occur in a narrow vein of cellular quartz in andesite near the head of the North Fork of Lost River (Shannon, 1926).

Colorless to white octahedral crystals occur on Summit Creek near where the Ketchum to Mackay road crosses the divide. The crystals are in Ordovician slate in a talus slope with platy pseudomorphous quartz (Shannon, 1926).

Fluorite crystals occur in the Phi Kappa Mine (8040 level) in Phi Kappa Canyon. The crystals occur on a crust of fluorite in a small vuggy zone along faults. Crusts are about 2.5 cm thick, the inner portion is colorless to light green and the outer portion and euhedral crystals are colorless or pink (with a bluish tint). In other areas, the crystals are light green. They are translucent to transparent and octahedral in form. Most have only four faces protruding from the crust and may be coated with a druse of fluorite or have a thin iron oxide coating.

Mineralization is in argillites, limestones, slate and quartzite that have been intruded by granitic and diabasic dikes. The ore is primarily in metasomatically replaced limestone. Much of the limestone of the ore zone has been replaced by diopside and grossular with up to 5% sulfide minerals, including small crystals of yellowish to amber colored garnet, small epidote crystals, massive pyrite, galena and sphalerite. There may be a few crystals of galena (Shannon, 1926; Tuchek and Ridenour, 1981; personal).

Crystals have been found in several mines of the Bayhorse District, about 9 miles southwest of Challis in T. 13 N., R. 18 E. The main district is on Bayhorse Creek, but fluorite mineralization extends northerly to Keystone Mountain, Garden Creek and Daugherty Creek into an area about 6 miles west of Challis. Fluorite occurs as small colorless to white cubes on crusts of hemimorphite in the Pacific Mine in the Bayhorse District (Shannon, 1926).

In the northern part, the fluorite cubes are up to 2 cm but few are over 1 cm. Most are colorless, white or light lavender, and are often translucent. Small amounts of quartz and calcite occurs with the fluorite. Mineralization is everywhere the dolomite is fractured and is especially concentrated where it is highly fractured and brecciated. There is much box work of paper-thin silica that is lined with small cubes of fluorite, especially on Keystone Mountain. The fluorite cubes are mostly under 1 cm across.

In the large cut at about 9,220 feet elevation on Keystone Mountain, small fluorite cubes (Photos. 172, 173) are abundant. In the south end of the cut, they occur with small crystals of barite which are mostly small (<5 mm across). In this same cut, the lavender fluorite appears to be only in the first few cavities near the contact of the box work with the non-brecciated silicified dolomite. The next cavities inwards contain colorless fluorite only. There is a zone of light purple fluorite in the floor of the cut at the southern end (below the barite occurrence on the wall of the cut) and another occurrence in an outcrop on the hillside below the cut.

In other cuts, pits and trenches nearby, there are similar occurrences of lavender to purple crystals. Most of these, if found in float, have been bruised and rounded from movement. Interestingly, most of the purple crystals are larger than the crystals in the boxwork, with some up to 2.5 cm across, or larger. The surfaces of these show some "step growth" and are not usually smooth like those of the smaller crystals.

Quartz is locally common, and occurs as drusy coatings or larger crystals, mostly less than 2 cm in length. These may be associated with fluorite, or have fluorite coating them. One 10 cm crystal (flat on the cavity wall) was seen with a fluorite coating.

In the Daugherty Gulch and Garden Creek areas, there has been production of fluorite from a few mines and prospects. Most are developed on fluorite veins which are massive or are vuggy consisting of 2-4 inches of fluorite on each side of the vein with crystal faces projecting into the open space. There is breccia development on some of the prospects with cubic crystals lining cavities in the breccia. Generally the crystals have etched surfaces and fractures. Some are nearly smooth-faced cubes (Photos. 174, 175), but most show step growth that in some areas is somewhat curved. Most crystals are under 1.5 cm, but some are over 2.5 cm across. Fresh crystals that have not been exposed to light are often a pale blue-green to sea-green color, but they change color to pale lavender on exposure to sun light. Many show a pale fluorescence, best in long wave ultraviolet light, especially in the center of the crystal with the color being a light purplish to lavender. These also have a light bluish phosphorescence that lasts several seconds after the ultraviolet source has been removed.

Not many specimens have been produced from these mines. They are in a silicified dolomite breccia that is extremely hard and tough, and there are few cavities with good crystals. Nearly all of the crystals have rough and etched faces and are unattractive, but some can be made to look pleasing by the application of mineral oil. (Anderson, 1954, personal).

In the Alta Mining District, on Little Fall Creek, fluorite is uncommon in the Purple Spar claims. Mineralization is on the northeast side of the creek around 9,000 feet elevation north of where the road crosses the creek. Fluorite occurs with chalcedonic and drusy quartz. The fluorite is white, green and lavender, as either fine to coarse grained vein material or euhedral crystals on chalcedony, drusy quartz and wall rock in breccia along a fault zone. Most of the fluorite occurs as coatings of octahedrons on the breccia, but is coated with drusy quartz and white chalcedony. Sometimes, more than one layer of drusy quartz is present, and the chalcedony is often absent. Rarely, there are open cavities in which a late-stage fluorite has been deposited on the last drusy quartz layer.

The fluorite is generally in octahedral crystals, with smooth to frosted surfaces. Most of it is translucent, and usually colorless. Sometimes the crystals are pale green, pinkish or light lavender (Photos. 176-178). Cubic crystals are rare, as are octahedral crystals formed from "stacks" of tiny cubes. Rarely, the octahedrons have stepped-growth surfaces with complex crystals at the corners. A rare open, weathered cavity has a secondary drusy coating of colorless gypsum crystals coating the fluorite or drusy quartz. This layer of gypsum will fall off, or can easily be removed.

Barite was found in one cavity. It occurred as small crystals, 1 mm thick and up to 6 mm across, of a thin plate-like habit. The crystals formed a few small groups with fluorite, and are zoned alternating white and colorless.

Mineralization is in interbedded quartzite and argillite. These rocks have been folded and faulted; fluorite occurs in veins and breccia zones along the faults. Some of the fluorite-rich zones are as much as 50 feet across, but most are narrow. Fluorite is more common towards the southwestern end of the mineralized zone, and quartz more abundant in the northeastern end.

Colorless to green crystals occur in the Bright Star Mine, 0.25 mile northwest of Highway 93 on the nose of the ridge northeast of Copper Creek. The deposit is in the NE$\frac{1}{4}$ Sec. 30, T. 11 N., R. 14 E. Cubic crystals to 2.5 cm were found in veins with minute circular flakes of gold in hematite-stained rock five feet below the portal of the shaft. Underground, crystals have been found in several veins in a shear zone (Choate, 1962).

Tetrahedral crystals of colorless to pale lavender color have been found in the Giant Spar Mine 0.25 mile south of the Salmon River northeast of Stanley. The mine is southwest across Little Casino Creek from Big Casino Creek in Sec. 29, T. 11 N., R. 14 E. Crystals are associated with very small pyrite crystals and chalcedony in vugs in veins (Choate, 1962).

Nearby in the Homestake Mine, fluorite occurs as cubic crystals. The mine is in the adjoining parts of the SE$^1/_4$ Sec. 30 and NE$^1/_4$ Sec. 31 about 0.33 mile south of the Salmon River between Little Casino Creek and the ridge crest to the west. The cubes are colorless and lavender, and it also occurs as vein fillings and crusts. Mineralization is most prominent in the upper adit where it occurs in brecciated rhyolite. Subhedral pyritohedrons of pyrite are associated. Each pyritohedron is about 4 mm across and contains a crystal of gold about 2 mm across (Choate, 1962; personal).

Fluorite crystals have been reported to 2.5 cm or more on the ridge northwest of Loon Creek Summit. Specimens to several centimeters across are reported to occur there. In a breccia zone in the area of cliffs and benches at the head of a small basin on the east side of the ridge, small stilbite crystals, tiny goethite pseudomorphs of pyrite and small green cubes of fluorite occur in altered volcanic rocks (personal).

Idaho County: Transparent colorless, green and purple crystals can be found in vugs in quartz veins in the Big Squaw fluorspar deposit (Noussan Mine). Mineralization is in a gneissic quartz monzonite, biotite gneiss, pegmatite and aplite. The deposit is just east of the center of Sec. 27, T. 25 N., R. 12 E. on the east side of the Salmon River in the River of No Return Wilderness. Crystals have also been found in overburden at 3,900 feet on the section line between Secs. 27 and 28, 0.25 mile north of the southeast corner of Sec. 27 (Weiss and Schmitt, 1972).

Lemhi County: Excellent quality fluorite crystals to large size have been found in the mines of the Meyers Cove District which is 1-3 miles south of Meyers Cover, about 38 air miles southwest of Salmon. The mines are located in T. 17-18 N., R. 16-17 E. Most deposits are on the crest of the ridge between Fluorspar Gulch and Dirck Creek. Mineralization is along northeast trending shear zones, often of large size. Several adits and other workings have been developed on these zones.

Early stage fluorite occurs as white, purple or green masses and coarse-grained aggregates. A second stage fluorite is similar in color, but forms concentric bands and has a columnar habit. Colorless crystals are late forming, have a cubic habit and are generally small (less than 1.5 cm across) but may be several centimeters across (Photo. 179-181). They occur in vugs with barite and chalcedony and in a few deposits stibnite is associated. Some of the cubes are coated with a druse of microcrystals. The barite has been found as colorless and white crystals to 3 cm, and rarely, to 10 cm (Anderson, 1943, 1954; Cox, 1951).

At the M & M Mine, cubic crystals of a light purplish color can be found on the dump. Up the road northerly a short distance, white, cubic crystals can be found in the roadcut and road bed. Small clusters of crystals that are up to about 2 cm across have been found (Photo. 179).

About half way from there to the next mine to the north, there is an exposure of light purplish cubic crystals in a breccia in a roadcut. Small groups have been found there. At the mine at the end of this road, small purplish crystals and crusts of cubic crystals have been found (personal).

Fluorite is rare in the cavities of the Crags batholith in the Yellowjacket Mountains west of Cobalt. One deeply etched crystal, about 1 cm across was found on the back side of a matrix specimen of albite and microcline. The crystal was colorless with a purple center, and had a square cross section and was flattened, apparently from growing in the narrow space where the matrix had separated from the walls of the cavity (personal).

Colorless fluorite crystals are uncommon at the Missouri Belle Mine as complex micro crystals in cavities with quartz crystals (Photo. 182). These tiny crystals are less than 4 mm across. Light purple to lavender crystals and masses occur with garnet, epidote and quartz in the contact mineralization at the deposit (personal).

In the quartz veins of the Ima Mine at Patterson, fluorite forms small grains or crystals frozen in the quartz. These typically are colorless or pale green. Microcrystals are uncommon as sharp cubes in cavities (Photo. 183) (personal).

Owyhee County: Small grains of fluorite, some of them cubic, occur with pyrargyrite on comb quartz in the east drift of the Silver City Mine in the Silver City District. Pale lavender octahedrons up to 3 mm across occur in a tunnel below the Blaine tunnel on the south side of Long Gulch. These fluorite crystals occur on adularia crystals (Shannon, 1926).

Valley County: Fluorite is reported to occur on the ridge southeast of Fish Lake, north east of Yellow Pine, in Sec. 1, T. 19 N., R. 8 E. Brilliant purple fluorite crystals occur in dark brown dikes that cut through the rocks of the ridge (personal).

Fluorite is uncommon in small cavities in the Logan Creek stock west of Big Creek. This area can be reached by a road up Logan Creek, and a hike up a trail. Boulders on the north side of a meadow contain small quartz crystals and rarely small fluorite crystals and fluorite was reported further to the west in the stock (Leonard and Marvin, 1984; personal).

FORNACITE

$Pb_2Cu(AsO_4)(CrO_4)(OH)$, monoclinic
Crystals steep pyramidal, rounded; generally in aggregates. Deep olive-green, greenish yellow; transparent to translucent. A rare mineral, found in the oxidized zone of some hydrothermal lead- and copper-bearing ore deposits.

Clark County: Very tiny crystals of fornacite have been found in one small cavity in the altered limestone of the Weimer Mine. The tiny crystals are thin plates, bright green color, and are associated with duftite, mimetite and wulfenite on calcite (Photo. 184). This is the first reported occurrence of this mineral in Idaho and the appearance and color of the crystals are similar to those recently found in Montana (personal).

FORSTERITE

Mg_2SiO_4, orthorhombic
Forms a series with fayalite, Fe2SiO4, together they are known as olivine. Generally granular masses or grains; crystals are generally combinations of prisms, pinacoids and a dipyramid. Olive, grayish green or brown in color. A common rock-forming mineral in many types of igneous rocks, especially basalt, gabbro and peridotite.

Lemhi County: At the skarn on Quartzite Canyon in the Spring Mountain District forsterite is common in several areas. Mostly it forms light brown masses that replace limestone, but also occurs as well formed crystals in cavities in these masses and as anhedral to euhedral crystals on magnetite crystals in the magnetite zones. In the massive forsterite, the crystals are light off white to tan color and tabular to blocky (Photo. 185). They are common to about 6 mm across but have been seen up to at least 3 cm across. In the magnetite, they are colorless transparent to white opaque, and are mostly small tabular crystals, up to about 10 mm, mostly 2-4 mm. Many show numerous fractures. Associated minerals in the forsterite include calcite, ludwigite, spinel, magnetite, magnesioferrite and spinel (personal).

Photo.138 Calcite, 1.2 cm high, McKinzie Creek, Idaho County.

Photo. 137 Calcite, 1.5 cm across, McKinzie Creek, Idaho County.

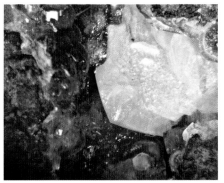

Photo. 141 Cerussite twin, 2 mm across, Iron Mask Mine, Lemhi County.

Photo. 139 Calcite and rosasite, flat crystal is 4 mm across, Excelsior Mine, Lemhi County.

Photo. 140 Prismatic cerussite crystals, many are twinned, to 3 mm, Confidence Mine, Fourth of July Creek, Custer County.

Photo. 142 Cerussite twin, long crystal is 3 mm, Iron Mask Mine, Lemhi County.

FREIBERGITE

$(Ag,Cu,Fe)_{12}(Sb,As)_4S_{13}$, cubic

Member of the tetrahedrite group, forms a series with tetrahedrite. Tetrahedral crystals, massive or coarse granular to compact. Steel gray to iron-black, opaque. Occurs in silver-bearing ores.

Shoshone County: Tetrahedrite, commonly silver bearing, is one of the main ore minerals in the Coeur d'Alene Mining District in Shoshone County. Rarely, the tetrahedrite contains enough silver to be the mineral freibergite. Some tiny crystals from the Sunshine Mine have often been reported to be freibergite, but most often they are only silver-bearing tetrahedrite. The freibergite crystals are rare in cavities with quartz and siderite (Photo. 186) (personal).

GADOLINITE-(Ce)

$(Ce,La,Nd,Y)_2FeBe_2Si_2O_{10}$, monoclinic

Crystals often prismatic sometimes flattened; mostly rough, massive, compact. Color black, greenish black, brown, rarely light green; translucent to transparent. Occurs in granites and granite pegmatites; fluorite and allanite is associated.

Unknown County: Shannon (1926) lists gadolinite as occurring at an unspecified locality in Idaho. The identification and analysis was done in Russia. No information was given on the gadolinite, nor on an unknown green mineral included in it. The Russian reference is: Chernik. Journ. Soc. Phys. Chim. Russe., Vol. 36, pp. 25-27 and 287-301, 1904.

GALENA

PbS, cubic

Most common as cubes; these may be modified by the octahedron. Lead-gray color and a perfect cubic cleavage. A common mineral in ore veins, associated with sphalerite, chalcopyrite, pyrite, cerussite, barite and fluorite. Often contains silver. It occurs in many mining districts in the state, but only a few have been known to produce crystals, and these are not large or noteworthy.

Blaine County: Galena is common in many of the mining districts in this county, but is generally massive and granular and rarely forms euhedral crystals. It is most abundant in the Ketchum-Hailey area, generally known as the Wood River District.

Galena forms small cubic and octahedral crystals in the St. Louis and Reliance mines in the Era District. The crystals are uncommon and associated with wurtzite. In the Reliance Mine they are also associated with jamesonite (Shannon, 1926).

Boise and Gem Counties: Octahedral crystals occur in the Lincoln Mine in the Westview District (combined Willow Creek, Pearl and Rock Creek Districts between Emmett and Horseshoe Bend). They occur in vugs in masses of brown sphalerite. Much of the galena in this district is auriferous. Many of the mines in this district have produced galena. Few of them have produced euhedral crystals, but there may be a small potential for them (Shannon, 1926).

Boundary County: Galena occurs with malachite in quartz on Leonia Knob in the NE$\frac{1}{4}$NE$\frac{1}{4}$ Sec. 21, T. 61 N., R. 3 E. The quartz is fractured and contains crystal-lined cavities. Cubic crystals of galena occur up to 3 mm across and have been found in the dump and in talus below the dump (Miller, 1973).

Custer County: Small imperfect cuboctahedral crystals occur in the Utah Boy No. 5

Photo. 144 Cerussite, 2.5 mm long, Little Giant Mine, Shoshone County.

Photo. 143 Cerussite, twinned specimen 3.5 cm across, 9 level, Jersey orebody, Bunker Hill Mine, Shoshone County.

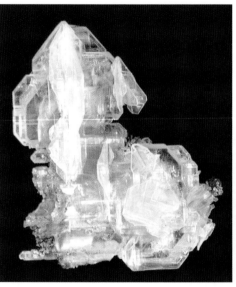

Photo. 145 Cerussite, 6 cm across, Monarch Mine, Shoshone County; Rock Currier specimen and photograph.

Photo. 146 Cerussite, 4 cm high, Monarch Mine, Shoshone County; Rock Currier specimen and photograph.

Photo. 148 Chlorite, 2.1 cm across, Iron Mountain, Washington County.

Photo.147 Chabazite crystals with one heulandite crystal, near Russell Bar, Idaho County.

Photo. 149 Chlorargyrite, cubic crystal and small mass, cube is about 0.5 mm across, with quartz, Stone Cabin Mine, Owyhee County.

Photo. 150 Chlorite and unknown minerals forming a pseudomorph of an unknown mineral (2.8 cm high), Iron Mountain, Washington County.

Photo. 151 Chlorite and unknown minerals forming a pseudomorph of an unknown mineral (2.7 cm long), with a chlorite crystal, Iron Mountain, Washington County.

Photo. 152 Chrysocolla pseudomorphs of aurichalcite, individual crystals are 1-1.5 mm in length, near Blizzard Mountain, Blaine County.

tunnel of the Ramshorn Mine in the Bayhorse District. The crystals are in cavities in siderite and tetrahedrite (Shannon, 1926).

Small cubes of galena and pyrite have been found in the workings of the Alto Silver-Quartz group of claims on the west side of the North Fork of Little Fall Creek, west of Mackay near Trail Creek Summit. Mineralization is in quartz and calcite in sheared calcareous slate, argillite and sandstone. Small galena cubes occur in a vein of iron-stained coarse honeycombed quartz. Some cavities are lined with smithsonite and cerussite. The workings include pits, cuts, adits and one shaft (Tuchek and Ridenour, 1981; Umpleby et al, 1930).

Fremont County: Galena forms cubes and fine grained masses of steel galena in the Birch Creek (Scott?) Mine in the Birch Creek District (in Clark County?). It is associated with anglesite, cerussite, wulfenite and smithsonite. Cubic crystals of galena up to 2 cm across occur in yellow jasper (Shannon, 1926).

Lemhi County: In the Blue Wing District, galena forms fine grained masses and some small cubes, but it is not common in the ores of the district. Associated minerals include pyrite, sphalerite, tetrahedrite, huebnerite, molybdenite and chalcopyrite (Shannon, 1926).

Small crystals have been collected from the veins in the Silver Star Mine in Gold Star Gulch in Secs. 10 and 11, T. 23 N., R. 22 E. and other mines in the area. The crystals occur with cerussite, pyromorphite, sphalerite, pyrite, malachite, azurite and anglesite in vugs in quartz veins. Mines in Gold Star Gulch have produced the best specimens, but those in Freeman Creek have produced some too (Anderson, 1959).

Silver-bearing galena was the prominent ore in the Spring Mountain District. Mines there include the Colorado, Elizabeth, Excelsior, Galena, Iron Mask, Lemhi Union, Red Warrior and Teddy. Secondary minerals have been reported, but it is not known if any of the galena occurred as crystals (personal; Shannon, 1926).

Shoshone County: Some of the numerous mines of the Coeur d'Alene District have been some of the greatest producers of galena ore in the world, unfortunately, few of them have produced any euhedral crystals of noteworthy quality. The galena is often pure or may be combined with other ore minerals including sphalerite, pyrrhotite, tetrahedrite or chalcopyrite. It is fine to coarse-grained massive material; cavities are virtually nonexistent.

Veins may be wide; a portion of the Hercules vein was reported to be 40 feet wide, nearly pure galena. The galena is often silver-bearing, so it makes a desirable ore. Following are just a few of the mines of the district that have produced galena: Bunker Hill, Last Chance, Tyler, Hercules, Tiger-Poorman, Hecla, Standard-Mammoth, Star, Morning, Hunter, Highland-Surprise, Nabob, Lookout Mountain and Hypotheek (personal; Shannon, 1926).

GALENOBISMUTITE

$PbSi_2S_4$, orthorhombic

Elongated, lath-like crystals; most commonly massive, fibrous or columnar. Light gray to tin-white; may be tarnished yellow or iridescent. Rare, associated with bismuthinite, tetrahedrite, galena, quartz and pyrite.

Boise County: Galenobismutite occurs in the Belshazzar Mine near the Jerusalem Valley Road 2 miles west of Quartzburg, in Secs. 17 and 18, T. 7 N., R. 4 E. It has also been reported in the Mountain Chief Mine in Secs. 18 and 19 on a tributary of Canyon Creek about 3.5 miles west of Placerville. It occurs with pyrite and quartz in a vein and forms elongated prisms embedded in quartz or minute deeply striated crystals. These project into cavities formed between quartz crystals. At the Gold Hill Mine it occurs as scattered small patches and small crystal aggregates in quartz seams and as needle-shaped and lath-shaped crystals in other sulfides. It is light gray and tarnishes yellow (Anderson, 1947a; Shannon, 1926).

GARNET

A group with at least 14 species known. The most common are magnesium-iron, manganese, calcium-aluminum, calcium-iron or calcium-chromium silicates. Several of the species form solid solution series, thus most garnets are not pure and contain elements of at least two species. Only those garnets that have not been identified as to species are described below, see separate species listings for other occurrences.

Bonner County: Tiny crystals of garnet occur in the skarn at the Vulcan Mine northeast of Lakeview on the east side of Lake Pend Oreille with diopside and scheelite. The garnet and diopside form vuggy masses with the small vugs lined with the brown garnet crystals or diopside crystals. No identification work has been done on the garnets, but typically in a skarn they are andradite and grossular combination. Garnet crystals are dodecahedrons and up to about 6 mm across. Some are sharp distinct crystals, but many are subhedral and they are often fractured (personal).

Clearwater County: Euhedral crystals of reddish brown garnets (probably grossular/ andradite) occur in the canyon sides of Dicks Creek on the north side of the reservoir above the Dworshak Dam. The garnets occur in a skarn zone with diopside and epidote as trapezohedrons up to at least 4 cm in diameter. Water covers most of the skarn zone when the reservoir is full. The deposit is accessible only by boat and the garnet zone is only above water when the reservoir is low. Crystals are sharp and well formed, but are highly fractured and have dull surfaces (personal).

Custer County: Excellent crystals have been found east of Hailey near the Alta Copper claims (also known as the Basin group) on the north side of the valley near the head of the Big Lost river at 8,000 to 8,250 feet elevation. The crystals are sharply formed euhedral crystals of light to dark amber color. They are the most abundant mineral of the deposit, but epidote, prehnite (in radiating aggregates of tabular crystals), wollastonite, diopside, augite, fluorite, galena, pyrite, sphalerite and pyrrhotite are associated. Mineralization occurs in contact metamorphic deposits in limey slate and clayey quartzite (Umpleby et al, 1930).

Garnets occur in small calcite seams in gray limestone near Goat Lake in the White Cloud Mountains. These occur in talus below the large cliffs just east of the lake. The tiny red-brown crystals are under 3 mm across (personal).

Idaho County: Small dodecahedral crystals of garnet can be found at Ruby Rapids on the Salmon River, 7.3 miles east of Highway 95. These are the first rapids above the first bridge across the Salmon River above Riggins. The reddish dodecahedral crystals are generally small, mostly less than 6 mm across, but can be found up to more than 3 cm across (Photo. 187). They can be found in the gravels between boulders along the river, in the gneissic rock and in the gneiss and soil above the road (personal).

Owyhee County: Purplish red trapezohedrons occur along the road and creek 1 mile west of Silver City. The crystals are up to 2.5 cm in diameter. They occur scattered in an aggregate of mica and feldspar and some of them are reportedly gemmy (Beckwith, 1972).

Tiny to small garnets of undetermined composition occur with hedenbergite in the skarn on South Mountain. In a zone of intergrown hedenbergite alongside the road to the summit near the junction of the road that crosses to the east side of the ridge, cavities between hedenbergite contain the reddish orange dodecahedral crystals (Photo. 188) (personal).

Photo. 153 Azurite and chrysocolla pseudomorphs of azurite, field of view 1.4 cm, Weimer Mine, Clark County.

Photo. 154 Chrysocolla pseudomorphs of malachite, Keystone Mountain silver mines, Custer County.

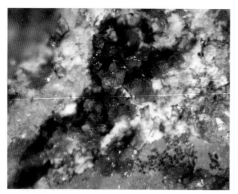

Photo.155 Conichalcite, spheres are 0.2-0.4 mm across, Keystone Mountain silver mines, Custer County.

Photo. 156 Microcrystalline masses of covellite replacing tetrahedrite, Ima Mine, Lemhi County.

Photo. 157 Cowlesite, spherical groups are 1-1.5 mm across, Pinehurst, Adams County.

Photo. 158 Cuprite octahedrons coated with malachite, single on left is 0.7 mm, with malachite and azurite, Iron Dike Mine, Lemhi County.

Photo. 159 Cyanotrichite, groups are 0.5-1.2 mm across, Iron Dike Mine, Junction District, Lemhi County.

Photo. 160 Cyanotrichite, 1.2 mm, on brochantite, Iron Dike Mine, Junction District, Lemhi County.

Photo. 161 Descloizite and vanadinite, two stages of microcrystals of descloizite, the brown crystals are an early stage that formed before and during vanadinite deposition and the orange crystals are a rare second stage that was deposited after vanadinite, Iron Mask Mine, Lemhi County.

Shoshone County: Garnet crystals, probably almandine, to over 2.5 cm can be found along Glover Creek near the bridge over the creek (above Homestead Creek). The crystals are subhedral to euhedral and are a dark reddish black color. They have a trapezohedral habit and occur in the soil, in the roadcut and creek bank. A few of them cut poor quality star stones, but most of them are highly fractured or show the partings where layers of included mica have weathered (personal).

In the area around Larkins and Mallard Peaks, crystals to 4 cm occur in the schist and gneiss country rock. They form dodecahedrons and trapezohedrons and are probably almandine. Crystals are most prominent in a transitional zone between schist and the overlying quartzite in an area northwest of Larkins Peak and between Mallard Peak and the Nub (Hietanen, 1968).

Brownish garnets are uncommon in a zone in a roadcut on Trail Creek, a fork of Floodwood Creek. The crystals are mostly up to about 1 cm across, but larger crystals to about 3 cm have been found. The complex crystals are frozen in a white matrix of undetermined composition (Photo. 189). The roadcut is a short distance north of where the road crosses the creek (personal).

Valley County: At the Golden Cup Mine on the south fork of Smith Creek, in a glacial cirque about 2 miles northwest of the Big Creek Lodge, at an elevation of 6,800 feet on the north side of Logan Creek, there is a large garnet tactite. Three adits are developed on the Red Garnet claims on the tactite which is in a small pendant of dolomitic marble, biotite schist and quartzite in a granodiorite stock. Stibnite occurs in a vein along the west contact of the tactite and pyrite and chalcopyrite occur in a gossan on the north contact (Kirkpatrick, 1974).

Several miles southeast of the above location, in Sec. 1, T. 20 N., R. 9 E., red garnets occur in marble, on the west side of Marble Mountain. Numerous outcrops above 8,800 feet elevation contain the small garnet crystals (personal).

Garnet crystals occur with epidote and quartz crystals in a skarn zone exposed in a roadcut about .25 miles east of the Sloans Peak Lookout jeep trail, east of Donnelly. Access is gained by taking the Paddy Flat Road (#388) to road number 389 for about 11 miles. Turn south on road number 401 towards the lookout turnoff at the top of a ridge then east to the roadcut.

Garnet crystals (probably grossular) vary from tiny to about 2 cm, but mostly less than 6 mm. Small crystals are generally orange (often translucent to transparent) and the color darkens as the size increases. Epidote is mostly small to about 1 cm. Quartz crystals are uncommon, but massive gray to smoky quartz is common in the western part of the deposit. Quartz crystals occur in cavities in the quartz and in the fine-grained massive diopside with the quartz. Some coarse garnet crystals also occur frozen in the quartz and may be exposed in matrix by carefully chipping away the quartz (personal).

In a few small zones east of Granite Lake (north of McCall), reddish garnet crystals occur in concentrations in gneiss. Crystals were seen in three areas, exposed on outcrops as crystals frozen in the rock or as individual crystals weathered out and lying free (personal).

Washington County: Tiny to small crystals of yellow garnet can be found in the skarn deposits on upper Brownlee Creek. Associated minerals malachite and chrysocolla. The small garnets are most common in a small mine in the mid-part of the district, just north of a sharp switchback (personal).

GEOCRONITE

$Pb_{14}(Sb,As)_6S_{23}$, monoclinic

Crystals tabular, usually massive, granular or earthy. Light lead-gray to grayish blue; metallic; opaque. In calcareous contact deposits and veins in limestones.

Bonner County: Specimens from the Hope Mine, Clark Fork District, that are labeled jordanite apparently are geocronite (Douglas et al, 1954).

Custer County: Geocronite has been found in the Livingston Mine, Mackay District, on the 2800 level. A U.S. National Museum specimen with Custer County listed as the locality, may be from the Livingston Mine too (Douglas et al, 1954).

Another locality for geocronite is the numerous mines and prospects of the Slate Creek area south of Clayton. Geocronite forms intergrowths with jamesonite in some of the veins. It is uncommon and may be only microscopic (Kern, 1972).

GERSDORFFITE

NiAsS, cubic

Crystals mostly octahedral, often modified; also lamellar and granular. Silver-white to steel-gray. Occurs with other nickel minerals in vein deposits. Rare.

Shoshone County: Crystalline aggregates of gersdorffite occur in a small mineralized zone in a prospect 1 mile above the mouth of Slate Creek, near Avery. It forms masses of small crystals less than 1 mm across which are separated by quartz. Rose red crusts of small crystals and masses of erythrite occur in cavities in the vein. Other sulfides, quartz and chlorite are associated (Shannon, 1926).

GLADITE

$CuPbBi_5S_9$, orthorhombic

Crystals prismatic, in granular masses; lead gray, opaque. Occurs with other bismuth minerals.

Blaine County: Gladite forms the elongated crystals in masses of ore at the Peace of Mine on Pole Creek, east of Alturas Lake. The ore consists of elongated subhedral to euhedral grains of gladite and aikinite forming crystals under 4 mm in length. Small cavities in the ore contain tiny crystals of gray aikinite. Identification of the gladite was by X-ray diffraction and microprobe analysis confirmed the aikinite identification (personal).

GLAUCOPHANE

$Na_2(Mg,Fe)_3Al_2Si_8O_{22}(OH)_2$, monoclinic

A member of the amphibole group; forms a series with ferroglaucophane. Crystals slender prismatic; massive, fibrous or granular. Grayish, bluish black, lavender, blue; translucent, vitreous to dull. Occurs in crystalline schists with chlorite, muscovite and epidote.

Lemhi County: Coarse black needle-like aggregates of glaucophane have been found on fractures in massive actinolite. The occurrence is on the east side of Indian Creek west of the town of North Fork (Anderson, 1928).

Photo. 162 Two stages of microcrystals of descloizite, brown crystals
0.2-0.8 mm across, Iron mask Mine, Lemhi County.

Photo. 164 Duftite, disk-like to
spherical crystals and groups, 0.2-0.3
mm, Weimer Mine, Clark County.

Photo. 163 Diopside, 8 mm, Colorado claim,
Lemhi County.

Photo. 165 Elbaite, 1.4 cm, Seven Devils
                              Mountains,
                              Adams County;
                              Norm and
                              Carla Radford
                              specimen.

Photo. 166 A doubly terminated epidote
crystal on quartz, 5 mm long, Peacock Mine,
Seven Devils District, Adams County.

Photo. 168 Ferberite with tiny goethite pseudomorphs of pyrite, view is 2.4 cm across. Corral Creek, Camas County.

Photo. 167 Elbaite, 1.6 cm long, Seven Devils Mountains, Adams County, Norm and Carla Radford specimen.

Photo. 170 Epidote, micro, with pyroxene and quartz, Bruce Canyon, Lemhi County.

Photo. 169 Epidote, showing twinning, 4.9 cm high, Genesee, Latah County.

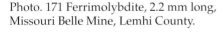

Photo. 171 Ferrimolybdite, 2.2 mm long, Missouri Belle Mine, Lemhi County.

GOETHITE

FeO(OH), orthorhombic

Common as a pseudomorph of other minerals, massive or stalactitic; rarely in prismatic crystals. These are usually flattened and striated. Yellowish brown to dark brown. A common oxidation product of weathered iron-bearing minerals.

Benewah County: Goethite pseudomorphs of pyrite can be found in roadcuts 10 miles north of Tensed. The cubes are up to 3 cm across (larger in unreported nearby locations) and are sharp and striated. They are scattered in layers in a soft, silty sandstone of the Precambrian Belt supergroup. Crystals can be found in the cuts along Highway 95 from about mile post 391 to the second cut north of mile post 392. Most of these cuts are benched and stepped back, making it easy to climb around on them in search of crystals. There are two or three layers containing the crystals in each cut. One of the best areas is the southern end of the seventh bench of the cut immediately north of mile post 392, where the crystals can be found in a layer a little more than a foot thick. Most of these cuts are now becoming overgrown by pine trees (Stinchfield, 1979; personal).

Goethite forms interesting massive deposits on a hillside near Desmet. The deposit has been prospected for iron ore. The goethite forms irregular masses and veins in oxidized quartzite. It is mostly black and commonly lines openings with smooth, irregular, nearly botryoidal or stalactitic coatings. In cross section, the stalactites can be seen to have a layered radiating structure. The deposit has been exposed in a small cut which is now slumped, so that very little is exposed (personal).

Blaine County: Cellular sponges of finely fibrous goethite occur in the Narrow Gauge shaft (Shannon, 1926).

Boise, Custer and Elmore Counties: Goethite forms pseudomorphs after pyrite and siderite in the crystal-bearing cavities of the Sawtooth Mountains (Photos. 60, 70). The pseudomorphs are generally sharp and clean.

In some cavities, goethite and limonite, form small hemispherical masses associated with smoky quartz, microcline and albite. In other cavities, these iron oxides form dark brown spongy masses, thin coatings or crusts (personal).

Clearwater County: Goethite (described as limonite) pseudomorphs of pyrite occur on the Lolo claim in the Weippe District. They have faces of the cube and pyritohedron. Specimens up to 2 cm in diameter have been collected (Shannon, 1926).

Custer County: Tiny goethite pseudomorphs of pyrite occur northwest of Loon Creek Summit in the area of the fluorite occurrence. The tiny crystals occur on quartz in cavities in altered volcanic rocks (Photo. 190). Tiny green cubes of fluorite and tiny white stilbite crystals are associated (personal).

Lemhi County: Goethite forms small botryoidal masses with an internal radial fibrous structure in quartz in the Big Chief Mine in the Blackbird District (Shannon, 1926).

Shoshone County: Goethite occurs in the oxidized ores of several of the mines in the Coeur d'Alene District. Shannon (1926) reports good specimens from a prospect on Milo Gulch and shallow workings on Kellogg Peak. It also occurs in the outcrop of the Caledonia vein and in the Palisade Mine on Pine Creek.

Goethite has been found in the Bunker Hill Mine, including some spectacular stalactites. Generally, it occurs as small masses, layers and coatings; these are often associated with cerussite. The goethite is often soft and porous, and sometimes, it forms thin rods that penetrate cerussite crystals (personal).

Massive and botryoidal goethite can be found in the mining roadcuts west of the Little Giant Mine south of Mullan (see pyromorphite for mine location). Goethite forms irregular masses and veins in oxidized quartzite. It is mostly black and commonly lines openings with smooth, irregular, nearly botryoidal or stalactitic coatings. These are generally thin. The deposit has been exposed in two places in the roadcut west of the mine and may occur in other areas nearby.

Similar material has been found along Placer Creek where it has been found as thick layers and masses with a botryoidal surface. The thick layers are composed of several thinner layers of compact, nearly parallel, acicular goethite fibers (Photo. 191). At both locations, the surfaces of the layers are usually black, smooth and shiny (personal).

Goethite pseudomorphs of pyrite occur in siltite of the Belt supergroup on Hord Gulch, south of Wallace (Photo. 192). These are dark brown, well-formed cubic crystals; they have been found in an old road bed on the north side of the gulch where the rock has been exposed during bulldozing of the road. Crystals occur to at least 2 cm across (personal).

GOLD

Au, cubic

Crystals are most often octahedrons with modifications; may be in arborescent groups. Crystals are irregular or poorly formed. Most often it is in the form of scales, plates, nuggets or masses. Yellow color; becomes lighter as the silver content increases. In veins with various sulfides and quartz or disseminated in rocks.

Blaine County: Free gold occurs in the Camas No. 2 and Tip Top mines in the Camas District. Pyrrhotite, pyrite, chalcopyrite and galena are associated. The Hailey gold belt contains free gold with pyrrhotite, chalcopyrite, galena and sphalerite (Shannon, 1926).

Coarse free gold occurs in several mines in the Red Warrior District. It forms irregular flakes in rusty quartz in the Golden Eagle Mine and flakes in minute cavities in bluish quartz in the Wide West Mine. Pyrite, sphalerite and auriferous pyrite are associated at the latter locality (Shannon, 1926).

Boise County: Gold occurs as rounded and flat nuggets and flakes in many of the streams of the Boise Basin around Idaho City, Placerville and Quartzburg. Some of the nuggets of gold and gold with quartz have been up to 4-5 cm across and about five ounces in weight. The placer gravels are found in recent stream valleys and old terraces. Monazite, garnet, magnetite, ilmenite, polycrase, samarskite and columbite occur with the gold. Some of the better streams include Moore, Elk and Fall Creeks and the Payette River which were heavily placer mined and dredged (Ballard, 1924; personal).

Numerous lode mines in the district contain free gold in quartz or sulfides. Pyrite, sphalerite, cerussite, galena, galenobismutite and other minerals are associated. Some of the most notable mines include the Gold Hill, Carroll-Driscoll, Ivanhoe, Golden Chariot, Buena Vista, Mineral Hill, Morning Star, Mountain Queen, Ebenezer, Kempner and Overlook. The gold in these mines varies from free gold in quartz (sometimes in vugs) to free gold in sulfides (Jones, 1917; Shannon, 1926).

The Mountain Chief Mine, including the Ebenezer claim, is on the southwest end of the porphyry belt, 3.5 miles from Placerville. The claims extend from the summit of the divide between Fall and Canyon Creek to Canyon Creek. Stibnite and pyrite crystals occur on drusy quartz. Coarse gold occurs in the quartz veins (Jones, 1917).

The Carroll-Driscoll Mine is northeast of the end lines of the Gold Hill group and extends to Garden Valley Pass, in the Quartzburg District. Coarse gold occurs in quartz veins with calcite, pyrite, galena, sphalerite and tetrahedrite. Most of the sulfides have been ground up in gouge along the sheared veins. Pyrite forms well-developed crystal aggre-

Photo. 172 Fluorite, 3.2 cm across, Keystone Mountain, Custer County.

Photo. 173 Fluorite, 4.6 cm across, Keystone Mountain, Custer County.

Photo. 174 Cubic fluorite crystals, many penetration twins, from the Garden Creek-Daugherty Gulch area, specimen has been treated with mineral oil, specimen is 11.5 cm across, Custer County.

Photo. 175 Cubic fluorite crystals, many penetration twins, from the Garden Creek-Daugherty Gulch area, specimen has been treated with mineral oil, largest crystals are 1.4 cm across, Custer County.

Photo. 176 Fluorite, light pink octahedrons on quartz, specimen 16.4 cm across, Purple Spar claims, Custer County.

Photo. 177 Fluorite octahedrons on quartz, specimen 7 cm across, Purple Spar claims, Custer County.

Photo. 178 Fluorite with coating of drusy quartz, specimen 7.8 cm across, Purple Spar claims, Custer County.

gates or single crystals (Jones, 1917)

Clearwater County: Coarse placer gold has been produced from several districts in the county. The Pierce District has produced gold from several creeks. Pierce is the location of the first significant discovery of placer gold in the state in 1860 (Shannon, 1926; personal).

Custer County: The Loon Creek District has produced gold from lode and placer mines. Some of the mines in both types of deposits were quite rich. Nuggets have been found that were nearly one ounce in weight. Placer deposits in the Stanley Basin District produced gold that was about the size of grains of wheat. Some of this was associated with native amalgam, cinnabar and brannerite (Shannon, 1926).

Some coarse gold, including a nugget weighing almost a kilogram (nearly 36 ounces), was found in the Yankee Fork District near the Morrison vein. Most of the gold of this district was fine grained. The mines also produced pyrite, sphalerite, tetrahedrite, arsenopyrite, pyrargyrite, miargyrite and aguilarite (Anderson, 1949; Shannon, 1926).

Gold was produced from the Iron Crown Mine near the head of Joe's Gulch north of Stanley. It formed irregular blebs, sheets and wires intimately associated with oxidized pyrite on rhyolite (Photo. 193). Some specimens have been found on the dumps in the past. Mineralization is in the rhyolite along a porphyry dike (Choate, 1962).

Elmore County: Skeletal gold was common in the oxidized ore in the Neal District. The gold veins are in fissures along minor shears in granite (Shannon, 1926).

Grains and thin scales of gold occur in the Rocky Bar District 45 miles east-northeast of Boise in T. 3-5 N., R. 11 E. The grains are of small size but are visible in fractures in the country rock and vein quartz. It occurs with quartz, arsenopyrite, pyrite, sphalerite, galena and chalcopyrite in the Empire, Vishnu, Idaho, Ada Elmore and other mines. In some veins, the quartz is vuggy and lined with small crystals (Anderson, 1943b; Wagner, 1939).

Idaho County: Coarse gold has been recovered from the placers in the Elk City District. Much of the gold was in nuggets with quartz or in large boulders of quartz in the streams. Few gold veins were found. The Black Pine Mine produced specimens of small grains of gold surrounding galena in quartz with disseminated sphalerite, pyrite and tetrahedrite (Shannon, 1926).

Extensive placer deposits were worked in the Florence District, which is located south of Grangeville, north of the Salmon River, east of Slate Creek. Some of the gold was coarse and as nuggets with quartz. Lode deposits contain coarse gold with comb quartz. The placer deposits contain allanite as flat black crystals to 1.5 cm in length, titanite as fragments to 6 mm, zircon as slightly yellowish crystals less than 6 mm and gold as irregular grains mostly of small size. Monazite crystals of a yellow color, dull luster and subhedral shape were found in the deposits along Grouse Creek (Reed, 1939).

There was extensive placer mining in the Dixie District southeast of Grangeville, south of Elk City. Most of the gold was a pennyweight ($^1/_{20}$ ounce) or smaller, but it was visible in veins in the lode deposits. Pyrite crystals were associated in many of the lodes and a lead vanadate or chromate was reported in the Comstock Mine (Capps, 1939; personal).

Extensive placer deposits were worked in the Warren District. The gold is generally coarse and is associated with garnet and monazite. Veins in the district contain native gold with native silver, sphalerite, arsenopyrite, pyrite and galena. Gold is more common in the sphalerite than in the pyrite in the Goodenough vein. Veinlets of quartz in the granite of the Rescue Mine contain gold foil (Shannon, 1926).

The Marshall Mountain District has been a gold producer sporadically. During the 1980s, there was a period of activity and a few specimens of gold leaf in quartz reached the mineral market (Photo. 194) (personal).

Latah County: Gold has been produced from lode and placer deposits and much of the gold was coarse. Deposits occur in the Hoodoo and Goldhill (Blackfoot) Districts. Camas, Jerome and Boulder Creeks were good producers in the latter district. Most of the lode deposits had little or no production.

Much coarse placer gold was produced from the upper Palouse River and several tributaries including Poorman Gulch. Portions of the river were mined with a floating dredge and portions of the tributaries were also heavily placered (Hubbard, 1956; personal).

Lemhi County: Native gold occurs in the lode mines of the Carmen Creek District. Flakes of native gold occur with bornite and chlorargyrite in the oxidized vein of the Carmen Creek Mine (Shannon, 1926).

Gold forms coarse flakes, grains and nuggets in the quartz lenses in brecciated zones in the Eldorado Mine and other mines in the Eldorado (Geertson) District. Chalcopyrite and galena are associated. The Ranger Mine at the head of the upper branch of Geertson Creek at about 9,000 feet elevation, just over the ridge from Kirtley Creek, contains some coarse gold. A mineralized quartz vein occurs in Precambrian quartzite. Some placer deposits occur in the district (Shannon, 1926).

In the McDevitt District, free gold occurs in the Copper Queen Mine. It is associated with bornite, chalcopyrite and chalcocite in a quartz vein (Shannon, 1926).

The White Horse Mine in the Kirtley Creek District, 6 miles northeast of Salmon, contains coarse gold in quartz. The grains of gold are associated with the oxidation products of pyrite, chalcopyrite and galena. In the Oro Cache group of claims, gold is visible in quartz and oxidized pyrite with silver-bearing galena in sheared rock and quartz. The Oro Cache group is in the NE$\frac{1}{4}$ Sec. 35, T. 23 N., R. 23 E.; mineralization extends across the border into Montana.

Visible gold occurs in the copper ores in the Bell Mine on the south side of Freeman Creek in Sec. 4, T. 22 N., R. 23 E. at 6,800 feet elevation. Several open cuts and short adits were developed on the property, but only one adit was open in 1949. Chrysocolla and malachite can be found on the dump, with native gold visible in some of the malachite. Gold also occurs in placer deposits of the district (Mackenzie, 1949).

Fine to coarse gold and nuggets occur in the placer deposits of the Leesburg District. Many streams around Leesburg have been worked up to the present, although most production was before the turn of the century. Much of the gold is coarse and nuggets as large as an ounce and a half were recovered.

Production from these lodes was primarily from the oxidized zones in upper workings. Gold in lower workings is tied up in sulfides hindering production, although there has been production of native gold in quartz as well as gold in oxides (Shockey, 1957; personal).

There is only one occurrence of gold in the Texas District. This is the Martha vein in the Allie Mine, in limestone. Fine leaf and flake gold are imbedded in limonite (Shannon, 1926).

Some of the mines in the area of the North Fork quadrangle, T. 22-25 N., R. 21-23 E., produced gold. It occurs as visible grains in quartz veins. Several of the mines in the area contain crystals of secondary lead, zinc and copper minerals, including anglesite, cerussite and pyromorphite in the Silver Star Mine in Gold Star Gulch (Anderson, 1959).

Small nuggets of gold up to 1 cm across occur in bornite in the Copper Queen Mine on the South Fork of Agency Creek, 1 mile north of the Wonder lode in Sec. 15, T. 19 N., R. 25 E. Bornite and other copper minerals fill spaces between breccia fragments in a fault breccia zone up to 20 feet wide. Gold is most abundant where the vein cuts a diorite dike. The host rock is a light-gray to tan micaceous quartzite of the Belt supergroup. Similar mineralization with gold occurs in the vein of the Blue Lupine Mine. This is parallel to the

Photo. 179 Fluorite from a vein that cuts across the road near the M & M Mine, the specimen is 4.2 cm across; the surface layer of the fluorite is white, interior is nearly colorless, Myers Cove, Lemhi County.

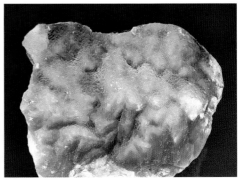

Photo. 180 Fluorite consisting of a crust of banded lavender cubes coated by a thin layer of nearly colorless tiny cubes, specimen 6.5 cm across, Anderson Mine, Myers Cove, Lemhi County.

Photo. 181 Fluorite, largest crystal is 1.2 cm across, Anderson Mine, Myers Cove, Lemhi County.

Photo. 182 Fluorite, complex micro crystal in quartz cavity, Missouri Belle Mine, Lemhi County.

Photo. 184 Fornacite, group on top right is 0.2 mm across, Weimer Mine, Clark County.

Photo. 183 Fluorite, micro crystal in quartz greenish yellow coating may be segnitite, Ima Mine, Lemhi County.

Photo. 185 White to light tan colored crystals of forsterite with brown crystals of vesuvianite, large forsterite is 1.2 cm across, Quartzite Canyon, Lemhi County.

Photo. 187 Garnet, 1.2 cm across, Ruby Rapids, Idaho County.

Photo. 188 Garnet on hedenbergite, garnet on right is 4 cm across, South Mountain, Owyhee County.

Photo. 186 Friebergite with siderite, Sunshine Mine, Shoshone County.

Photo. 190 Goethite pseudomorphs of pyrite, crystals are under 0.8 mm across, near Loon Creek Summit, Custer County.

Photo. 191 Garnet, 3 cm across, Trail Creek, Shoshone County.

main Copper Queen Mine (Sharp and Cavender, 1962).

Mineralization is along a fault zone, with gouge and breccia, that is up to five feet wide. Pyrite, chalcopyrite, galena, malachite and azurite are associated with the gold. Other mines in the area contain similar mineralization (Anderson, 1957).

Six miles northwest of Salmon, in the mines and prospects along Wallace, Diamond and Bird Creeks, gold occurs as grains up to 1 mm across. Mineralization is in quartz veins; the mines are 2 to 4 miles west of the Salmon River (Biddle, 1985).

Owyhee County: Rich veins of gold and electrum (gold containing more than 20% silver) occurred in the mines on War Eagle and Florida Mountains in the Silver City District. Rich specimens containing layers of gold, electrum and ruby silver minerals were taken from these mines; unfortunately nearly all of it went to the smelter and very little to the cabinets of mineral collections anywhere. The gold formed fillings in cavities with several copper and silver sulfides and quartz and orthoclase. Some excellent specimens have been collected from the many mines including grains of mossy gold in cavities in quartz from the Black Jack Mine. Gold with acanthite and native silver occurred in the Ida Elmore, Mahogany and Minnesota mines. The Ida Elmore Mine has also produced specimens with gold in large grains in bluish quartz with disseminated sphalerite and galena and specimens of crystalline spongy gold. Placer deposits were very rich and produced coarse gold, some of it crystalline (Shannon, 1926; personal).

Some of the mines in the Silver City area, were incredibly rich, although mineralization was shallow, often not extending down more than a few hundred feet. There were thick veins of silver minerals, gold and electrum. Dake (1956) described one specimen he saw: "We saw in the collection of an old timer (yes it was high graded in 1874) a specimen measuring about 10 x 12 x 15 cm and made up of alternating seams of ruby silver and pure electrum. Some of the veins of electrum were a 1.2 cm thick. We tried to buy the specimen, but it was not for sale and was valued at $475 in gold and silver alone."

Shoshone County: The biggest gold producer in the northern part of the Idaho Panhandle is the Murray District north of the Coeur d'Alene District. Coarse gold was produced from placer deposits in Prichard, Eagle and Beaver Creeks and their tributaries. There has been production in recent years with some nuggets as large as eight ounces being found and many mining claimants continue to do some work and recover a few nuggets each year.

The lode mines contained fine to coarse gold in quartz with pyrite, chalcopyrite, galena and sphalerite. Some of the primary mines are the Crown Point (Photo. 195), Golden Chest, Gold Coin, Four Square, Ophir Mountain, Yosemite, Daddy, Mother Lode, Treasure Box, Buckeye and Occident mines. In recent years, there has been some activity in several of these mines. Specimens of gold nuggets (Photo. 196) and gold in quartz have been produced from placer deposits and gold in quartz from the lode mines (Shenon, 1938; personal).

Native gold is not generally seen in the Coeur d'Alene District. There was one occurrence of it in the Stanley Mine above Burke. In this deposit, gold formed thin, frost-like films on cracks in stibnite (Shannon, 1926).

Gold occurs in the gravels of the upper portion of the St. Joe River and a few of its tributaries. The gold is generally fine, but can be panned, in small quantities, from the surface gravels. Small pink crystals of almandine occur with the gold (personal).

Valley County: The Thunder Mountain District produced gold from rhyolite; mining has been sporadic up to recent times. At the Sunnyside Mine, a mineralized rhyolite breccia contained gold mixed with clay along fractures and joints. Mossy and dendritic gold could be panned out of crushed rhyolite. The mineralized flow varies from 15 to 30 feet thick and overlies a barren rhyolite flow.

The gold contains silver near the amount of electrum. The Dewey Mine contains gold in seams in a rhyolite tuff. Some of the gold is associated with pyrite nodules which contain leaf gold in their centers. Charred logs of large size are included in the rhyolite and are frequently impregnated with gold (Shannon, 1926).

GOSLARITE

$ZnSO_4 \cdot 7H_2O$, orthorhombic

Common as an efflorescence or efflorescent crust; massive, granular, fibrous and stalactitic. Crystals are colorless, sometimes white, greenish, bluish, brownish. Transparent to translucent. Soluble in water. Widespread; a post-mining efflorescence in mines that contain sphalerite or other zinc minerals.

Custer County: Goslarite forms coatings on specimens of sphalerite that have oxidized on the dump of the Livingston Mine at the head of Jim Creek in the Boulder Creek District, 60 miles northwest of Mackay. Associated minerals include jamesonite, galena, chalcopyrite, tetrahedrite, wurtzite, pyrite, pyrrhotite and cerussite (Kiilsgaard, 1949).

GRAPHITE

C, hexagonal (trigonal)

Thin, hexagonal tabular crystals; usually coarse to fine foliated masses. Soft; may have greasy feel. Iron-black to steel-gray. In rocks of intense regional or igneous metamorphism.

Valley County: Graphite occurs at a prospect northeast of McCall in Sec. 35, T. 19 N., R. 4 E.; the prospect lies alongside the road to Yellow Pine (personal).

Graphite has also been found as poorly formed crystals with pyrite cubes in the adits above the highway at Lucile Bar on the Salmon River about 10 miles north of Riggins (personal).

GRATONITE

$Pb_9As_4S_{15}$, hexagonal (trigonal)

Prismatic crystals or massive. Dark lead-gray color. Occurs in cavities in pyrite-bearing ore with enargite, tetrahedrite and realgar. Uncommon.

Lemhi County: Gratonite forms micro rhombic crystals in fractures in quartz in the Ima Mine in the Blue Wing District in Sec. 23, T. 14 N., R. 23 E. on the north side of Patterson Creek, 65 miles south of Salmon. The crystals are associated with crystals of huebnerite, microcline, scheelite, calcite, galena, chalcopyrite, molybdenite, molybdite, fluorite, tetrahedrite, erythrite and other metallic minerals. Most of these are anhedral, sometimes euhedral, grains in massive material.

The gratonite crystals have a similar occurrence and occur in, often replacing, chalcopyrite and galena. Mineralization is in quartz veins in a fracture system in granite. The huebnerite crystals are often euhedral and up to 7 cm in length. Reported secondary minerals include anglesite and pyromorphite after galena and azurite, malachite, covellite and chalcocite after chalcopyrite. Other minerals include pyrite and rhodochrosite. (Anderson, 1948b).

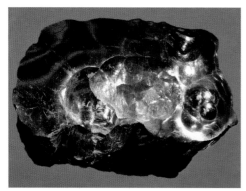

Photo. 191 Goethite, 16 cm across, Placer Creek, Shoshone County; Norm and Carla Radford specimen.

Photo. 192 Goethite pseudomorph of pyrite, 1.8 cm high, Hord Gulch, Shoshone County.

Photo. 193 Gold in quartz, 5 mm across, Iron Crown Mine, Custer County.

Photo. 194 Gold on quartz, gold leaf is 7 mm across, probably Marshall Mountain District, Idaho County.

Photo. 195 Gold in quartz, exposed gold is 2.3 cm, Crown Point Mine, Potosi Gulch, Murray, Shoshone County; Norm and Carla Radford specimen.

Photo. 196 Gold with quartz, 2 cm high, Reeder Gulch, Murray, Shoshone County; Norm and Carla Radford specimen.

Photo. 197 Grossular, 5.4 cm across, note reddish brown outer layer over light greenish inner zone, Buckskin Ridge, Thompson Creek Mine, near Clayton, Custer County; Norm and Carla Radford specimen.

Photo. 198 Grossular, large crystal is 2.4 cm across, Harpster, Idaho County; Norm and Carla Radford specimen.

Photo. 200 Grossular, 1.5 cm across, Iron Mountain, Washington County.

Photo. 199 Grossular, Quartzite Canyon, Spring Mountain District, Lemhi County.

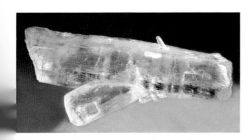

Photo. 202 Gyrolite, double sphere, 6 mm across each, Pinehurst, Adams County.

Photo. 201 Gypsum from the roadcut north of Weiser, 6.8 cm long, Washington County.

GREENOCKITE

CdS, hexagonal
Dimorphous with hawleyite. Occurs in hemimorphic pyramidal crystals or as an earthy coating. Yellow or orange. Forms an earthy coating on zinc minerals or rarely as crystals in amygdaloidal cavities in basic igneous rocks.

Blaine County: Shannon (1926) reports that greenockite had been tentatively identified in the Plughof (Lark) Mine, 2 miles southwest of Bellevue. It forms yellow coatings on oxidized ore.

GROSSULAR

$Ca_3Al_2(SiO_4)_3$, cubic
Garnet group, forms a series with andradite, hydrogrossular and uvarovite. Cinnamon-brown, orange, white or green. Transparent to translucent. Garnets are common in metamorphic rocks and sometimes in igneous rocks.

Adams County: Trapezohedral crystals occur at the White Mountain Mine in the Seven Devils District. Crystals are cinnamon-brown in color and are associated with epidote and calcite. Grayish brown masses and imperfect dodecahedral crystals of grossular occur in the Arkansas Mine. They average about 1 cm in diameter and are scattered through calcite with fine grained diopside (Shannon, 1926).

Custer County: Grossular occurred in the contact rock on Buckskin Ridge above Thompson Creek. The crystals were greenish gray inside with a thin reddish brown layer on the outside (Photo. 197). They formed a coarse druse in cavities in massive garnet rock. This area was stripped away in preparation of the open pit Thompson Creek molybdenum mine (personal).

Idaho County: Orange crystals of garnet, probably grossular, occur in the tactites near Harpster (Photo. 198). The crystals often have brilliant surfaces and are translucent. Crystals up to about 2.5 cm in diameter have been found in cavities; other calc-silicate minerals are associated (personal).

Lemhi County: Grossular occurs in the skarn on Quartzite Canyon in the Spring Mountain District. It forms white, pink and orange to red masses along the contact of the skarn with the intrusive rock. Although the lighter colored grossular occur only as masses, the red grossular does form crystals. Tiny yellow crystals have been found in the lower part of the eastern end of the skarn zone above the access road, but they are rare (Photo. 199) (personal).

Washington County: Dodecahedral crystals of grossular occur in the pit on Iron Mountain. In one area, light brown grossular crystals are in cavities in altered and oxidized skarn with chlorite (Photo. 200). Most crystals are under about 1 cm across. A massive grossular zone contains narrow, vertical cavities with large grossular crystals to at least 12 cm across lining the cavity walls. Unfortunately, these crystals are highly shattered and even though they are intact when exposed, most readily fall apart, often to tiny grains and fragments, when disturbed. The crystals are light brown, mostly dull and consist of less than a half crystal projecting above the cavity wall.

Other minerals in the pit include bundles of dravite, magnetite, phlogopite and chlorite pseudomorphs of one or more unknown minerals. The pit is about 100 feet long, but the steep sides are slumping and caving, burying the rock and mineral exposures in loose debris. Vegetation has overgrown the dump (personal).

GUANAJUATITE

Bi_2Se_3, orthorhombic
Acicular crystals, striated lengthwise; massive, foliated or granular. Bluish gray color. Rare, with other bismuth minerals.

Lemhi County: Dark gray grains and small masses of guanajuatite occur in quartz in a prospect on Kirtley Creek. The occurrence is 1.5 miles from the mouth of the creek 9 miles northeast of Salmon (Shannon, 1926).

GYPSUM

$CaSO_4 \cdot 2H_2O$, monoclinic
Prismatic crystals, often diamond-shaped; more commonly in granular masses. Color-less, white, gray or yellow; transparent to translucent. A common mineral in sedimentary rocks; also occurs in oxidation zones of ore deposits.

Bannock County: Small crystals of gypsum occur with sulfur 5 miles east of Soda Springs (Shannon, 1926).

Boise, Custer and Elmore Counties: Gypsum is an uncommon granular coating in cavities in the granite of the Sawtooth Mountains. It has been positively identified in one cavity and similar material as coatings and masses has been found in others (personal).

Lemhi County: Gypsum is common in the veins in the mines of the Little Eightmile District. It forms small veinlets cutting the veins and fills cavities. Tabular crystals line a few of the cavities in the lead-silver veins and acicular crystals up to 9 mm in length project from the tabular crystals (Thune, 1941).

Shoshone County: Gypsum occurs in the Bunker Hill Mine in oxidized areas. It forms colorless to white elongated prismatic crystals. Long crystals, to 3 cm or more commonly diverging from a common point and smaller crystals project from them in branch-like groups. It also forms crusts of small crystals or grains (personal).

Washington County: Gypsum forms colorless, translucent to transparent, elongated, prismatic crystals in sediments near Midvale. Individual crystals are up to 15 cm in length; often two or more crystals are intergrown and sometimes they form a group of large radiating crystals. The sides of the prisms are nearly smooth with small growth features and the terminations are more irregular (personal).

One locality is in clay in the roadcut at the pass 7.7 miles north of Weiser. The clay layer often slumps and slides out towards the road. The Highway Department has posted "No Digging" signs, but it is possible to find crystals weathered out on the surface. The crystals are transparent colorless, variety selenite and are generally prismatic. Terminations are mostly crude, but the other faces are often smooth and lustrous or somewhat pitted (Photo. 201). Most crystals are under 6 cm long, but they have been found to at least 20 cm (personal).

A zone of dark gray to black breccia can be found in the central portion of the cut. Small white crystals of calcite can be found in this breccia, which runs up the cut to the top of the hill on the west side (personal).

GYROLITE

$Na(Ca,Mg,Fe)_{16}(Si,Al)_{24}O_{60}(OH)_7 \cdot 15H_2O$, hexagonal
Lamellar radial structures, massive; colorless to white, transparent to translucent.

Photo. 203 Gyrolite spheres with apophyllite, spheres are 6 mm across, Pinehurst, Adams County.

Photo. 205 Hedenbergite, 4 cm high, South Mountain, Owyhee County.

Photo. 204 Hedenbergite and garnet, large hedenbergite is 1.2 cm high, South Mountain, Owyhee County.

Photo. 206 Hemimorphite, sphere in center is 3 mm across, near Blizzard Mountain, Blaine County.

Photo. 207 Hemimorphite and rosasite, hemimorphite crystals up to 3 mm long, Excelsior claim group, Lemhi County.

Photo. 208 Hemimorphite, light blue, 6.3 cm across, Tiger Mine, Mackay District, Custer County; Norm and Carla Radford specimen.

Photo. 209 Hemimorphite with clusters of tiny quartz crystals, micro, Excelsior claim group, Lemhi County.

A secondary mineral formed by the alteration of lime silicates; often associated with apophyllite and zeolite group minerals.

Adams County: Gyrolite occurs with zeolites, apophyllite and calcite in small cavities in basalts south of Pinehurst. This is the first reported occurrence of this mineral in Idaho. There are good exposures in roadcuts along Highway 95, especially in the roadcuts 0.8 mile north of mile post 177 up to mile post 178. It forms hemispheres of two types (Photo. 202, 203). The first deposited are wavy platy crystals forming large hemispheres, up to 1.5 cm across. These are colorless and transparent and occur as single hemispheres or a few hemispheres scattered across cavity walls up to complete cavity coatings. The second to form are white hemispheres, smaller, under about 8 mm. These are less compact and are composed of very thin plates of gyrolite.

Apophyllite and chabazite are commonly associated, the Apophyllite sometimes encloses the small white gyrolite hemispheres. Other minerals in these cavities include levyne, offretite, cowlesite, tacharanite, thomsonite, phillipsite, stilbite, calcite and mesolite.

The highway was rebuilt in this area in 2000 and all the roadcuts were heavily blasted and quarried. Most of the cuts are not suitable to collecting after the construction; large boulders were used as road-fill and rip rap along the river throughout this area (personal).

HALLOYSITE

$Al_2Si_2O_5(OH)_4$, monoclinic

A kaolinite-serpentine group mineral. Tubular, ultramicroscopic in size, compact to mealy masses; mostly colorless to white, also yellowish to reddish. Widespread, often associated with kaolinite, a common clay mineral formed by the weathering or hydrothermal alteration of feldspars and other aluminous silicate minerals.

Boise, Custer and Elmore County: Halloysite has been identified by X-ray diffraction as one of the minerals, along with albite, replacing an unknown prismatic mineral in a white granite in the Sawtooth Mountains. The broken pieces of the pseudomorph were thought to be apatite and display a subhedral hexagonal cross section. The color is cream to purplish-pink (personal).

HEDENBERGITE

$CaFeSi_2O_6$, monoclinic

A member of the pyroxene group; forms a series with diopside and johannsenite. Prismatic, fibrous or lamellar masses; brown to black. Found in contact metamorphic lime-silicate rocks and crystalline limestone.

Custer County: Greenish to brownish, bladed fibrous masses of hedenbergite have been reported with galena in the Basin prospect on the mountain north of Park Creek, at the Trail Creek-Summit Creek divide. Epidote, garnet and prehnite occur in the same adit in a metamorphosed calcareous shale (Shannon, 1926).

Owyhee County: Hedenbergite is associated with ilvaite, calcite, sphalerite and chalcopyrite in the contact metamorphic rocks in the South Mountain District. It forms euhedral crystals up to 3 cm in length, but varies from fine grained masses to coarse masses of fibrous blades (Photo. 204, 205). Cavities are filled with quartz, calcite rhombs, nailhead calcite and pyrite. Azurite is associated in the Laxey Mine and bindheimite is associated in the Golconda Mine.

The hedenbergite is in a zone that extends from the Laxey portal southeast to the Texas shaft and 1,200 feet further to the Standard shaft. The zone consists of a hedenbergite-ilvaite-rich contact rock. Excellent crystals of both hedenbergite and ilvaite can be found in some cavities in the zone (Shannon, 1926; Sorenson, 1927; personal).

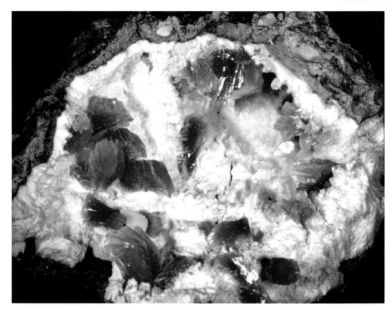

Photo. 210 heulandite-Ca on mordenite, specimen is 12.5 cm across, Rat's Nest claim, Custer County.

Photo. 211 heulandite-Ca an unusually large group of coarse crystals, bow-tie like group in front is 6 cm high, Rat's Nest claim Custer County.

HELVITE

$Mn_4Be_3(SiO_4)_3S$, cubic

Forms a series with danalite and another with genthelvite. Crystals are most often tetrahedrons; may be octahedrons. Sometimes as rounded aggregates. Brown, reddish, gray, yellowish gray, yellow, yellowish green; transparent to translucent. Primary occurrence is in granite pegmatites, syenites and nepheline syenite pegmatites.

Boise, Custer and Elmore Counties: Helvite can be found in cavities in the granitic rocks of the Sawtooth batholith with smoky quartz, microcline and albite. It is uncommon, but several cavities with helvite have been found. Crystals are tetrahedral and are commonly twinned (positive and negative tetrahedrons) (Photo. 58). Spinel law twins are rare but have been found. Most specimens are less than 6 mm across, but they have been found up to 3.6 cm across.

Surfaces vary from etched and pitted to brilliant, although most are dull. In nearly all crystals, the color is cinnamon-brown, although a few are lighter. It is a late-forming mineral that occurs on albite and microcline, associated with quartz, topaz, masutomilite and zinnwaldite.

Helvite is apparently uncommon in the Sawtooth Mountains, but locally may be abundant and occur in several cavities in a small area. Fine specimens of helvite on smoky quartz, albite or microcline have been collected, but are rare (personal).

HEMATITE

Fe_2O_3, hexagonal (trigonal)

Tabular crystals with hexagonal outline, sometimes in rose-like groups or in botryoidal to reniform masses. Reddish brown to black. A common mineral in all types of rocks and ore deposits.

Adams County: The specular variety of hematite is common in the ore deposits of the Seven Devils District. It forms thick curved scales in massive bornite and thin plates parallel to the face of garnet or epidote crystals. Broad plates and sheaves of specular hematite occur in epidote of the Copper Boy Mine. Large curved hematite plates occur with bornite and garnets in the Peacock Mine, and small specular masses common (Shannon, 1926; personal).

Bannock County: Hematite forms very thin minute tabular crystals with calcite and quartz crystals in vugs in a garnet rock on Lanes Creek. The crystals display only the basal pinacoid and very flat hexagonal pyramid. The locality is in the $NW^1/_4$ Sec. 9, T. 6 S., R. 43 E. (Shannon, 1926).

Boise, Custer and Elmore Counties: Hematite is fairly common in the miarolitic cavities of the Sawtooth batholith where it occurs with microcline, albite, smoky quartz and aquamarine. Most often it forms small plate-like crystals between feldspar crystals, but does form larger, well-formed crystals. Individual hexagonal crystals are commonly around 6-8 mm across and about 2 mm thick. Clusters of crystals forming what is commonly called a rose have been found (Photo. 62). These may be as much as 3 cm across.

Lemhi County: Hematite forms crystals up to 1 cm across in veins of specular hematite at the Black Angus prospect 3 miles south of Poison Creek in Secs. 2 and 3, T. 17 N., R. 21 E. in the McKim Creek iron deposits, about 30 miles south of Salmon. Large masses of black specular hematite can be found. Mineralization is in a phyllitic quartzite above the Lemhi quartzite. Magnetite occurs along the margins of the veins; most of it is altered to hematite (Soregaroli, 1961; personal).

Tiny scales of hematite are uncommon in the cavities in the rocks of the Crags batholith, west of Cobalt. The tiny scales are sharp, euhedral crystals up to about 3 mm across and 0.2 mm in thickness. They occur in cavities between albite crystals with anatase (personal).

Shoshone County: Hematite is common in many of the mines in the Coeur d'Alene District. Most of it is specular or massive and not of interest to collectors. It can be found with other iron oxides.

In some of the mines on the West Fork of Pine Creek, on the west end of the district, it forms compact, fibrous botryoidal and stalactitic masses (Shannon, 1926).

Washington County: Large masses of hematite can be found in a steep 1,000 foot section of a stream channel on Iron Mountain, 6 miles east of Mineral (about 22 miles north of Weiser). Lenses of crystalline hematite are exposed at the top of the slope in a siliceous porphyry intrusion. Prospect developments expose the lenses. The hematite lenses grade into pyrite at shallow depth. This appears to be at the contact of a granitic intrusive and garnet-bearing rock (Shannon, 1926).

HEMIMORPHITE

$Zn_4Si_2O_7(OH)_2 \cdot H_2O$, orthorhombic

Forms tabular to nearly acicular crystals, often in divergent or parallel groups; also massive and granular. White with a bluish or greenish tint, yellow or brown; translucent to transparent. Occurs in oxidation zones of zinc deposits associated with sphalerite, smithsonite, anglesite, cerussite and galena.

Blaine County: Crusts of hemimorphite crystals line cavities in gossan at a prospect on the northwest side of the saddle north of Blizzard Mountain. The tiny crystals are up to about 1.5 mm in length and have the common thin lath shape. They form radial groups and crusts lining the cavities or perched on quartz (Photo. 206). Aurichalcite and chrysocolla pseudomorphs of aurichalcite are associated (personal).

Cassia County: In the Black Pine District, hemimorphite forms bluish white to white radiating sheaves and druses of tabular crystals on the host rock. It is associated with jamesonite, scorodite, smithsonite and barite; cinnabar is also reported (Shannon, 1926).

Custer County: Hemimorphite forms acicular crystals on smithsonite in the Champion claims in the Mackay District (Alder Creek side). These claims are located at 8,000 feet elevation south of Cliff Creek and south-southeast of the Empire Mine. Specimens of minute blade-like crystals of colorless hemimorphite with aurichalcite have been found above the No. 4 level of the Empire Mine (Shannon, 1926).

In the Tiger Mine near Mackay, hemimorphite has been found forming crusts in oxidized ores of the mine (Photo. 208). It forms crusts to 6-8 mm or more thick that are composed of tiny acicular crystals with a light blue color (personal).

In the Red Bird, Beardsley, River View and Pacific mines in the Bayhorse District, hemimorphite occurs as bundles of white columnar or vertically elongated crystals in cavities in oxidized lead-silver ores. The Red Bird Mine specimens are botryoidal masses of limonite-stained hemimorphite crystals with small white cubes of fluorite. Hemimorphite in the Pacific Mine forms sheaves of white crystals in cavities or colorless crystals on druses of quartz crystals with cerussite. In the Beardsley Mine, the crystals form druses with malachite and calcite on chrysocolla or a siliceous matrix (Shannon, 1926).

Lemhi County: In the Pittsburg-Idaho Mine and other mines in the Texas District, hemimorphite forms acicular crystals in oxidized lead-silver ores. Most crystals are on drusy smithsonite. Deeply striated long acicular crystals coat cavities in the 400 foot level of the Flat vein in the Pittsburg-Idaho Mine (Shannon, 1926).

Hemimorphite is uncommon on the dumps of the Iron Mask and Excelsior mines in Horseshoe Gulch in the Spring Mountain District. It occurs as tiny crystals, under 6 mm in length, of the typical lath-like habit. It occurs alone at the Iron Mask mines, but may be with rosasite, hydrozincite(?) and calcite at the Excelsior Mine (Photo. 209, 207). In some of the cavities, hemimorphite is coated with a very fine druse of quartz crystals or have tiny groups of quartz crystals perched on hemimorphite crystals. The hemimorphite is mostly colorless to white but is sometimes pale blue (personal).

Owyhee County: Drusy crusts of hemimorphite occur in the Laxey Mine in the South Mountain District. The crystals are of the common habit, lining cavities. The tiny crystals are mostly under 2 mm in length and are colorless to white. It has also been reported in other mines in the district including the Bay State Mine (personal; Shannon, 1926).

Shoshone County: Small crystals of hemimorphite have been found in the Bunker Hill Mine. These were found as white spherulites in 1972 and again in 1979. The spherulites consist of tiny crystals radiating from a point, and are up to 6 mm across (Photo. 14). Individual crystal groups were up to 7.5 x 10 cm across (Radford and Crowley, 1981; personal).

HEULANDITE

$(Na,Ca)_{2-3}Al_3(Al,Si)_2Si_{13}O_{36} \cdot 12H_2O$, monoclinic

Zeolite group. Prismatic crystals that often have orthorhombic symmetry; often diamond shaped. Colorless, white, yellow or red; transparent to translucent. A secondary mineral that is most common in volcanic rocks with other zeolites, quartz and calcite.

Adams County: Minute crystals of heulandite occur with chabazite and stilbite in massive garnet on the Blue Jacket claim in the Seven Devils District. The crystals are thin, six sided and zoned (Shannon, 1926).

Heulandite occurs with other zeolites, apophyllite, calcite and quartz in small cavities in Columbia River basalt south of Pinehurst. There are exposures in roadcuts along Highway 95 from about one half mile north of mile post 176 to mile post 178. Heulandite is most common as colorless tiny crystals forming drusy coatings lining cavities, occasionally, crystals are up to about 6 mm across (personal).

Blaine County: Heulandite is reported to occur at an undisclosed location between Hailey and Ketchum. The crystals are reported to be up to 2.5 cm long, white to pink in color and with calcite in an outcrop of volcanic rock on the east side of the river (personal).

Boise, Custer and Elmore Counties: Tiny crystals of heulandite were found intergrown with aquamarine in a white boulder of granite in the Sawtooth Mountains. The small pod consisted of tiny colorless to white crystals to about 6 mm long with aquamarine from up to about 1 cm in length. Identification was by X-ray diffraction and was not positive, but may be another zeolite.

Custer County: Heulandite was reported as pink to red coatings on mordenite nodules and as tiny crystals in small nodules in an andesitic layer interbedded with tuffaceous sediments in the Challis volcanics south of Challis (Ross and Shannon, 1924). The locality was not described as to its exact locality, nor were fine collector quality crystals described. This occurrence has been located and is a small pit, accessible through private land. The pit is slumped and overgrown and has not been known to produce significant mordenite or heulandite in recent years (personal). It is the type locality for heulandite-Na (now that heulandite has been split into separate species). The heulandite-Na at the locality was reported by Ross and Shannon (1926) as having some free standing microcrystals, but no free standing crystals have been reported in recent years.

A new discovery in the area is of very fine quality heulandite-Ca crystals in large cavities on what is now the Rat's Nest claim. These occur as scattered crystals or drusy coatings in cavities on a mordenite lining. The heulandite crystals are commonly 1 cm long and often up to 2.5 cm long, with crystals rarely to 5 cm long, of typical habits. The crystals are colorless to medium pink or rarely dark pink. Excellent specimens with crystals scattered across matrix pieces up to more than a 45 cm have been found (Photo. 210-212). The quality of the heulandite crystals and the large matrix specimens are equal to any in the world.

Some of the large cavities are filled with calcite, sometimes platy. If the cavity is not completely filled, on occasion, heulandite and calcite crystals may occur on the platy calcite surfaces. Some very fine specimens with mordenite have been found, but typically the mordenite covers the heulandite so that it is poorly exposed. If matted, the mordenite is not attractive, but it can be removed.

The locality is poorly exposed on a very steep hillside. The altered andesitic layer that contains the heulandite and mordenite weathers at the same rate as the enclosing tuffaceous sediments. Excavating material with hand tools is very difficult, so specimen production has been done with equipment. Access to this location is through private land, and it is not open to collecting.

This same zone produces some quartz geodes, rarely with a pale amethystine color. Typically these geodes are small, under 7 cm across, and nearly filled with quartz crystals so as to have only a small opening. They can be up to more than 15 cm across and have a thin blue-gray agate shell with a drusy quartz lining. Rarely, heulandite crystals have been found in a quartz geode (Photo. 213). The only other macro minerals seen at this locality are stilbite and laumontite. Stilbite has been seen in only few of the cavities as single white crystals to about 2.5 cm long, mostly smaller and as groups and clusters. Laumontite occurs in some of the heulandite-calcite-mordenite cavities as groups of the common prismatic crystals. The longest laumontite seen was 8 mm, sometimes they have a pale pinkish color, and as is typical of this mineral, it loses water and disintegrates after being exposed (personal).

Heulandite-Na, occurs in several localities in the region around Challis. At the Rat's Nest claim, tiny crystals line small cavities in the matrix of the large heulandite-Ca lined cavities (Photo. 214). These small cavities are locally abundant. It was also seen in tuffaceous rock near the mouth of Morgan Creek, and in volcanic rocks up Deer Creek (personal).

Similar appearing crystals occur in a greenish tuff just north of the north end of 2nd Street at the edge of Challis. Here, the tiny orange-red crystals (Photo. 215) occur in thin vuggy veinlets (personal).

Elmore County: Tiny white crystals of heulandite have been tentatively identified by x-ray diffraction from Steel Mountain. The tiny crystals occur on the sides of white microcline crystals, and are 1-2 mm across and up to about 3 mm in length.

Idaho County: Heulandite is uncommon in cavities in Columbia River basalt in the quarry at the intersection of the Hazard Creek Road at Highway 95. The crystals are transparent, tiny and line cavities. They are associated with mordenite and chalcedony (personal).

Small crystals of heulandite occur with analcime, calcite and mordenite in small cavities in Columbia River basalt near Russell Bar in roadcuts along Highway 95 from mile post 218 for about 0.3 miles south. All cavities are small, mostly less than 3 cm across and almond-shaped. Most crystals are drusy coatings but occasionally they are up to about 4 mm across. They are generally colorless and transparent (personal).

Heulandite forms tiny crystals lining vesicles in Columbia River basalt in the cut along Highway 95 on the north side of Skookumchuck Creek. The crystals are tiny and are associated with analcime, apophyllite, chabazite and a white acicular zeolite (personal).

Heulandite occurs in vesicles in Columbia River basalt on the east side of the Little Salmon River just south of Boulder Creek south of Pinehurst. Large vesicles have shells of granular heulandite or radial-structured apophyllite. Some large vesicles are filled with globular aggregates of radial prehnite. Small amygdules are filled with granular heulandite that sometimes enclose groups of natrolite. The basalt crops out in bluffs above the river. Access is difficult, there are no roads on that side of the river, but it can be crossed when the water is low (Hamilton, 1963).

HISINGERITE

$Fe_2Si_2O_5(OH)_4 \cdot 2H_2O$, monoclinic

Massive, compact, finely crystalline or fibrous. Black to brownish black; resinous. A common mineral that can be found in many geologic settings as an alteration product.

Blaine County: Hisingerite is common replacing siderite along cracks in the rock of the Minnie Moore Mine near Bellevue. It has a blood-red color when exposed, but upon drying out becomes brown in color and highly fractured (Shannon, 1926).

HORNBLENDE

$(Ca,Na)_{2-3}(Mg,Fe,Al)_5(Al,Si)_8O_{22}(OH)_2$, monoclinic

Member of the amphibole group; now considered two minerals—ferrohornblende and magnesiohornblende. Prismatic crystals; sometimes fibrous or columnar. Dark green to black; translucent on thin edges. An important rock-forming mineral in igneous and metamorphic rocks.

Shoshone County: Black blades of hornblende form sheaves up to 2 cm in length in metamorphosed rocks west of West Sister Peak along the St. Joe River. The occurrence is in a cherty rock that has the appearance of limestone but contains no carbonate. Similar blades occur in a gray carbonate-bearing rock northwest of the Sisters. Greenish black blades are reported in the same area (Shannon, 1926).

HUEBNERITE

$MnWO_4$, monoclinic

Forms a series with ferberite, $FeWO4$; the intermediate members are called wolframite. Prismatic, most often long prismatic; sometimes flattened or tabular. Yellowish brown to reddish brown or uncommonly brownish black; translucent to transparent. In quartz-rich veins, pegmatitic veins, hydrothermal veins and other deposits.

Blaine County: Huebnerite occurs in a quartz vein near the top of Blizzard Mountain, about five miles west of the Martin town site (approximately in $SE^{1/}_4$ Sec. 14, T. 2 N., R. 23 E.). The vein has cavities lined with drusy quartz, and the blades of huebnerite occur frozen in the quartz (Cook, 1956; Kerr, 1946; personal).

Butte County: Huebnerite has been found in the Golden Chariot Mine and possibly other mines in the Lava Creek District. The Golden Chariot Mine is in Sec. 15, T. 2 N., R. 24 E. The Hub Mine and properties are in Secs. 8, 9, 16 and 17 and the Martin property is in Sec. 22 of the same township. The Ella and Hornsilver mines are in Sec. 11, T. 3 N., R. 24 E., and the Last Chance and St. Louis mines are in Sec. 15 of that township. The Reliance Mine is 0.5 mile north of the St. Louis.

The huebnerite has a characteristic form of platy aggregates or black crystals and bladed masses or acicular crystals on quartz crystals in the mines of the Golden Chariot group. It occurs with quartz, which occurs as amethyst and delicate cellular network pseudomorphs of calcite. Epidote and specular hematite are associated (Anderson, 1929).

Lemhi County: Huebnerite occurs in the Blue Wing District and has been mined as tungsten ore. The Ima Mine is the only mine that has produced ore in the district. It is on the northwest side of Patterson Creek, about 25 miles east of Challis, in Sec. 23, T. 14 N., R. 23 E. The huebnerite is associated with tetrahedrite, galena, sphalerite, pyrite and molybdenite in a quartz vein, sometimes associated with a pegmatite. It forms reddish brown blades up to 7 cm in length, mostly less than 3 cm, frozen in white quartz veins in granite, or rarely as smaller euhedral crystals in cavities (Photo. 216).

Some blades penetrate and replace fluorite and rhodochrosite. Microcline is associated as coarse and fine subhedral crystals and pyrite as cubes and modified cubes to 5 cm, sometimes embedded in masses of molybdenite. Gratonite forms micro rhombic crystals and scheelite forms pale yellow to white crusts and druses in cavities in the quartz. Siderite, calcite, galena, chalcopyrite, bornite, cuprite, sphalerite and other metallic minerals are also associated. The limited oxidized zone has azurite, brochantite, malachite and segnitite (Anderson, 1948b; Callaghan and Lemmon, 1941; Kerr, 1946; personal; Umpleby, 1913a).

Valley County: Huebnerite occurs at the New Snowbird Mine 4.75 miles northwest of the settlement of Big Creek. The mine is on the headwaters of Smith Creek, 1.2 miles northeast of Elk Summit. Subhedral prismatic crystals are frozen in milky quartz with small patches and veinlets of scheelite. The huebnerite is dark brown and up to 1 cm in length. Mineralization is in a silicified shear zone in granodiorite of the Idaho batholith (Kirkpatrick, 1974; Leonard et al, 1968).

A similar occurrence can be found in the Red Bluff Mine between the middle and south forks of Smith Creek at an elevation of 8,000 feet. Here a steeply dipping quartz vein and smaller similar veins cut a quartz and feldspar gneiss. The veins are cut by porphyritic dacite dikes and both the veins and dikes are highly fractured and silicified.

The quartz contains huebnerite and scheelite associated with pyrite, sphalerite, galena and chalcopyrite. Huebnerite crystals are euhedral, although some are cut by veinlets of scheelite. Scheelite occurs on fracture surfaces in quartz and also on joint faces in the dikes (Kirkpatrick, 1974).

At the White Metal prospect on the north side of the south fork of Smith Creek there are several quartz lenses that contain huebnerite crystals. These are at an elevation of 8,200 feet. The huebnerite crystals form blades to 5 cm in length, and scheelite coats fracture surfaces and forms veinlets in the quartz (Kirkpatrick, 1974).

HYDROCERUSSITE

$Pb_3(CO_3)_2(OH)_2$, hexagonal (trigonal)
Crystals have hexagonal outline; thin to thick tabular, flattened; steep pyramidal. Colorless, white, gray; transparent to translucent. An uncommon secondary mineral in oxidized

ores of lead bearing deposits with cerussite and other minerals.

Shoshone County: Hydrocerussite has been found in the Bunker Hill Mine. Specimens were found in the 1950s and 1960s that were tentatively identified as this mineral. In the 1970s, it was identified as the mineral making up the core and bases of elongated, tapering, rounded crystals of cerussite. Apparently these were originally hydrocerussite crystals that had been partially replaced by cerussite. There have been other reports of hydrocerussite in the mines of the Coeur d'Alene District, but they have not been confirmed by analysis (personal).

HYDROZINCITE

$Zn_5(CO_3)_2(OH)_6$, monoclinic
A secondary mineral found in the oxidized portion of zinc-bearing deposits often associated with other secondary minerals. Commonly as masses, coatings and fibrous, stalactitic or reniform masses; uncommon crystals are lath-like or bladed and have pointed terminations. Colorless, white, gray, yellow to brown, pink and green.

Lemhi County: Tiny, white, spherical masses of what appear to be hydrozincite of micro size are uncommon with hemimorphite and rosasite on the dump of the Excelsior Mine in the Spring Mountain District. The tiny white masses have been seen on only a few specimens (personal).

ILVAITE

$CaFe_2Fe(SiO_4)_2(OH)$, orthorhombic and monoclinic

Prismatic, vertically striated; columnar or massive. Iron-black or dark grayish black. In magnetite orebodies, with zinc and copper ores and contact deposits.

Owyhee County: Ilvaite occurs with hedenbergite, garnet, pyrrhotite, chalcopyrite, sphalerite and galena in contact metamorphic rocks and ore deposits in the area around the Golconda and Laxey mines, South Mountain District. The contact metamorphic zone is along the contact of schists, quartzites and marble with granite and granodiorite. The ilvaite and hedenbergite vary from scattered crystals to masses of imperfect crystals.

Large ilvaite crystals occur in calcite masses (Photo. 217), and large excellent, terminated, sometimes doubly terminated, prismatic crystals occur on groups of quartz crystals (Photos. 218, 219) and in soft limonitic gossan. Some are over 7 cm in length, and all are black in color. Many are lustrous, but most are a little dull to sometimes quite dull. Crystals are typically prismatic and often striated. The most common forms are m(110) and s(120), sometimes with a(100), b(010) and d(140) with terminations having the faces o and r.

Drusy calcite coats some specimens. In areas, ilvaite is abundant and in masses of crudely shaped crystals. Specimens have been produced from the mines in the district, but generally not in association with the ore minerals. In the mines and in the surrounding country rock, ilvaite does occur with quartz crystals and with calcite crystals. There is no mining in the district now and mineral production is minimal (personal; Shannon, 1926; Sorenson, 1927).

JAMESONITE

$Pb_4FeSb_6S_{14}$, monoclinic

Subparallel aggregates of prismatic crystals, these may form columnar masses; in masses of needles, massive or fibrous. Grayish black, sometimes tarnished iridescent. In hydrothermal veins associated with stibnite, pyrite, sphalerite and galena.

Blaine County: Jamesonite has been reported in the Reliance Mine, Era District. It is associated with pyrite, chalcopyrite, sphalerite, galena and quartz (Shannon, 1926).

Cassia County: Slender needle-like crystals of jamesonite have been found in some of the mines of the Black Pine District in T. 15 S., R. 29 E. It also occurs as masses or groups of parallel needles. The crystals are associated with barite (massive and crystals replacing calcite and quartz), cinnabar (sooty or dust-like coatings on quartz and barite), smithsonite (crystals, crusts and reniform; white, brown, green or blue color), scorodite (leek green crystals, massive or botryoidal) and some jasperoid in veins (Shannon, 1926).

Custer County: Subparallel aggregates of prismatic crystals have been found in the Livingston Mine at the head of Jim Creek at 9,300 feet elevation. The mine is 60 miles northwest of Mackay in the Boulder Creek District. Some of the jamesonite is coated with an earthy yellow alteration product. Galena, chalcopyrite, tetrahedrite, wurtzite, pyrite, pyrrhotite, arsenopyrite, anglesite, cerussite and goslarite are associated. The galena may form small crystals and the cerussite forms small crystals and crystalline masses. The goslarite forms an oxidation product of sphalerite on specimens on the dump (Kiilsgaard, 1949).

Similar jamesonite can be found in the Lakeview Mine (Crater Mine) on the south shore of Crater Lake in the cirque at the head of Livingston Creek, 1 mile northwest of the Livingston Mine. Pyrite and sphalerite occur with the jamesonite in an argillite host rock (Kiilsgaard, 1949).

Jamesonite forms grains in the Little Livingston Mine in the east canyon wall of Livingston Creek at the northwest end of Railroad Ridge. Various silver minerals and cerussite are associated in argillite of the Milligen formation (Kiilsgaard, 1949).

It is also reported at the head of Slate Creek near the summit of Railroad Ridge with quartz, pyrite, siderite and arsenopyrite. Individual grains are reported to be 5-10 mm across, have a blackish gray color and a brilliant luster. It is possible that this is the same occurrence as described above, or is the same mineralized zone (Shannon, 1925a).

Lemhi County: Acicular crystals of jamesonite occur in the stibnite veins in the Buckhorn Mine in the Little Eightmile (Junction) District about 450 feet from the portal of the main adit. The stibnite veins cut a 55 foot wide altered dacite dike. It also occurs as fibrous masses, and is associated with boulangerite and stibnite (Thune, 1941).

Owyhee County: Jamesonite (identification not positive, may be owyheeite or boulangerite) occurs as radiating prismatic fibers up to 1 cm in length in cavities in rhyolite in the 800 level of the DeLamar Mine. Similar crystals occur in quartz and project into cavities in the Rising Star Mine in the Flint District with argentiferous tetrahedrite. It has also been reported in the Black Jack-Trade Dollar vein (Piper and Laney, 1926; Shannon, 1926).

Shoshone County: Acicular crystals of jamesonite form masses in quartz and partially fill small cavities in quartz in the Sunshine Mine. Individual crystals are typically up to 1-1.5 cm in length (personal).

JAROSITE

$KFe_3(SO_4)_2(OH)_6$, hexagonal (trigonal)

Generally in microscopic crystals as masses or crusts, fibrous or earthy. Ocherous, amber yellow to dark brown; translucent. Forms as a secondary mineral in oxidized iron-rich ore deposits with limonite.

Custer County: A brecciated and silicified zone in limestone on Cherry Creek in the Mackay District (Alder Creek side) contains excellent, but tiny, crystals of jarosite. The crystals are thick and tabular, golden brown in color and up to 2 mm in diameter and form masses in quartzite (Fig. 15). The exact locality is not reported but is given briefly as "quartzite just above limestone, Cherry Creek" and "went up Cherry Creek until I came to iron-stained quartzite outcrop, then went to top of ridge and found limestone-quartzite contact" (Shannon, 1926).

Lemhi County: Jarosite forms yellow to yellow brown microcrystalline coatings lining cavities in the quartz veins of the Ima Mine on Patterson Creek. It occurs with azurite, malachite, mimetite and wulfenite. The veins also contain small red blades of huebnerite (personal).

Owyhee County: Jarosite forms small masses of tiny yellow to yellow-brown crystals in cavities with quartz in the altered volcanic rocks at the Stone Cabin Mine on Florida Mountain. These vary from compact masses to groups of distinct tiny crystals (Photo. 220). Similar jarosite occurs in the nearby DeLamar Mine and was reported during mining operations there. Both mines are now closed and are being rehabilitated (personal).

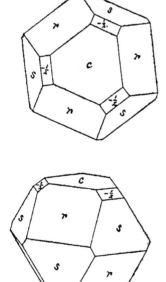

Fig. 15 Jarosite, Cherry Creek, Mackay (Alder Creek) District, Custer County; crystal drawings from Shannon (1926).

JOSEITE

Bi_4TeS_2, hexagonal

Irregular laminated masses. Grayish black to steel-gray, tarnishes darker or iridescent. Occurs in granular limestone or veins with other bismuth minerals.

Custer County: Joseite has been reported in the mines of Washington and Germania Basins with pyrrhotite, sphalerite, galena, arsenopyrite, stibnite and other bismuth minerals and possibly maldonite and tetradymite. Mineralization is in granitic rocks and in the Wood River formation. Production has been principally of lead, silver and gold (Ross, 1963).

KAINOSITE-(Y)

$Ca_2(Y,Ce)_2Si_4O_{12}(CO_3)\cdot H_2O$, orthorhombic
Short to long prismatic crystals, granular. Light yellowish brown to chestnut brown; also colorless, yellow, light rose to light red. Transparent to translucent. In granite pegmatites, Alpine clefts and in magnetite ore.

Boundary County: Kainosite-(Y) occurs as anhedral grains in a thorite-bearing quartz vein on the northwestern end of Hall Mountain, east of Porthill overlooking the Kootenai River Valley. The vein is intruded into a diorite dike near the center of the southern boundary of the NW$^{1}/_{4}$ Sec. 13, T. 65 N., R. 1 W. The kainosite grains are colorless to white, and are present only in portions of the vein with the highest radioactivity. Thorite varies from 5 to 60% of the vein. Individual kainosite grains are adjacent to or intergrown with allanite or, sometimes, calcite. Other minerals in the vein include chlorite, magnetite and apatite (Adams et al, 1964).

KERMESITE

Sb_2S_2O, triclinic (pseudomonoclinic)
Generally forms lath-shaped crystals, tufted radiating aggregates or powder-like masses or coatings. Color is a distinctive cherry-red. It is an alteration product of stibnite and is commonly associated with the other antimony mineral oxidation products, including cervantite, stibiconite and valentinite.

Elmore County: Kermesite occurs with the other antimony oxidation products, stibnite and native antimony, in the Hermada antimony mine on the East Fork of Swanholm Creek, 20 miles west of Atlanta. Kermesite, with the other secondary minerals, is common in the surface oxidized zones. Mineralization is in quartz veins, and stibnite is the primary ore mineral. The mine is developed with an adit and pit, and there is similar mineralization at other locations in a two square mile area around the Hermada (Popoff, 1953).

Shoshone County: Kermesite, valentinite and stibnite occur in the Stanley antimony mine in Gorge Gulch above Burke. It forms thin coatings of powder with a deep red to brownish red color. Quartz and minor amounts of gold are associated (Shannon, 1926).

KYANITE

Al_2SiO_5, triclinic

Trimorphous with andalusite and sillimanite. Long tabular crystals; often bladed aggregates. Most often blue, also white, gray or green. An accessory mineral in schist and gneiss. Common associates are staurolite, garnet and corundum.

Shoshone County: Crystals to 2.5 cm are abundant in several areas on the east side of Goat Mountain near the summit and in a belt that extends easterly to Blackdome Peak on the west side of Goat Mountain. There are good exposures of kyanite-bearing mica schist and gneiss along the road to Blackdome Peak. Some of the kyanite is translucent; it is colorless to pale blue and crystals are up to 15 cm in length (Photo. 221). Poor to good quality garnet crystals, staurolite and andalusite occur with the kyanite (Abbott and Prater, 1954; personal).

On Moses Butte, kyanite occurs in rocks north of the peak (Photo. 222). Individual crystals are light blue, mostly around 4 cm long, but some are up to about twice that length. Pinkish red almandine crystals under 2.5 cm occur to the south and large crude granular almandine crystals can be found on the southeast slope of the mountain (personal).

Blue prisms of kyanite up to 3 cm in length occur 2.5 miles south of Trimmed Tree Mountain. The crystals are in a coarse matrix of chlorite, biotite, feldspar and black tourmaline (Shannon, 1926).

Good quality crystals occur in similar rock in an area about 1 mile northwest of Larkins Peak. These are up to 4 cm in length, are brownish red or bluish color and subhedral to euhedral. Many of them have clean bright surfaces. Garnet crystals are abundant in much of the gneiss. Lower quality crystals cover a large area around Larkins and Mallard Peak (Hietanen, 1968).

Kyanite occurs with staurolite in a wide zone around Peggy Peak, Papoose Mountain and Bathtub Mountain. Some of the kyanite is altered to muscovite, especially in the area around Peggy Peak. Muscovite pseudomorphs of kyanite are as much as 35 cm in length (Hietanen, 1962).

LABRADORITE

$(Na,Ca)Al(Al,Si)Si_2O_8$, triclinic

A member of the plagioclase feldspars, with a composition of 50% to 70% anorthite $(CaAl_2Si_2O_8)$ and the remainder albite $(NaAlSi_3O_8)$. Tabular crystals; commonly twinned. Colorless, white or gray; transparent to translucent. Common rock-forming mineral.

Clark County: Gem quality crystals of labradorite can be found in the cinders of Cinder Butte southeast of Spencer. From Spencer, follow the gravel road that runs southeasterly from town for 14.5 miles to paved Clark County highway A-2. The butte can be seen about 3.5 miles to the south and is accessible from the highway via a dirt road 3.2 miles south of the intersection. The north side of the butte has a large pit that has been excavated for cinders.

The butte is a large cinder cone and consists of black and red cinders that vary from about 1 cm across to more than 10 cm across. Labradorite crystals range from less than 1 cm to more than 3 cm in length. Most of them are white and highly fractured, but gem quality crystals and crystal fragments are common. The color of these pieces varies from colorless to bright yellow.

Individual crystals can be found weathered out of the cinders in the dirt along the access road and pit edge and amongst the cinders. Most specimens will be found as broken crystal fragments, but fine quality crystals, mostly twinned, can be found (Photo. 223). These may be coated with red iron oxides. The locality described below is about 15 miles to the southeast (personal).

Fremont County: Labradorite occurs in the black porphyritic rocks of Mac's Butte about 18 miles north of St. Anthony. Crystals are pale yellow and transparent. They average about 5 mm in length but reach a length of 2.5 cm. Crystals are scarce to abundant in a black volcanic rock and loose on the surface of the ground (Shannon, 1926).

LAUMONTITE

$CaAl_2Si_4O_{12} \cdot 4H_2O$, monoclinic

Member of the zeolite group. Generally long prismatic crystals with oblique terminations, fibrous, columnar, radiating or divergent. White, gray, yellowish, pink or brownish transparent to translucent. Often becomes powdery on exposure due to changes from water loss. Common in veins and cavities in basalt and related rocks with other zeolites, also in decomposed granite, pegmatites and in metallic mineral deposits.

Blaine County: Crystals up to 2 mm in length line cavities in a chloritized rock at the

Bellevue King prospect in the Wood River District. They line seams in the rock and form veins up to 2 cm thick which have calcite-filled centers. The crystals are of the common habit (Shannon, 1926).

Boise, Custer and Elmore Counties: Small crystals of laumontite are rare in miarolitic cavities in the Sawtooth Mountains. Small crystals, to about 8 mm long, were abundant in a long, irregular, tube-like cavity in a boulder. The laumontite was at the bases of smoky quartz crystals with albite. The mineral was also found in another cavity (personal).

Custer County: Laumontite is rare in the heulandite-mordenite bearing geodes of the Rat's Nest claim. See the heulandite section for a complete description of the occurrence. The laumontite occurs in clusters of crystals up to about 8 mm long, generally they are white but some are a pale pink color (Photo. 224). Naturally, like all laumontite, they disintegrate as they lose water after exposure (personal).

Kootenai County: Laumontite is reported to have occurred with stilbite, prehnite and other minerals in a fracture in a diabasic rock at Post Falls (Shannon, 1926). This is one of those "lost" localities that probably consisted of an isolated cavity, probably in a dark phase of the migmatites that form the hills and mountains south of Post Falls.

Lemhi County: Laumontite is uncommon in one area of the skarn on Quartzite Canyon in the Spring Mountain District. It has been found as tiny crystals associated with mesolite, natrolite and thomsonite on fracture surfaces (personal).

LEAD

Pb, cubic

Octahedral, dodecahedral or cubic; crystals rare. Usually masses, plates or sheets. Lead-gray color; rare.

Blaine County: In the Jay Gould Mine in the Wood River District in Secs. 15 and 22, T. 2 N., R. 17 E., native lead occurred with minium in masses of galena. The lead formed small rounded grains from 3 to 5 mm in diameter and irregular reniform bunches up to 25 grams in weight. These masses were coated with minium. It also occurred in fractures in quartz which is stained by minium (Shannon, 1926; Umpleby et al, 1930).

Shoshone County: Native lead occurred as stout wires in the Mammoth Mine at Mace. It was associated with galena (Shannon, 1926).

LEADHILLITE

$Pb_4(SO_4)(CO_3)_2(OH)_2$, monoclinic

Dimorphous with susannite. Prismatic crystals that are usually pseudohexagonal and tabular, massive or granular. Colorless to white, gray, pale green, pale blue or yellow. A secondary mineral in oxidized lead deposits with pyromorphite, cerussite, anglesite and linarite.

Blaine County: Leadhillite occurs with other lead minerals including litharge and native lead in the Mineral Hill District near Hailey (Palache, 1944).

Shoshone County: Leadhillite occurred in the Caledonia Mine with cerussite, linarite and possibly caledonite. It formed small irregular masses of a greenish to brownish white color. It also formed minute tabular crystals on galena and chalcopyrite in the Lookout Mountain Mine on Pine Creek. The leadhillite crystals are pseudohexagonal in habit and are coated with or replaced by cerussite (Shannon, 1926).

LEVYNE

$(Ca,Na_2,K_2)_3Al_6Si_{12}O_{36} \cdot 18H_2O$, trigonal

A zeolite group mineral. Crystals thin tabular, sometimes sheaf-like aggregates. Colorless, white, grayish, yellowish or reddish, transparent to translucent. Associated with other zeolites in volcanic rocks.

Ada County: Levyne occurs in cavities in volcanic rock at the Lucky Peak Dam, 10 miles east of Boise. This is the first known occurrence of this mineral in Idaho. Mineralization is both above and below the road. Levyne has been found below the road in the western part of the picnic area. Levyne forms platy crystals to about 4 mm across and less than 1 mm thick. The levyne is colorless and transparent, but the surfaces are white and are coated with submicroscopic fibers of offretite-erionite (Photo. 225). Chabazite, phillipsite and thomsonite can also be found in cavities in these rocks, especially in the eastern part of the picnic area. Calcite and calcite with chabazite are common in the rocks exposed in the roadcuts above the picnic area (Ream, 1991).

Adams County: Levyne is uncommon with other zeolites, apophyllite, calcite and quartz in small cavities in basalts south of Pinehurst. This is the second reported occurrence of this mineral in Idaho (see Ada County above). There are good exposures in roadcuts along this stretch of Highway 95 and many of them contain vesicles lined with zeolites. Levyne has been found in the roadcut about 0.3 miles north of mile post 177. It occurs as white, thin plates, up to about 4 mm across on a druse of tiny, unidentified crystals. It also occurs in the roadcut 0.8 miles north of mile post 177 where it forms plates about 1 mm thick and 2-4 mm across (Photo. 226), two cavities were seen with levyne crystals that extend across the cavities and are up to about 1.2 cm across. Tiny spheres of cowlesite and crystals of phillipsite are associated (personal).

LIBETHENITE

$Cu_2(PO_4)(OH)$, orthorhombic

Libethenite forms short prismatic crystals that are usually poorly formed, also grains and blebs. The fracture is conchoidal to uneven and the luster vitreous. Color varies from light to dark olive green or deep green to black, and it is translucent. It is a secondary mineral that occurs with secondary copper and iron minerals.

Custer County: The Star Group of claims in the Slate Creek area, south of Clayton, consists of four adits located in the Silver Rule Creek drainage. Three are reportedly caved at the portal and one is caved inside. Mineralization consists of quartz and calcite veins that lie at low angles in beds of the Milligen argillite. Brecciation occurs along faults in the mines.

Alteration is intense so that jamesonite and pyrite are the only primary minerals remaining. Secondary minerals include libethenite, azurite, malachite and limonite. The libethenite forms botryoidal crusts of dark green color that coat microfractures (Kern, 1972).

LILLIANITE

$Pb_3Bi_2S_6$, orthorhombic

Prismatic crystals rare; platy crystals, massive granular or radiating fibrous. Steel-gray opaque, metallic. Found in lead-bismuth ore deposits.

Boise County: Lillianite has been reported in the mines of the Quartzburg mineral zone in the Boise Basin, 20 miles northeast of Boise. It occurs with bismuthinite and matildite in vein deposits (Ballard, 1924).

LINARITE

$PbCu(SO_4)(OH)_2$, monoclinic

Elongated prismatic crystals as singles or groups; often forming crusts. Deep azure-blue; translucent. A secondary mineral in oxidized copper and lead ores with malachite, brochantite, cerussite, anglesite, aurichalcite and chrysocolla.

Butte County: Bright blue crusts of intergrown parallel crystals of linarite occur in the Wilbert Mine (formerly Daisy Black) in the Dome District with cerussite and other secondary minerals. It has been reported in the No. 3 tunnel with cerussite and smithsonite (Ross, 1933; Umpleby, 1917).

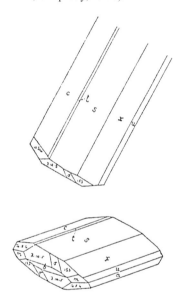

Fig. 16 Linarite, Pacific Mine, Custer County; crystal drawings from Shannon (1926).

Custer County: Linarite forms minute crystals in small vugs in the Pacific Mine in the Bayhorse District. It is deposited from the oxidation of galena and tetrahedrite in white quartz. Most of the linarite does not form euhedral crystals, but some microcrystals have been found in minute cavities (Fig. 16) (Shannon, 1926).

Elmore County: Films, crusts and minute blue crystals of linarite occur sparingly in the Atlanta Mine in the Atlanta District. It is associated with anglesite in cracks in coarse grained argentiferous galena with stephanite and pyrargyrite. The linarite crystals are generally submicroscopic (Anderson, 1939; Shannon, 1926).

Owyhee County: The Monkey Mine in the South Mountain District, contains linarite as stains, crusts and minute blue crystals. Bindheimite is associated in gray anglesite, coating coarse galena. In the Laxey Mine, linarite forms crusts of poorly formed intergrown blue crystals (Shannon, 1926).

Shoshone County: The Caledonia Mine produced some specimens of linarite. These were rosettes up to 1 cm in diameter of flat bladed crystals. They were on a joint surface in a mass of quartzite fragments cemented by cerussite and covellite. Other specimens were of linarite, limonite, leadhillite and caledonite on massive cerussite. The linarite occurred on the cerussite and associated limonite as minute flat prismatic crystals. They were bright blue in color and had a more adamantine luster than the associated azurite that they had been mistaken for. It has also been reported from the Sierra Nevada Mine in Deadwood Gulch, near the Caledonia Mine Shannon, 1926).

The Lookout Mountain Mine on Pine Creek produced some specimens of linarite. These consisted of a fine blue crust of indistinct columnar crystals associated with caledonite, leadhillite and cerussite on galena and chalcopyrite (Shannon, 1926).

A large crystal of linarite was reported from the Hercules Mine at Burke. The crystal was in a cavity in a mass of cerussite (Shannon, 1926).

Tiny to small elongated crystals of linarite were also found at the Sherman Mine (personal).

LINDGRENITE

$Cu_3(MoO_4)_2(OH)_2$, monoclinic

Tabular or platy crystals or massive. Green, yellowish green; in thin plates. Occurs as a secondary mineral with limonite, hematite and copper minerals.

Adams County: Lindgrenite is uncommon in the Helena Mine, northeast of Cuprum, in the Seven Devils District in the SE¼ Sec. 25, T. 21 N., R. 3 W. (Other sources have given the location of the mine as about 3 miles to the north in Sec. 3, at the head of Copper Creek at the Helena town site.) It forms veinlets, crusts and drusy crusts. Some of the veinlets are composed of poorly developed tabular crystals parallel to the vein walls. Some of the drusy crusts consist of fair quality crystals in radiating tabular clusters. The crystals are yellowish green to deep green. Molybdenite, chrysocolla, brochantite and powellite pseudomorphs of molybdenite occur in the same veins. Powellite also forms pale green waxy botryoidal masses in cavities. This occurrence of lindgrenite was the first discovery of it in the United States (1935) and only the second in the world. Mineralization in the Helena Mine is in a tactite along the contact of a diorite and marble (Cannon and Grimaldi, 1953; Cook, 1954).

LITHARGE

PbO, tetragonal

Forms as an alteration product of massicot either as a coating on the massicot or as crusts. Greasy to dull luster; red color; transparent.

Blaine County: Litharge is reported from the Mineral Hill District near Hailey where it occurs with native lead and leadhillite (Palache, 1944).

LUDLAMITE

$(Fe,Mg,Mn)_3(PO_4)_2 \cdot 4H_2O$, monoclinic

Generally prismatic and tabular, sometimes in parallel aggregates or massive or granular. Bright green to apple-green; translucent. A secondary mineral occurring with other phosphate minerals.

Lemhi County: In the Blackbird District, ludlamite occurs with vivianite as tabular crystals and stacks of crystals to about 2 cm high (Photos. 45, 46). Most crystals are about 8 mm to 12 mm across, and occur as tablet-shaped crystals with the c(001) face dominant. Sharp, single crystals, groups and composite crystals on matrix have been collected. It was especially noted in the Blackbird Mine.

Ludlamite is associated with most of the other minerals that occur in the mines of the district, including pyrite, pyrrhotite, chalcopyrite, cobaltite, safflorite, quartz and biotite. Generally ludlamite is found in cavities and thin open fractures in veins in the sulfide ore and siderite. Often it occurs on a crumbly matrix, so specimens must be handled carefully (Glass and Vhay, 1949; personal) .

LUDWIGITE

Mg_2FeBO_5, orthorhombic

Forms a series with vonsenite. Most commonly as fibrous masses, the fibers diverging or interwoven. Sometimes granular or as rosettes of acicular crystals. Black to greenish black. Occurs in contact metamorphic deposits with magnetite, diopside and szaibelyite (commonly an alteration product of ludwigite).

Lemhi County: Very fine specimens of ludwigite occur in the skarn on Quartzite Canyon in the Spring Mountain District and to the west at the head of Bruce Canyon. Generally it occurs as the usual acicular crystals forming groups and tufts, but in one small zone it forms prismatic crystals up to 3 cm across and 6 cm long (Photos. 227, 228). Clusters of crystals 3-6 mm across and 4-6 cm long are common in this area, where they occur frozen in white marble. Most of these crystals are fractured and fall apart when the marble is etched away with a weak acid.

Ludwigite is also associated with magnetite along the road to Bruce Canyon, and at the Bruce Estate magnetite deposit at the top of Bruce Canyon. In these two areas, it forms small crystals with magnetite crystals. The ludwigite is partially to completely altered to an unknown brown mineral. Associated minerals include spinel, forsterite and calcite. Calcite fills the voids where the crystals occur, but a few good quality specimens have been obtained by etching away the calcite with a weak acid. Most often the ludwigite and the magnetite crystals are fractured and fall apart when the calcite is dissolved, but a few good specimens have been collected (Photo. 229) (personal).

MAGNESIOFERRITE

$MgFe_2O_4$, cubic

Member of the spinel group, as small octahedral crystals, granular or massive. Black or brownish black; strongly magnetic. Can be easily mistaken for magnetite and for spinel. An uncommon mineral mostly found in metamorphosed dolostones; in combustion-metamorphosed marls and burning coal piles and in kimberlites and carbonatites.

Lemhi County: Magnesioferrite occurs as crystals in the skarn on Quartzite Canyon in the Spring Mountain District. Crystals occur frozen in marble where it forms lustrous, black, octahedral crystals under 2 mm across (personal).

MAGNETITE

$FeFe_2O_4$, cubic

Forms a series with jacobsite and with magnesioferrite. Commonly forms octahedral crystals; also granular masses. Iron-black; strongly magnetic, may act as a natural magnet. It is a common ore of iron, occurs as an accessory mineral in igneous rocks and is common in crystalline metamorphic rocks.

Boise, Custer and Elmore Counties: Magnetite is rare in the granite of the Sawtooth Mountains. It has been found in a few miarolitic cavities as microcrystals on quartz, albite and microcline. Individual crystals are up to 2 mm across and are modified octahedrons, often rounded. Most have striated surfaces with triangular faces (personal).

Custer County: Magnetite can be found in the contact metamorphic deposits in Custer County, especially in the Mackay District, with garnet and chalcopyrite (Shannon, 1926).

Magnetite occurs in several mines and prospects of the Mackay Mining District south of Mackay. Very good crystals to 1 cm were found in a small prospect pit on "Windy Ridge," high up to the west (Photo. 230). The small dodecahedral crystals are associated with small orange-brown garnet crystals and subhedral yellow green diopside crystals.

Magnetite crystals also occur at the other mines in the main part of the district. It may be associated with calcite and chrysocolla (personal).

Elmore County: Tiny crystals of magnetite occur with microcline, albite and smoky quartz in miarolitic cavities in the Steel Mountain stock. The crystals are generally octahedral, although they are usually intergrown masses with only a few octahedral faces showing, often with triangular markings. The black masses are mostly less than 4 mm across (personal).

Lemhi County: In the McKim Creek iron deposits, 3 miles south of Poison Creek, magnetite occurs as crystals along specular hematite veins. Much of the magnetite is altered to hematite which forms large masses of specular material. The Black Angus deposit is in Secs. 2 and 3, T. 17 N., R. 21 E. Mineralization is in quartzite.

In the Fire Fly claim, in the $SW\frac{1}{4}NW\frac{1}{4}$ Sec. 25, T. 18 N., R. 21 E., magnetite forms octahedrons in a quartz vein. Vugs in the vein are lined with quartz crystals to 2 cm, magnetite octahedrons, pyrite cubes, chalcopyrite and chrysocolla (Soregaroli, 1961; personal).

Magnetite occurs as euhedral crystals in the skarn on Quartzite Canyon in the Spring Mountain District. Crystals can be found as crystals frozen in forsterite and as crystals in cavities in massive magnetite. In the forsterite, the octahedral crystals are generally up to about 1 cm across and are associated with acicular ludwigite.

To the west of the main forsterite zone in Quartzite Canyon, at the head of Bruce Canyon, there is a large magnetite mass on the Bruce Estate claims. The magnetite has cavities that are lined with octahedrons of magnetite. Generally these crystals are under 2 cm across, but may be up to 8 cm; they vary from dull and rough surfaces to rarely lustrous surfaces (Photos. 231, 232). Small crystals of white forsterite or diopside and acicular ludwigite (often replaced by unknown iron oxides or hydroxides) occur with the magnetite crystals. One small layer of calcite with "floater" crystals of magnetite and olive green spherical clusters of very fine acicular ludwigite was seen. Most of the magnetite is pitted and has rough surfaces, but a few good specimens have been obtained by etching out the calcite that fills the magnetite cavities (personal).

The magnetite pod has been developed with a small cut on the upper level, and a road and adit on a lower level about 100 feet below. The adit apparently follows a zone of minor copper mineralization. Small amounts of chrysocolla and malachite can be seen in this zone. Few good specimens have been produced from this deposit. The magnetite is mostly pitted, often fractured and crystals fall apart after the calcite has been etched away (personal).

Washington County: Dodecahedral crystals of magnetite occur in the open pit on Iron Mountain. Crystals occur scattered through the chlorite zones in the pit, but the best crystals were found in a small area in a small massive magnetite pod. Dull crystals line the cavity walls and occasionally project up to form complete or nearly complete dodecahedrons. Most crystals are 1 to 1.5 cm across, but they occur up to about 4 cm. Surfaces vary from dull and rough, to fairly smooth (Photos. 233, 234). Oxidation of the magnetite has damaged the crystals in most cavities. Cavity occurrence in the magnetite mass is irregular and sporadic. Associated minerals in the skarn exposed in the pit includes chlorite, dravite, grossular, phlogopite and quartz (personal).

MALACHITE

$Cu_2(CO_3)(OH)_2$, monoclinic
Prismatic, most crystals are long slender prismatic to acicular, needle-like or fibrous; also forms crusts or coatings. Often replaces azurite. Bright green; translucent. A common mineral found in the oxidized zones of copper-bearing deposits with azurite, native copper, chalcopyrite, pyrite and iron oxides.

Adams County: Malachite was common in the Seven Devils District, second only to chrysocolla. The Arkansaw-Decorah-Marguerite, Peacock and South Peacock mines are principal localities. Most of the malachite occurs as small masses and grains, often mixed with chrysocolla, although there are some acicular groups of small size (Shannon, 1926; personal).

Bannock County: Malachite forms radiating groups and prismatic fibers that form tufts in quartz in the Moonlight tunnel of the Pocatello Gold and Copper Mining Co. in the Fort Hall District. It occurs in copper ore that consists of bornite that is mostly altered to copper pitch (Shannon, 1926).

Bear Lake County: In the Humming Bird Mine in Paris Canyon in the Bear River Range, in Sec. 1(?), T. 13 S., R. 42 E., malachite forms radially fibrous masses. Some of it is scattered through quartz which has been stained red by hematite. The veins consist of brecciated quartz and contain jasperoid, and tetrahedrite and azurite are associated (Mansfield, 1927; Shannon, 1926).

The Bonanza claim (also known as the Duke claim) in Sec. 10, T. 14 S., R. 45 E., has produced some malachite. This has been found in an inclined shaft about 0.25 mile south of the main Bonanza shaft. The malachite forms seams and veins, some of it in or associated with fossil wood that has been replaced by chalcocite.

This is part of a north-south mineralized zone that runs north from T. 11 S. to T. 14 S., R. 45 E., a few miles northeast, east and southeast of Montpelier. Numerous prospects have been excavated in green, maroon and brown shales of the Triassic age "Red Bed" sedimentary rocks. Green malachite staining is common on fracture and bedding surfaces and is concentrated in carbonized wood in the sediments. Chalcocite and some covellite also occurs with the carbonized wood. Occasionally, the malachite forms small acicular crystals (Gale, 1910; Mansfield, 1927).

Blaine County: Malachite occurs as stains and crusts in the Copper Bluff prospect in Basinger Canyon, northeast of Clyde. It is associated with azurite and chrysocolla (Shannon, 1926).

Clark County: Needle-like crystals of malachite occur in vugs in the veins of the Weimer Copper Co. Mine in the Skull Canyon District 2 miles east of the old site of Kaufman.

Some of the crystals are well-terminated prisms, either stout or acicular These may form radial clusters of bright green crystals more than 5 mm in length, as tufts or radial groups. Common are flat lying crystals, crusts and masses coating fractures (Photo. 235-237). Azurite is associated as thin crusts coating fractures or rarely groups or hemispheres of bladed crystals (Shannon, 1926; personal).

Custer County: Velvety crusts and botryoidal coatings of malachite occur in the Ramshorn and Hoosier mines in the Bayhorse District. These crusts are in cavities in partly oxidized tetrahedrite and gossan and may be associated with chalcopyrite, bindheimite and azurite (Shannon, 1926; personal).

In the Turtle Mine, in Sec. 14, T. 12 N., R. 18 E., malachite and azurite form drusy coatings of microscopic crystals and masses in cavities. Mineralization is in a quartz vein; galena and tetrahedrite are associated (Pontius, 1982).

Small tufts of malachite occur in cavities on quartz with cerussite and other minerals in the small zone of mineralized breccia in the small cut near the top of Keystone Mountain. The cut is a prospect in a fluorite-bearing breccia deposit and one small area shows minor mineralization with oxidized metallic minerals. Azurite, quartz and unidentified micro minerals are also associated (personal).

There is a similar occurrence down the mountain on the north side at the old silver mines. Here malachite occurs as tufts and groups of fine acicular crystals associated with chrysocolla pseudomorphs of malachite and several other secondary minerals with quartz and fluorite. These are all of micro size (personal).

Along the Salmon River, about one mile east of Spud Creek, downstream of Clayton tiny crystals of malachite form coatings in the oxidized vein material with chalcopyrite in a prospect. The small adit is located about 250 feet above the river, on the south side. The minerals are tiny and suitable for micro specimens only (personal).

Latah County: Malachite occurs in the Pinnel vein of the Gold Hill Mine in the Gold Hill Mining District, about 3 miles northeast of Harvard. The mine is at the head of Jack Gulch and is the most extensively developed mine in the district. The Pinnel vein has been opened on two levels. Malachite forms thin coatings and acicular crystals that commonly occur in tuft-like clusters and rosettes lining cavities. The rosettes and tufts are up to 1 cm across; azurite, chrysocolla and cuprite are associated. The mines and prospects of this area are heavily overgrown with most workings caved and the small dumps hidden in the vegetation (Faich, 1937; personal).

Lemhi County: In the Spring Mountain District, malachite occurs sparingly in the western adit of the Iron Mask Mine. It was found as micro prismatic crystals coating fracture surfaces on dolomite. Minor amounts of chrysocolla were associated (personal).

To the west, malachite was found on the dumps of the two shafts of the Hope prospects. Here it occurred in quartz with specular hematite and quartz crystals. The malachite formed small masses in tiny cavities, radial groups in the cavities and rarely excellent single transparent rhombic crystals in the cavities (Photos. 238, 239). Minor coatings of chrysocolla are associated. The cavities are lined with tiny quartz crystals and the malachite is perched on, and sometimes included in, the quartz. Very little malachite was found on these dumps (personal).

Malachite occurs with azurite, brochantite and cyanotrichite in the Junction District. In the Iron Dike Mine on the east side of Stroud Gulch, it occurs as thick coatings and crusts, granular masses and fibrous masses in gossan. Little malachite is exposed in the pit, but an occasional specimen has been found on the dump. Malachite sometimes replaces small crystals of azurite or rarely cuprite (Photo. 240-242). The amount of malachite and other minerals was small. There is very little mineralization showing in the pit walls and only an occasional piece can be found on the dumps. The small adit is in barren gray limestone (personal).

Malachite can be found at the Blue Jay Mine, west of Leadore, on Big Eightmile Creek, with malachite and chrysocolla. The mine is developed as an open pit and several cuts that expose a copper-mineralized breccia in diorite. This same type of mineralization is exposed in a couple of areas down the ridge along the access road. There appears to be more chrysocolla in the lower zones.

Malachite forms thin layers (Photo. 243) with similar azurite, and thicker layers of chrysocolla. Large surfaces of malachite and chrysocolla can be found, but most of the azurite occurs as patches only 1-2 cm across. In the upper pit of the mine, a black coating (tenorite or melaconite?) covers much of the other minerals. The mine is accessible by a road from the Big Eightmile Creek road a couple of miles before the campground at the end of the road (personal).

Malachite forms thin seams and coatings on fracture surfaces in the oxidized portions of the copper-bearing deposits in the Blackbird District. It was especially common in the oxidized ores of the Black Pine Mine where it formed botryoidal masses and acicular crystals (Purdue, 1975; personal).

Owyhee County: Microcrystals of malachite occur with azurite, calcite, cerussite, covellite and other secondary minerals in the oxidized portions of the ore bodies of the Laxey Mine and nearby mines on South Mountain. Malachite forms elongated to fibrous crystals and microcrystalline crusts that often coat other minerals (Photo. 244) (personal).

Shoshone County: Malachite occurs at the Hansy Mine. The adits of this mine are located on the west side of Olentange Creek, a tributary of Loop Creek. Malachite forms typical fine green needles and masses in gossan (Photos. 245, 246) (personal).

Malachite occurs as tufts and acicular crystals in the oxidized ores of the Monitor Mine north of the Hansy Mine near the Montana border. The tufts and radiating groups of micro crystals (Photo. 247) are associated with aurichalcite, azurite, chrysocolla, chrysocolla ps. of malachite, zalesiite and a pale green unknown mineral that rarely forms microscopic hemispheres of tiny needles. Malachite is locally abundant (personal).

Several mines in the Coeur d'Alene District produced malachite, but few of them contained any that were noteworthy as specimens. The Caledonia Mine produced fibrous or mammillary malachite with cerussite and cuprite and acicular crystals in spongy limonite. Thin coatings of malachite colored cerussite green. Radiating acicular malachite occurred in limonite in the Hypotheek Mine (Shannon, 1926).

The Empire (Horst-Powell) Mine and Handspike mines, north of Kingston, on the Little North Fork of the Coeur d'Alene River have produced specimens of malachite. These have radiating acicular prisms embedded in soft limonite or on quartz and masses of compact acicular crystals (Photos. 248, 249). Individual crystals are rarely up to 1 cm or more in length and clusters may be a few centimeters across. Crusts of compact malachite have also been reported from this mine. Small amounts of other copper minerals also have been noted; much of the dumps of this mine have been washed away by waters of the Coeur d'Alene River (Shannon, 1926; personal).

Valley County: At the Red Metal Mine, south of Profile Gap, malachite occurs with azurite, cerussite, silver and other unidentified secondary minerals. The malachite forms tufts and compact masses of fibers. Silver forms microscopic sheets and wires and the other secondary minerals form tiny crystals (personal).

Washington County: Coatings and rare crystals of malachite can be found in the skarn deposits on upper Brownlee Creek. Associated minerals include quartz (as crude white crystals), garnet and chrysocolla (personal).

MALDONITE

Au_2Bi, cubic

Forms octahedral crystals, granular masses and thin coatings. Pinkish silver-white but tarnishes to copper-red to black. Occurs in veins and other deposits with gold, scheelite and apatite.

Custer County: Maldonite was reported at the Empire Mine in Washington Basin (Shannon, 1926).

MANDARINOITE

$Fe_2Se_3O_9 \cdot 6H_2O$, monoclinic

Known from only four localities in the world. Yellowish green crystalline aggregates. Microcrystals in silver deposits with chlorargyrite and quartz.

Owyhee County: Mandarinoite forms yellowish green crystalline aggregates with chlorargyrite and quartz in the silver ores of the DeLamar Mine. Specimens were found on the 6316-foot bench of this open-pit mine, near level 2 of the pre-1916 underground workings. This bench has been mined out, and no mandarinoite has been found elsewhere in the mine.

The mandarinoite occurred in open veinlets, where it formed pale lime-green crystals up to 0.5 mm in length. Crystals were in subparallel groups and isolated radiating rosette-like clusters up to 1.5 mm in diameter on drusy quartz (Photos. 250, 251). Most crystals were bright, shiny and transparent; others have some dull, frosted faces. The crystals are elongate parallel to [001] and slightly flattened on {100}. Twinning with (100) as the twin plane and the composition plane occurs in most crystals. Only three forms are known: a{100}, m{110} and d{011}.

Chlorargyrite occurs as smooth, rounded, irregular masses and as rounded cubic crystals with a pinkish brown color on both the quartz and the mandarinoite. Other secondary minerals in the mine include goethite, silver, covellite and copper. The primary minerals are pyrite, marcasite, naumannite, aguilarite, acanthite, pyrargyrite, miargyrite, chalcopyrite, sphalerite and gold. Mineralization is in northwest-trending siliceous veins in a quartz-feldspar rhyolite porphyry of middle Miocene age (Lasmanis et al, 1981).

MARCASITE

FeS_2, orthorhombic
Crystals tabular, often twinned forming cockscomb groups; usually in radiating forms or reniform. Pale bronze-yellow to almost white; tarnishes yellow to brown. In veins with lead and zinc minerals.

Lemhi County: Spherical nodules of marcasite occur in Tertiary beds of loosely cemented clayey sandstone 1 mile south of Salmon. The nodules are up to 4 cm across. Most specimens are dull on the outside and show a granular but weakly radiating structure inside (Shannon, 1926; Umpleby, 1913a).

MARIALITE

$3NaAlSi_3O_8 \cdot NaCl$, tetragonal
Scapolite group mineral; most minerals of the scapolite group are intermediate in composition. Marialite and meionite crystals prismatic, granular and massive. Colorless, white, gray, pink, violet or other colors; transparent to opaque. Occurs in regionally metamorphosed rocks, marbles, calcareous gneisses, granulites and greenschist, also in skarns and pegmatites.

See "Scapolite" for locality descriptions; most scapolite specimens have not been identified by species in Idaho.

MASSICOT

PbO, orthorhombic
Dimorphous with litharge. Massive, earthy to scaly; yellow, reddish yellow. Translucent. An oxidation product of lead ore deposits; associated with galena, secondary lead minerals, copper or antimony minerals and iron oxides.

Shoshone County: Massicot forms thin coatings of micrograins and scales on oxidized ores of the Bunker Hill Mine. Specimens of cerussite and anglesite crystals often have thin coatings with a light yellow or greenish yellow color. It also is likely to have been present in several other mines. Shannon (1926) reported bindheimite in Mammoth, Last Chance, Tyler, Caledonia, Northern Light, Lookout Mountain, Carbonate and Hypotheek mines. More recent studies indicate that the bindheimite is probably all massicot (Radford and Crowley, 1981; personal).

MASUTOMILITE

$K(Li,Al,Mn)_3(Si,Al)_4O_{10}(F,OH)_2$, monoclinic

Mica group, known in only a few localities in the world, including in Japan and Czechoslovakia. Typical mica habit, purplish pink or yellow to golden brown. Occurs in granitic rocks with smoky quartz, microcline and zinnwaldite.

Boise, Custer and Elmore Counties: Masutomilite occurs in miarolitic cavities in the granite of the Sawtooth batholith. Studies indicate that masutomilite is fairly common. The micas in the cavities in the Sawtooth batholith are generally either or both of two micas, zinnwaldite as dark brown to green crystals, and masutomilite as golden to golden brown crystals, typically as zoned crystals with the two intergrown. Individual crystals are well-formed, occurring as books up to 5 cm across and 2 cm in length, although they are generally weathered and cleaved. Masutomilite is associated with albite, microcline, smoky quartz, topaz and other minerals (personal).

MATILDITE

$AgBiS_2$, hexagonal

Usually massive or granular; rarely prismatic crystals. Iron-black to gray. In metallic ore deposits with galena, sphalerite, tetrahedrite, pyrite and chalcopyrite.

Boise County: Matildite has been reported from some of the mines in the Quartzburg mineral zone in the Boise Basin, 20 miles northeast of Boise. It is associated with bismuthinite and lillianite in vein deposits (Ballard, 1924).

MEIONITE

$3CaAl_2Si_2O_8 \cdot CaCO_3$, tetragonal

Scapolite group mineral; most minerals of the scapolite group are intermediate in composition. Same characteristics as marialite: crystals prismatic, granular and massive. Colorless, white, gray, pink, violet or other colors; transparent to opaque. Occurs in regionally metamorphosed rocks, marbles, calcareous gneisses, granulites and greenschist, also in skarns and pegmatites.

Lemhi County: Tiny crystals of meionite have been identified with magnetite and diopside in the skarn along Quartzite Canyon in the Spring Mountain District. These were found in fractures in the massive skarn (personal).

MELANTERITE

$FeSO_4 \cdot 7H_2O$, monoclinic

Green; soluble in water. Crystals are equant to short prismatic, thick tabular or octahedral; most often pulverulent aggregates, crusts, stalactitic or fibrous. A widespread, common mineral formed as a weathering product of pyrite and marcasite; found as an efflorescence in pyrite-bearing orebodies.

Butte County: Melanterite has been found in the Last Chance Mine on Champagne Creek, Sec. 15, T., 3 N., R. 24 E., with large crystals of barite. Pyrite and other sulfides have been found (Anderson, 1929).

MESOLITE

$Na_2Ca_2Al_6Si_9O_{30} \cdot H_2O$, monoclinic

Member of zeolite group. Generally in fine, acicular crystals with square cross section; often in groups radiating from a common point, or crusts lining cavities. Colorless to white. Brittle. Found in volcanic rocks with other zeolites.

Adams County: Mesolite is commonly the white acicular zeolite associated with other zeolites along Highway 95 in an area south of Pinehurst. This area is described under analcime and gyrolite. Small cavities contain fine acicular or hair-like crystals of mesolite, often in hemispherical groups, associated with other zeolites and other minerals (Photo. 252) (personal).

Boise County: Very thin needles of mesolite occur in cavities in basalt along Highway 55 in a roadcut and small pit on private land, about 1 mile north of Gardena. Calcite, chabazite, stilbite and thomsonite are associated (personal).

Custer County: Mesolite occurs in cavities in sandy sediments interbedded with volcanic rocks in an undisclosed area near Challis. The mesolite lines cavities as fine hairs and is associated with stilbite and possibly other zeolites (Photo. 253). Individual crystals are up to about 1.5 cm in length (personal).

Idaho County: In the basalts along Race Creek, on private ranch land, mesolite lines cavities and is associated with calcite and stilbite. Mesolite crystals are mostly under 1 cm long (Photo. 254), but have been reported to large size. A large cavity, 3 x 4 x 6 feet, was reported to have been found lined with mesolite to 5 cm in length. In much of this area, where there are cavities, they are under 6 inches across and the zeolites are all small. The zeolites occur in outcrops of the Columbia river basalts (personal).

Mesolite may also occur on the east side of the Little Salmon River across from the zeolite occurrences listed for Adams County in the area south of Pinehurst. See the analcime and gyrolite listings for more information (personal).

Lemhi County: Mesolite is uncommon in one area of the skarn zone along Quartzite Canyon. It has been found as 1.2 cm crystals in radiating groups on fracture surfaces and in thin veinlets (personal)

METACINNABAR

HgS, cubic

Dimorphous with cinnabar. Massive or tetrahedral. Grayish black. Associated with cinnabar, stibnite, marcasite, native mercury, realgar, calcite and barite.

Blaine County: Small spherical globules of metacinnabar occur on cinnabar, coating cavities in the Dockwell tunnel near the head of Deer Creek in the Hailey District. These black globules are less than 1 mm in diameter (Shannon, 1926).

METAVARISCITE

$AlPO_4 \cdot 2H_2O$, monoclinic

Dimorphous with variscite. Crystals minute, thin to thick tabular, slightly elongated or tabular. Pale green, transparent to translucent. Forms from the weathering of phosphatic rocks.

Fremont County: Metavariscite occurs with variscite on a ridge on the south side of

Two Top Creek northeast of Mack's Inn. Variscite forms nodules and masses from a few centimeters to several centimeters across. Many of them have narrow cavities or fractures that are lined with tiny micro crystals of metavariscite and some variscite. The crystals are medium green and translucent to transparent and up to about 3 mm across (Photo. 255, 348). Carbonate-apatite and wardite are uncommon associations. The occurrence is claimed and being mined for gem variscite nodules (personal communications).

MIARGYRITE

$AgSbS_2$, monoclinic

Thick tabular crystals, deeply striated or massive. Iron-black to steel-gray; thin splinters are translucent and deep blood-red color. In veins with galena, pyrite, calcite, barite, quartz and other silver minerals.

Boise County: Miargyrite crystals were found with silver, proustite, pyrargyrite, owyheeite, tetrahedrite, chalcopyrite, galena, sphalerite, gold, quartz and calcite in the veins of the Crown Point and Banner mines in the Banner District on Banner Creek. The mines are at an elevation of 6,000 feet at the headwaters of the creek, which is a tributary of the Boise River. Mineralization is in narrow veins filling fissures in Tertiary porphyry dikes cutting the Idaho batholith.

Most of the minerals form minute to coarse grains and masses. Rarely they form minute crystals on drusy quartz. The silver has only been reported from the lower levels of the Banner Mine (Anderson and Rasor, 1934).

Custer County: Some very fine euhedral crystals of miargyrite occur in the mines of the Yankee Fork District on the Yankee Fork of the Salmon River in T. 12-13 N., R. 15 E. These are with pyrargyrite, acanthite, chlorargyrite, covellite, malachite, azurite, silver and gold (Anderson, 1949; Cass, 1973).

Elmore County: Small black crystals of miargyrite have been found on quartz druses in mines in the Atlanta District. The crystals were associated with pyrargyrite, silver, acanthite and chalcopyrite (Anderson, 1939).

Owyhee County: Miargyrite occurs in many of the mines of the Silver City District. It has been especially plentiful in the Flint and Trade Dollar-Black Jack vein on War Eagle Mountain. In the Henrietta Mine, it forms crusts of crystals on quartz. The well-formed crystals average more than 2 mm across and are dull or heavily striated. Crystals in the Henrietta Mine were steel-black with a metallic luster (Fig. 17). Crusts of microcrystals, mostly less than 3 mm across, often on quartz, were generally dull and etched, and the following forms have been identified a(100), m(101), t(111), d(311), c(001), s(211), k(124) (Asher 1967; Piper and Laney, 1926; Shannon, 1926).

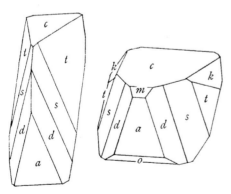

Fig. 17 Miargyrite, Henrietta Mine, Owyhee County; crystal drawings from Shannon (1926).

MICROCLINE

$KAlSi_3O_8$, triclinic

Dimorphous with orthoclase. Prismatic with angles close to those of orthoclase; commonly twinned on the Carlsbad law, but less commonly on the Baveno and Manebach laws. White to pale yellow; rarely green or bluish green (known as amazonite). Translucent to transparent. A common rock-forming mineral in igneous rocks, especially pegmatites. Associated with plagioclase feldspars and quartz.

Boise, Custer and Elmore Counties: Microcline is common in miarolitic cavities, in both the granite and pegmatites, in the Sawtooth Mountains. It forms light pink to medium pink, and sometimes white, crystals generally to about 2 cm. Larger crystals to at least 10 cm are uncommon. The larger crystals may be fresh and sharp, but most often they are partially altered, full of holes or parting along the cleavage planes. Some of the potassium feldspar crystals in the cavities are orthoclase, but most are microcline. Albite, smoky quartz, muscovite, zinnwaldite, masutomilite, topaz, spessartine and aquamarine are associated.

Untwinned crystals are most numerous, but Baveno twins are common, Manebach twins are less common, and Carlsbad twins and combinations have been found. The Manebach twins often form a chevron termination. Some plates of pink microcline consist of numerous curved crystals lying on their sides; albite may be present forming white crystals between the microcline crystals. Microcline can be found throughout the Sawtooth batholith, but it is a minor mineral in most aquamarine cavities. It is usually pink and a major mineral in topaz cavities. It is associated with most of the other minerals (personal).

Camas County: Microcline (not positively identified, may be orthoclase) occurs in the small miarolitic cavities in the Soldier Mountain stock of Smoky Dome northwest of Fairfield. These white to pink crystals are up to at least 4 cm high. All crystals seen have pitted and etched faces. Albite, epidote, magnetite, prehnite and smoky quartz crystals are sometimes perched on the microcline. Cavities are uncommon in the granites of this stock, and are small (personal).

Cassia County: Microcline crystals are uncommon in cavities in the granitic rocks of the City of Rocks, southeast of Oakley. Crystals of microcline to several centimeters have been found in miarolitic cavities in pegmatites and in the rock. Small smoky quartz crystals are associated. The rock outcrops are weathered and rounded, and most exposed cavities are weathered out, rounded and empty (personal).

Kootenai County: Brilliant white crystals of microcline have been found in cavities in pegmatite in the Precambrian gneiss on Red Hog, a large hill southwest of Coeur d'Alene. Crystals have been found that are up to 6 cm in length and twinned on the Baveno law. Commonly they are sharp with clean faces. Smoky quartz and beryl have been found with the microcline. Cavities are scarce in the pegmatites that may be exposed in roadcuts on the hill. The hill is heavily vegetated and the roadcuts are old, slumped and overgrown. There are very few outcrops, and there is a small potential for more material in the area (personal).

A similar occurrence is a few miles to the northwest along Cougar Gulch. Cavities are scarce in pegmatites along the roads of the area (personal).

Lemhi County: Fine crystals of microcline can be found in the area where aquamarine occurs in the Crags batholith in the Yellowjacket Mountains between Yellowjacket Lake and Golden Trout Lake and westerly into the Bighorn Crags. Crystals and occurrences are similar to those of the Sawtooth Mountains. In this area, outcrops are less common and are generally weathered and rounded. Few cavities remain intact; most are weathered smooth and rounded.

A few cavities still contain microcline crystals that are white and have brilliant surfaces. These form untwinned crystals and Baveno, Manebach and Carlsbad twins up to at least 5 cm in length (Photo. 256, 257). Other microcline crystals are pink, and are commonly somewhat to severely altered and etched. A few fine specimens have been found in the miarolitic cavities with smoky quartz, muscovite and albite. Aquamarine and topaz may also be associated, but are rare (personal).

Shoshone County: White to pinkish crystals occur in the rocks of one of the Gem stocks in Ninemile Creek. The occurrence is near the Success Mine on a point of the hill. Most crystals are about 2.5 cm in length and are Carlsbad twins. They are phenocrysts frozen in the monzonite of the stock (Shannon, 1926).

MIMETITE

$Pb_5(AsO_4)_3Cl$, monoclinic (pseudohexagonal)

Pseudohexagonal, prismatic in rounded barrel-shaped forms or spindle-shaped. Sometimes acicular, reniform or botryoidal. Yellow to yellowish brown, orange-yellow, orange-red, brownish red or grayish; transparent to translucent. A secondary mineral in the oxidized portion of lead deposits associated with pyromorphite, smithsonite, anglesite, malachite, wulfenite and mottramite.

Bear Lake County: Light yellow-green micro crystals of mimetite have been found at the Blackstone Mine west of Montpelier (Photo. 258). The tiny crystals are rare, scattered on matrix in the oxide ores with pyromorphite, wulfenite and cerussite (Mansfield, 1927; Richards, 1910; Shannon, 1926).

Custer County: Hexagonal prismatic crystals of mimetite were found in the Ramshorn Mine in the Bayhorse District. These minute crystals were yellow in color and occurred on cerussite in cavities in the galena-tetrahedrite ore. Most of them were replaced by bayldonite (Shannon, 1926).

Lemhi County: Mimetite has recently been identified in a selection of secondary minerals from the Ima Mine. Here it occurs as tiny colorless to cream colored acicular or prismatic crystals in parallel to radiating groups. Crystal length is generally under 1 mm (Photos. 259-261). Most crystals have a yellow to brown coating of bindheimite and segnitite, and may occur on bayldonite but generally they are on quartz. Malachite, azurite and other secondary minerals are associated (personal).

MINIUM

Pb_2PbO_4, tetragonal

Uncommonly in microscopic crystalline scales, generally massive or earthy. Scarlet-red or brownish red, may have a yellowish tint. A secondary mineral formed from the alteration of galena or cerussite.

Blaine County: Minium was found in the Jay Gould Mine and other mines of the Wood River District. It coated native lead or occurred in quartz with native lead. It was also found in the oxidized zone of the Plughof (Lark) Mine, 2 miles southwest of Bellevue (Shannon, 1926).

Custer County: Minium has been reported in the upper portion of the Beardsley vein in the Bayhorse District (Shannon, 1926).

Lemhi County: Fine specimens of minium occur with plattnerite and siderite in the Democrat Mine near Gilmore. It forms a bright red powder in small cavities in oxidized ore near the surface of the Pittsburgh-Idaho Mine in the Texas District (Shannon, 1926).

Owyhee County: Dusty, bright red crystals of minium have been reported from the Golconda Mine on South Mountain. These microcrystals are associated with anglesite cerussite and bindheimite in an oxidized lead ore (Sorenson, 1927).

Shoshone County: Minium was found with galena in the Silver Dollar claim in Idaho Gulch 2 miles east of Murray (Shannon, 1926).

MOLYBDENITE

MoS_2, hexagonal

Tabular hexagonal crystals sometimes tapering or barrel-shaped prisms. Most often foliated or massive; lead-gray. An accessory mineral in many granites and pegmatites or in vein deposits with wolframite, scheelite and fluorite.

Boise, Custer and Elmore Counties: Molybdenite is rare in the Sawtooth Mountains, and has been found in small quantities in only about three locations. It occurs as small flakes with the typical gray color, up to about 1 cm across (personal).

Boundary County: Molybdenite forms rosettes up to 1 cm in diameter in quartz with muscovite in a prospect 21 miles southwest of Porthill. Crusts of molybdite are replacing some of the molybdenite (Shannon, 1926). This occurrence is probably the one in the area of Phoebe Tip.

On the north side of the peak, at the Parker Molybdenum Mine in Secs. 16 and 21, T. 64 N., R. 4 W., molybdenite occurs in a quartz-molybdenite-sericite-dike. An adit and an inclined shaft have been developed on the dike. To the south, at the International Molybdenum Co. Mine in Sec. 27, T. 64 N., R. 4 W., a similar occurrence has been prospected.

Molybdenite is reported to occur with cassiterite in pegmatitic quartz dikes, and cassiterite is disseminated in biotite granodiorite and in aplite dikes. The cassiterite generally forms small elbow twinned crystals, mostly around 0.2 mm across. The molybdenite forms large subhedral to euhedral crystals as plates and rosettes (Baker, 1979).

Molybdenite occurs near Copeland near the road to the Dora and Tungsten Hill mines, perhaps in Sec. 9, T. 64 N., R. 1 E. (Livingston, 1919).

Custer County: Molybdenite crystals to 2 cm have been found at the White Mountain prospect. They are scattered through quartz veins in quartz monzonite. The prospect is at the 9,000 foot level on the south side of Summit Creek in Sec. 20, T. 6 N., R. 19 E. It is reached from the junction of Little Fall and Summit Creeks by hiking about 1 mile south to the outer end of a north-facing cirque (Kirkemo et al, 1965).

A similar occurrence is on the Anda or Walton Moly claim group about 1.5 miles northwest of the mouth of Little Fall Creek at an elevation of 8,300 feet. Quartz veins with molybdenite can be found in Tertiary quartz monzonite, Paleozoic sediments (argillites and slate) and aplite dikes. The veins with molybdenite are 20 to 40 feet in length, and contain molybdenite as rosettes up to 2 cm or more across (Kirkemo et al, 1965; Tuchek and Ridenour, 1981).

Small molybdenite crystals occur in quartz in a breccia zone in quartz monzonite in a prospect on the south side of Washington Basin. The small crystals and masses are up to at least 6 mm across; small grains and masses of pyrite and galena are associated. Small stilbite crystals coat cavities in the breccia. The prospect is on the north facing valley wall east of the old mill site (personal).

Elmore County: Molybdenite occurs in the Rinebold and Decker-Hortenstine mines in the Rocky Bar District along Roaring River. It forms scales and flakes that occur singly or form masses along quartz veins and intrusive dikes in granite. Pyrite, phlogopite-biotite, chalcopyrite, sphalerite, fluorite and calcite are associated. Molybdite is uncommon, but wulfenite is associated at the Rinebold Mine.

The Rinebold Mine is on the East Fork of Roaring River about 0.3 mile above its mouth at 5,500 to 6,000 feet elevation. Adits, cuts and pits have been dug on the property. Wulfenite has been found in two adits on the west side of the East Fork about 60 to 110 feet above the river. The Decker-Hortenstine Mine is on Roaring River about 2 miles upstream from the East Fork at 7,000 feet elevation, and another prospected area is on the south branch of the East Fork (Schrader, 1924).

Idaho County: Molybdenite forms rosettes up to about 2.5 cm across in prospects south of Josephine Lake, on the north side of Squaw Point in Sec. 28, T. 22 N., R. 4 E. The prospects are at about 7,800 feet elevation, above and to the southwest of two tarns. Crystals have a rough hexagonal shape; mineralization is in a dark red-brown skarn (personal).

Lemhi County: Molybdenite occurs at the Missouri Belle Mine near the Montana border, northwest of North Fork. Sharp hexagonal molybdenite crystals occur frozen in quartz and as groups in cavities in quartz. Most common, are subhedral crystals and crystalline masses frozen in quartz or in cavities (Photo. 262). Molybdenite is associated with ferrimolybdite and with pyrite. Often it surrounds pyrite or is included in pyrite (personal).

MOLYBDITE

MoO_3, orthorhombic

Fibrous, flattened needles or thin platy crystals; generally in masses and aggregates. Crystals may be elongated and striated parallel to the c axis. Dark gray to canary yellow, greenish yellow or green; sometimes nearly colorless. An oxidation product of molybdenite; in quartz veins and other deposits with molybdenite.

Adams County: Olive green earthy molybdite is associated with powellite in the Peacock Mine in the Seven Devils District. It occurs in a rock that consists mostly of garnet with bornite, and probably is an alteration product of the powellite (Shannon, 1926).

Boundary County: Thick silky pale yellow films and crusts of molybdite coat quartz in diorite at the Parker Mountain Mine 21 miles by trail southwest of Porthill. Molybdenite is associated (Shannon, 1926).

MONAZITE

$(Ce,La,Nd,Th)PO_4$, monoclinic

Now recognized as two minerals—monazite-(Ce) and monazite-(La). Flattened or elongated crystals. Yellowish or reddish brown to brown; may be shades of yellow, greenish or nearly white. Subtranslucent to translucent. An accessory mineral in granitic rocks and gneissic metamorphic rocks. Often in the alluvial and colluvial deposits formed from these.

Boise County: Small crystals of monazite can be collected in the gravels of the streams in the Idaho City and Centerville areas of the Boise Basin. Most crystals are well-formed and are golden-yellow to amber or orange-brown in color. They average less than 1 mm across, but some crystals are as large as 5 mm. During gold placer mining it was noted in some quantity with the gold, ilmenite, magnetite and zircon. It can be panned out of the gravels or, in some areas, the granitic soils of the valley sides (Shannon, 1926).

Boise, Custer and Elmore Counties: Monazite occurs as microcrystals in aggregates to about 2 mm across in the Sawtooth Mountains. These have been found in one cavity and were yellow in color (personal).

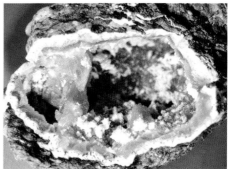

Photo. 213 Heulandite-Ca and mordenite in a small geode with a blue chalcedony lining, 4.4 cm across, Rat's Nest claim, Custer County.

Photo. 212 Heulandite-Ca lining a geode 20 cm across, Rat's Nest claim, Custer County.

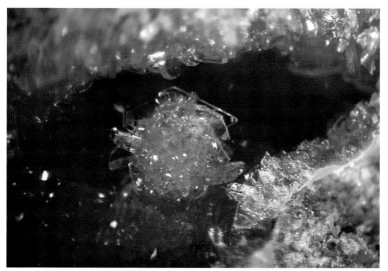

Photo. 214 Heulandite-Na lining a cavity 2 cm across, Rat's Nest claim, Custer County.

Photo. 215 Heulandite-Na, microcrystals, near 2nd Street, Challis, Custer County.

Clearwater County: Yellow crystals of monazite, similar to those of Boise County, can be found in the placer deposits in the Pierce area. Titanite is associated in sand concentrates that consist of ilmenite and pink garnets (Shannon, 1926).

Lemhi County: Monazite crystals up to 2 cm in length occur in a pegmatite dike in gneiss on the Snowdrift claim about 0.5 mile north of the Salmon River on the east side of a small gulch. This is 3 miles east of Shoup in Sec. 16, T. 24 N., R. 19 E. The crystals are in the two to four and a half foot thick intermediate zone of a dike in the upper cut of the prospect (Trites and Tooker, 1953).

Anhedral to euhedral crystals can be found in the metamorphic rocks of a mineralized belt that is 1.5 miles wide by 18 miles long and extends from the canyon of Dump Creek, about 4 miles below the town of North Fork, northwesterly into Montana. The Silver King Mine is one of the best localities. Most crystals are less than 1.7 cm long, but some are larger. They are a honey-brown to reddish color and are mildly radioactive. They occur with rutile, allanite, garnet, actinolite and other minerals. The crystals are more prevalent in the deposits to the west end of the belt (Anderson, 1958).

MORDENITE

$(Ca,Na_2,K_2)Al_2Si_{10}O_{24} \cdot 7H_2O$, orthorhombic

A member of the zeolite group. In fibrous masses or hair-like to needle-like crystals. Colorless to white or pinkish; translucent. A secondary mineral in volcanic rocks associated with other zeolites, calcite and quartz.

Custer County: Mordenite occurs with heulandite, analcime, calcite, quartz and chlorite in Miocene age volcanic rocks interbedded with lake sediments about 15 miles south of Challis. It forms felted aggregates, radial fibrous masses and compact porcelaneous masses. The cottony felted masses are the most abundant and are up to 30 cm in diameter. These occur in vesicles that are lined with a crust of small heulandite crystals. A thin shell of chalcedony is often deposited on the heulandite. The occurrence has received little interest from collectors in recent years and is not known to produce good specimens of any of these minerals (Shannon, 1926; personal).

In the same area, very fine mordenite specimens have been found at a new discovery at what is now the Rat's Nest claim. Here mordenite, often reported as the best in the world, has been recovered in specimens with mordenite "hairs" to over 2.5 cm long on and associated with heulandite-Ca (Photo. 263-265). Specimens of both minerals or of mordenite only have been collected at the locality. The cavities have been seen up to 3 feet across, but are most common under 1 foot across. Sometimes the mordenite forms mounds or stalactitic growths.

The cavities may also contain calcite, especially of the argentine habit, which may be large plates that span the cavities. The plates typically are white and are most often in parallel groups or occasionally as individual plates that intersect at various angles. Small amounts of stilbite and laumontite are sometimes associated and orange to red crystals of heulandite-Na are often in small cavities in the matrix (personal).

Idaho County: Small tufts of mordenite occur with analcime, calcite and heulandite in small cavities in Columbia River basalt in roadcuts along Highway 95 from mile post 218 for about 0.3 miles south, a short distance upstream of Russell Bar on the Salmon River. The cavities are small, mostly less than 1 cm across and oval-shaped. Mordenite occurs as tiny tufts either scattered or completely lining a cavity, generally coating heulandite crystals (Photo. 266). Individual heulandite crystals are a few millimeters across and the mordenite crystals a few millimeters in length. These are in cavities that are mostly about 1-3 cm across and around 1 cm high. The heulandite and mordenite were deposited on a green clay that shrinks when it dies out, so the mordenite and heulandite often fall off the matrix after being removed from the rock. In another part of the roadcut, small pink chabazite crystals have been found (personal).

Several miles south of Pinehurst in a quarry just south of Hazard Creek, Mordenite occurs in cavities in Columbia River basalt. Small tufts of mordenite were rarely found lining cavities with tiny heulandite crystals (Photo. 267). The mordenite occurs in tufts or as fine coatings lining the cavities. Pyrite was found in other cavities (personal).

MUSCOVITE

$KAl_2(Si_3Al)O_{10}(OH,F)_2$, monoclinic (pseudohexagonal)

Pseudohexagonal crystals. In tabular crystals; foliated in small to large sheets. Transparent to colorless in thin sheets; may be yellow, brown, green or red. A common rock-forming mineral in rocks of all types in most geologic environments.

Adams County: Muscovite forms large books in the mica mine west of Mica Hill in Sec. 8, T. 15 N., R. 2 E., 12 miles southeast of Council. Microcrystals of chalcopyrite can be found, and beryl is reported. The Muscovite forms books up to 20 cm across (personal).

Boise, Custer and Elmore Counties: Muscovite is less common in cavities in the Sawtooth batholith than two other micas, masutomilite and zinnwaldite. It forms small books and scaly coatings with a gray to greenish gray color. Occasionally, it is pink to purplish pink. X-ray analysis indicates that some of this (especially some of the pink material) may be lepidolite, but more work needs to be done. The scaly coatings can be found on microcline, albite and smoky quartz (personal).

Clearwater County: Sections of books of muscovite can be found in colluvial deposits near the old Fohl picnic area 0.3 mile west from the Pierce Divide. Associated minerals include topaz and smoky quartz (personal).

Latah County: Mica-bearing pegmatites have been mined for sheet mica in the Avon District. The occurrence covers a large area in T. 41 N., R. 2 W. from 3 to 6 miles north of Avon. The principal producer was the Muscovite Mine which produced from both underground and surface workings. Light greenish beryl crystals, some over 30 cm in length and 20 cm across, occur in the pegmatite. The last production and extensive exploration from these mines and prospects was in the 1950s, so they are largely slumped and overgrown (Shannon, 1926; personal).

Photo. 218 Ilvaite on quartz, 2.8 cm, South Mountain, Owyhee County.

Photo. 216 Huebnerite, 1.5 mm long, Ima Mine, Lemhi County.

Photo. 217 Ilvaite, doubly terminated crystals on a thin plate of calcite, specimen 8.8 cm across, Laxey Mine, Owyhee County.

Photo. 219 Ilvaite and quartz, specimen 13 cm across, South Mountain, Owyhee County; Joan and Bryant Harris specimen.

Photo. 221 Kyanite, 3.6 cm long, Goat Mountain road, Shoshone County.

Photo. 220 Jarosite, tiny crystals with quartz, Stone Cabin Mine, Owyhee County.

Photo. 222 Kyanite, 3.5 cm long, Moses Butte, Shoshone County.

Photo. 223 A twinned crystal of labradorite with an iron oxide coating on some faces, 1.9 cm, Cinder Butte, Clark County.

Photo. 224 Laumontite fresh from a cavity, individual crystals are 3 to 8 mm in length, Rat's Nest claim, Custer County.

Photo. 225 , Levyne on a cavity lining of thomsonite, large levyne crystal is 6 mm across, Lucky Peak Dam, Ada County.

NATROLITE

$Na_2Al_2Si_3O_{10} \cdot 2H_2O$, orthorhombic
Dimorphous with tetranatrolite; member of the zeolite group. Crystals long prismatic, often radiating groups; some fibrous, massive or granular. Colorless or white; transparent to translucent. A secondary mineral that occurs in cavities in volcanic rock. Generally associated with other zeolites, quartz and calcite.

Idaho County: Natrolite is reported to occur with prehnite, apophyllite and heulandite in vesicles in Columbia River basalt south of Pinehurst on the east side of the Little Salmon River south of Boulder Creek. The natrolite forms rosettes in granular heulandite in small amygdules. The basalt crops out in the bluffs above the river (Hamilton, 1963).

Small crystals of natrolite occur with analcime and stilbite in small cavities in Columbia River basalt near Russell Bar in roadcuts along Highway 95 just south of mile post 218. All cavities are small, mostly less than 1 cm across, and oval-shaped. Natrolite is uncommon as tiny needle-like crystals (personal).

In a roadcut, 2 miles up Slate Creek from Highway 95, natrolite occurs as small hair-like crystals with analcime. The roadcut is small, but the white zeolite-bearing pockets in the black basalt can easily be seen. The rock is hard and cavities larger than 3 cm across with the larger crystals of analcime, up to about 2 cm across, and natrolite, up to about 1.5 cm long, are uncommon (personal).

Lemhi County: Natrolite is uncommon in one area of the skarn zone along Quartzite Canyon. The micro crystals have been found associated with mesolite, thomsonite and laumontite on fracture surfaces (personal).

NAUMANNITE

Ag_2Se, orthorhombic (pseudocubic)
Pseudocubic, mostly in granular masses or thin plates, but may form cubes. Iron-black. Occurs in quartz veins with other selenides.

Custer County: Blue-gray grains of naumannite occur in the ores of several mines in the Yankee Fork District. It forms minute grains with pyrite, chalcopyrite and tetrahedrite. The minerals occur in crustified veins with quartz and calcite (Shannon, 1926).

Lemhi County: Microscopic grains of naumannite occur in the ores of the Monument and Parker Mountain mines of the Gravel Range District. The grains are in quartz veins with adularia (Shannon, 1926).

Owyhee County: Several of the mines in the Silver City District produced naumannite

The DeLamar Mine was the first reported occurrence of this mineral in the United States (Shannon, 1920). It formed sectile and malleable nodules and masses in clay in the veins. It was often mistaken for acanthite, but has a lighter blue-gray color and is more malleable and sectile (Piper and Laney, 1926; Shannon, 1920).

The DeLamar Mine was reopened and operated as an open pit mine in the 1970s and 1980s. Naumannite occurred as grains with other silver minerals, pyrite, chalcopyrite and mandarinoite, and occasionally as gray microcrystals in small cavities with tiny quartz crystals (Photo. 268) (Lasmanis, et al 1981; personal).

NICKELINE

NiAs, hexagonal
Pyramidal crystals rare, generally massive, reniform with columnar structure. Pale copper-red, tarnished gray to blackish. Occurs with other nickel minerals, pyrrhotite and chalcopyrite or in veins with cobalt minerals.

Lemhi County: Small indistinct nickeline crystals occur in the veins of the Togo Mine, Blackbird District. The crystals are pale copper-red color and generally have a dark tarnish. They are associated with smaltite and other nickel and cobalt minerals (Shannon, 1926).

NITER

KNO_3, orthorhombic
Crystals bipyramidal; most often in thin crusts, tufts and acicular crystals, massive or granular. Vitreous luster; transparent; colorless, white or gray. Common as an efflorescence in arid regions, often in caves; with nitratine, epsomite and gypsum.

Clark County: Niter occurs in a lava cave near Dubois. It is derived from a surface deposit of bird guano (Palache, 1951).

NITRATINE

$NaNO_3$, hexagonal (trigonal)
Crystals are rhombohedral, but usually massive granular, as an incrustation. Vitreous luster, colorless, white, reddish brown, gray, lemon-yellow; transparent. Water soluble, found in arid climates as an efflorescence or in soil.

Owyhee County: Nitratine is reported to occur near Homedale (Palache, 1951).

Photo. 226 Levyne, crystals 2-2.5 mm across, on phillipsite and heulandite with tiny clay crystallizations on the levyne; surfaces appear to have a thin offretite-erionite coating, Pinehurst area, Adams County.

Photo. 228 Ludwigite, 9 cm across; the brown surface alteration has been removed showing the pitted surface of the unaltered portion of the ludwigite, Quartzite Canyon, Lemhi County.

Photo. 227 Ludwigite, 10.5 cm across, with coating of unknown alteration, Quartzite Canyon, Lemhi County.

Photo. 229 Ludwigite and magnetite, magnetite is 1 cm across, Quartzite Canyon, Lemhi County.

Photo. 230 Dodecahedral crystals of magnetite with garnet and diopside, large magnetite crystal is 8 mm across, Windy Ridge area, Mackay District, Custer County.

Photo. 231 Magnetite, modified octahedrons, with minor ludwigite, specimen 7.6 cm across, Bruce Estate prospect, Lemhi County.

Photo. 233 Dodecahedral crystals of magnetite, largest is 2 cm across, Iron Mountain, Washington County.

Photo. 232 Magnetite, modified octahedron, 2.6 cm across, Bruce Estate prospect, Lemhi County.

Photo. 234 Dodecahedral crystals of magnetite, largest is 3.2 cm across, Iron Mountain, Washington County.

OFFRETITE

$(K_2,Ca)_5Al_{10}Si_{26}O_{72} \cdot 30H_2O$, trigonal

Offretite is probably always intergrown with erionite; it is very difficult to determine which is dominant, even with various laboratory techniques. Both are zeolite group minerals. Offretite crystals typically long prismatic, fine fibrous, minute. Colorless, white, yellow to golden; transparent to translucent. Occurs with other zeolites in volcanic rocks. Often intergrown with erionite as a very fine crystalline coating projecting from the surfaces of levyne; for the purpose of clarity, offretite is used in this text.

Ada County: Offretite occurs as submicroscopic fibers on the surfaces of levyne crystals at the Lucky Peak Dam about 10 miles east of Boise. The minerals occur in cavities in volcanic rock along the road immediately south of the dam for about a quarter mile towards the boat launch. Levyne has been found below the road, in the western part of the picnic area. The best collecting is late in the summer and fall when water level is low. Other minerals in cavities in the rocks include calcite, chabazite and phillipsite. This is the first reported occurrence of this mineral in Idaho (Ream, 1991).

Adams County: Offretite occurs as submicroscopic fibers on the surfaces of levyne crystals in the small cavities in basalts south of Pinehurst where it occurs with chabazite, apophyllite, mesolite, calcite and other minerals. It was found at the roadcut 0.3 miles north of milepost 177 and at the roadcut 0.8 miles north of that milepost (personal, Ream, 1999)

OLIVENITE

$Cu_2AsO_4(OH)$, orthorhombic

Forms a series with adamite. Short to long prismatic to acicular or globular shapes with fibrous structure, tabular or massive and granular. Shades of olive-green, greenish brown or rarely straw-yellow, grayish green or grayish white; translucent to opaque. Occurs in the oxidized portions of ore deposits.

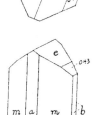

Fig. 18 Olivenite, Blackbird District, Lemhi County; crystal drawings from Shannon (1926).

Lemhi County: Druses of dark olive-green crystals coating cavities in a cellular quartz can be found in the Nickel Plate Mine on the Little Deer Creek side of the Divide, 2 miles northeast of the Uncle Sam Mine in the Blackbird District (Fig. 18). Cobaltite and a bright yellow-green alteration product of scorodite and olivenite are associated. The olivenite crystals are dull and of small size; they occur in small cavities in a cellular quartz (Shannon, 1926).

ORTHOCLASE

$KAlSi_3O_8$, monoclinic

Dimorphous with microcline. Prismatic, often twinned on the Carlsbad, Baveno or Manebach laws. Colorless, white, gray or pink; adularia is the colorless translucent to transparent variety. Sanidine is a glassy, often transparent, variety in igneous rocks. One of the most common rock-forming minerals.

Boise, Custer and Elmore Counties: Orthoclase is uncommon in the cavities in the granites of the Sawtooth batholith. It has been identified in a few cavities as white to flesh-colored crystals up to about 3 cm in length, but microcline is the most common potassium feldspar in the cavities. Smoky quartz, spessartine and muscovite are associated.

The adularia variety of orthoclase is also rare in these cavities. In one cavity, it was found as an overgrowth on the earlier formed orthoclase forming colorless coatings and as single crystals. A few doubly terminated blocky, twinned crystals up to 1.5 cm in length were found in this cavity (personal).

Bonner County: Orthoclase forms phenocrysts in the quartz monzonites and diorites of the Kaniksu batholith and satellite intrusive bodies. They can be found in several areas in the Selkirk Mountains and in several outcrops south and southeast of Sandpoint (Photo. 269). In many areas, the rock has been deeply weathered in situ, allowing the large crystals to be removed intact. They have been found up to at least 10 cm in length and are generally Baveno or Carlsbad twins. Small mica inclusions are common, but the crystals are mostly solid.

Crystals have been found in roadcuts and outcrops along Pack River and Caribou Creek. North of Priest River, they can be found along the upper part of Quartz Creek. Smaller crystals, around 2-3 cm in length, can be found in the roadcuts and outcrops southeast of Sandpoint along the highway to Bottle Bay. South of Sagle, large glacial float boulders of Kaniksu batholith rocks, contain Carlsbad twins up to at least 10 cm in length. The large boulders can be found along the railroad tracks, east of the highway, about 2 miles southwest of Sagle. The boulders are mostly weathered and can be easily broken apart, freeing the large orthoclase crystals (personal).

Boundary County: Rocks of the Kaniksu batholith contain orthoclase crystals in the Selkirk Mountains in Boundary County the same as in Bonner County. They can be found in several roadcuts and outcrops including those along portions of Ruby, Snow and Myrtle Creeks. In these areas the large phenocrysts, commonly 3-6 cm long, are frozen in fresh, solid rock. On occasion, the rock is weathered, and the individual phenocrysts can be removed (personal).

Cassia County: Crystals of an unreported species of feldspar occur as phenocrysts in the granite of the City of Rocks, southeast of Oakley; these are probably orthoclase. The crystals are up to 15 cm in length and weather out of the granite. They can be found lying on the surface of the ground or loose on the rock surfaces. Miarolitic cavities in the granitic rock and the uncommon pegmatites, contain microcline and smoky quartz crystals (Anderson, 1931; personal).

Kootenai County: The quartz monzonite of Chilco Mountain contains orthoclase up to 4 cm long. Some of the crystals have a light pink color. They have been found on the

Photo. 235 Malachite and calcite, field of view is 1.8 cm, Weimer Mine, Clark County.

Photo. 237 Malachite on quartz, hemispheres are around 1 mm across, Weimer Mine, Clark County.

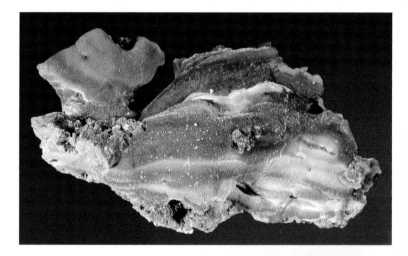

Photo. 236 Malachite, 4.8 cm across, Weimer Mine, Clark County.

Photo. 238 Malachite, tufts are 2 mm across, Hope prospect, Lemhi County.

Photo. 239 Malachite, crystals are 1.5 mm across, Hope prospect, Lemhi County.

Photo. 240 Malachite, small spherical groups are 3 mm across. Iron Dike Mine, Junction District, Lemhi County.

Photo. 242 Malachite pseudomorphs of azurite, field of view 2.3 cm, Iron Dike Mine, Junction District, Lemhi County.

Photo. 241 Malachite pseudomorphs of azurite on azurite, pseudomorphs are 7 mm long, Iron Dike Mine, Junction District, Lemhi County.

Photo. 243 Malachite crusts, specimen is 4.9 cm across, Blue Jay Mine, Lemhi County.

southwest side of the mountain and elsewhere (Shannon, 1926).

Lemhi County: Phenocrysts of orthoclase weather out of the rock in the Blackbird District and cover the ground in some areas. These crystals are rounded, Carlsbad twins or nearly spherical masses. The country rock is a porphyritic granite or granite gneiss and crystals are up to 5 cm in diameter (Shannon, 1926; personal).

Microscopic crystals of the adularia variety of orthoclase occur in the ores of the Gravel Range District. The rhombic crystals are associated with sulfides and selenides in fissure fillings in rhyolite (Shannon, 1926).

Owyhee County: Excellent specimens of the adularia variety of orthoclase (Shannon used the term "valencianite" for adularia formed in ore deposit veins) can be found in the Silver City District. It forms large white crystals lining cavities in several of the veins in the district and is associated with several metallic minerals in the Booneville, Black Jack, Trade Dollar and Cumberland mines. Crystals were found in all deposits regardless of whether the veins were in rhyolite, granite or basalt.

Some specimens contain inclusions of chalcopyrite and acanthite or fillings of chalcopyrite in cracks. Small transparent crystals coat the surfaces of lamellar quartz that is described elsewhere in this text. Small quartz crystals are associated in the Blaine tunnel, and fluorite is associated with the orthoclase in a mine on the south side of Long Gulch below the Blaine tunnel.

The crystals are typically wedge-shaped and often have a light yellowish to tan coloration but the interior is white to nearly colorless. These valencianite crystals, associated with small quartz crystals were common in many of the mines. Typically, the crystals are 6-12 mm across (personal; Shannon, 1926).

OWYHEEITE

$Pb_{10-2x}Ag_{3+x}Sb_{11+x}S2_8$ (x= -0.13 to +0.20), orthorhombic
Acicular or massive with an indistinct fibrous structure. Light steel-gray to silver-white; tarnishes to yellowish color. In vein deposits with other silver minerals.

Boise County: In the Banner District, owyheeite occurs as small grains and perhaps microcrystals with other silver minerals in the mines on Banner Creek. Associated minerals include proustite, pyrargyrite, miargyrite, silver, gold, galena, chalcopyrite, tetrahedrite, quartz and calcite. Mineralization is in quartz veins filling fissures in Tertiary porphyry dikes that intrude the Idaho batholith along shear zones; most of the minerals are found coating or filling fractures in the quartz veins (Anderson and Rasor, 1934).

Owyhee County: The mineral owyheeite was first recognized and described from a specimen from the Poorman Mine in the Silver City District. It occurs in white quartz in a typical fissure vein of the district. Open fissures in the vein are lined with quartz crystals. The owyheeite forms needle-like crystals that are embedded in the tips of the quartz crystals and project into the voids filling the cavities. Only minor amounts of pyrargyrite, yellow grains of sphalerite and nests of sericite are associated.

Fine-grained masses of the mineral are very light gray to almost silver white. A few minute needle-like crystals occur in small cavities in the quartz. Upon exposure, the owyheeite turns a faint yellow color (Piper, 1926; Shannon, 1921, 1926).

PALYGORSKITE

$(Mg,Al)_2Si_4O_{10}(OH) \cdot 4H_2O$, monoclinic (and orthorhombic)

Crystals are lath-shaped, elongated to fibrous, in bundles, as flexible sheets (mountain leather). White to gray; translucent. Occurs in hydrothermal veins or altered serpentine or granitic rocks.

Lemhi County: Palygorskite is uncommon as tiny fibrous white masses with magnetite and ludwigite in the skarn zone along Quartzite Canyon in the Spring Mountain District. Associated are white masses that may be serpentine and sericite (personal).

PARISITE-(Ce)

$Ca(Ce,La)_2(CO_3)_3F_2$, monoclinic, pseudohexagonal

Doubly terminated pyramidal crystals; many forms but oscillatory and sceptered due to intergrowths. Brownish yellow, brown, yellow; transparent to translucent. Found in alkalic massifs, granite pegmatites and REE-rich carbonatites.

Elmore County: One crystal of what has been tentatively identified as parasite-(Ce) was found on a specimen of albite, potassium feldspar and smoky quartz from the granite of the Steel Mountain stock. The crystal was a medium amber color, doubly terminated steeply dipyramidal lying flat on the back side of a plate of feldspar and quartz (Photo. 270). One termination was sacrificed for analysis by electron microprobe. It has not been X-rayed to further establish the identification. This is the first report of this mineral in Idaho. Aeschynite-(Ce) and other REE-bearing minerals, yet unidentified, have been found in other cavities in the granite. All of these are rare and mostly microscopic (personal).

PAULINGITE

$(K_2,Ca,Na_2,Ba)_5Al_{10}Si_{32}O_{84} \cdot 34\text{-}44H_2O$, cubic

Zeolite group. Rhombic dodecahedral crystals. Colorless; transparent. Uncommon, may be locally abundant. Found with other zeolites, quartz and pyrite in vesicles in basalt.

Idaho County: Paulingite has been found near Riggins, but the exact location is not known. Specimens were of a reddish brown vesicular basalt with vesicles up to about 1 cm across containing paulingite microcrystals. Phillipsite, also in microcrystals, occurs with the paulingite. The paulingite forms dodecahedrons that line the cavities.

At the time discovered, it marked the first find of the mineral in abundance, unfortu-

Photo. 244 Malachite coating altered hedenbergite crystals, field of view 2.6 cm across, Laxey Mine, South Mountain, Owyhee County.

Photo. 245 Blocky malachite crystals, 0.4 mm across, Hansy Mine, Shoshone County.

Photo. 246 Malachite, 2 mm long, Hansy Mine, Shoshone County.

Photo. 247 Malachite, groups are 1-1.5 mm across, Monitor Mine, Shoshone County.

Photo. 248 Malachite, crystals in front are 1.1 cm in length, Empire Mine, Shoshone County.

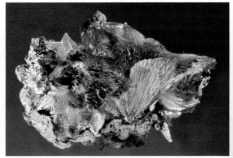

Photo. 249 Malachite, specimen is 3.2 cm across, Empire Mine, Shoshone County.

Photo. 250 Mandarinoite, upper group 0.8 mm, DeLamar Mine, Owyhee County; Dan Behnke photograph.

Photo. 251 Mandarinoite, group 1.3 mm across, DeLamar Mine, Owyhee County; Dan Behnke photograph.

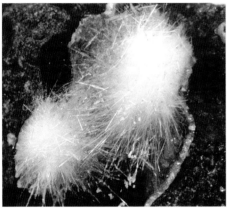

Photo. 252 Mesolite on heulandite, cavity is 1 cm across, Pinehurst, Adams County.

Photo. 253 Mesolite and stilbite, 7.2 cm across, Challis area, Custer County.

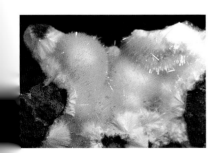

Photo. 254 Mesolite, area of view is 2.6 cm, Race Creek, Idaho County.

Photo. 255 Metavariscite, Two Top Creek, individual platy crystals are 1.2 mm across, Fremont County.

nately, the locality is unknown. Specimens were given to the University of Washington Geology Department, by a graduate student, for laboratory classes to use as samples of basalt. The student had reportedly collected them near the junction of Papoose Creek and Squaw Creek, unaware that the vesicles contained what was, at that time, a rare mineral; when paulingite was recognized in the specimens, he was unable to direct anyone to the right outcrop.

Flows of the Columbia River basalt are extensive and are typically about 50 to 150 feet thick in this area. The lower flows in the valley in the vicinity of the junction of the two creeks have the red color and vesicular tops. So far, collectors have only been able to find outcrops with vesicles that contain calcite, other zeolites in tiny crystals, chalcedony and opal, but no paulingite. The zeolites noted in the area include heulandite, analcime, phillipsite, chabazite, mesolite and some thomsonite, all as tiny crystals (Tschernich and Wise, 1982).

PEARCEITE

$Ag_{16}As_2S_{11}$, monoclinic
Crystals are tabular hexagonal prisms that have beveled edges. Black. Occurs in silver ore deposits with acanthite and other silver minerals and sulfides, quartz and barite.

Bonner County: Pearceite has been reported with silver and antimony sulfides from the Conjecture Mine in the Lakeview District. Cavities in the veins of the upper levels of the mine contain small crystals of the minerals. The pearceite partially replaces galena associated with ankerite and sphalerite (Shannon, 1926).

PENFIELDITE

$Pb_2Cl_3(OH)$, hexagonal
Prismatic, elongated or tabular. Colorless to white, also yellowish or bluish tinge. Transparent. Occurs with other secondary lead minerals in oxidized portions of ore deposits.

Shoshone County: Small white crystals of penfieldite have been reported from the Little Giant Mine with pyromorphite. The crystals are reported to be less than 6 mm in length and white in color. The occurrence is in the back of the adit, above the decline. At this zone, pyromorphite occurs as bright green, translucent, tiny crystals, up to about 3 mm in length (personal).

PENTLANDITE

$(Fe,Ni,)_9S_8$, cubic
Mostly occurs massive or in granular aggregates. Color is light bronze-yellow with a metallic luster. It has no cleavage and a conchoidal fracture. Associated with pyrrhotite, mostly in highly basic rocks; may occur with chalcopyrite, cubanite and related minerals.

Custer County: Pentlandite occurs in a few of the mines and prospects in the Slate Creek area. It apparently forms small grains and blebs in quartz and in other metallic minerals. Pyrrhotite, chalcopyrite, tetrahedrite, marcasite and possibly cubanite are associated. Libethenite, geocronite, digenite and argentopyrite also occur in the mines on Slate Creek (Kern, 1972).

PETZITE

Ag_3AuTe_2, cubic
Massive or fine granular to compact. Steel-gray or iron-gray to iron-black. Occurs with other tellurides in veins.

Idaho County: Petzite has been reported in the Black Diamond Mine in the Dixie District associated with gold; the identification was not confirmed (Shannon, 1926).

PHENAKITE

Be_2SiO_4, hexagonal (trigonal)
Crystals generally rhombohedral, sometimes prismatic; either typically with complex development. Luster vitreous; colorless to white and transparent or translucent. A rare mineral found in pegmatitic dikes or miarolitic cavities in granitic rocks. Occurs with topaz, beryl, microcline, apatite, quartz and chrysoberyl.

Boise, Custer and Elmore Counties: Phenakite has been found as tiny crystals in the miarolitic cavities in the Sawtooth Mountains; the identification was confirmed by X-ray analysis of two specimens. Prismatic crystals are typically about 1 mm in length, up to 2 mm and are terminated by third order pyramids (Photo. 69). Rhombic crystals are smaller, up to about 1 mm across. Crystals of both habits are colorless to very pale pink and are associated with topaz, smoky quartz, microcline, albite and zinnwaldite (personal).

Elmore County: Phenakite is rare in miarolitic cavities in the Steel Mountain stock. Only one crystal has been reported, perched on microcline. The crystal is complex, has a rounded appearance, about 6 mm across and is colorless. Smoky quartz is associated (personal).

Kootenai County: Phenakite has been reported in the pegmatites on Red Hog, 10 miles southwest of Coeur d'Alene. It was found in a cavity in a pegmatite with albite, muscovite, beryl, microcline and smoky quartz (personal).

PHILLIPSITE

$(K,Na,Ca)_{1-2}(Si,Al)_8O_{16} \cdot 6H_2O$, monoclinic
A zeolite group mineral. Crystals are penetrating twins, often elongated, often simulating orthorhombic or tetragonal forms, also in spherulites. Colorless, white, yellowish or reddish; transparent to translucent. Occurs with other zeolites in volcanic rocks; also in saline lake deposits and calcareous deep sea deposits.

Ada County: Phillipsite occurs as microcrystals lining cavities in volcanic rocks at the Lucky Peak Dam about 10 miles east of Boise. The tiny colorless crystals are mostly less than 2 mm across. Rarely, phillipsite forms spheres on a coating of thomsonite (Photo. 271). Calcite, chabazite, levyne and offretite are associated (personal).

Adams County: Phillipsite can be found with analcime, cowlesite, levyne, chabazite, thomsonite and gyrolite in vesicles in Columbia River basalt in the roadcut that is 0.8 mile north of mile post 177 on highway 95, south of Pinehurst. The phillipsite crystals are colorless to milky, less than 4 mm long and line vesicles (Photo. 272). The crystals are blocky to elongated and often twinned. It probably occurs in the outcrops to the south too (personal).

Idaho County: Tiny crystals of phillipsite can be found in the vesicluar Columbia

Photo. 256 Microcline and albite, specimen is 7.8 cm across, Crags batholith, Lemhi County.

Photo. 258 Mimetite, 1.2 mm across, Blackstone Mine, Bear Lake County.

Photo. 257 Microcline, an elongated Manebach twin, 6 cm high, Crags batholith, Lemhi County.

Photo. 259 Prismatic mimetite showing an unusual tapering habit, with yellow segnitite coating, Ima Mine, Lemhi County.

Photo. 260 Colorless mimetite on bayldonite, crystals 0.7 mm long, Ima Mine, Lemhi County.

Photo. 261 Colorless prismatic mimetite, up to 0.8 mm long, with yellow segnitite coating, Ima Mine, Lemhi County.

Photo. 262 A very fine crystal of molybdenite in quartz, Missouri Belle Mine, Lemhi County.

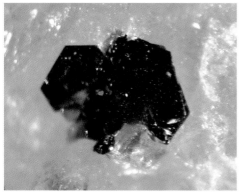

Photo. 263 Mordenite with heulandite, specimen is 16.5 cm across, the pinkish color is due to the pink color of the heulandite showing through the mordenite coating, Rat's Nest claim, Custer County.

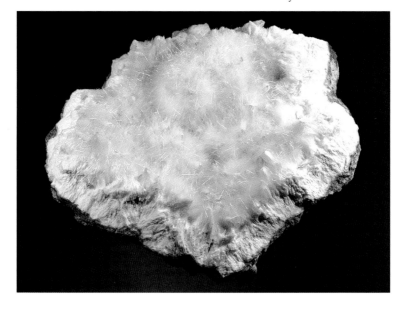

River basalt in the roadcut along Highway 95 at mile post 227 on the White Bird grade, north of White Bird. Phillipsite crystals are transparent to white and less than 3 mm long. Sometimes they are coated with tiny cream colored calcite crystals and also occur with chabazite (personal).

PHLOGOPITE

$KMg_3AlSi_3O_{10}(OH,F)_2$, monoclinic, hexagonal

Mica group mineral. Prismatic crystals, often coarse; also scales and plates. Yellowish brown to brownish red, colorless, white, greenish, grayish. Mostly found in metamorphic limestones and ultrabasic rocks.

Lemhi County: Tiny crystals of phlogopite occur in the oxidized zone of the Ima Mine. The colorless crystals with hexagonal cross section occur as single thin plates or clusters on vuggy quartz. Azurite, malachite and other secondary minerals are associated. Identification of the phlogopite was by X-ray analysis (personal).

Washington County: Phlogopite occurs as large crystals forming spherical groups frozen in calcite in the pit on Iron Mountain. These spheres are mostly 20-40 cm across. Partial crystals of phlogopite are up to 30 cm across. They are green to somewhat silvery green. Analysis shows that most are partially altered to chlorite and possibly other minerals, but they are dominantly phlogopite. These large phlogopite have a similar appearance to the small chlorite crystals that occur elsewhere in the skarn. Analysis has shown that they can be distinguished by size, all the small crystals are chlorite and only the large crystals frozen in the calcite are phlogopite. The skarn also contains some cavities with poor to good quality brown garnets and rarely magnetite (personal).

PHOSPHOVANADYLITE

$(Ba,Ca,K,Na)_x[(V,Al)_4P_2(O,OH)_{16}] \cdot 12H_2O$, cubic, pale greenish-blue cubes 20-50 microns on edge, coat phosphatic organic-rich mudstone.

Caribou County: Phosphovanadylite is a new mineral identified and described from material that occurs with sincosite at Monsanto's Enoch Valley Mine, Soda Springs. It occurs in the Phosphoria formation as coatings of tiny cubic crystals on organic-rich mudstone in a thin layer in a pit. The greenish-blue crystals darken to greenish-black (probably due to oxidation) over several month's time (Medrano, et al, 1998).

PHOSPHURANYLITE

$Ca(UO_2)_3(PO_4)_2(OH)_2 \cdot 6H_2O$, orthorhombic

Microscopic rectangular plates, scales and laths, sometimes forming crusts. Deep yellow to golden yellow. A widespread secondary mineral in weathered zones with autunite and uranophane.

Custer County: Phosphuranylite occurs northeast of Stanley in T. 11 N., R. 13-14 E. It forms small soft bright green and yellow grains with renardite, autunite, uraninite, marcasite and stibnite. Mineralization is in rocks of the Idaho batholith and in arkosic conglomerate at the base of the Challis formation. Numerous claims were located on the occurrences and pits, cuts and trenches have been dug and a few adits driven on the mineralized zones. There has been some production from these mines.

The uranium mineralization is along fractures and fault zones and some is disseminated in the rock along the fractures. The minerals occur as micro to small crystals coating the surfaces. The Lightning, Aspen and Copperite group of claims in Secs. 1 and 12, T. 11 N., R. 13 E. along Basin and Hay Creeks may have the been mineralized. There are several bulldozer cuts in rocks of the batholith and necks and plugs of Challis volcanics. There is a fault zone in a pit on the south side of Hay Creek that is well-mineralized. Another good locality may be the Hardee claims in the S$\frac{1}{2}$ Sec. 10, T. 11 N., R. 14 E., on the ridge west of the West Fork of Upper Harden Creek where a fault in granodiorite is exposed in a bull-dozer pit. There is considerable fracturing of the rock providing an abundance of surfaces for the uranium minerals. Throughout this area, most of the pits, trenches and other work-ings are slumped, caved and overgrown, so that mineralized zones are difficult to locate (Kern, 1959; personal).

PLATTNERITE

PbO_2, tetragonal
Rarely in prismatic crystals, generally in botryoidal masses or nodular. Iron-black to brownish black. In oxidized portions of lead-bearing ore deposits, associated with cerussite, pyromorphite and smithsonite.

Lemhi County: Plattnerite occurred embedded in red minium in the Democrat Mine in the Gilmore District (Shannon, 1926).

Tiny black acicular prisms of what may be plattnerite are uncommon on some of the vanadinite from the Iron Mask Mine, Spring Mountain District. The black crystals, less than 1 mm in length have been seen on a few specimens (Photo. 273) (personal).

Shoshone County: Excellent examples of plattnerite were collected in the You Like Mine in the early history of the Coeur d'Alene District. It formed rounded nodules and botryoidal masses in the near-surface workings. A few crystals of white pyromorphite were associated. The outsides of the plattnerite nodules were reddish brown and the interiors were iron-black. Several of them were quite large being up to 10 x 12 x 20 cm and oth-ers up to 200 pounds were reported. A few cavities in the nodules contained microscopic plattnerite crystals (Shannon, 1926).

The Mammoth Mine produced similar plattnerite masses up to 100 pounds in weight. Botryoidal masses were found in the Hercules Mine at Burke and massive plattnerite was found in the Last Chance and Caledonia workings of the Bunker Hill Mine. Plattnerite also occurred in the Tamarack Mine near Burke (Photo. 20) and the Senator Stewart Mine near Kellogg (Radford and Crowley, 1981; Shannon, 1926).

PLUMBOJAROSITE

$PbFe_6(SO_4)_4(OH)_{12}$, hexagonal (trigonal)
Forms crusts, masses and lumps of microscopic hexagonal plates; also pulverulent and earthy. Golden brown to dark brown; dull to glistening or silky luster. A secondary mineral in the oxidized lead ores in arid regions with other secondary lead minerals.

Custer County: At the old silver mines on Keystone Mountain, plumbojarosite is un-common as tiny plates and flakes of a yellow to yellow-brown to dark amber color (Photo. 274). These are on quartz associated with chrysocolla and other secondary minerals. The yellow to yellow-brown flakes form finely crystalline groups and compact masses and the darker colored crystals are mostly scattered or in small groups. Identification was by

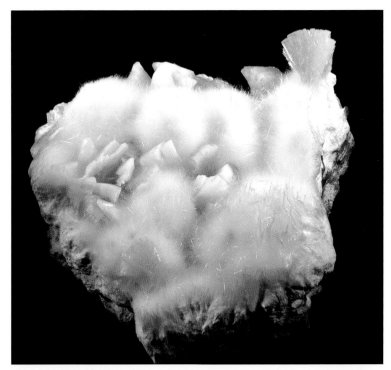

Photo. 264 Mordenite with heulandite, specimen 11.2 cm across, Rat's Nest claim, Custer County.

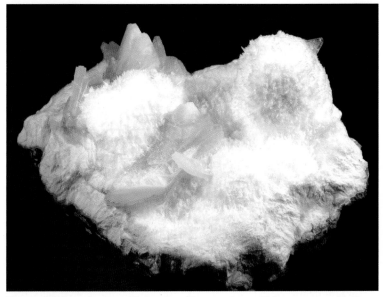

Photo. 265 Mordenite with heulandite, specimen 11.5 cm across, Rat's Nest claim, Custer County.

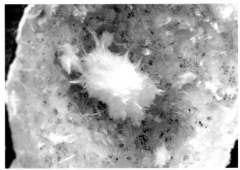

Photo. 266 Mordenite and heulandite, the heulandite is colorless but looks greenish because it sits on greenish clay, specimen is 3 cm across, near Russell Bar, Idaho County.

Photo. 267 Mordenite on tiny heulandite crystals, cavity is 3.5 cm across, Hazard Creek, Idaho County.

Photo. 268 Naumannite with quartz, field of view 4 mm across, DeLamar Mine, Owyhee County.

Photo. 269 Orthoclase crystal from the Kaniksu batholith, Lignite Road, Lake Pend Oreille, Bonner County.

Photo. 270 Parisite-(Ce), 5 mm long, Steel Mountain, Elmore County.

microprobe and X-ray analysis. The fine flakes are common, but the coarse dark amber crystals are uncommon (personal).

Lemhi County: Plumbojarosite was uncommon in the Kaufman and Weaver mines. It occurs with other lead and silver minerals (Palache et al, 1951).

POLHEMUSITE

(Zn,Hg)S, tetragonal

Irregular grains, tetragonal prisms and dipyramids, black color. Microscopic only. Occurs with stibnite and mercury minerals.

Valley County: Polhemusite was first identified and described from microscopic grains in the ores of the B and B deposit, Big Creek District, and it is now known from only one other. It occurs as tiny grains or prismatic and dipyramidal crystals with stibnite, cinnabar, mercurian sphalerite and zincian metacinnabar in a quartz rich gangue. The largest grains or crystals apparently are only 20 microns across. The deposit is a replacement deposit of stibnite in a silicified zone in granodiorite of the Idaho batholith within the Thunder Mountain caldera. Small quartz crystals and stibnite crystals are uncommon. The prospect is located on the north side of Profile summit and is accessible by an old road off the road to Big Creek where a small pit was developed (Leonard, et al, 1978; personal).

POLYBASITE

$(Ag,Cu)_{16}Sb_2S_{11}$, monoclinic (pseudohexagonal)

Pseudohexagonal, in tabular crystals or massive; iron-black. Found in silver veins with pyrargyrite, tetrahedrite and other silver minerals.

Blaine County: Polybasite has been found in the Parker Mine in Elkhorn Gulch, 4 miles east of Ketchum in Sec. 14, T. 4 N., R. 18 E. It occurs with galena, sphalerite, tetrahedrite, pyrite, chalcocite, quartz and siderite in veins in argillites of the Milligen formation (Umpleby et al, 1930).

Bonner County: Well-formed crystals of polybasite were common in the Talache Mine 10 miles south of Sandpoint. The mine is located in the $SE^{1/}_4$ Sec. 6, T. 55 N., R. 1 W. on the west side of Lake Pend Oreille. The crystals were uncommon above the 800 level but fine crystals were frequently found on chalcopyrite coating joints in deeper levels. Generally, polybasite occurs as grains and blebs to about 8 mm across. Mineralization is in the Little Joe vein in rocks of the St. Regis and Revett formations of the Belt supergroup. Galena, sphalerite and tetrahedrite are associated with the polybasite (Humphreys and Leatham, 1936; Sampson, 1928; Savage, 1967).

Polybasite occurred as a thin platy layer along joints in ore, with native silver in the Blue Bird Mine in the Talache District. The plates had tabular faces of the basal pinacoid with triangular makings, but do not display crystal outlines (Shannon, 1926).

Butte County: Polybasite has been found in the ores of the Hub Mine in the Lava Creek District in Secs. 8, 9 and 17, T. 2 N., R. 24 E., 2 miles southwest of the Martin town site. Microcrystals of proustite, pyrite, stephanite and native silver are associated (Anderson, 1929; Shannon, 1926).

Elmore County: Small iron-black crystals and microscopic grains occur coating drusy quartz in some mines of the Atlanta District. The crystals are flattened hexagonal tabular prisms that are mostly less than 1 mm across (Photo. 275). They have beveled edges that show triangular striations on the basal faces. Some crystal aggregates show twinning. Other silver minerals, including acanthite, miargyrite, pyrargyrite, xanthoconite and sulfides, are associated (Anderson, 1939).

Owyhee County: The mines of the Silver City, DeLamar and Flint Districts contained polybasite in small masses showing the distinct cleavage of the mineral. The masses are steel gray and up to 1 cm across in the DeLamar Mine and are similar in the Poorman and other mines of the Silver City District. The specimens are similar to tetrahedrite in appearance.

Minute, sharp, brilliant crystals of polybasite line drusy cavities in quartz in a drift in the Rich Gulch Mine on the west slope of Florida Mountain. The crystals are black in color and hexagonal in outline with hexagonal and triangular markings (Shannon, 1926).

In the Flint District, it formed distinct crystals, tabular plates and masses. It is intergrown with pyrargyrite, miargyrite, stephanite and tetrahedrite (Piper and Laney, 1926).

POLYCRASE-(Y)

$(Y,Ca,Ce,U,Th)(Ti,Nb,Ta)_2O_6$, orthorhombic
Short prismatic, often flattened, crystals or massive. Black, may have a greenish or brownish tint. Occurs in granite pegmatites with muscovite, ilmenite, monazite, zircon and garnet.

Boise County: Square prismatic to thin tabular crystals of polycrase occur in the placer concentrates of the Centerville and Idaho City Districts. They are rough crystals and are brownish or greenish black in color. Some of them are up to 1 cm across and all have a thin yellow alteration crust. The crystals resemble samarskite and in the Idaho City concentrates are associated with samarskite and columbite (Shannon, 1926).

POWELLITE

$CaMoO_4$, tetragonal
Crystals pyramidal or thin tabular, pulverulent or as crusts; often forms pseudomorphs after molybdenite. Straw-yellow, brown, greenish yellow, pale greenish blue, dirty white to gray, blue and nearly black; transparent. A secondary mineral in molybdenum-bearing ore deposits.

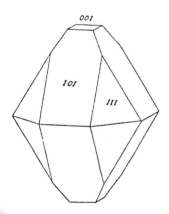

Fig. 19 Powellite, Seven Devils District, Adams County; crystal drawing from Shannon (1926).

Adams County: Powellite is rare at the Peacock Mine in the Seven Devils District (Fig. 19) which is the type locality for this mineral. It forms small yellow dipyramidal crystals up to 3 mm, resembling scheelite, on light brown garnet with bornite. The crystal forms observed are c(001), p(111) and e(101) and the interfacial angles are very close to those of scheelite. The discovery of powellite in the Peacock Mine was the first discovery of the mineral (Cook, 1954; Shannon, 1926).

It also occurs in the Helena Mine 1 mile northwest of Landore. Supergene powellite replaces molybdenite and scheelite and powellite are altered to cuprotungstite (Cook, 1954; Shannon, 1926).

In the Alaska Mine, just southeast of Lockwood Saddle, about 5 miles north of Cuprum, powellite is uncommon. It

Photo. 271 Spheres of phillipsite in cavities with thomsonite lining, large sphere on right is nearly 6 mm across, Lucky Peak Dam, Ada County.

Photo. 272 Phillipsite on gyrolite, near Pinehurst, Adams County.

Photo. 273 Tiny elongated microcrystals of plattnerite on vanadinite, Iron Mask Mine, Lemhi County.

Photo. 274 Plumbojarosite on quartz, 0.6 mm, old silver mines, Keystone Mountain, Custer County.

Photo. 275 Pseudohexagonal tabular crystals of polybasite, 0.5 mm across, with unknown gray mineral, Atlanta District, Elmore County.

Photo. 277 Pyrargyrite, 1.2 mm high with orange-amber xanthoconite crystals at the base, Atlanta District, Elmore County.

Photo. 276 Prehnite with epidote and quartz, prehnite crystal in center is 6 mm across, light iron stain and white clay coating, Smoky Dome, Camas County.

Photo. 278 Pyrargyrite, terminated crystal on right is 0.8 mm, Atlanta District, Elmore County.

Photo. 279 Pyrite, 1.5 high, Custer County; Harvard Mineralogical Museum specimen.

Photo. 280 Pyrite in phyllite, surface is altered to goethite, 1.3 cm, near Lucile, Idaho County.

Photo. 281 Pyrite, the octahedral crystals are 1-2.5 mm across, Highway 12, near Russian Creek, Idaho County.

occurs with scheelite, malachite, azurite, garnet, epidote and diopside (Cook, 1954).

Custer County: In the Bayhorse District, powellite forms dirty white pearly plates up to 1 cm across. The plates are an alteration product of molybdenite and are interleaved with it. Molybdite is associated (Shannon, 1926).

PREHNITE

$Ca_2Al_2Si_3O_{10}(OH)_2$, orthorhombic

Crystals are tabular, often forming rounded groups, also reniform or stalactitic. Light green to white; translucent. A secondary mineral in cavities in basalt associated with zeolites and calcite. Also occurs in skarn deposits with lime-silicate minerals.

Camas County: Prehnite is uncommon to rare in the miarolitic cavities in the Tertiary granite of the Soldier Mountain stock of Smoky Dome northwest of Fairfield. The tiny pale greenish crystals are square tabular to pointed and occur in stacks and groups (Photo. 276) perched on microcline with albite, epidote and smoky quartz (personal).

Custer County: Contact metamorphic rocks, at the Basin group of claims, contain many of the lime-silicate minerals. The claims are north across Park Creek from Trail Creek Summit. The contact rocks have formed in limey slate and clayey quartzite. Prehnite occurs as radiating aggregates of tabular crystals and garnet forms sharp euhedral crystals of light to dark amber color. Associated minerals include epidote, wollastonite, diopside, augite, fluorite, galena, pyrite, chalcopyrite, sphalerite and pyrrhotite (Shannon, 1926; Umpleby et al, 1930).

Elmore County: Small, spindle-shaped and tabular crystals of prehnite have been found in a miarolitic cavity in granite in the Steel Mountain stock. The small crystals are up to about 6 mm, generally in curved groups and have a very light green tint. They occur with epidote, smoky quartz, albite and microcline (personal).

Idaho County: Prehnite is reported in the Columbia River basalts south of Riggins. The locality is on the east side of the Little Salmon River south of Boulder Creek. The amygdaloidal basalt forms bluffs that overlook the river. Prehnite is reported as globular aggregates of radial structure with apophyllite, heulandite and natrolite (Hamilton, 1963).

Kootenai County: Near Post Falls, prehnite was found associated with stilbite, laumontite and other zeolites in a seam in diabase. It formed minute tabular crystals lining cavities and granular masses filling cavities (Shannon, 1926).

PROUSTITE

Ag_3AsS_3, hexagonal (trigonal)

Dimorphous with xanthoconite. Prismatic, rhombohedral or scalenohedral crystals or massive. Scarlet or vermillion; translucent. One of the ruby silver minerals; found in silver veins with pyrargyrite.

Blaine County: Proustite occurs in the Pilgrim Mine near the head of Beaver Creek at 8,200 feet elevation. The mine is 0.7 mile southwest of the Silver King Mine and 8 miles from the Stanley-Ketchum Road in Sawtooth Valley, south of Alturas Lake. Pyrargyrite galena and sphalerite form crystals in a quartz vein in granite (Ballard, 1922).

It also occurs as small grains in the oxidized ores in the Ella Mine in Ella Canyon. Associated minerals include acanthite, chlorargyrite and tetrahedrite (Shannon, 1926).

Boise County: Proustite occurs with pyrargyrite, miargyrite, owyheeite, silver, gold galena, chalcopyrite, tetrahedrite, quartz and calcite in quartz veins in the mines of the Ban ner District on Banner Creek. Most of the minerals occur as minute to coarse grains, but minute crystals on drusy quartz have been found (Anderson and Rasor, 1934).

Butte County: Minute crystals of proustite are embedded in the quartz-siderite gangue and intergrown with pyrite in the Hub Mine in the Lava Creek District. The mine is at 6,200-6,900 feet elevation at the corners of Secs. 8, 9 and 17, T. 2 N., R. 24 E. Proustite and stephanite form microcrystals embedded in the gangue and intergrown with pyrite, or as veinlets that cut across sulfide mineralization. Sheets and wires of silver, polybasite and other silver minerals are associated (Anderson, 1929; Shannon, 1926).

Elmore County: Proustite has been found in the Atlanta and Tahoma mines in the Atlanta District. It forms vermilion to aurora-red crystals on slickensided surfaces in the Atlanta lode. The crystals are small acute rhombs capped by obtuse rhombs and basal pinacoids. Pyrargyrite and other silver minerals and sulfides are associated (Anderson, 1939).

Lemhi County: Small red crusts of proustite occur in the Carmen Creek District. A similar occurrence is reported in the ores of the Texas District (Shannon, 1926).

Owyhee County: Proustite was common in most mines of the Silver City, Flint and De Lamar Districts. One mass weighing 500 pounds, with crystal faces, was found in the Poorman Mine. When broken, it proved to be solid crystalline throughout. Part of the mass was sent to the Paris Exposition of 1867 where it reportedly was awarded a gold medal. This would be one of the largest and most remarkable occurrences of proustite known. Proustite was abundant in the Trade Dollar vein. Pyrargyrite, miargyrite and other silver minerals were associated (Piper and Laney, 1926; Shannon, 1936).

Shoshone County: Flattened and distorted crystals and thin films of proustite were found in the Polaris and Big Creek mines on Big Creek and in the Yankee Boy Mine. It was most common in fractures in the wall rocks, not with the argentiferous tetrahedrite and galena of the veins (Shannon, 1926).

PSILOMELANE

Preferred usage is for massive hard, unidentified, manganese oxides, but also used for the mineral romanechite ($BaMnMn_8O_{16}(OH)_4$, orthorhombic).

Massive, botryoidal or stalactitic. Black or brownish. Formed from oxidation of veins or weathered rock formations.

Lemhi County: Psilomelane occurs in the incline shaft in the No. 4 tunnel of the Patterson Creek tungsten mine (now the Ima Mine) in the Blue Wing District. It forms dull black plumose-fibrous aggregates on drusy quartz (Shannon, 1926).

PYRARGYRITE

Ag_3SbS_3, hexagonal (trigonal)

Prismatic or scalenohedral crystals; massive. Deep red; translucent. Occurs in silver veins; more common than proustite. Associated with proustite, acanthite, tetrahedrite, calcite and quartz.

Blaine County: Pyrargyrite occurs in the Pilgrim Mine near the head of Beaver Creek at 8,200 feet elevation, 0.7 mile southwest of the Silver King Mine. Crystals of galena and sphalerite with proustite are associated in a quartz vein in granite (Ballard, 1939).

Boise County: Pyrargyrite was found in the gold veins of the Washington claim in the Idaho City District. It was abundant with stephanite in a quartz vein, but near the surface

Photo. 283 Tiny cubes of pyrite with quartz, Stone Cabin Mine, Florida Mountain, Owyhee County.

Photo. 282 Pyrite, large crystal is 1.4 x 1.6 cm, DeLamar Mine, Owyhee County.

Photo. 285 Pyromorphite, micro, Blackstone Mine, Bear Lake County.

Photo. 284 Pyrite, unusual crystal with interesting surface features and modifications, 5 cm across; Iowa Gold Mine "Quartzling," Idaho; now an unknown location; Harvard Mineralogical Museum specimen.

Photo. 286 Pyromorphite, crystals to 3 mm, Laxey Mine, South Mountain, Owyhee County.

both minerals were altered to chlorargyrite (Shannon, 1926).

In the silver mines of the Banner District, pyrargyrite was found with stephanite and sphalerite. These minerals occurred as grains between the quartz crystals on comb quartz in a vein. Proustite, miargyrite, tetrahedrite, chalcopyrite, galena, gold and silver are associated in some veins. Most mineralization consists of minute to coarse grains in quartz veins (Anderson and Leatham, 1934; Shannon, 1926).

Bonner County: Pyrargyrite occurs in several small adits north of Lakeview on the shore of Lake Pend Oreille in the SE$\frac{1}{4}$ Sec. 34, T. 54 N., R. 1 W. A few rich pockets of silver ore were found in the adits and microcrystals of sulfides have been reported in cavities. Mineralization is in rocks of the Wallace formation of the Belt supergroup. The adits are at lake level, and may be underwater during the summer high water level (Kun, 1974).

Microscopic crystals of pyrargyrite occur in the Conjecture Mine in the NE$\frac{1}{4}$NW$\frac{1}{4}$ Sec. 26, T. 53 N., R. 1 W., 4 miles south of Lakeview on the south end of Lake Pend Oreille. The crystals are associated with several silver sulpharsenides and sulphantimonides, galena, tetrahedrite, acanthite, sphalerite, chalcopyrite, huebnerite, wolframite, boulangerite, stibnite and rhodochrosite which form very small and microcrystals in the upper workings of the mine (Kun, 1974; Savage, 1967).

Custer County: Euhedral crystals of pyrargyrite have been found in mines of the Yankee Fork District on the Yankee Fork of the Salmon River. The crystals occur in drusy vugs with miargyrite, enargite, acanthite, chlorargyrite, covellite, malachite, azurite and gold. In the Dickens Mine, the minerals occur in crustified vuggy veins (Anderson, 1949; Cass, 1973).

Elmore County: The Atlanta District contained pyrargyrite as an important ore mineral (Photos. 277, 278). In the Monarch Mine it formed a vein 6 cm in width with a parallel streak of quartz containing silver. Most of the pyrargyrite was granular masses, but it did form crystals. Stephanite, acanthite and stromeyerite were associated (Shannon, 1926).

In the Atlanta lode, pyrargyrite was abundant as small crystals and microscopic grains. Gold, stephanite, polybasite, miargyrite, galena and tetrahedrite were associated (Anderson, 1939).

Owyhee County: Pyrargyrite was a common mineral in the mines of the Silver City, Flint and DeLamar District. It formed euhedral crystals in cavities on other minerals and grains in masses intergrown with other minerals. In the Henrietta vein, it occurred as euhedral crystals on quartz with polybasite, miargyrite, stephanite and tetrahedrite (Asher, 1967; Piper and Laney, 1926; Shannon, 1926).

Nuggets of pyrargyrite, miargyrite and acanthite occur in streaks of kaolin in crevices in the DeLamar Mine. It is associated with fluorite on crusts of quartz crystals in a stope in a raise in the east drift of the Silver City Mine.

Steel-gray crystals of miargyrite and deep red transparent crystals of pyrargyrite were found on quartz in the Henrietta Mine (Fig. 20). Some of these crystals were large

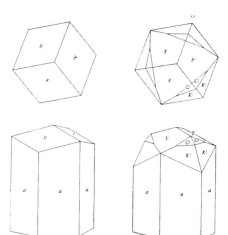

Fig. 20 Pyrargyrite, Henrietta Mine, Silver City District, Owyhee County; crystal drawings from Shannon (1926).

enough for measurement on the goniometer. The following forms were identified; simple crystals displayed only the prism (1010) and rhombohedron (1122); more complex crystals exhibited the forms (4151) and (4152). Excellent pyrargyrite crystals to 2 mm occurred on quartz crystals in cavities in the California or Marguerite shaft on War Eagle Mountain. Acanthite and chalcopyrite are disseminated in the quartz of the vein (Shannon, 1926).

Shoshone County: Thin films of pyrargyrite were found coating joints in the 2,000 foot level of the Standard-Mammoth Mine at Mace. Minute crystals and thin films were found in the Bunker Hill Mine and a few specimens were produced in 1979 (Radford and Crowley, 1981; Shannon, 1926).

Valley County: Pyrargyrite crystals have been found in the Dewey Mine in the valley at the head of Mule Creek. It is accessible from Monumental Creek. Crystals (apparently of small size) occur in one vein in the mine. One zone in the mine had pyrite nodules with leaf gold in the centers (Shenon and Reed, 1936).

PYRITE

FeS_2, cubic

Commonly as cubes, pyritohedrons and octahedrons or combinations of these; massive, granular, reniform or stalactitic. Pale brass-yellow. The most common of the sulfides, occurs in most types of ore deposits and disseminated in many rock types. Both a primary and a secondary mineral. Common with chalcopyrite, galena, sphalerite and quartz.

Blaine County: Highly modified pyrite crystals occur in the Croesus Mine in the Hailey gold belt, in Scorpion Gulch in Secs. 29 and 30, T. 2 N., R. 18 E., about 3.5 miles southwest of Hailey. They are up to 5 mm in diameter and are highly lustrous. Crystals are also reported from the Camas, Tip Top and Wide West mines (Shannon, 1926).

Crystals were found in the Le Despencer Mine on the north side of Deer Creek about 1 mile upstream from Clarendon Hot Springs, near Hailey. The crystals are in the altered granite adjoining the mineralized veins which contain galena, sphalerite, quartz and calcite (Umpleby et al, 1939).

Modified pyrite crystals occur in calcite in the Parker Mine in the Warm Springs District, about 4 miles east of Ketchum in Elkhorn Gulch. Polybasite, galena, pyrite, sphalerite, quartz and calcite are associated (Shannon, 1926; Umpleby et al, 1930).

The Muldoon Mine in the Little Wood River (Muldoon) District produced pyrite pyritohedrons embedded in sericite (Shannon, 1926).

Near Hailey, pyrite occurs in the Broadway Mine on the east side of Hyndman Creek Valley about 3.5 miles from the Creek's mouth. Pyrite forms pyritohedrons to 1.7 cm in diameter in veins in shale. Quartz, galena and chalcopyrite are associated. Stibnite occurs on the ridge above the mine (Umpleby et al, 1930).

Boise County: Pyrite, in the Mountain Chief Mine in the Quartzburg District, occurs as masses of imperfect crystals. Some of the masses were up to 3 cm across. They are associated or intergrown with sphalerite, arsenopyrite and chalcopyrite. Pyrite also forms small cubes disseminated in the sericitized wall rock of some veins (Shannon, 1926).

Good pyritohedral crystals up to 1.5 cm across occur in the Carroll-Driscoll Mine These are as aggregates or single crystals in sericite gouge. Some of the crystals are highly modified (Jones, 1917; Shannon, 1926).

The quartz porphyry on the Gold Hill Mine contained disseminated pyritohedral crystals of small size. In addition, cubes with modifying faces occurred in sericitized feldspar phenocrysts in the porphyry (Shannon, 1926).

Auriferous pyrite forms cubes with sphalerite in ore in the Golden Age Mine in the Pioneerville District. Galena, sphalerite and tetrahedrite are associated in some quartz veins. Striated cubes occur in the Coon Dog No. 1 vein. These are up to 1 cm across and are imbedded in quartz with chalcopyrite, sphalerite and covellite. There is a similar occurrence in the tunnel of the Coon Dog No. 4 vein. Pyritohedral and cubic crystals occur in the Gem of the Mountains, Overlook and Blackbird mines (Shannon, 1926).

The Lincoln Mine in the Pearl (Westview) District contains small pyrite crystals. These show an oscillatory combination of the cube and pyritohedron and are in drusy cavities in sphalerite (Shannon, 1926).

Boise, Custer and Elmore Counties: Pyrite is uncommon in miarolitic cavities in granites of the Sawtooth batholith in the Sawtooth Mountains. It occurs as cubes; most are partially to completely altered to goethite. Associated minerals include albite, microcline, zinnwaldite and smoky quartz (personal).

Bonneville County: Pyrite can be found in the Robinson and Pittsburgh mines on the east slope of Caribou Mountain. Crystals of calcite and other minerals can be found with the pyrite crystals in cavities where xenoliths of limestone have weathered out. Other minerals include chalcopyrite and bornite. The mines are developed in Secs. 4 and 9, T. 4 S., R. 44 E.; there are several adits and other workings (Hamilton, 1961).

Boundary County: Pyrite crystals to about 1.2 cm across have been reported from the Buckhorn Mine in the eastern part of the county. The mine is developed with three adits in metasediments of the Belt supergroup of Precambrian age. Pyrite is the only metallic mineral conspicuous in a quartz gangue; some galena and siderite is present (Navratil, 1958).

Butte County: Striated crystals to 2.5 cm occur in most mines of the Lava Creek District in T. 2-3 N., R. 24 E., north of Craters of the Moon National Monument. Most of the crystals average about 6 mm across and are associated with other sulfides and gangue minerals. In the Last Chance Mine in T. 3 N., R. 24 E., pyrite forms pyritohedrons with reniform marcasite. The mine is on Champagne Creek (Anderson, 1929).

Clearwater County: Pyrite cubes up to 2 cm across occur in the Lolo M. & P. Co. Mine in the Musselshell (Weippe) District. Some of these are partially altered to limonite (Shannon, 1926).

Custer County: Pyrite has been found as lustrous modified cubes at an unreported locality in Custer County (Photo. 279).

At the Alto Silver claims on the south tributary of Little Fall Creek, small striated pyrite cubes occur in a vein of iron-stained coarse honeycombed quartz. Some cavities are lined with smithsonite and cerussite. Ore minerals include galena, sphalerite and chalcopyrite. Mineralization is in Paleozoic argillite and interbedded slate (Umpleby et al, 1930; Tuchek and Ridenour, 1981).

Idaho County: Cubes of pyrite occur in a schist in the Highway 95 roadcut on the east side of the highway, 0.2 mile south of the road to Lucile. There is no parking in the area and the roadcut is very close to the highway and has no shoulder. The crystals are cubes and elongated cubes, striated, lustrous and sometimes coated with a thin layer of goethite (Photo. 280). A few crystals can be found in float (personal).

Pyrite crystals occur in a rusty quartz vein in the western part of a roadcut 0.4 mile east of mile post 165 (1.2 miles west of Russian Creek) on Highway 12 several miles west of Lolo Pass. The tiny, lustrous octahedral crystals are up to about 3 mm across (Photo. 281). The quartz vein cuts gneiss, and a quartz vein to the east contains tiny stilbite crystals (personal).

Lemhi County: Coarse cubes of pyrite occur in the ore deposits of the Mackinaw District in quartz. Much of it contains gold (Shannon, 1916).

Interesting tabular pyrite crystals occur in the Rabbitfoot Mine, northeast of the Singheiser Mine, in the Gravel Range District, 8 miles south of Forney. These are in lithophysae in silicified rhyolite. The 2 mm diameter tabular crystals have a hexagonal outline. Shannon (1926) speculated that they may be pseudomorphous after mica, polybasite or pyrrhotite.

Crystals of pyrite can be found in the Singheiser Mine on the north side of Arrastre Creek about 1.5 miles above the junction of Arrastre and Silver Creeks in Sec. 25, T. 18 N., R. 17 E. Mineralization is in quartz with gold selenides (Trites and Tooker, 1953).

Owyhee County: Fine quality crystals of pyrite have been found in the pit of the DeLamar silver mine. Small cubic crystals in groups on matrix and pyrtohedrons to 2 cm were found in clay seams (Photo. 282). These were in a zone that has been mined out (personal).

In the Stone Cabin Mine, associated with the DeLamar Mine, pyrite formed cubic and complex crystals frozen in the altered rock and in cavities with quartz. Generally the crystals were tiny and were often associated with quartz crystals (Photo. 283) (personal).

Shoshone County: Pyrite is common in most ores of the county, but rarely as euhedral crystals. It does occur as cubes in the argillites in several localities. The cubes are often over 5 mm across and are altered to goethite in most areas. Brilliant druses of highly modified minute crystals occur in vugs in quartz in the Highland Surprise Mine on Highland Creek south of Pinehurst. A few specimens can be found on the dump (personal).

Pyritohedrons to 2 cm were found in the Yankee Boy Mine on Big Creek. These were found in sericitic shale. Spherical pyrite with an internally radiating structure has been found in the Greenhill-Cleveland Mine at Mace and the Gold Hunter Mine in Mullan. Tiny crystals were collected in 1979-1981 in the Bunker Hill Mine with calcite. These tiny crystals were up to about 4 mm across and were mostly cubic with some modified by the octahedron (Shannon, 1926; personal).

Valley County: At the Golden Cup Mine on the south fork of Smith Creek, in a glacial cirque about 2 miles northwest of the Big Creek Lodge, at an elevation of 8,000 feet, there are several small silicified shear zones in the metavolcanics of the Yellowjacket formation. Cavities in quartz are filled with chalcopyrite, pyrite and calcite; other mines in the area contain tungsten mineralization (Kirkpatrick, 1974).

Large nodules of pyrite in the Thunder Mountain District contained coarse leaf gold in their centers. The occurrence is in a volcanic tuff in the Dewey Mine (Shannon, 1926)

PYROLUSITE

MnO_2, tetragonal

Dimorphous with ramsdellite. Generally in radiating fibers or columns, granular masses or dendritic coatings; rarely in crystals. Iron-black. A supergene mineral; very common as dendrites on fracture surfaces.

Clark County: Spongy drusy masses of pyrolusite occur in the Scott (Birch Creek) Mine in the Birch Creek District. It was reported to be abundant in the ores of the mine (Shannon, 1926).

Lemhi County: Pyrolusite is abundant in oxidized portions of the lead-silver veins in the mines of the Little Eightmile District. It is massive and crystalline, but mostly forms sooty coatings or dendrites in fracture surfaces. In the manganiferous iron ores, it often forms veinlets that contain euhedral orthorhombic crystals that project perpendicularly from the fracture walls (Thune, 1941).

Shoshone County: Steel-gray crystalline rosettes of pyrolusite were found in the lower tunnel of the north Bunker Hill Mine. This occurrence was in a rusty brecciated quartz vein. Mossy masses of minute pyrolusite crystals on calcite crystals were found in cracks in the quartzite of the 800 level of the Hercules Mine (Shannon, 1926).

PYROMORPHITE

$Pb_5(PO_4)_3Cl$, hexagonal

Prismatic crystals, often barrel-shaped, commonly have cavernous terminations. May be reniform, botryoidal or granular. Colorless, green, yellow, orange, brown or grayish. A secondary mineral in the oxidized zone of lead deposits, associated with cerussite, smithsonite, hemimorphite, anglesite, malachite and limonite.

Blaine County: Pyromorphite has been found in the Eureka Mine in the SW$^{1}/_{4}$ Sec. 14, T. 2 N., R. 17 E., on Bullion Creek. The pyromorphite is reported with vanadinite and wulfenite in the outcrop above the main adit (Umpleby et al, 1930).

Bear Lake County: Small crystals of pyromorphite occur with cerussite, wulfenite and mimetite at the Blackstone Mine west of Montpelier on St. Charles Creek (Photo. 285). The short prismatic light brown crystals are rare (Mansfield, 1927; personal; Richards, 1910; Shannon, 1926).

Boise County: Pyromorphite is associated with cerussite in the Hall Brothers claim in Deadwood Basin in the Deadwood District. It forms tufts of minute acicular crystals of pale yellow-green color and larger imperfectly formed deep blue-green prisms (Shannon, 1926).

Small and microscopic crystals of pyromorphite occur in the Buckskin Mine 4 miles northeast of Placerville along the ridge between Ophir and Grimes Creek at 5,000 feet elevation. Similar crystals occur in the Last Chance Mine in the northern part of the Quartzburg mineral zone. Both mines are in the Boise Basin. Vanadinite, stibnite, galena and bismuthinite are associated in the Buckskin Mine (Ballard, 1924).

Bonner County: Very nice pyromorphite crystals of tiny to small size occurred in the Plum Creek prospect on Lunch Peak. Crystals were dominantly green to bright green, but some were yellow, especially the very fine, thin acicular crystals. Most crystals are under 6 mm in length and 1 mm across. They form coatings and radial groups in small cavities in white vein quartz (Photo. 287).

Tiny crystals of translucent to transparent cerussite and small quartz crystals are associated. Rarely, there are small gray anhedral to subhedral crystals included in the quartz that appear to be galena. Pyromorphite epimorphs (encrustation pseudomorphs) of calcite have been found. The pyromorphite occurred in at least one nearly vertical quartz vein in the diorite in a small pit along the road near the top of Lunch Peak. The pyromorphite specimens are some of the best microcrystals, perhaps the best, collected in recent years from Idaho. Unfortunately, the Forest Service rehabilitated the locality, bulldozing the remaining small amount of mineralized rock over the dump and filling and grading the pit in the summer of 1996 (personal).

Butte County: Small greenish crystals of pyromorphite have been found in the Pandora Mine on Boyle Mountain in the Lava Creek District in T. 2-3 N., R. 24 E. It is associated with chrysocolla that is opal-like in texture and blue, bluish gray or almost black (Anderson, 1929).

Cassia County: Pyromorphite occurs in several mines of the Conner Creek Valley in Sec. 8, T. 13 S., R. 25 E. The Big Bertha claims are at the summit of the wide flat ridge between Conner Creek and Howell Creek at 8,000 feet elevation, 2 miles northwest of the Melcher Mine. The pyromorphite crystals are prismatic or barrel-shaped and are yellow-green to deep green or brown in color. They are most common in the near-surface workings along the north side of Conner Creek with galena (as cubic crystals), sphalerite, pyrite, malachite, chalcopyrite, cerussite and quartz (Anderson, 1931).

Clark County: Pyromorphite has been found in the Scott Mine in the Birch Creek District in Sec. 31, T. 9 N., R. 31 E. It is associated with galena, anglesite, cerussite, wulfenite, plumbojarosite, smithsonite, siderite and barite. There are several shafts and drifts developed in Paleozoic limestone, shale and quartzite (Trites and Tooker, 1953).

Elmore County: Small crystals occur in the Jacobs prospect in the Volcano District. Numerous small barrel-shaped crystals with a deep green color were found coating a fracture surface in a 15 inch wide quartz vein. The Jacobs prospect is in the SE$^1/_4$ Sec. 14, T. 2 S., R. 10 E. (Allen, 1940).

Idaho County: Small imperfect crystals occur in the Mallard Creek prospect in the Dixie District. They are green and small and are associated with galena and light yellow sphalerite on quartz. Minute yellow-green crystals occur in the Comstock Mine in rusty quartz (Shannon, 1926).

Lemhi County: Minute yellow-green crystals of pyromorphite coat quartz in the Isis claim in the Mineral Hill District, 7 miles north of Shoup (Shannon, 1926).

Pyromorphite is rare in mines of the Texas District around the town of Gilmore. Crystals are short, deeply striated, hexagonal prisms (Umpleby, 1913).

Pyromorphite has been found in the mines of the Eldorado District, east to northeast of Baker. It has been found in the War Eagle Mine, on the crest of the ridge north of Pratt Creek, about 2 miles west of the Goldstone Mine which is at the head of Pratt Creek at 9,000 feet elevation. Mineralization is in a quartz vein in Precambrian metasediments. Sulfides are scattered through the quartz and include galena, pyrite and chalcopyrite. The oxidized surface ores contain some pyromorphite and cerussite (Anderson, 1957).

The Virginia Mine is on the East Fork of Sandy Creek on the high ridge and cliffs on the north side of the canyon. There are seven adits, one of which is over 400 feet in length. A quartz vein in Precambrian quartzite contains galena, chalcopyrite and pyrite. The oxidized ores contain several secondary minerals, including pyromorphite, azurite, malachite, chrysocolla and cerussite (Anderson, 1957).

Owyhee County: tiny crystals of pyromorphite occur with other secondary minerals in the oxidized ores of the mines on the northwest side of South Mountain. The tiny crystals have been found at the Laxey and other mines associated with chrysocolla, azurite, malachite and cerussite (Photos. 286, 288) (personal).

Shoshone County: The Coeur d'Alene District has produced excellent specimens of pyromorphite from several mines (Photos. 18, 19, 21-33, 291, 292). Shannon (1926) said that some of these were equal to those from any other locality in the world. The colors from the district included shades of green, colorless, pink, gray and brown. It generally forms drusy crusts of small crystals coating rock fragments, but crystals up to about 3 cm have been found. Most of the crystals only showed the unit prism and basal pinacoid, but the faces of the unit pyramid were common. Some of the crystals were barrel-shaped, and some of the larger crystals were cavernous.

Generally it is a solitary mineral, but a few specimens were found with cerussite and rarely, minute crystals of wulfenite. Some of the upper oxidized workings of the mines contained extensive areas with pyromorphite crystals which produced excellent specimens.

Some of the better occurrences include the Hercules Mine at Burke and the Standard Mammoth Mine at Mace. Plattnerite was associated with pyromorphite in the You Like

Mine, part of the Morning Mine development. The crystals were up to 1 cm long, white or gray in color and some were stained brown by coatings of plattnerite.

Pyromorphite is common in the Little Giant Mine on Silver Creek, south of Mullan. Crystals are gray, gray-green and green in color. Most of them are under 1 cm in length, but have been found up to 2 cm; micro crystals are common (Photos. 31, 32, 289, 290).

Pyromorphite formed colorless crystals in ocherous limonite, or stout pale green minute prisms in the surface workings of the Evolution prospect near Osburn. Cup-shaped crystals were found in the Sandow tunnel where it crosses the Caledonia vein. Good specimens were also reported in the Omaha Mine which became part of the Caledonia Mine. Green and pink crystals were found in the Caledonia Mine.

Pyromorphite has been found in the outcrop of the Northern Light Mine south of Pinehurst. Specimens were found in the Lookout Mountain Mine east of the forks of Pine Creek, high on the canyon side above the creek.

Excellent specimens were found in the Sierra Nevada and Senator-Stewart mines on Deadwood Gulch. Pyromorphite was reported in the Quaker tunnel. The dumps of the Senator-Stewart mines contain small crystals of yellowish green to green pyromorphite; most crystals are less than 5 mm in length. These dumps are on the property of the Bunker Hill Limited Partnership and are not open to collecting. The Bunker Hill Mine has produced many fine specimens of pyromorphite in several colors and habits. An unusually fine discovery was made in some upper workings in the early 1980s just before the mine closed. These consisted of yellow to reddish orange arsenian pyromorphite with a botryoidal to prismatic habit and yellow, yellow-green to bright green crystals of prismatic habit. Individual crystals were up to more than 2.5 cm in length. Specimen mining activities later in the 1980s produced more pyromorphite crystals, but not in as spectacular quality specimens. After an exchange of ownership, renewed specimen mining again produced high quality yellow to green and orange pyromorphite specimens in the late 1980s and 1990s (Radford and Crowley, 1981; Shannon, 1926; personal).

PYROPHANITE

$MnTiO_3$, hexagonal (trigonal)
Fine scaly, small tabular crystals or embedded grains. Deep blood-red, greenish yellow, brownish red. Metallic to submetallic. In manganese deposits, associated with garnet in manganese-bearing deposits.
Boise, Custer and Elmore Counties: Pyrophanite has been identified as zones in hematite crystals in one of the miarolitic cavities in the granite of the Sawtooth batholith north of Ardeth Lake. Microprobe analysis of two crystals, from one cavity, indicated that the central zone contained manganese and titanium and no iron. Similar tests of crystals from three other cavities showed only iron (personal).

PYROSTILPNITE

Ag_3SbS_3, monoclinic
Dimorphous with pyrargyrite. Crystals tabular or lath-like sometimes in sheaf-like aggregates. Hyacinth red. Occurs with the ruby silver minerals.
Owyhee County: The rare mineral, pyrostilpnite, was found in the Henrietta Mine in the Silver City District. One fiery red, markedly striated crystal, 1.5 mm in diameter was found with miargyrite. This crystal was destroyed in identification. Apparently no other

crystals are known to have been preserved from this locality, but Shannon (1926) believes that it may have been relatively common in the mine (Piper and Laney, 1926).

PYRRHOTITE

$Fe_{1-x}S$ (x = 0-0.17), monoclinic and hexagonal

Mostly massive or granular; may form tabular or pyramidal crystals. Brownish bronze; magnetic. Occurs in vein and contact metamorphic deposits as well as igneous rocks. Pyrrhotite is common in many of the ore deposits of the state.

Blaine County: Pyrrhotite was common in the ores of the Croesus, Camas and Tip Top mines. Associated minerals include arsenopyrite, chalcopyrite, galena and pyrite. Most of these sulfides were gold-bearing. In the Rosetta District, pyrrhotite occurred in the coarse ores of the Golden Glow and other mines (Shannon, 1926).

Custer County: Small crystals enclosed in chalcopyrite and quartz occur in the Lost Packer Mine in the Loon Creek District. Azurite and malachite are also reported. Pyrrhotite was also found in the mines of the Seafoam district where it occurred with galena, pyrite and sphalerite. Pyrrhotite was also reported from the Mackay District and from the Washington Basin District (Shannon, 1926).

Owyhee County: Crystals of pyrrhotite have been found in the Texas orebody on South Mountain. The brilliant crystals to about 1.5 cm across occur with sphalerite and quartz (Photo. 293). Matrix specimens, in which all three minerals are lustrous, and specimens that are large size have been collected (personal).

QUARTZ

SiO_2, hexagonal (trigonal)

Mostly prismatic crystals with striations parallel to the a axis on the prism faces; terminated by positive and negative rhombohedrons. Common in massive forms including coarse to fine grained crystalline to flint-like or cryptocrystalline masses. Mostly colorless or white, also violet to purple (amethyst), gray to black (smoky quartz), light pink or rose (rose quartz) or yellow (citrine); transparent to translucent. Occurs in rocks of all types; an important constituent of igneous rocks. Crystals occur in cavities of many types, associated with feldspars, metallic minerals and silicates. The most abundant mineral in the earth's crust.

Adams County: Small crystals with chalcocite occur in vugs at the Lime Peak Mine in the Snake River Canyon about 0.5 mile north of Homestead in the Seven Devils District (Cook, 1954).

Slightly water worn quartz crystals and fragments occur in the placer deposits of Rock Flat about 5 miles northwest of McCall. The locality is along both sides of Highway 55 and the highway to the Brundage recreation area. Spinel, corundum, gold and other minerals are associated. Crystals of corundum can be found in most areas around the intersection of these highways; quartz is uncommon (Beckwith, 1972; personal).

Quartz occurs in several of the mines in the Seven Devils District. In the South Peacock Mine, it occurs as small crystals mostly under 3 cm long, some large. Most are white, but they may also be colorless. A few are colored reddish by inclusions. Few of these crystals are simple sharp prismatic crystals, most show overgrowths or tiny quartz crystals on the surfaces of large crystals (Photo. 295). They may be associated with malachite, garnet, hematite and epidote (personal).

Blaine County: Amethyst crystals line geodes from the Tertiary basalts in the area covered by the Hailey quadrangle. They are most common along Pole Creek, a tributary of the Little Wood River. The amethyst is rare, and most geodes are lined with colorless quartz crystals. Phantoms of amethyst occur in some of the colorless crystals (Shannon, 1926).

Quartz crystals can be found in cavities in limestone in the Stormy Galore Mine and other mines near the head of West Richmond Gulch at 7,500 feet elevation. Galena, sphalerite, chalcopyrite and pyrite are associated (Umpleby, 1914).

Boise County: Small crystals and drusy coatings of crystals occur in the gold veins in the Quartzburg, Idaho City and other districts of the county (Shannon, 1926).

Boise, Custer and Elmore Counties: Excellent crystals of smoky quartz can be found in the granitic rocks of the Sawtooth batholith (Photos. 71, 72, 75, 76, 82). Crystals occur in miarolitic cavities in the granite and pegmatites. Most cavities have collapsed, so good matrix specimens are uncommon, especially with crystals larger than about 2 cm.

High quality, gemmy, smoky crystals are common in small sizes, up to about 3 cm in length. Larger crystals may be gemmy in part, but often are cloudy or only translucent, although many large crystals are gemmy. Individual crystals have been found as large as 40 cm in length (and possibly larger) and 20 cm in width. Individual crystals vary from light smoky to black. Surfaces may be brilliant and clean, frosted, or coated with microcrystals of muscovite, bertrandite, hematite or clay.

Albite and microcline are the most common minerals associated with the quartz, but masutomilite, zinnwaldite, hematite and ilmenite are common in some areas. Fluorite, topaz, spessartine and aquamarine may also occur, and helvite has been found.

Fine matrix specimens of smoky quartz on feldspar matrix have been collected. These may have any of the other minerals associated on very fine quality specimens, and are common in smaller sizes, with smoky quartz to about 2 cm in length. These small specimens are rarely in good to excellent condition, displaying little alteration or weathering of the feldspar (personal).

Boise and Gem Counties: Small quartz crystals occur in the mines and prospects of the Westview District which spans the county boundary between Emmett and Horseshoe Bend. Associated minerals include galena, calcite, dolomite and gold (Shannon, 1926).

Boundary County: Quartz crystals occur in the Elba claim on Leonia Knob in the NE$\frac{1}{4}$NE$\frac{1}{4}$ Sec. 21, T. 61 N., R. 3 E. The quartz in the mine is fractured and vuggy. Some of the cavities are lined with quartz crystals; associated minerals are galena and malachite (Miller, 1973).

Butte County: Crystals have been found in the Lava Creek District, north-northwest of Craters of the Moon National Monument in T. 2-3 N., R. 24 E. Quartz occurs as drusy coatings, amethyst and pseudomorphic after plates of calcite. It forms drusy coatings on Blizzard Mountain with tungsten minerals in the Golden Chariot Mine. Some of the crystals are up to 2 cm long and amethystine. Delicate cellular networks of quartz pseudomorphs of calcite have been found in some of the mines (Anderson, 1929).

Quartz-lined geodes occur along Antelope and Road Creeks near Arco. Some of the crystals are amethystine. The geodes weather out of the volcanic rocks of the area (Beckwith, 1972).

Amethyst lines geodes in green volcanic rock on a ridge above Thompson Creek, west of Muldoon. The geodes have agate rinds and are about 6 to 10 cm across. The amethyst color is light. It is also reported that amethyst occurs in quartz veins on a ridge about one mile to the west (personal).

Camas County: Vuggy quartz veins occur in the Princess Blue Ribbon Mine in the Willow Creek Mining District, 27 miles southwest of Hailey. The district is in Secs. 33 and 34, T. 2 N., R. 16 E. The quartz crystals in the veins are sprinkled with sulfides and other minerals, including, galena, sphalerite, chalcopyrite, pyrite, chalcocite, malachite and gold (Milner, 1950).

Smoky quartz occurs in miarolitic cavities in the Hall Gulch pluton one to 10 miles southwest of Hill City. A portion of the intrusive extends westerly into Elmore County. Cavities are common but are generally small, mostly less than 4 mm across. Orthoclase (microcline?) crystals also occur in the cavities; individual crystals of quartz and orthoclase are rarely more than 1 cm in length. The granites of this pluton are poorly exposed, and the few outcrops are rounded and weathered (De Long, 1986).

Clearwater County: Quartz crystals to 5 cm or longer can be found on the west side of Pot Mountain. The mountain is in the bend of the North Fork of the Clearwater River in

Sec. 11, T. 39 N., R. 8 E. Crystals have been found in the soil and in the rock, apparently in quartz veins (personal).

Smoky quartz occurs in uncommon miarolitic cavities in the granitic rocks of the Bungalow stock in the area around Bungalow on the North Fork of the Clearwater River (Photo. 294). Crystals to several centimeters in length have been found with feldspar. Some crystal cavities have been found that are associated with small pegmatite bodies, that form irregular pods and lenses.

Feldspar crystals consist of microcline of a pinkish color and of white albite; most of these crystals are small. Minor amounts of muscovite are associated, but other minerals have not been reported. Most of the cavities are under 12 cm across, but larger cavities have been found.

The granitic rocks of the stock are Tertiary in age and generally gray in color. Outcrops and exposure vary from solid, fresh-looking rock to grussic (soft gravelly) material. Most of the hillsides are steep and tree covered with only a few rock outcrops (personal).

Smoky quartz crystals and fragments of crystals occur in an alluvial (or colluvial?) deposit on the ridge 0.3 mile west of the old Fohl Picnic area at Pierce Divide. The deposit consists of rounded and angular cobbles and clay. Pieces or complete crystals of black and colored tourmaline and topaz crystals, along with fragments of muscovite crystals are associated.

The origin of the deposit is unclear. Some smoky quartz crystals are complete and only slightly damaged, yet the next specimen found may be nearly rounded. Rock fragments also occur both rounded and sharp angular. There are pegmatites in the area (personal).

Custer County: Doubly terminated quartz crystals can be found in the mines of the Bayhorse District. These are up to 2.5 cm in length and occur embedded in siderite (Shannon, 1926).

Tiny to small crystals of quartz occur with stilbite and other zeolites in the volcanic rocks on Lime Creek. This mineralized area is 1.9 miles up the creek on a jeep trail from Highway 93. Stilbite, quartz and a minor amount of heulandite and other zeolites occur in seams and cavities, sometimes in cavities that are lined with blue and white agate. Quartz crystals are mostly tiny, under about 6 mm in length, but have been seen up to about 1.5 cm long. Rarely, these crystals are sceptered (Photo. 296) (personal).

Quartz crystal-lined geodes up to 30 cm in diameter can be found in the upper valley of Lost River. These have been found in the basaltic lava flows in several areas of the valley (Shannon, 1926).

Quartz crystals occur in veins in quartzite and gneiss at the head of Wildhorse Canyon. The canyon is at the eastern base of Hyndman Peak (Beckwith, 1972; Shannon, 1926).

Amethyst-lined geodes, like those in Blaine County, occur in the basalts in the low hills near the junction of the North Fork of Lost River with the main stream (Shannon, 1926).

Amethyst lines some geodes in some of the volcanic rocks along Challis Creek. Specific locations have not been reported. Geodes with a blue agate rind, lined with colorless quartz or amethyst are found where they have weathered on the surface (Photo. 297). Geodes up to 20 cm across with a coarse drusy coating of amethyst have on occasion been sold to mineral collectors (personal).

In the Yankee Fork Mining District, quartz is a common vein mineral. Some veins have vugs that are lined with a coarse comb or druse of crystals. Rarely, a coarse-grained amethystine variety can be found, especially on Estes Mountain (Stiles, 1976).

Quartz occurs in near-horizontal veins on the north side of this Mountain north of Custer. The veins are several inches wide and often vuggy and lined with quartz (Photo. 298). Some of these have amethystine layers (Photo. 299). Crystals have been found both above and below the road. Most of the comb quartz crusts only have narrow openings, but some are larger with stubby terminations.

Rarely, there are cavities, and one cavity about 2 feet across was noted that was filled with rough, crude crystals. These were generally grayish and some were slightly amethystine. Another flattened cavity in a quartz vein contained several quartz crystals to 6 cm long. Some of these showed pale amethystine color, and some were scepters (Photo. 300) (personal).

In the Alta Mining District, on Little Fall Creek, quartz can be found in the Purple Spar claims. Mineralization is on the northeast side of the creek around 9,000 feet elevation. Access is by taking the road up Little Fall Creek, from a couple of miles east of Trail Creek Summit. Mineralization is on the northeasterly side of the valley.

Fluorite occurs with drusy and chalcedonic quartz in veins in the cliffs. These veins contain a few cavities lined with drusy quartz which may be upon a fluorite layer, or occasionally have fluorite crystals sitting on the drusy quartz. The quartz varies from typical even drusy coatings to irregular coatings forming mounds and projections. There also are brecciated areas where drusy quartz coats breccia fragments (personal).

Tiny quartz crystals, rarely pale amethystine, occur in the uncommon geodes on the Rat's Nest claim with heulandite and mordenite. Quartz geodes are uncommon in large sizes; small quartz-lined geodes, rarely also containing tiny heulandite crystals, are uncommon but occur scattered through the deposit. The tiny amygdaloidal cavities lined with the red-orange heulandite-Na crystals sometimes also contain a few tiny quartz crystals (personal).

In an area near Antelope Flats, very fine quality quartz pseudomorphs of apophyllite have been found in geodes in decomposed volcanic rock. Most of the geodes of the area are lined with quartz crystals, rarely light amethyst, or with unattractive white spiky quartz and mordenite, but a few are lined with the pseudomorphs. The pseudomorphs are interesting mineralogically and are rare in the world. In this area, they have several forms and appearances (Photos. 302-304).

Most consist of a tiny druse of quartz crystals, either white or light gray (nearly colorless) forming the surface of the apophyllite crystal. Others are massive quartz and have a smooth or rough surface. Many of these have rounded groups of very tiny white quartz crystals around the base of the pseudomorphs. Most crystals with the drusy quartz surfaces are hollow and have cavernous terminations, and may have tiny calcite crystals coated with quartz in the cavities. Some of the cavernous pseudomorphs have nearly the entire termination faces of the apophyllite form missing so that only the short prism faces, now quartz of course, remain. Rarely, there are a few small analcime crystals associated with the smooth-faced pseudomorphs.

Most of the pseudomorphs with the drusy quartz surfaces are under about 3 cm long, but a few were found with crystals to 9 cm. Most of those with smooth faces are under 2 cm, but have been found to 4 cm (personal).

Elmore County: Drusy quartz coats cavities in quartz veins in the Vishnu Mine and other mines in the Rocky Bar District. Crystals are up to 1.5 cm long and are associated with arsenopyrite, sphalerite, galena and pyrite (Wagner, 1939).

Smoky quartz crystals have been found to 30 cm in length in the placer deposit of the Dismal Swamp area northwest of Rocky Bar. The crystals have been found with gold, topaz, and other heavy minerals. Dismal Swamp is a small basin in which the crystals have weathered from the surrounding granitic rocks where they originated in miarolitic cavities, and possibly in pegmatites. Cavities are uncommon, but have been found in the few outcrops of the area (Beckwith, 1972; personal).

Small quartz crystals occur in the veins in the mines of the Volcano District. They occur as coarse comb linings and druses lining fractures. Crystals vary from about 6 mm to a maximum of about 2.5 cm in length and are white in color (Allen, 1940).

Smoky quartz can be found in miarolitic cavities in the granite of the Steel Mountain stock, near Dismal Swamp, northwest of Rocky Bar. Most cavities are small, being less than 7 cm across; thus most quartz crystals are small, less than 2 cm in length. One weathered, nearly empty, larger cavity (approximately 0.6 x 0.6 x 1 m across) was found. Smoky quartz crystals are relatively common up to about 2 cm in length, and have been found up to 30 cm in length (the few large crystals from the one large cavity). The smaller crystals are often gemmy, light to dark brown, and the larger crystals nearly black. Surfaces are often brilliant, but may have a frosted appearance. Associated minerals include microcline, albite, magnetite, chlorite, titanite and rarely REE minerals. There are few rock exposures on this granite stock, most of it is rounded and overgrown (personal).

Gem County: Smoky quartz crystals occur in the pegmatites with schorl and aquamarine on Ola ridge, east of Ola. Crystals are mostly small, less than 6 cm long, but have been reported to 12 cm. Rarely small scepters with colorless to white scepters on smoky stems have been found (Photo. 305) (personal).

Idaho County: Quartz crystals are scarce in a massive quartz knob northeast of Burghdorf. Crystals are a few to several centimeters long and transparent, but scarce. The quartz mass forms the top of Crystal Butte (personal).

Quartz crystals with rutile inclusions have been found at an undisclosed location near Golden on the south Fork of the Clearwater River east of Grangeville. The quartz crystals are up to at least 5 cm in length, partially colorless and contain red and golden rutile needles (Photos. 301, 314). Other quartz crystals have also been found including colorless to white sceptered crystals (Photo. 306) (personal).

Kootenai County: Smoky Quartz has been found in cavities in pegmatite dikes in the Precambrian gneiss on Red Hog, a large hill 10 miles southwest of Coeur d'Alene and in miarolitic cavities in small granitic intrusions on the west side of the hill. This locality is private land and has a deep soil cover and moderate vegetation cover. Cavities have been found where they have been exposed in roadcuts.

Smoky quartz and some rock crystal (possibly bleached smoky quartz) have been found as euhedral crystals up to at least 10 cm in length. Generally these are clean and sharp, often brilliant. Most of them are black or very dark brown; some are gem quality.

Cavities are collapsed and are generally of small size, less than 30 cm across. Microcline, and sometimes albite, is commonly associated and beryl is reported (personal).

A similar occurrence can be found along the Cougar Gulch road a few miles to the northwest. The pegmatites are uncommonly exposed in roadcuts, crystal cavities are rare. One cavity in a thin pegmatite, nearly flat-lying, in a roadcut, produced several high quality smoky quartz crystals to 7 cm. The best of these were generally 2 to 3 cm in length, medium and brilliant with nearly flawless interiors.

The cavity was filled with clay and about 15 cm wide, by 40 cm deep by 12 cm high. It only yielded a few quartz crystals and pieces of microcline (personal).

Quartz has also been found on Mica Peak. Small white crystals to more than 5 cm in length have been found (Photo. 307) (personal).

Latah County: Crystals to 7 cm occur near Bank Gulch in the NW$\frac{1}{4}$ Sec. 23, T. 42 N, R. 2 W. The crystals are in a wide vein along a fault. Pyrite forms cubes partially altered to limonite in the area, and locally there are crystalline aggregates of schorl (McNeill, 1971).

Quartz crystals to 7 cm across and Japan law twin crystals have been found in a field several miles northeast of Troy. The location has not been thoroughly studied to determine the source of the crystals. This is the only known location of Japan law twin quartz in the state (personal).

Lemhi County: Crystals of large size have been found in several localities in the areas east and north of Leesburg in T. 21-22 N., R. 20-21 E. Specific areas include the head of Sawpit Creek, head of Pollard Creek and its tributaries, and in the cirque at the head of Rapps Creek. Most crystals are 5 cm or smaller and are abundant in some areas as druses. Crystals to 15 cm in length have been reported, but crystals over 1 cm are uncommon. Many of them are tinted bluish or yellowish by thin coatings of cryptocrystalline quartz with a drusy surface or stained yellow by iron oxides, but most are colorless.

They occur in quartz veins in gray quartzite; the veins have iron oxidation and bleaching along them. Pyrite and wolframite are associated but rare; most of the pyrite has been altered to iron oxides. Brilliant black crusts of iron oxides are locally abundant. A damaged smoky quartz crystal, about 5 cm in length, was reportedly found in talus at the headwaters of the southern fork of Pollard Creek. Single colorless quartz crystals have also been reported to have been found on talus slopes (personal; Shockey, 1957).

Crystals to large size have been found on Crystal Gulch, a tributary of Indian Creek, 6 miles west of North Fork. One locality is in the north side of Crystal Gulch, just above its confluence with Indian Creek. The other locality is about 1 mile east on both sides of the north fork of Crystal Gulch. The crystals vary from less than 2.5 cm in length to crystals that are over 50 pounds in weight. They are partially milky and fractured and partially clear. They occur in chlorite pockets in a gneissic porphyritic diorite, of the Idaho batholith. These chlorite-quartz crystal pockets are along diorite or gabbro dikes. They are scattered over a large area and are irregular and unpredictable.

Pockets and good crystals are uncommon. At the locality on the north side of Crystal Gulch, above the confluence of the Gulch with Indian Creek, the U.S. Bureau of Mines dug trenches and drove a short adit exploring for crystals. These workings are caved and slumped. At the portal of the adit, a natural outcrop is coated with calcite rhombs that are coated with chlorite. Yellowish amber titanite crystals occur frozen in the calcite. These small crystals can be seen where the calcite has been weathered or broken. A thin coating of dark green microcrystals of chlorite(?) coat the surface of the calcite. A similar occurrence was noted about 0.2 mile up the canyon (Herdlick, 1948; personal).

Similar quartz crystals have been found near the headwaters of Squaw Creek, about 7 miles northwest of the Crystal Gulch locality. The crystals occur with chlorite. The largest found here weighed about 70 pounds (Herdlick, 1948).

Northwest of this area, along the border with Montana, smoky quartz, albite and microcline occur in miarolitic cavities and small pegmatites in the granite of the Painted Rocks Lake stock. Most of the stock lies to the north in Montana but it does extend an unknown distance into Idaho. The occurrence runs for several miles along border from the Cathedral Rock area westerly to and beyond Blue Joint. The area is heavily timbered, so exposures are uncommon. The cavities occur in small pegmatites as well as the main granite body (personal).

Brilliant smoky quartz crystals have been found in the porphyritic granitic rock of the Crags batholith, west of Cobalt. They occur in miarolitic cavities in the rocks of the Yellowjacket Mountains from Yellowjacket Lake to Golden Trout Lake and in the Bighorn Crags to the northwest. The granite is deeply weathered and crumbly in the lower exposures. Below most cliffs there is little or no blocky talus, but only gravelly tree-covered slopes. Ridges are often rounded, although steep to vertical cliffs are dominant in the upper portions of the outcrops. Yellowjacket Lake lies in a cirque-like depression, that is shadowed by high ridges and cliffs on the south and west sides.

Most of the miarolitic cavities are weathered and empty, and large holes formed where the crumbly rock has weathered away around fractures are common. Some of these cavities are over three feet across. Pegmatites occur as small dikes, or more commonly as irregular pods. A weathered cavity over 3 x 4 x 6 feet was seen in one of the unusually large pegmatite pods. Most of the pegmatite bodies are less than two feet across.

Microcline crystals are white and often brilliant, or pink and often etched. Smoky quartz crystals are generally less than 5 cm in length (Photo. 308), and most are less than 2.5 cm but may be more than 8 cm in length. They are dark brown to black and have brilliant surfaces. Some specimens have a colorless or milky quartz overgrowth that forms a phantom crystal when the smoky inner portion is visible. Specimens with quartz oriented along the crystallographic axis of the microcline were seen (personal).

Crystals are associated with hematite and magnetite in the iron deposits in the McKim Creek area, 30 miles southwest of Salmon. In the veins of the Fire Fly claim in the SW$^1/_4$ NW$^1/_4$, Sec. 25, T. 18 N., R. 21 E., south of Poison Creek, quartz veins have vuggy zones which are lined with quartz crystals up to 2 cm in length. Magnetite as octahedrons, pyrite as cubes, chalcopyrite and chrysocolla are associated (Soregaroli, 1961).

Quartz crystals, some amethystine, line agate nodules found along Cabin and Ringle Creeks. Individual crystals are as much as 1.2 cm across. The nodules are up to 25 cm across, but most are around 4-8 cm. Stilbite lines fractures in some nodules (Soregaroli, 1961).

A few specimens of quartz have been found in the Blackbird District. These have been recovered in groups with crystals up to 10 cm in length (personal).

Owyhee County: Crusts of drusy quartz and often larger crystals were found in cavities in the veins of most of the districts of the county. Some good specimens were found on the dump of the Blaine tunnel and in the Banner vein on Long Gulch. The terminations are often dominated by the positive rhombohedron so that the crystals appear to have only three sides and look triangular in cross section. The quartz crystals also often taper rapidly and may step down in cross section to form a "reverse scepter." Often crystals are coated with a layer that is finely crystalline or chalcedonic or have a drusy coating of very fine quartz crystals. In the mineralized portions of the quartz veins, the silver minerals were commonly on the quartz crystals (personal, Shannon, 1926).

Quartz of a platy pseudomorphic habit occurred in abundance in the DeLamar, Webfoot, Chautauqua and other mines of the Silver City and nearby districts. It forms a "cellular network of thin, straight intersecting laminae of quartz," often with a drusy coating. Each plate consists "of a narrow median line adjoined on both sides by quartz, projecting as minute crystals on the laminae" (Shannon, 1926).

The angles of the intersecting plates do not seem to follow any law or represent the angles of any mineral. Orthoclase (referred to as the valencianite variety by Shannon) is associated with this quartz in several of the mines. Thick tabular plates of calcite, in a cellular aggregate, identical to the habit of the quartz was found in the Owyhee shaft and the dump of the tunnel on the south side of Long Gulch below the Blaine tunnel. It is believed that the quartz is pseudomorphous after this type of calcite (Piper and Laney, 1926; Shannon, 1926).

Doubly terminated quartz crystals occur in the Rising Star vein in clay-filled cavities. Crystals occur with orthoclase in the veins of the Flint District and in the Banner Mine on Florida Mountain. Reticulated naumannite was reported on drusy quartz in the Banner Mine (Piper and Laney, 1926).

Dake (1956) reports geodes lined with quartz crystals on War Eagle Mountain, and pale colored amethyst crystals on some of the mine dumps on the mountain.

Small and tiny quartz crystals occur in geodes and veins in the DeLamar Mine. Sometimes they are associated with naumannite and other silver minerals (personal).

Shoshone County: Small crystals of quartz have been found in several of the mines of the Coeur d'Alene Mining District. In the Sunshine Mine, small specimens with milky to colorless quartz crystals to about 2 cm in length have been found. Good quality crystals of siderite and tetrahedrite have also been found. Similar specimens with quartz and siderite occur in the Silver Summit Mine and in the Galena Mine (Photo. 35) with quartz to about 3 cm in length. Small crystals of quartz have been found with calcite and sphalerite crystals in the Bunker Hill Mine (Photo. 38) (personal).

Quartz crystals occur on O'Donnell Creek near Stocking Meadows. The transparent crystals are mostly up to about 3 cm in length, and sometimes up to about 6 cm. They are occasionally recovered in clusters. Some of the crystals have inclusions of an unknown acicular dark green or dark brown mineral at the base. Crystals have been recovered by digging in the soil and following quartz veins. This location has been under claim on occasion (personal).

Quartz crystals have been found at an undisclosed locality near Clarkia. These crystals form clusters with crystals from 1 to about 6 cm in length. The prism faces are overgrown with a somewhat skeletal white quartz and some tiny crystals project from the prisms near their bases (Photo. 309) (personal).

Twin Falls County: Chalcedony lines thundereggs in a roadcut at Rabbit Springs, 4.5 miles north of the Nevada border, on Highway 93. The chalcedony fluoresces under ultraviolet light. The Highway Department has smoothed and graded the outcrop, but the small geodes litter the surface. Bluish agate and small geodic cavities lined with small quartz crystals can be found in a small pit 0.2 miles to the SE. There was a rest stop at this location, but it was recently removed by the Highway Department (personal).

Valley County: Quartz crystals, often smoky, can be found with epidote and orange to red garnets in a skarn exposed in a roadcut about 0.25 miles east of the Sloans Peak Lookout jeep trail, east of Donnelly. Access is gained by taking the Paddy Flat Road (#388) to road number 389 for about 11 miles. Turn south on road number 401 towards the lookout turnoff at the top of a ridge then east to the roadcut.

Quartz crystals are uncommon, but massive gray to smoky quartz is common in the western part of the deposit. Quartz crystals occur in cavities in the quartz and in the fine-grained massive diopside with the quartz. Many of the quartz crystals have a brilliant, gemmy, medium smoky color. Epidote is mostly small to about 1 cm, garnet crystals are tiny to about 2 cm, but mostly less than 6 mm. Small crystals are orange and the color darkens as the size increases. Some coarse garnet crystals are frozen in the quartz and may be exposed in matrix by carefully chipping away the quartz (personal, Joe Dorris personal communication).

Quartz occurs in small cavities in the Logan Creek stock west of Big Creek. This area can be reached by a road up Logan Creek, and a hike up a trail along the creek to a meadow. Boulders on the north side of the meadow contain small quartz crystals and rarely small fluorite crystals in small cavities. A few cavities occur in the cliffs above. A mile further west, a larger cavity containing crystals to better than 4 cm long was found (personal).

Quartz crystals, in groups and clusters can be found in hydrothermal veins with pyrite, galena and molybdenite in the prospects and mine east of Twin Peaks, in Sec. 35, T. 18 N., R. 4 E., southeast of McCall. The quartz is generally milky, but sharp crystals can be found up to about 1.2 cm in length (personal).

Quartz crystals to large size have been reported from Green Mountain in Sec. 6 and 7

T. 17 N., R. 5 E. The quartz crystals have been reported up to more than 30 cm in length. Garnet and epidote crystals occur frozen in the rock, and may occur as euhedral crystals in cavities (personal).

Rutilated and rock clear quartz were found with epidote at prospects east of Donnelly, off the Paddy Flat road, southeast of McCall. The quartz crystals have been found up to 10 cm in length, and fine brilliant epidote up to 2.5 cm. Three pits were dug in a search for radio quality quartz during WW II. Since then, the pits and dumps have become slumped and overgrown. The crystals occur as singles in decomposed rock and clay soil (personal).

Quartz crystals occur in miarolitic cavities in the granitic rocks southwest of Wolf Fang Peak, on the north side of Elk Creek (personal).

Smoky quartz crystals occur on the ridge just north of Cascade. Miarolitic cavities containing microcline and quartz are uncommon, but some were of large size. This is private land, and some areas have homes built on them (Beckwith, 1972; personal).

Washington County: Quartz crystals, some amethystine, occur in the Beacon Hill and Hog Creek areas northwest and north of Weiser. These are found in geodes (Beckwith, 1972).

REALGAR

AsS, monoclinic
Short prismatic crystals, striated along c-axis; mostly massive, granular, compact. Dark red to orangish red; transparent to translucent. Found in low temperature hydrothermal vein deposits with orpiment and stibnite; also a sublimation product or hot springs deposit.

Unknown county: Realgar has not been documented as occurring in good crystals or of any noteworthy occurrence in the state. An old specimen from a private collection, labeled as coming from Idaho has numerous realgar crystals in cavities in a black siliceous matrix. The realgar crystals are mostly bright red, some orangeish red and are up to 1.1 cm in length. On this specimen most of the crystals have been broken (personal).

RENARDITE

$Pb(UO_2)_4(PO_4)_2(OH)_4 \cdot 7H_2O$, orthorhombic
Probably equal to dewindtite. Forms drusy coatings of minute flattened crystals, also lath-like; microcrystalline crusts; fibrous. Lemon-yellow, yellow or brownish yellow; translucent to transparent. A secondary mineral associated with torbernite and other secondary uranium minerals.

Custer County: Renardite has been found in T. 11 N., R. 13-14 E., north of Stanley. It occurs as soft bright green and yellow grains in rocks of the Idaho batholith and arkosic conglomerate at the base of the Challis formation. Phosphuranylite, autunite, uraninite, marcasite and stibnite are associated (Kern, 1959).

RHODOCHROSITE

$MgCO_3$, hexagonal (trigonal)
Forms series with calcite and with siderite. Rare in rhombohedral crystals, mostly massive or granular. Pink or rose-red; transparent to translucent. Occurs in veins with silver, lead and copper minerals.

Bonner County: Massive rhodochrosite occurs in the Conjecture Mine, south of Lakeview. Shannon (1926) reported it to be with quartz and pale pink in color. Metallic minerals associated include galena, pyrite, sphalerite and tetrahedrite. The ores contain small cavities in the upper levels which are lined with microcrystals of various lead, silver and zinc minerals. It is possible that there may be some microcrystals of rhodochrosite too.

The mine has extensive underground workings, but is presently flooded. Even though there are several million tons of low to moderate grade silver ore reportedly blocked out, the mine is scheduled to be rehabilitated (personal).

Lemhi County: Minute crystals of rhodochrosite can be found on fracture surfaces in the Kittie Burton Mine in the Indian Creek District. It occurs in the ores associated with malachite, azurite and earthy iron and manganese oxides (Shannon, 1926).

Excellent crystals of rhodochrosite have been reported from the Blackbird District. These are of small size and uncommon (Shannon, 1926; Umpleby, 1913a).

Rhodochrosite occurs as white to light pink masses in the Ima Mine, frozen in the vein quartz. Crystals have not been reported in the cavities in the quartz veins (personal).

ROSASITE

$(Cu,Zn)_2(CO_3)(OH)_2$, monoclinic
Commonly various shades of blue to blue green, also green. Rare as tiny acicular crystals in radial groups; most often occurs as hemispheres, botryoidal crusts and masses. An uncommon mineral in the oxidized zone of copper-zinc bearing ore deposits.

Lemhi County: On the dumps of the pits and shaft of the Excelsior Mine on the east side of Horseshoe Gulch, in the Spring Mountain District, small fillings and uncommonly hemispheres of rosasite occur in oxidized dolomite. This is the first reported occurrence of rosasite in the state. The hemispheres are less than 3 mm across, and the irregular masses filling cavities are less than 2 cm in maximum dimension (Photo. 310). Rarely, a small cavity contains tiny crystals of rosasite which may be associated with the rosasite hemispheres (Photos. 311, 312). Associated minerals include hemimorphite and calcite. The mines are high on the east side of a steep-walled cirque. There is very little of the rosasite-bearing material on the dumps, and only a small percentage of the material contains cavities; the rosasite is mostly small masses and veinlets (personal).

ROSCOELITE

$K(V,Al,Mg)_2AlSi_3O_{10}(OH)_2$, monoclinic
A mica group mineral, uncommon. Generally as minute scales, rosettes and stellate groups. Clove-brown to greenish brown, dark green. An early stage gangue mineral in low-temperature Au-Ag-Te deposits and oxidized portions of low-temperature sedimentary U-V deposits.

Custer County: Roscoelite has been identified in the Washington Basin District. It occurs as small scales and crystals in a prospect near the Empire vein. The small bright dark green translucent crystals occur in small cavities and fractures in the wall rock of a small trench (Photo. 313). Grains of pyrite and sphalerite are associated (personal).

RUTILE

TiO_2, tetragonal
Trimorphous with anatase and brookite. Crystals are prismatic and vertically striated and often acicular. Elbow twins are common, often repeated. Yellow, red, reddish brown to black; subtranslucent to transparent. Occurs in granite, pegmatites and many metamorphic rocks.

Boise County: Rutile crystals are uncommon in the black sand concentrates of the gold-bearing gravels of the county. A prismatic crystal 6 mm long was found in some concentrates from Centerville. The crystal was terminated by the pyramid and the prism faces were deeply striated. The crushed fragments showed a yellowish green color (Shannon, 1926).

Boise, Custer and Elmore Counties: Rutile is uncommon in miarolitic cavities in the granites of the Sawtooth Mountains, and has been positively identified from only one cavity, but is tentatively identified from several others. In the identified occurrence, it forms twinned aggregates of platy crystals, black in color, and up to about 1 cm across.

In other cavities, it is expected to be one of the minerals that occurs as red to black blade-like and needle-like inclusions in smoky quartz and topaz; the other mineral is ferrocolumbite. These inclusions are locally common and typically occur as a few single blades or needles or as radiating groups of several crystals. Typically, they are included in the outer 1-2 mm of the quartz or topaz. Individual crystals are mostly about 2-5 mm in length and very thin (personal).

Clearwater County: Crystal fragments and water worn pebbles of rutile up to 2 cm in diameter are common in some placer gravels in the Pierce area. They are brown, yellow or greenish in small fragments, but the larger pieces are reddish black. Tourmaline, corundum, epidote, ilmenite and other rare minerals are associated (Shannon, 1926).

Rutile has been found in two adjacent localities near Mason Butte in the southeastern part of the county. One locality is the headwaters of Cedar Creek at the base of Mason Butte in the SE$\frac{1}{4}$ Sec. 1 and NE$\frac{1}{4}$ Sec. 12, T. 38 N., R. 1 W. Rutile occurs as pebbles in the gravels of the alluvium (Hubbard, 1957).

The other locality is in Sec. 13, T. 38 N., R. 1 W., about five miles southwest of Cavendish. Rutile occurs as pebbles in the bed of a logging road about 300 feet from the junction of the logging road with a dirt access road (personal).

Idaho County: Quartz crystals with rutile inclusions have been found at an undisclosed location east of Grangeville near Golden on the south Fork of the Clearwater River. The quartz crystals are up to at least 5 cm in length, partially colorless and contain red and golden rutile needles (Photos. 301, 314). Other quartz crystals have also been found including colorless to white sceptered crystals. Grossular has also been reported in this area (personal).

Lemhi County: Rutile occurs in the Blue Boar vein in the Tendoy Copper Queen Mine in Sec. 15, T. 19 N., R. 25 E. and the Blue Ridge prospect which is in a basin at the head of Camp Gulch which enters the South Fork of Agency Creek from the east at the mine. Shafts and cuts have been developed on the vein. Mineralization includes jasperoid, montmorillonite, pyrite, hematite and rutile in quartz. The rutile forms honeybrown roughly prismatic striated crystals in white vein quartz and irregular masses in gray quartzite. Irregular cavities in the quartz are lined with drusy quartz, siliceous box work or montmorillonite (Schipper, 1955; Sharp and Cavender, 1962).

Shoshone County: Steel-gray needles of rutile were found in quartz in the Lookout Mountain Mine south of Pinehurst. The specimen was found as float and not in the mine (Shannon, 1926).

Valley County: Rutilated quartz has been found with clear quartz epidote at prospects east of Donnelly, off the Paddy Flat road, southeast of McCall. Quartz crystals have been found up to about 10 cm long. The deposit was prospected for quartz during WW II. Since then, the pits and dumps have become slumped and overgrown. The crystals occur as singles in decomposed rock and clay soil weathering out of a quartz vein in a contact zone (personal).

SAFFLORITE

$CoAs_2$, orthorhombic

Dimorphous with clinosafflorite. Crystals resemble arsenopyrite, may be massive with a fibrous structure. Tin-white; tarnishes to dark gray. Occurs with other cobalt and nickel minerals, silver, bismuth and loellingite in vein deposits.

Lemhi County: Safflorite can be found with cobaltite and chalcopyrite in the Calus Mine, which is located in Sec. 21, T. 21 N., R. 18 E. on the hillside north of Blackbird. Mineralization is in a quartz, pyrite, biotite, ankerite and siderite gangue (Trites and Tooker, 1953). Safflorite may occur in the Blackbird and other mines of the district.

SAMARSKITE-(Y)

$(Y,Ce,U,Fe)_3(Nb,Ta,Ti)_5O_{16}$, monoclinic

Prismatic, sometimes tabular; often massive. Velvet black, may have a brownish tint. Occurs in granite pegmatites with ferrocolumbite, monazite, zircon, muscovite, albite and garnet.

Boise County: Samarskite-(Y) is associated with columbite, zircon, garnet and monazite in the concentrates of the gold-bearing gravels of the Idaho City District. It forms pitted terminated crystals and grains with a black color (Shannon, 1926).

Samarskite-(Y), consisting of fine grains to coarse crystals, occurs in the pegmatite of the Columbite Mine 3 miles south of the South Fork of the Payette River on the crest of the ridge between Wash and Horn Creeks in Sec. 24, T. 8 N., R 4 E. A 309 pound crystal with a columbite core and a 100 pound crystal were found, during mining operations, near the west portal of the tunnel which as been driven completely through the ridge. The tunnel cuts through a zoned pegmatite (Fryklund, 1951).

At the Mirandeborde prospects, on the west side of Wash Creek, opposite the Bowman prospects, samarskite-(Y) forms grains in pegmatite. Columbite is associated. This is the largest pegmatite of the group in this area. There are other prospects, pits and adits developed on small pegmatites in this area (Fryklund, 1951).

SCAPOLITE

Scapolite is the old name, now discredited as a species, for the minerals of the scapolite group: marialite and meionite. None of the occurrences in Idaho have been identified as to species.

Shoshone County: Scapolite is abundant in areas in the schists that have formed from the metamorphism of the Precambrian age Belt Supergroup rocks in the St. Joe and Clearwater Rivers area. It is especially common in the area around Avery and can be seen in outcrops and roadcuts along the St. Joe River.

It forms small, rounded grains, mostly less than 6 mm across. These are white and on the exposed surfaces they can easily be seen in contrast against the darker schist or phyllite matrix where they create a speckled outcrop (personal).

SCHEELITE

$CaWO_4$, tetragonal

Octahedral or less commonly tabular; may be massive or granular. Colorless to white, yellowish, pale yellow or brownish. Transparent. An important tungsten ore mineral. Found in contact metamorphic deposits, quartz veins or pegmatites; associated with wolframite, epidote, tremolite, garnet, diopside and chalcopyrite.

Bonner County: Tiny crystals of scheelite occur in the skarn at the Vulcan Mine northeast of Lakeview on the east side of Lake Pend Oreille. There is a large exposure of the skarn along the new section of the road northerly of Lakeview. This is the main road around the lake and separates from the road to Lakeview at a junction about a half mile south of Lakeview. After the road crosses Gold Creek and switches back to the west it cuts through a small exposure of the skarn at 1.5 miles from the creek; the main exposure is 0.2 mile further west. The main exposure is a garnet-diopside mass with many small cavities and locally abundant pyrite. The pyrite is oxidizing and one can detect the odor of sulfur while driving by this rusty roadcut.

There is an adit in the central part of the cut, nearly completely buried by slumping debris and another small digging at the top of the cut near the east end. There are tiny green crystals of diopside, brown garnet crystals to about 6 mm and tiny yellow to white scheelite crystals rarely as large as 2 mm (Photo. 315). These are distorted octahedrons and also subhedral crystals, somewhat rounded. The scheelite occurs in the central part of the roadcut with the garnet and diopside in the numerous small cavities. The smaller exposure down the road has a similar occurrence (personal).

The main Vulcan Mine is accessible by the old road, either by continuing westerly and then northerly on the new road to a junction, or by going north out of Lakeview. The main Vulcan Mine is in an oxidized intrusive rock with quartz veins containing pyrite and reportedly arsenic. The large rusty dump can be seen along the road. There are two other adits along the road down near Gold Creek just west of the junction with the jeep trail that goes along the creek (personal).

Boundary County: Fine to coarse crystals of scheelite occur in a drusy quartz vein in diorite near Copeland. The coarse crystals can be found in limonite-filled cavities, but most of the scheelite is fine grained and massive (Shannon, 1926).

Custer County: Scheelite partially fills cavities in massive garnet, and is sometimes euhedral, in the Phoenix Mine, Mackay District. Mineralization is in a tactite in a shear zone at the contact of granite of the White Knob stock and limestone and marble. Powellite and olive-gray, red-brown to black garnets are associated. The mine is on the ridge near the head of Mammoth Canyon, 3 miles west of Mackay in T. 6 N., R. 23 E. (Cook, 1956).

Scheelite occurs with epidote, vesuvianite, garnet, calcite, pyrite, molybdenite diopside and actinolite at the Wildhorse Mine deposits northwest of Mackay on Wildhorse Creek. There are several tactite zones in the valley that have been mined or prospected for tungsten. The Hard to Find deposit is on the left fork of Wildhorse Creek about 1,000 feet above the main fork. The largest tactite zone occurs in this deposit. The Beaver claims are on the east side of the creek, about 0.9 mile north of the mill. The Steep Climb deposit is about 300 feet elevation above the mill on the west side of the creek and the DMEA adit is above the mill. There are several tactite zones in a cirque at the Pine Mouse claims about 1.4 miles northwest of the mill.

Scheelite forms large white crystals, and epidote forms short euhedral crystals. Mineralization is associated with alaskite dikes that have formed from the metamorphism of beds of marble in gneiss. The best exposures of the tactite is in the Hard to Find cut where it is exposed intermittently along its 600 foot length. Crystals have been reported to be "of large size," but are uncommon, even in micro size. More common are massive, altered occurrences of the minerals with dark, earthy oxides. The pits and cuts are slumped and overgrown (Heungwon, 1955; Pattee, 1968; personal).

Idaho County: Scheelite occurs as yellow-brown masses in the Charity Mine in the Warren District. There are some crystal faces in the masses. Some pockets of scheelite contained coarse gold. It is known to occur in other mines in the district, including the Little Giant (Shannon, 1926).

Lemhi County: The Ima Mine in the Blue Wing District contains scheelite. It forms thin crusts with a white to pale yellow color, lining cavities in coarse quartz associated with huebnerite (Shannon, 1926).

Scheelite occurs in several of the mines along Freeman Creek. In a quartz vein in Sec. 2, T. 22 N., R. 23 E., crystals of scheelite can be found with small amounts of limonite. It occurs in one of several quartz veins that can be found along the walls of several mafic dikes next to the Miner Lake fault. Muscovite, galena and pyrite also occur in the quartz (Mackenzie, 1949).

Shoshone County: Scheelite occurs in several of the mines of the Murray District, north of the Coeur d'Alene District. The Golden Chest and Golden Winnie mines are the most noted occurrences. These are best known as gold mines and are in a district that was principally a gold district. Rich placer deposits were worked prior to 1900 and intermittently up to the 1940s.

Scheelite occurs in quartz veins in masses up to 10 cm across. A few crystals have been found as drusy coatings on fracture surfaces. Gold-bearing pyrite and other sulfides are associated (Shannon, 1926; personal).

SCHORL

$NaFe_3Al_6(BO_3)_3Si_6O_{18}(OH)_4$, hexagonal (trigonal)

Forms a series with dravite; member of the tourmaline group. Prismatic and vertically striated; often coarse to fine columnar in parallel or radiating structure. Black, dark blue on thin edges. Occurs in granite pegmatites, other igneous rocks and many metamorphic rocks. Many of the occurrences given below were actually listed as" tourmaline" in the references. It is probable that most of them are schorl (some may be dravite).

Blaine County: Schorl forms imperfect crystals in talus blocks of pegmatite at the head of the cirque on the south flank of Mount Hyndman (Shannon, 1926).

Aggregates of radial fibers of tourmaline (schorl or dravite) in spherical masses up to 5 mm across were found on a mining claim in the Lava Creek District, 20 miles west of Arco.

They are greenish to brownish black in color (Shannon, 1926).

Schorl occurs in the area around Hailey in T. 1-2 N., R. 17-18 E. It forms masses and radiating groups frozen in complex lime-silicate contact rock. Wollastonite, vesuvianite, actinolite, apatite, diopside, garnet, augite and several metallic minerals occur with the schorl (Umpleby et al, 1930).

Boundary County: Small crystals of tourmaline, probably schorl, occur in a narrow pegmatite in a roadcut on the Trout Creek Road, about one mile west of the West Side Road, 10 miles west of Bonners Ferry. Individual crystals are up to about 1.9 cm in length (Navratil, 1959).

Clearwater County: Fragments of euhedral crystals of schorl up to 2 cm in diameter occur in placer gravels at Pierce. Corundum, epidote and garnet are associated (Shannon, 1926).

Pieces of black tourmaline crystals occur in an alluvial (colluvial?) deposit near the site of the Fohl Picnic area on the ridge west of the Pierce Divide. Pieces to several centimeters long have been reported. Muscovite, smoky quartz and topaz are associated, and pieces of elbaite crystals have been reported (personal).

Gem County: Brilliant black crystals of schorl have been collected at several small pegmatites northeast of Ola (Photo. 316). One deposit which has been worked by collectors is accessible by taking the High Valley-Squaw Creek Road (road to Smiths Ferry) which turns east from the highway 0.2 mile north of the Ola Cafe. Follow this road for 4.3 miles up the mountain. At this point take a left fork and follow it for 0.4 mile to three forks in the road. Take the right fork and follow it for 1.6 miles. The pegmatite is on the ridge on the right, about 100 feet above the road. From the east, turn off of Highway 55 at the Cougar Mountain. Lodge onto the High Valley-Squaw Creek Road and follow it for 13.5 miles to Ola Summit, then 1 mile to the road to the pegmatite.

Schorl crystals occur in a zone in the pegmatite, exposed just below the thin soil near the ridge top. Single crystals, mostly doubly terminated have been found up to at least 22 cm in length. They also occur as groups and intergrown. Crystals are frozen in the feldspar matrix of the pegmatite, but weathering has partially decomposed the pegmatite and released the schorl. The pegmatite has been heavily worked, so that a collector needs to move much material to find a productive zone. A few smoky quartz crystals of small size occur with the schorl. Beryl has been reported from another pegmatite nearby (personal).

Other pegmatites in the area have had claims located on them and have been mined for specimens. One such claims is the Joint Venture claim #1 from which black, lustrous schorl crystals have been mined (Photo. 317) (personal).

Latah County: Schorl is rare to common in the mica-bearing pegmatites that have been mined for sheet mica in the Avon District. The occurrence covers a large area in T. 41 N., R. 2 W. from 3 to 6 miles north of Avon. The principal producer was the Muscovite Mine which produced from both underground and surface workings. Schorl crystals can be found that are from less than 1 cm to more than 12 cm in length. Most of the larger crystals have rough surfaces, and many have a flattened form. Light greenish colored beryl crystals, to large size (up to at least 20 cm across), occur in the pegmatite too. These are highly fractured and have rough to moderately smooth surfaces.

The last production and extensive exploration from these mines and prospects was in the 1950s, so they are largely slumped and overgrown. Crystals can be found on the dumps and in the pegmatite exposures in the walls of the pits of the Muscovite Mine. In the other mines and prospects of the district, the various crystals have been found on the dumps and in the walls of the cuts, trenches and pits, but schorl and beryl are scarce. A few reddish garnet crystals have also been found (Shannon, 1926; personal).

Shoshone County: A few clusters of black tourmaline crystals (probably schorl) occur in quartz on top of Moses Butte. The crystals are several centimeters long and occur in parallel groups. Below this outcrop is a zone with large granular almandine crystals (personal).

Elongated or fibrous crystals of schorl are reported to occur in metamorphic rocks in several locations south of the St. Joe River. Some of the crystals are up to 2 cm in length. Black needles of schorl occur in feldspar with green chlorite and kyanite from a locality 2.5 miles south of Trimmed Tree Mountain. Bundles of small crystals have also been found near the summit of Moses Butte frozen in quartz (personal; Shannon, 1926).

SCORODITE

$FeAsO_4 \cdot 2H_2O$, orthorhombic

Forms a series with mansfieldite. Crystals are usually pyramidal or tabular; may be prismatic or massive to earthy. Pale leek-green or grayish green to liver-brown; transparent. A secondary mineral in oxidized arsenic-bearing ores with vivianite, beudantite and quartz.

Blaine County: Thin crystals of scorodite occur in the Golden Bell Mine at the head of Minnie Gulch, Hailey District. The mineralization occurs in granodiorite (Shannon, 1926).

Microcrystalline crusts of green scorodite occur in the Eagle Bird Mine near the head of Garfield Canyon. The mine is located at 9,100 feet elevation almost on the line separating Secs. 35 and 26, T. 4 N., R. 21 E. Arsenopyrite, cerussite and anglesite are associated (Anderson and Wagner, 1946).

The Idaho Muldoon Mine contains microcrystalline crusts of green scorodite. The mine is in Sec. 7, T. 3 N., R. 22 E. on the east wall of Muldoon Creek at 7,800 feet elevation. Associated minerals include arsenopyrite, galena, pyrite, chalcopyrite, cerussite, anglesite and malachite (Anderson and Wagner, 1946).

Cassia County: Pale leek-green prismatic crystals and blackish olive-green botryoidal scorodite occur with cinnabar in prospects near Black Pine. Several mines including the Hazel Pine and Valantine have produced scorodite. Barite, realgar, smithsonite (as small curved brown, green or blue crystals or crusts) and jamesonite (as slender acicular crystals) occur with the scorodite in cavities in quartz veins (Anderson, 1931; Shannon, 1926).

Gem County: Scorodite can be found in mines of the Pearl-Horseshoe gold belt (Westview District) extending across the county line into Boise County. It has been reported from the Lincoln Mine 1 mile southwest of Pearl and the Lucky Ridge Mine west-northwest of Crown Point near the crest of the ridge facing the Payette River. Green scorodite forms microcrystalline crusts in gossan of the oxidized surface ore. Arsenopyrite, pyrite, galena, sphalerite, boulangerite, stibnite, pyrargyrite and possibly owyheeite are associated (Anderson and Rasor, 1934).

Lemhi County: In the Blackbird District, scorodite replaces cobaltite and coats fractures. Generally it is a yellow-green color and forms earthy crusts and masses. In the Nickel Plate Mine, it is associated with olivenite (Shannon, 1926).

SEGNITITE

$HPbFe_3(AsO_4)_2(OH)_6$, hexagonal

Occurs as rhombohedral or pseudo-octahedral crystals of tiny to small size; also as drusy coatings, spherical clusters or spongy aggregates. Greenish brown to yellowish brown to dark brown; transparent to translucent. A rare mineral in the oxidized portion of lead- and arsenic-bearing ore deposits.

Lemhi County: The rare mineral segnitite has recently been identified at the Ima Mine, Lemhi County. Here it occurs as rare yellow to brown and green microcrystalline coatings associated with beudantite, mimetite and wulfenite (Photo. 318). The individual crystals of the coatings are less than 0.1 mm across. Few small areas of the dumps show any of these secondary minerals. This is the first reported occurrence of segnitite in Idaho and it was only recently reported in Montana (Nikischer, 2004); there are only a few other occurrences in the United States of this rare mineral (personal).

SEPIOLITE

$Mg_4Si_6O_{15}O(OH)_2 \cdot 6H_2O$, orthorhombic

Massive, fine fibrous, earthy or often compact nodular; dry porous masses will float on water. Clay-like, grayish, yellowish, bluish green or reddish. Nearly opaque and dull. Occurs as an alteration of serpentine or magnesite; uncommon as an authigenic mineral in lacustrine deposits.

Lemhi County: Sepiolite is common in fractures in the mines of the Little Eightmile District. Generally it fills fractures in the lead-silver veins, but also occurs in the host rock adjoining the veins. Some of the fillings are as much as 2.5 cm thick. These fillings are formed by intermixed microscopic fibers and amorphous masses. It has a soapy feel and varies from colorless to blue-green (Thune, 1941).

SIDERITE

$FeCO_3$, hexagonal (trigonal)

Forms a series with magnesite and a series with rhodochrosite. Crystals as rhombohedrons, often with curved faces; most often cleavable granular, compact or earthy. Light to dark brown; transparent to translucent. Occurs in sedimentary rocks and as a gangue mineral in ore deposits.

Blaine County: Siderite is a common gangue mineral in the mines of several districts in the county. It has been found in the Elkhorn, Hailey, Rosetta, Warm Springs and Smoky Districts. It is associated with several gold, silver, lead and zinc minerals, but is mostly massive in form. There may be small crystals in some of the mines of these districts (Shannon, 1926).

Boise, Custer and Elmore Counties: Siderite is uncommon in the cavities of the granite of the Sawtooth Mountains, and is partially to completely altered to dark iron oxides. It occurs as small rhombs or combinations of flattened acute rhombs with nearly circular form, either as singles or groups (Photo. 60). They occur on the feldspar matrix or on smoky quartz. Most crystals are less than 6-7 mm across, but have been found up to 6 cm across.

These altered crystals have a brown to dark brown (almost black) color. When broken, some of them display a tan colored center that appears to be unaltered siderite. To the author's knowledge, no completely unaltered siderite crystals have been found. Quartz, microcline, albite, topaz, zinnwaldite, masutomilite and aquamarine are associated (personal).

Custer County: Siderite is a common mineral in many of the veins of the mining districts in the county. In the Bayhorse District it forms one of the gangue minerals in most of the mines. Small vugs contain minute crystals of siderite, arsenopyrite, tetrahedrite and chalcopyrite in the Utah Boy No. 5 tunnel of the Ramshorn Mine (Shannon, 1926). Similar small crystals probably occur in other mines of the district.

Idaho County: Specimens of siderite (sphaerosiderite) can be found in vesicles in the basalt of a roadcut 15 miles northwest of Grangeville. The roadcut is along Highway 95 on the northeast side of the highway at the southeast end of the connecting loop into Cottonwood. It is between mile posts 254 and 255 and is the largest one in the area. The siderite forms hemispheres and spheres to 1.7 cm. They are reddish brown or purplish with an iridescence when fresh and black when altered to goethite (Photo. 319). Jasper can be found in the southeast end of the cut (personal, Stinchfield, 1979). Siderite is quite common in vesicles in the Columbia River basalts. Collectors who are interested in this spheroidal form of siderite will probably have good luck searching other outcrops of the basalt in western Idaho.

Kootenai County: Siderite forms spheres (sphaerosiderite) in vesicles in the Columbia River basalt in the western part of the county (Photo. 320). Fine specimens with spheres to about 1 cm across have been found along Cougar Gulch, southwest of Coeur d'Alene. The siderite spheres are dark brown to nearly black on the surface, and lighter color, often greenish brown inside. Those with the dark colors are probably altered to goethite on the surface, and some may be altered completely. Brown spheres have been found at Rutledge Point on the east edge of Coeur d'Alene. Similar occurrences can be found in other outcrops of the basalt in the area, including the new Interstate 90 roadcuts to the east (personal).

Lemhi County: Minute crystals occur in veins in the Blue Wing District. It is common in other mines of the county and has been reported in the Blackbird District (Shannon, 1926).

Siderite is the most abundant gangue mineral in the mines of the Little Eightmile District. It occurs as masses and as rhombohedral crystals lining cavities in the primary ores (Thune, 1941).

Shoshone County: Good crystal specimens are not common, but siderite is the most common gangue mineral in most of the lead-silver mines of the Coeur d'Alene District and many of the other districts of the Idaho Panhandle. It varies from fine to coarsely crystalline masses. Most of it is a cream to buff color, but often is amber to dark brown. Much of it weathers to a dark brown or reddish brown color on exposure. Crystals are uncommon, but do occur in cavities and typically are sharp rhombs.

It is rare as small rhombohedral crystals of a yellowish to dark honey-yellow color in a few cavities in the Sunshine Mine. In these cavities, it is associated with tetrahedrite and quartz crystals; a few excellent small specimens have been produced in recent years. Similar specimens of siderite and quartz have been found in the Galena Mine (Photo. 35) and in the Silver Summit Mine. The siderite forms rhombic crystals up to about 1.5 cm across (personal).

Small translucent brown rhombohedrons line cavities in quartz in the Gold Hunter Mine. Boulangerite needles fill the vugs and often impale rhombs of siderite (Shannon, 1926).

Siderite crystals to 5 cm have been found in the Richmond and Monitor Mines near the headwaters of Loop Creek. These mines and other prospects are 20 miles southeast of Wallace in Secs. 8-10, 15 and 16, T. 46 N., R. 7 E. near the Idaho-Montana border. Crystals are partially embedded in quartz or as a druse lining cavities in veins in the rocks of the Belt supergroup. Micro crystals of malachite and zalesiite are associated but uncommon to rare at the Monitor Mine and malachite is associated at the Richmond Mine (personal; Umpleby and Jones, 1923).

SILVER

Ag, cubic

As cubes, octahedrons or dodecahedrons, mostly in groups of parallel crystals; commonly in elongated, reticulated, arborescent and wiry forms; massive or as scales or coatings. Silver-white; tarnishes gray to black. Most common in oxidized portions of silver-bearing ore deposits. Forms a series with gold. Associated with calcite, barite, silver sulfides and arsenides, cerussite and other metallic minerals.

Blaine County: Thin folia and grains of silver occur in several mines of the Wood River District. The Bullion Mine, in Secs. 15 and 22, T. 2 N., R. 17 E. was one of the better producers of silver. Native silver was associated with mossy grains of acanthite in altered granite. Silver was abundant in some parts of the vein in the Jennie P. prospect (previously Montezuma) in the SW$^1/_4$ Sec. 15, T. 1 N., R. 17 E. It occurs with chlorargyrite, galena, sphalerite, chalcopyrite and pyrite. Thin films of silver were uncommon in the Croesus Mine in Scorpion Gulch, about 3.5 miles southwest of Hailey in Secs. 29 and 30, T. 1 N., R. 18 E. It was most common on the 800 level near the shaft. Mineralization is in lenses in quartz diorite. Some cerussite and smithsonite were associated with the silver and pyrite, chalcopyrite, arsenopyrite, pyrrhotite and quartz were found in the mine (Shannon, 1926; Umpleby et al, 1930).

Wire silver has been found in a prospect at the head of Smiley Creek. It also occurs in the Webfoot Mine at 8,000 feet elevation on Smiley Creek about 1.4 miles from Vienna, and the Solace Mine 0.25 mile upstream. Proustite, arsenopyrite, tetrahedrite, chlorargyrite, pyrite, galena, sphalerite and chalcopyrite have also been reported. The metallic minerals fill cracks and fractures in quartz and silicified granite (Ross, 1927).

Boise County: Native silver was common in the Poorman Mine and uncommon in the lower levels of the Banner Mine, Banner District. It was associated with pyrargyrite, chlorargyrite, polybasite, argentiferous galena and gold. It generally occurred as scales, flakes or thin sheets in fractures that cross the veins and also as fine wires twisted around quartz crystals or rarely as wire nests in vugs. Proustite, miargyrite, owyheeite, tetrahedrite, chalcopyrite, sphalerite, quartz and calcite also occur in the veins. Most of the minerals form minute to coarse grains and masses and rarely form microscopic crystals on drusy quartz.

The district is located at 6,000 feet elevation on the headwaters of Banner Creek, a tributary of the Boise River, 75 miles northeast of Boise. Mineralization consists of quartz veins filling fissures in Tertiary porphyry dikes that intrude the Idaho batholith along shear zones (Anderson and Rasor, 1934; Shannon, 1926).

Silver forms wires and scales in the ores of the Subrosa claim and near Grimes Pass and many other mines of the Boise Basin in T. 5-8 N., R. 4-7 E. It has been reported in the vicinity of the Washington Mine northeast of Idaho City. Silver minerals, galena, sphalerite and pyrite are associated. These are at shallow depths in the surface ores. It also forms wires and foils in vugs in primary ore at depth (Ballard, 1924).

Bonner County: Native silver was uncommon in oxidized zones of the Weber and other mines in the Lakeview District. It generally occurred as thin scales or coatings on fracture surfaces or as grains in the gangue (Shannon, 1926).

Butte County: Wires and sheets of silver have been found in the Hub Mine on the South Fork of Lava Creek and other mines of the district. The mine is 2.5 miles east of the Martin town site at 6,200-6,600 feet elevation in Secs. 8, 9, 16 and 17, T. 2 N., R. 24 E. Mineralization is late Tertiary ores, mostly oxidized. Pyrargyrite, copper, acanthite, malachite, azurite, chlorargyrite, galena, pyrite, sphalerite, chalcopyrite and other minerals are associated. Smithsonite forms botryoidal crusts lining cavities, sometimes with columnar crystals of hemimorphite in some mines of the area (Anderson, 1929).

Custer County: Wire-like filaments of silver occurred in cavities in the oxidized ores of late Tertiary deposits. It was associated with acanthite and chlorargyrite in manganese oxides in the Yankee Fork District, and was found with gold in the Charles Dickens and Golden Sunbeam mines. In the Anderson Mine, silver was reported to occur on quartz as micro crystals and wires.

The Skylark and River View Mines in the Bayhorse District, contained leaf and wire silver. The Skylark Mine is on the north side of Bayhorse Canyon west of and above the Ramshorn Mine, about 2 miles west of Bayhorse. The River View Mine is east of Bayhorse on the south side of the canyon (personal; Shannon, 1926).

Silver has also been reported in the General Custer Mine. Proustite, polybasite and other secondary minerals are associated (Umpleby, 1913b).

Elmore County: The Old Monarch Mine and other mines in the Atlanta District, contained native silver in the oxidized surface ores. Excellent wire silver was found above the 250 level of the Monarch Mine in the Pettit orebody. Small wires in drusy clefts on and between quartz crystals were found in the mines. A 6 cm vein of rusty quartz in the Old Monarch Mine contained abundant native silver and a similar vein contained ruby silver (Shannon, 1926).

Idaho County: The Little Giant vein in the Warren District, produced silver with silver bromides, tellurides and acanthite (Shannon, 1926).

Lemhi County: Silver was rare in the Texas District and in the Gold Flint Mine in the Mackinaw District (Shannon, 1926).

Owyhee County: Pure native silver was uncommon in the veins of the Silver City District, but silver, mixed with gold in the form of electrum, was common in most of the veins associated with several silver sulfides. Silver and electrum formed small masses, veins, sheets and tiny wires. In the Afterthought Mine at the head of the East Fork of Sinker Creek, 2 miles southeast of Silver City, wire silver was found with silver sulfides; these were reported to be abundant on the 4th and 5th levels. A similar occurrence is in the Never Sweat Mine in the same area. Both mines are in Sec. 9, T. 5 S., R. 3 W. It occurred in many mines on War Eagle Mountain where it formed small sheets, grains and thin layers. The Poorman (Photo. 321) and War Eagle mines (Photos. 322, 323) were noted for its occurrence with silver minerals (Salman, 1972; Shannon, 1926; Walker, 1965).

Shoshone County: The oxidized ores of the mines of the Coeur d'Alene District contained native silver in several habits associated with cerussite and anglesite (Photos. 37, 39). It occurred in the cerussite ores in several mines, including the Mammoth, Morning, You Like, Hercules, Poorman, Tyler, Bunker Hill, Caledonia and Sierra Nevada. The silver occurred as arborescent wires, coarse single wires, and small, thin plates. The wires varied from short to several cm in length, as singles scattered on matrix, often with cerussite, or as masses of intergrown wires (personal; Shannon, 1926).

Valley County: At the Red Metal Mine on Ellison Creek, south of Profile Gap, Big Creek District, silver is rare as wires and sheets on fracture surfaces (Photo. 324). Small sheets, wires and granular masses coated fracture surfaces and small cavities. Associated minerals include azurite, malachite and several unidentified secondary minerals that form coatings and groups of tiny crystals. The mine was developed as a gold mine, but also produced considerable silver. It is reported that the grade of some of the ore was so high that "much of it was shipped by parcel post" (Shenon and Ross, 1936). Only small quantities of tiny secondary minerals can be seen on the dumps (personal).

SINCOSITE

$CaV_2(PO_4)_2(OH)_4 \cdot 3H_2O$, monoclinic (pseudotetragonal)

Crystals thin to thick tabular, usually square outline, often compact, irregular or scaly masses. Grass green, yellowish green to olive-green or brownish green. Transparent to translucent. In cavities in silicious gold ore; as thin veinlets in carbonaceous shale.

Bear Lake County: Sincosite occurs as greenish brown plates, films and masses on black matrix near Bloomington (personal).

SMITHSONITE

$ZnCO_3$, hexagonal (trigonal)

Rarely as rhombohedral or scalenohedral crystals; mostly reniform, botryoidal or as crusts. Colorless, brown, white, green, blue or pink. Forms in zinc deposits in limestone or carbonate-bearing vein deposits. Associates are sphalerite, cerussite, galena, calcite and limonite.

Blaine County: Smithsonite formed botryoidal crusts with a gray to green color in prospects high on the mountain south of Trail Creek near Ketchum. It occurs with cerussite in the Ella Mine in Ella Canyon, Era District and in the mine of the Kusa Mining Co. on Boulder Creek in the Wood River region (Shannon, 1926).

Butte County: Smithsonite formed a vein near the Johnson Mine, 2 miles northwest of the Wilbert Mine in the Dome District, south of Dome. The vein was about 14 inches wide, and cut magnesian limestone. The smithsonite was yellowish-gray in color and had a rough botryoidal and drusy surface (Shannon, 1926).

Clark County: Smithsonite has been found in the Scott Mine in the Birch Creek District in Sec. 31, T. 9 N., R. 31 E. It occurs in Paleozoic limestone, shale and quartzite with anglesite, cerussite, wulfenite, plumbojarosite and pyromorphite. The mine has been developed with several shafts and drifts (Trites and Tooker, 1953).

Smithsonite occurs in the Buckhorn Mine in Metta Basin northwest of Gloved Peak in Sec. 17, T. 8 N., R. 29 E. It occurs with galena, barite and malachite (Anderson, 1948a).

Custer County: Sheaves of hemimorphite are on druses of smithsonite in the Beardsley Mine in the Bayhorse District. Both hemimorphite and fluorite occur on smithsonite in unusually vuggy ore in the Red Bird Mine of the same district on the east side of Squaw Creek, 5 miles above its confluence with the Salmon River. It has been reported in other mines of the district associated with hemimorphite and the copper carbonates (Shannon, 1926).

Smithsonite has been found in the Starr-Hope Mine in the Copper Basin District (Shannon, 1926).

Crusts of smithsonite occur in vugs in iron-stained quartz on the Alto Silver claims on the south tributary of Little Fall Creek. There are two adits (now caved) near the head of the creek at about 9,100 feet elevation. Veins to about 6 inches thick occur in interbedded argillite and slate. Cavities in the veins are lined with smithsonite and cerussite with small striated cubes of pyrite, sphalerite, chalcopyrite and galena (Tuchek and Ridenour, 1981 Umpleby, 1930).

Lemhi County: In the Texas District, smithsonite is common in the oxidized lead-silver ores. It formed botryoidal coatings in cavities and as stringers along joints. These were most common in the Pittsburgh-Idaho Mine (Shannon, 1926).

Yellowish to reddish brown crusts of smithsonite occur with malachite, galena, sphalerite, cerussite and anglesite in the Viola Mine. The mine is in Secs. 14 and 15, T. 12 N., R. 29 E. at 9,000 feet on the ridge about 1.5 miles northeast of the site of the old smelter at the Nicholia town site (Anderson and Wagner, 1944).

Smithsonite forms microcrystals in the lead-silver veins in the mines of the Little Eight-mile District. The crystals are yellow and line cavities in association with sphalerite, galena and pyrite. They occur in an uncommon needle-like habit. Smithsonite also forms coatings in the cavities (Thune, 1941).

Owyhee County: Smithsonite forms grayish green to brownish botryoidal crusts in the Bay State tunnel on South Mountain. The crusts are associated with prismatic cerussite crystals lining cavities (Sorenson, 1927).

SPESSARTINE

$Mn_3Al_2(SiO_4)_3$, cubic

Forms a series with almandine; member of garnet group. Forms dodecahedrons or trapezohedrons; may be massive granular. Brownish to red or orange; transparent to translucent. Most commonly in pegmatite dikes and rhyolites.

Boise, Custer and Elmore Counties: Spessartine crystals can be found in cavities in several areas in the Sawtooth Mountains. Most crystals are less than 6 mm across, but can be up to at least 2.5 cm. They occur as coatings of tiny crystals or single crystals scattered over microcline, albite and smoky quartz in cavities or may nearly coat the entire pocket. Crystals are yellow, orange, orangeish red to dark red or almost black in color, and some are gemmy. They do not occur everywhere as the smoky quartz, microcline and albite do, but tend to be abundant in areas and absent elsewhere (personal).

Clearwater County: Small purplish red spessartine crystals can be collected in the gold placers in the Pierce District. They are mostly less than 3 cm in diameter and of trapezohedral habit. These may be found on Rhodes and Cow Creeks. Larger crystals occur in metamorphic rock in other areas of the county (Shannon, 1926).

Elmore County: A few tiny spessartine-almandine crystals were found in one miarolitic cavity in granite in the Steel Mountain stock. The stock is northwest of Rocky Bar, near Dismal Swamp. The spessartine occurs as tiny, etched, crystals with a bright orange color. A few are included in smoky quartz. Microcline, chlorite and albite are associated (personal).

SPHALERITE

(Zn,Fe)S, cubic

Trimorphous with matraite and wurtzite. Tetrahedral, dodecahedral and cubic crystals uncommon; mostly in cleavable masses. White (rarely), yellow, brown to black (darkens with increasing iron content), red; transparent to translucent. Commonly associated with galena, chalcopyrite, pyrite, marcasite, smithsonite and calcite in veins and in replacement deposits in limestone.

Sphalerite is common in many of the mining districts of the state. Only the localities that have produced interesting specimens are described below; elsewhere, the sphalerite is reportedly massive and does not form subhedral to euhedral crystals.

Boise County: The Lincoln Mine in the Pearl (now Westview) District contains small crystals of sphalerite. The crystals occur in cavities in massive sphalerite as a combination of the positive and negative tetrahedron associated with pyritohedral crystals of pyrite. The sphalerite has a dark brown color (Shannon, 1926).

Butte County: Sphalerite occurs as coarse crystals in the Paymaster Mine and other mines in the Lava Creek District in T. 2-3 N., R. 24 E. Generally, it forms small crystals or masses with galena and pyrite to 2.5 cm and soapy masses of beidellite(?) (reported as leverrierite by Anderson, 1929).

Custer County: Sphalerite forms tetrahedrons in the Empire Mine in the Washington Basin District. These crystals occur in small vugs in quartz and sphalerite, and are modified by cube faces. Galena, arsenopyrite and other sulfide minerals are associated (Shannon, 1926).

Owyhee County: Excellent specimens of sphalerite crystals have been recovered at the Texas orebody on South Mountain (Photos. 293, 325). Fine matrix specimens to 15 cm, or more, have been collected with crystals up to about 1.5 cm across. Individual crystals are black and lustrous. Small quartz crystals and brilliant pyrrhotite crystals are commonly associated (personal).

Shoshone County: Although a common ore mineral in the mines of the Idaho Panhandle, where it occurs as granular and compact masses in the veins, particularly in the Coeur d'Alene District, sphalerite is uncommon as euhedral crystals. Minute reddish crystals were found in vugs in the Amy Matchless Mine south of Pinehurst on the east side of Pine Creek. Ruby red crystals were found in a crack in the ore on the 1,600 foot level of the Greenhill-Cleveland Mine at Mace. Small honey-yellow crystals were reported from the Temby stope of the Bunker Hill Mine, but was generally rare in the mine (Shannon, 1926).

Small dark brown to nearly black crystals of sphalerite have been found in the 10 level, Quill orebody in the Bunker Hill Mine. Occasionally, a fine specimen with small sphalerite crystals (rarely up to about 1 cm across) accompanied by small quartz crystals, sometimes with calcite crystals, is recovered (Photo. 38) (personal).

SPINEL

$MgAl_2O_4$, cubic

Forms a series with megnesiochromite, hercynite and gahnite. Most common in octahedrons, sometimes twinned on the spinel law. Color is white, red, lavender, blue, green, brown and black. Most often translucent, but may be transparent. Common in metamorphic rocks, especially crystalline limestone, gneisses and serpentine; also in contact metamorphic deposits.

Custer County: Spinel occurs with chondrodite in crystalline limestone near the small tarn in a cirque at the head of Wildhorse Canyon on the east side of Mount Hyndman. The chondrodite forms rounded grains 1 to 2 mm across. Spinel is reported to be deep bottle green in color (Shannon, 1926).

Lemhi County: At the skarn on Quartzite Canyon in the Spring Mountain District, spinel forms tiny black crystals associated with forsterite, magnetite and ludwigite. Generally, it occurs in cavities in the massive forsterite with forsterite crystals, but sometimes occurs on ludwigite (Photos. 326-328). The octahedral crystals are generally under 3 mm, but a few have been seen to 6 mm (personal).

A similar occurrence is a few miles to the northwest on the Colorado claims on Lemhi Union Gulch. A skarn is exposed above the road next to an adit and in a small bulldozer cut on the top of the ridge above. The spinel crystals are similar to those described above and

Photo. 287 Pyromorphite crystals to 3 mm, Plum Creek prospect, Bonner County.

Photo. 288 Pyromorphite, crystals to 1.5 mm, Laxey Mine, South Mountain, Owyhee County.

Photo. 289 Pyromorphite on black botryoidal goethite, crystals to 0.6 mm, Little Giant Mine, Shoshone County.

Photo. 290 Stout, yellow, nearly transparent pyromorphite, largest crystal is 1 mm, Little Giant Mine, Shoshone County.

occur with diopside (Photo. 329). The largest seen was about 6 mm across (personal).

Valley County: Excellent micro octahedral crystals of spinel have been found at a small skarn north of McCall. The deposit is in the roadcut about 0.25 mile south of Deep Creek; similar zones have been reported along Deep Creek. The crystals are generally less than 2 mm across as sharp, brilliant octahedrons or as pitted octahedral crystals (Photo. 330). They occur individually or in groups with colorless, green or orange platy crystals with a micaceous habit. The colors of the spinel crystals are green, purple and black. Poor to fair quality crystals of epidote, titanite and grossular also occur in the deposit (personal).

STAUROLITE

$(Fe,Mg,Zn)_2Al_9(Si,Al)_4O_{22}(OH)_2$, monoclinic (pseudoorthorhombic)

Prismatic crystals often twinned, sometimes cruciform. Red-brown to brownish black; translucent. Occurs in schist, gneisses and slates; associated with kyanite and garnet.

Benewah County: Staurolite occurs along Carpenter Creek 5 miles south of its confluence with the St. Maries River. Crystals can be found in schist in roadcuts along the creek. They are often twinned and up to 4 cm in length (Sinkankas, 1976).

Shoshone County: In several areas south of the St. Joe River in the Avery area and to the southeast, staurolite is common in the metamorphic rocks. Some crystals to 10 cm have been found, but most are less than 2 cm in length. A 1 mile wide zone of staurolite-bearing schist extends from Angle Point to the northwest to the south side of Dominion Peak where it turns westerly and crosses the south side of East Sister. The schist is light brown to silvery gray, with distinct bedding. Staurolite generally forms the largest crystals with almandine, quartz, muscovite, biotite and plagioclase crystals and grains being smaller. In some areas the staurolite is altered to chlorite and muscovite. Kyanite is often associated, and muscovite pseudomorphs of kyanite, up to 35 cm in length, have been found in the area between Peggy Peak and Angle Point (Hietanen, 1962).

Brown crystals occur just north of the 6,320 foot summit between Bathtub Mountain and Junction Peak. The crystals are twinned and up to 4 cm in length. They also occur 0.75 mile southeast of Bathtub Mountain in thin bedded layers of schist. At this locality, there are numerous crystals to 2 cm with shiny prism faces. Other layers in the same area have large stubby crystals with dull faces. Some are altered to chlorite, but weather out of the rocks and maintain the appearance of good staurolite crystals.

Very nice crystals of brown staurolite occur in a schist along Trail 100 off the southeast side of Bathtub Mountain. The crystals occur in a thin layer in the schist along the ridge top 50 feet above the trail starting about 100 feet down the trail from the road. Crystals are dull to lustrous and commonly 1-3 cm long, but have been found up to at least 7 cm in length. Twins (both 60° and 90°) are common, but not abundant (Photo. 331).

A few crystals were also noted in float along the old road below the trail. It is not known if these are from the zone above or another zone (personal).

STEPHANITE

Ag_5SbS_4, orthorhombic

Short prismatic to tabular crystals or massive; iron-black. In silver deposits with acanthite, silver and other silver minerals, tetrahedrite, chalcopyrite, galena and pyrite.

Boise County: A silver vein north of the gold vein on the Washington claim in the Idaho City District contains stephanite with pyrargyrite and chlorargyrite. The brillian gray crystals occurred on comb quartz (Shannon, 1926).

Butte County: Small disseminated crystals of stephanite occur in quartz and intergrown with pyrite and proustite in the Hub Mine in the Lava Creek District. It is in small veinlets that cut the main ore veins. It is associated with proustite as microcrystals embedded in the gangue and intergrown with pyrite. The silver minerals also form veinlets that cut across the sulfide ore deposits (Shannon, 1926).

Elmore County: Stephanite was the most important silver mineral in the Atlanta District. It formed granular, imperfectly crystalline and columnar masses with pyrargyrite in comb quartz. It often filled the centers of veins which have pyrargyrite along the edge (Anderson, 1939; Shannon, 1926).

Owyhee County: Stephanite has been reported from the Flint District. It was found in the Rising Star and other mines intergrown with other minerals (Piper and Laney, 1926; Shannon, 1926).

Shoshone County: Well-formed crystals to 4 mm have been found in the "J" orebody in the Bunker Hill Mine on a drusy coating of pyrite (personal).

STIBICONITE

$SbSb_2O_6(OH)$, cubic
Massive or as a powder or crust. Pale yellow to yellowish white or reddish white; transparent. Forms from the oxidation of stibnite and other antimony minerals. Associated with cervantite, valentinite and stibnite.

Elmore County: Pale greenish yellow coatings and small grains of stibiconite occur in the quartz veins in the Hermada Mine on Swanholm Creek with native antimony, stibnite, kermesite and cervantite (Popoff, 1953).

Shoshone County: Stibiconite coats stibnite in the Stanley antimony mine in Gorge Gulch above Burke, Coeur d'Alene District. The crusts are 1 to 5 mm thick and are a dirty white color. Valentinite and cervantite are associated (Shannon, 1926).

The antimony mine near Glidden Pass contains fibrous or bladed pseudomorphs of stibiconite after stibnite. These are a dirty white color (Shannon, 1926).

STIBNITE

Sb_2S_3, orthorhombic
Dimorphous with metastibnite. Commonly in slender, striated prismatic crystals. These are sometimes bent or twisted; often in radiating groups. Lead-gray color. It is the most important antimony ore mineral. Forms as a low temperature mineral in hydrothermal vein deposits. Gold, realgar, marcasite, pyrite, cinnabar and quartz are associated.

Blaine County: The Broadway Mine on the east side of Hyndman Creek Valley about 3.5 miles from its mouth has produced sheaves of stibnite crystals. It occurs on the ridge above the mine with quartz and pyrite (as pyritohedrons to 1.7 cm). Mineralization is in quartz veins in argillite of the Milligen formation (Umpleby et al, 1930).

The North Star Mine, in North Star Gulch, in the $SE^{1/}_4$ Sec. 23, T. 4 N., R. 18 E., contains stibnite. The mine has been developed with two adits on a vein in the argillites of the Milligen formation. Stibnite fills some vugs and fractures in the vein; boulangerite is associated and is the most common antimony mineral. Other minerals include galena, arsenopyrite, sphalerite and quartz (Umpleby et al, 1930).

Radiating aggregates of needle-like crystals of stibnite have been found in the Inde-

Photo. 291 Pyromorphite, 5 cm across,
9 level, Jersey vein, Bunker Hill Mine,
Shoshone County; Norm and Carl Radford
specimen.

Photo. 292 Pyromorphite, 5 cm across,
Bunker Hill Mine, Shoshone County.

Photo. 293 Pyrrhotite, sphalerite and quartz, silvery blocky crystals
on right and left are pyrrhotite, specimen 9 cm across, Texas orebody,
South Mountain, Owyhee County; Norm and Carla Radford specimen.

Photo. 294 Smoky quartz, 5.5 cm long,
Headquarters (probably from the
Bungalow stock), Clearwater County;
Norm and Carla Radford specimen.

Photo. 295 Quartz with minor malachite coating, field of view 7.8 cm across, Peacock Mine, Seven Devils District, Adams County.

Photo. 296 Sceptered quartz crystal with normal quartz crystals, scepter is 1.2 cm in length, Lime Creek, Custer County.

Photo. 297 Amethyst crystals on agate from a geode, field of view 5.5 cm across; the back side has been polished, thus the smooth curving surface, Challis Creek, Custer County.

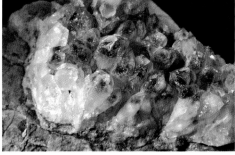

Photo. 298 Quartz, 3.3 cm across, Estes Mountain, Custer County.

Photo. 299 Amethyst-colored terminations in quartz from a vein on Estes Mountain, amethyst area 3.2 cm across, Custer County.

pendence Mine in Independence Creek in the N$^{1}/_{2}$ Sec. 23, T. 4 N., R. 18 E., more than 4 miles east of Ketchum. A shear zone in quartzite and argillite has been mineralized with tetrahedrite, galena, boulangerite, stibnite and pyrite (Umpleby et al, 1930).

Boise County: Stibnite forms thin spindle-shaped crystals in the Mountain Chief Mine located at the southwest end of the porphyry belt, 3.5 miles from Placerville. The claims extend from the summit of the divide between Fall and Canyon Creeks down to Canyon Creek. There are four adits developed on the veins, the lowest at 5,600 feet elevation. Mineralization occurs as a fissure filling in sheared granite and diorite porphyry and a lamprophyre dike along the shear. The stibnite spindles are between quartz crystals or extend across vugs in the quartz. Small pyrite crystals are sometimes associated, and gold occurs in the veins (Jones, 1917).

A similar occurrence is in the Belshazzar Mine which joins the Mountain Chief on the northeast and extends to Fall Creek. Three adits have been developed on the shear zone.

Stibnite forms large lustrous crystals to 4.2 cm at an undisclosed location. Specimens of these large crystals in diverging groups with calcite were collected and sold many years ago and are occasionally seen on display. They typically are labeled as being from Boise County with specific location given (Photo. 332) (personal).

Butte County: Coarse columnar, bladed and radiating groups of deeply striated crystals of stibnite to 3.5 cm have been found in a mineralized area in the Lava Creek District. Some of them are partially altered to stibiconite, cervantite or valentinite (to 7 mm in vugs as green prismatic crystals with waxy luster). The area is on the north branch of Lava Creek north of the Hub Mine in Sec. 4, T. 2 N., R. 24 E. (Anderson, 1929).

Elmore County: Stibnite occurs as the primary ore mineral in the Hermada Mine on Swanholm Creek. Mineralization is in narrow quartz veins, mostly less than 5 cm across. Stibnite generally forms small grains (Popoff, 1953).

Lemhi County: Stibnite has been found in mines of the Gravel Range (Singheiser) District 1 mile south of Meyers Cove on the west side of Camas Creek. It is most common on the western end of the district, and extends into the ridge northwest of the West Fork of Camas Creek near the western boundary of Sec. 6, T. 17 N., R. 17 E. It forms radiating clusters of needle-like crystals. These are up to 5 cm in length and some of them are covered and partially replaced by barite. Chalcedony, barite and fluorite are associated. In the southern part of the district, stibnite replaces chalcedony and fluorite (Anderson, 1943a; Ross, 1927, 1934).

Radiating acicular crystals of stibnite occur with boulangerite, pyrite, sphalerite, galena, arsenopyrite, pyrargyrite and jamesonite in veins in an altered dike in the Buckhorn Mine in the Little Eightmile (Junction) District. The veins are 450 feet from the portal in the main adit. The pyrargyrite forms thin films surrounding some of the stibnite crystals (Thune, 1941).

Owyhee County: Needles and blades of stibnite up to 5 cm in length were found in the Rising Star Mine, Flint District. These were in coarse white comb quartz. It occurred as masses and grains in several of the mines of the region (Shannon, 1926).

Blades and needles have been found in the Nugent Mine in Sec. 18, T. 4 S., R 3 W., 4 miles north-northwest of Silver City at the head of the gulch that leads north and east from Sinker Creek. Stibnite forms massive to delicately bladed crystals in an adit in sparse cavities in the Silver City granite (Piper and Laney, 1926).

In the Black Horse Mine in Sec. 3, T. 4 S., R. 3 W., it forms blades and grains in quartz veins in silicified granodiorite (Asher, 1967).

The Cosmopolitan Mine contains stibnite as blades in quartz veins in granodiorite. The crystals form excellent specimens and can be found a few thousand feet southwest of the mine buildings in pits and trenches in Sec. 8, T. 4 S., R. 3 W. (Asher, 1967).

Shoshone County: Stibnite formed coarse blades in quartz in the Stanley Antimony Mine in Gorge Gulch about 1 mile above Burke. Disseminated crystals of pyrite, sphalerite and arsenopyrite occur in the quartz, too (Shannon, 1926).

Stibnite has been found in the Gold Hunter Mine in the Morning District west of Mullan. It formed acicular crystals that formed nests in quartz. It also formed acicular crystals in the mines of the Star Antimony group on a ridge between Stewart Creek and the East Fork of Pine Creek, south of Pinehurst. It was rare as nests of crystals in vugs in quartz in a brecciated quartz vein in argillites of Prichard formation of the Belt supergroup (Umpleby and Jones, 1923).

A few small, acicular crystals are occasionally found in the 500 level of the Sunshine Mine. These specimens consist of sprays of dark gray crystals up to about 2 cm in length which are found in cavities in quartz (personal).

Valley County: Stibnite occurs in the Meadow Creek Mine which is located on the north side of Meadow Creek about 0.5 mile above its junction with the East Fork at 6,700 feet elevation. It forms masses with bladed habit, minute acicular crystals in veinlets, and drusy crystalline aggregates in vugs. Quartz, gold and arsenopyrite are associated. The stibnite veins crosscut the gold-arsenopyrite veins. Some of the stibnite is coated with cherry red to brownish red kermesite (Cooper, 1951; Currier, 1935).

The Hennesey lode on the south bluff of Sugar Creek about 0.5 mile above its confluence with the east fork contains stibnite as coarsely crystalline masses. There are two adits at the mine, about 400 feet apart (Currier, 1935).

Stibnite also occurs at the Red Garnet prospect on the north side of Logan Creek at an elevation of 6,800 feet. Here a large garnet tactite is exposed in a small pendant of dolomitic marble, biotite schist and quartzite in granodiorite. Two adits have been developed on the western contact of the tactite body along the stibnite vein. On the north side of the tactite, an adit has been driven in a gossan that contains pyrite and chalcopyrite (Kirkpatrick, 1974).

Stibnite occurs in the B and B deposit north of Profile Gap in the Big Creek District associated with cinnabar, metacinnabar and polhemusite. Most of the stibnite occurs as narrow veins consisting of compact intergrown crystals up to 2.5 cm or more long, but it also occurs as subhedral to euhedral crystals partially filling cavities lined with small quartz crystals, rarely, prismatic crystals of stibnite project into quartz lined cavities (Photo. 333) (personal).

STILBITE

$NaCa_2Al_5Si_{13}O_{36} \cdot 14H_2O$, monoclinic and triclinic

Zeolite group. Prismatic or tabular, commonly in sheaf-like aggregates. White; translucent. A secondary mineral found in cavities in volcanic rocks with other zeolites, calcite and quartz.

Adams County: Massive garnet from the Blue Jacket Mine in the Seven Devils District contains stilbite with heulandite and chabazite. The stilbite forms prisms and divergent groups of prisms up to 2 mm in length in small cavities (Shannon, 1926).

Stilbite can be found with other zeolite group minerals, calcite, apophyllite and quartz in cavities in the basalts along Highway 95 south of Pinehurst beginning at about one half mile north of mile post 176 northerly to mile post 178. Most cavities are small and the crystals are micro to small (personal).

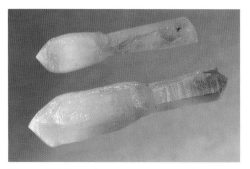

Photo. 300 Quartz scepters, longest is 3.6 cm and has an amethystine base, Estes Mountain, Custer County.

Photo. 301 Rutile inclusions in quartz, 7.2 cm long, near Golden, Idaho County; Norm and Carla Radford specimen.

Photo. 302 Quartz pseudomorph of apophyllite with smooth faces and associated tiny crude quartz crystals; large pseudomorph 2.8 cm high, Antelope Flats, Custer County.

Photo. 303 Quartz pseudomorph of apophyllite with smooth white faces, 12.5 cm across, Antelope Flats, Custer County.

Photo. 304 Quartz pseudomorph of apophyllite with drusy quartz forming the faces, cavernous terminations, large pseudomorph is 7 cm high, Antelope Flats, Custer County.

Photo. 305 Quartz scepter, 4.5 cm long, Ola Ridge, Gem County; Norm and Carla Radford specimen.

Blaine County: Several areas in the Minnie Moore Mine near Bellevue in the Wood River District contain stilbite. The east crosscut of the 1,000 foot level contains 3-4 mm crystals in fractures in shale. They are generally colorless (Shannon, 1926).

Blaine County: Small orange stilbite crystals line fracture surfaces in volcanic rocks 2.5 miles below Galena Summit. The stilbite is exposed on a ridge that runs off from the road. Minor amounts of heulandite occur in the area, too (personal).

Boise County: Small crystals of stilbite occur in a small quarry alongside Highway 55 one mile north of Gardena. Small cavities in basalt at this location also contain calcite, chabazite, mesolite and thomsonite. Some of these minerals also occur in the nearby roadcut (personal).

Boise, Custer and Elmore Counties: Micro to small crystals of stilbite are rare in the Sawtooth Mountains (Photos. 74, 77). At one location, crystals occur as coatings on joint surfaces in the granite. Individual crystals are less than 3 mm in length, have an amber to pinkish color, typical stilbite habit and are translucent. At another location, they were found in a few small miarolitic cavities with albite, microcline, smoky quartz and in one cavity, with specular hematite and aquamarine. Here, they formed crusts of tiny white crystals, some with brown feathery inclusions, or white crystals scattered on microcline (personal).

Custer County: Stilbite is uncommon on the Rat's Nest claim with heulandite and mordenite. A few geodes have been found with white stilbite crystals to 2.5 cm on calcite or with heulandite crystals. Until now, only two geodes have been found with stilbite. This is an active mining claim for mineral specimens and collecting is not permitted (personal).

Stilbite occurs with quartz and other zeolites in cavities in the volcanic rocks along Lime Creek about 7 miles southeast of Challis. These can be found in a canyon about 100 yards west of the road up the creek, about 1.9 miles from Highway 93. Stilbite occurs as white crystals of the common habit in cavities in stilbite veins and veins of blue agate (Photos. 334, 335). Small quartz crystals and small crystals of heulandite are sometimes associated with the stilbite. Stilbite crystals are mostly under 1.5 cm, but have been seen up to 3 cm in length. Generally they line cavity walls, but have been found on the surfaces of stalactitic growths of agate and quartz (personal).

Another occurrence of stilbite is east of the road in a small cut on the face of the hills that face the highway. Here, stilbite forms small veins. Cavities with clusters of stilbite crystals are uncommon in these veins (personal).

Small stilbite crystals (Photo. 336) occur with tiny goethite pseudomorphs of pyrite and small green cubes of fluorite in altered volcanic rocks northwest of Loon Creek Summit. These are in a breccia zone in the steep bare area at the head of a small basin on the east side of a ridge (personal).

Orangeish pink stilbite crystals form drusy coatings on fragments in a breccia in the altered quartz monzonite in a prospect on the south side of Washington Basin. The small crystals are up to 2 mm in length (Photo. 337). Minor amounts of pyrite, molybdenite and galena occur there as well. The prospect is above the south side of the valley, east of the old mill site (personal).

Tiny orange to red stilbite crystals occur on some joint surfaces and in thin seams in the diorite at Goat Lake in the White Cloud Mountains. These were found in talus below the cliff that rises above the lake on the east side. The stilbite crystals are fairly uniform in size, mostly around 3 mm long (personal).

Idaho County: Stilbite, as single crystals and large sheaf-like crystals, have been found in the Columbia River basalts along Race Creek, northwest of Riggins (Photo. 338). Individual crystals and groups are up to about 3 cm in length. Mesolite, chabazite, calcite and thomsonite are associated. They have also been reported elsewhere in the area around

Riggins (personal).

Small crystals of stilbite can be found in vesicles in Columbia River basalt 0.2 mile north of mile post 220, north of Skookumchuck Creek. The stilbite is less than 6 mm long and translucent to white associated with minor amounts of other zeolites (personal).

Tiny crystals of stilbite occur in vuggy quartz veins with subhedral grains of an unidentified green mineral in a roadcut) 0.4 miles east of mile post 165 on Highway 12. This location is near Russian Creek, several miles west of Lolo Pass. The white crystals are up to about 3 mm in length. The quartz vein cuts gneiss in a fractured zone; a quartz vein to the west has tiny pyrite crystals (personal).

Kootenai County: Specimens from a fracture in a diabase contained stilbite with prehnite and laumontite. The stilbite forms small colorless to slightly yellowish rectangular crystals. The location is unknown and is probably an anomaly in the gneiss of the Post Falls area (Shannon, 1926).

STRENGITE

$FePO_4 \cdot 2H_2O$, orthorhombic
Variscite group member. Crystals pseudo-octahedral, thin to thick tabular, stout prismatic, spherical aggregates with radial-fibrous structure. Colorless, violet, red; transparent to translucent. A secondary mineral formed from the alteration of iron-rich phosphates; especially in pegmatites.

Latah County: Strengite has been found in a small pegmatite near the Muscovite Mine on Mica Mountain north of Avon. The strengite occurs as intergrown reddish brown crystals about 1.5 x 3 mm. Vivianite forms blue alterations on the surfaces of the strengite crystals. Ferriferous ankerite is associated as fine-grained veinlets with a buff color. Unfortunately, the report on this occurrence does not provide an adequate description of the location so as to determine which of the several old pegmatite prospects in this area produced the strengite (Campbell, 1939).

STROMEYERITE

AgCuS, orthorhombic
Crystals prismatic, pseudohexagonal; massive. Dark steel-gray or blue on exposed surfaces. In veins with other silver minerals, chalcopyrite and tetrahedrite.

Elmore County: Stromeyerite occurred with acanthite, pyrargyrite, stephanite and xanthoconite in the Atlanta District (Shannon, 1926).

Owyhee County: Soft, gray grains of stromeyerite were found in the Rising Star Mine. These were up to 3 mm across and became deep blue when exposed. They were disseminated in quartz with stibnite, stephanite, acanthite and polybasite (Piper and Laney, 1926; Shannon, 1926).

Shoshone County: Dark gray sectile masses of stromeyerite, tarnished purple, cement quartzite fragments in the Caledonia Mine in the Coeur d'Alene District (Shannon, 1926).

SULFUR

S, orthorhombic
Dimorphous with rosickyite. Pyramidal or in masses imperfectly crystallized, massive

Photo. 307 quartz, upper crystal 5.6 cm, lower crystal 5.5 cm in length, Mica Peak, Kootenai County; Norm and Carla Radford

Photo. 306 Quartz scepter, 6.6 cm in length, near Golden, Idaho County; Norm and Carla Radford specimen.

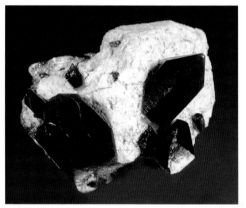

Photo. 308 Smoky quartz on microcline, 4.5 cm across, Crags batholith, Lemhi County.

Photo. 309 Quartz, milky to transparent; cluster is 8.2 cm across; Clarkia area, Shoshone County.

Photo. 310 Rosasite hemispheres, to 1.2 mm, with hemimorphite, microcrystals, Excelsior Mine, Spring Mountain District, Lemhi County.

Photo. 312 Groups of rosasite microcrystals, 0.6 mm, on quartz, Excelsior Mine, Spring Mountain District, Lemhi County.

Photo. 311 Rosasite, 0.3-0.5 mm, on quartz and hemimorphite, Excelsior Mine, Spring Mountain District, Lemhi County.

Photo. 313 Roscoelite crystals on quartz, crystals are 0.2-.03 mm across, Washington Basin, Custer County.

or stalactitic. Sulfur-yellow; may be colored gray, green or red by impurities. Transparent to translucent. Occurs at or near the craters of volcanoes, as a hot spring deposit from the oxidation of hydrogen sulfide or in sedimentary rocks.

Caribou County: Sulfur occurs with gypsum around several springs 5 miles east of Soda Springs. The springs are in the $SE\frac{1}{4}SW\frac{1}{4}$, Sec. 2 and $NE\frac{1}{4}NW\frac{1}{4}$ Sec. 11 in Sulphur Canyon and in the $SE\frac{1}{4}$ Sec. 11 and in the $NE\frac{1}{4}NE\frac{1}{4}$ Sec. 14. T. 9 S., R. 43 E. The two minerals cement the fragments of tuff, limestone and quartzite in a fault breccia. Small pyramidal crystals of sulfur line vugs in masses in the breccia. Unusual stalactites of sulfur occur in vertical crevices in the breccia on the south wall of the quarry on the Wood Canyon side of the divide. The stalactites are canary yellow when fresh, but become dull gray on exposure. Small crystals of gypsum are associated (Richards and Bridges, 1910; Shannon, 1926).

Custer County: Minute crystals of sulfur, occurred in small cavities in masses of chalcopyrite in the Lost Packer Mine. These were found in earthy limonite 30 feet below the surface (Shannon, 1926).

Lemhi County: Sulfur crystals have been found in the Ima Mine in the Blue Wing District in Sec. 23, T. 41 N., R. 23 E. They occur with huebnerite, fluorite, rhodochrosite, chalcopyrite, bornite, galena, sphalerite, azurite, malachite, chlorargyrite and pyrite (Callaghan and Lemmon, 1941).

Sulfur is uncommon in the mines of the Eightmile District. It partially fills cavities in the partly oxidized portions of the lead-silver deposits. Generally sulfur forms small spheroidal masses, but it rarely occurs as microscopic acute pyramidal crystals (Thune, 1941).

SYLVANITE

$(Au,Ag)_2Te_4$, monoclinic

Short prismatic or thick tabular crystals; bladed or granular. Steel-gray to silver-white somewhat yellow. In vein deposits with other tellurides, sulfides and pyrite.

Shoshone County: A silver-white telluride, which was probably sylvanite, was found in the Pilot claim in the Murray District (Shannon, 1926).

TACHARANITE

$Ca_{12}Al_2Si_{18}O_{51} \cdot 18H_2O$, monoclinic

White, soft, chalky masses; no crystals known. Occurs with zeolites and other hydrous calcium aluminium silicates. Similar to tobermorite in composition, characteristics and occurrence; cannot easily be distinguished from tobermorite. Tacharanite is apparently more common with zeolites and thus is listed here, although specimens have not been analyzed.

Adams County: In the area south of Pinehurst along highway 95 around mile posts 176 to 178, a mineral that is probably tacharanite occurs with analcime, chabazite, heulandite, levyne, cowlesite, phillipsite, stilbite, apophyllite and gyrolite, many of which are fairly common there. It has been found as small, rounded masses, mostly less than 3 mm across. This is the first and only known occurrence of this mineral in the state, and it is uncommon there (personal).

TENNANTITE

$(Cu,Fe)_{12}As_4S_{13}$, cubic

Forms a series with tetrahedrite. Tetrahedral crystals, granular or massive. Flint-gray to iron-black. Not as common as tetrahedrite, but the occurrence is about the same.

Bear Lake County: Tennantite has been found in the ores of the Hummingbird Mine, St. Charles District (Palache, 1944).

TETRADYMITE

Bi_2Te_2S, hexagonal (trigonal)

Rarely distinct pyramidal crystals: commonly foliated to granular masses or bladed. Pale steel-gray; tarnishes dull or iridescent. Occurs in gold-quartz veins and contact metamorphic deposits with galena, pyrite, tellurides and bismuth minerals.

Custer County: Tetradymite occurs in the Basin claims near Trail Creek, north of the divide. Tetradymite occurs as bluish gray grains in quartz and carbonate gangue. The occurrence is in contact metamorphic rocks with garnet, epidote, prehnite, vesuvianite and wollastonite. The lime-silicate rocks replace limey slate and clayey quartzite (Shannon, 1925b; Umpleby, et al, 1930).

Photo. 314 Rutile inclusions in quartz, 4.4 cm long, near Golden, Idaho County, Norm and Carla Radford specimen.

Photo. 315 Schorl 1.8 cm long, near Ola, Gem County.

Photo. 316 Scheelite on diopside, scheelite 0.8 mm, roadcut near Vulcan Mine, Bonner County.

Photo. 317 Schorl, 3.3 cm high, Joint Venture claim #1, near Ola, Gem County.

Photo. 318 Yellow to yellow-brown segnitite coating a group of mimetite crystals (right center) with colorless wulfenite plates, wulfenite crystals 0.6 mm across, Ima Mine, Lemhi County.

Photo. 319 Siderite in cavity in basalt, largest hemisphere is 7 mm across and is partially altered to goethite, Cottonwood, Idaho County.

Photo. 320 Siderite, brown with iridescence, hemisphere is 1.5 cm across, Rutledge Point, Kootenai County; Norm and Carla Radford specimen.

Photo. 321 Silver/electrum on quartz, several masses around 1 mm across, northern shaft, Poorman Mine, War Eagle Mountain, Silver City District, Owyhee County.

Photo. 322 Silver/electrum on quartz, large mass 4 mm across, War Eagle Mine, War Eagle Mountain, Silver City District, Owyhee County.

Photo. 323 Silver/electrum on quartz, field of view about 1.5 cm across, from the War Eagle Mine, War Eagle Mountain, Silver City District, Owyhee County.

TETRAHEDRITE

$(Cu,Fe)_{12}Sb_4S_{13}$, cubic

Forms a series with tennantite and another with freibergite. In tetrahedral crystals, massive or granular. Flint-gray to iron-black to dull black. A common sulfosalt and often a copper ore. May contain silver and form an important silver ore. Found in veins with copper, lead, zinc and silver minerals.

Blaine County: Tetrahedrite occurs in the mines of the Wood River District (Palache, 1944). Shannon (1926) reports that it occurs in massive form in several of the mines of that district and in other mines and district of the county.

Custer County: Minute crystals occur in the Ramshorn Mine in the Bayhorse District. These occur in vugs with crystals of arsenopyrite and siderite. A mossy crust of minute chalcopyrite crystals coat the other minerals (Shannon, 1926).

Shoshone County: Tetrahedrite is common in the Coeur d'Alene District and is the most important silver-bearing mineral in the Silver Belt of the Kellogg-Wallace area. Most of it is massive, but small crystals have been found in some veins. A few small crystals were found in the vein of the Yankee Boy Mine on Big Creek, and a few crystals occurred in the Hypotheek Mine on French Gulch south of Kingston. The crystals were in cracks in quartz with pyrite and arsenopyrite. Some of the crystals were up to 5 mm across and had shiny faces. This tetrahedrite and much of it in the mines on Pine Creek, were nonargentiferous, unlike the important silver-bearing tetrahedrite veins in the Silver Belt to the east (Shannon, 1926).

Small tetrahedrite crystals have been collected in the Sunshine Mine east of Kellogg, in recent years. These have been obtained by a few of the miners and geologists working in the lower levels of the workings. Most crystals are less than 8 mm across and form perfect or modified tetrahedrons of nearly black color (Photo. 34). Small crystals of dark honey colored siderite and small milky quartz crystals are associated. Crystals of tetrahedrite have been found in the Galena Mine, occasionally up to about 1 cm across, but usually smaller (personal).

THAUMASITE

$Ca_3Si(CO_3)(SO_4)(OH)_6 \cdot 12H_2O$, hexagonal

Ettringite group. Acicular to filiform crystals, usually massive, compact. Colorless, white; transparent to translucent. A late stage mineral in some sulfide ore deposits, in contact metamorphic zones.

Lemhi County: Microscopic needles of thaumasite are uncommon in one area of the skarn on Quartzite Canyon in the Spring Mountain District. These were found in one specimen on a fracture surface as felted masses (personal).

THOMSONITE

$NaCa_2Al_5Si_5O_{20} \cdot 6H_2O$

Zeolite group, crystals rare, prismatic; mostly columnar or radiating fibers forming spherical groups. White, reddish green or brown; transparent to translucent. A secondary mineral found in volcanic rocks with other zeolites.

Adams County: Thomsonite forms small crystals and spheres with other zeolites and quartz in small cavities in Columbia River basalt south of Pinehurst. There are good exposures in roadcuts along Highway 95 from about one half mile north of mile post 176 to mile post 178 (Photos. 339, 340). Thomsonite occurs in two main forms, both sitting on a cavity lining of tiny chabazite crystals; the first, or earliest deposited, are mostly compact hemispheres of a gray color. The second stage is of white hemispheres or small crystal clusters and single crystals. They are colorless, thin lath-like crystals up to about 2.5 mm in length. Hair-like needles of mesolite project from these (personal).

Blaine County: What may be thomsonite occurs as fiber-like crystals in the volcanic rocks on Little Smoky Creek northwest of Hailey. It is fine fibrous, white and radiates from the walls of cavities. The mineral was not positively identified (Shannon, 1926).

Boise County: Thomsonite occurs as vesicle fillings on Warm Spring Creek in the Bear Valley Quadrangle with chabazite. It forms radiating fine-fibrous fillings with a white color. Most of the vesicles are less than 3 mm in diameter (Shannon, 1926).

Small crystals of thomsonite occur in a small quarry alongside Highway 55 one mile north of Gardena. Small cavities in basalt at this location also contain calcite, chabazite, mesolite and stilbite and some of these also occur in the nearby roadcut (personal).

Elmore County: White blades of what is probably thomsonite occurs with chabazite 5 miles below Glenns Ferry on the Snake River. The blades are less than 2 mm in diameter (Shannon, 1926).

Idaho County: Thomsonite forms small spheres and vesicle linings in Columbia River basalt north of Skookumchuck Creek, about 0.2 miles north of mile post 220. Associated minerals include chabazite and stilbite (personal).

Kootenai County: What may be thomsonite occurred as small hemispheres of radiating needle-like crystals which served as the bases for stilbite crystals near Post Falls (Shannon, 1926).

Lemhi County: Thomsonite is uncommon in one area of the skarn on Quartzite Canyon in the Spring Mountain District. It has been found as tiny crystals associated with mesolite, natrolite and laumontite on fracture surfaces (personal).

THORITE

$ThSiO_4$, tetragonal

Dimorphous with huttonite. Short prismatic—similar to zircon in habit with a simple combination of prism and dipyramid; also massive. Orange-yellow, brownish yellow, yellow, orange, brown, brownish black, black or green. A widespread mineral in pegmatite, metasomatic rocks and hydrothermal veins.

Elmore County: Tiny amber colored crystals have been found in the small miarolitic cavities of the Steel Mountain stock. Microprobe analysis indicate they are thorite or possibly huttonite. These crystals are rare, and are associated with albite, potassium feldspar and smoky quartz (personal).

Lemhi County: Thorite occurs with copper minerals in the Wonder Lode Mine located in Sec. 22, T. 19 N., R. 25 E. on the South Fork of Agency Creek, 0.75 mile south of the Copper Queen Mine. One fissure-filling vein cuts the Precambrian age micaceous quartzite. Thorite forms brick-red blebs and irregular masses which are sparsely scattered through quartz in the western part of the vein. In the eastern part of the vein, thorite forms prismatic crystals and irregular blebs and masses. These are abundant where siderite is common in the quartz vein. Most crystals and blebs are fractured from shearing, but unbroken crystals of thorite and hematite coat some fractures. Chalcopyrite, sphalerite, malachite and azurite

Photo. 324 Silver, crystalline sheets and wires, field of view 1.2 cm across, Red Metal Mine, near Profile Gap, Valley County.

Photo. 326 Spinel, to 3 mm, on ludwigite, Quartzite Canyon, Spring Mountain District, Lemhi County.

Photo. 327 Spinel, around 1 mm, Quartzite Canyon, Spring Mountain District, Lemhi County.

Photo. 325 Sphalerite and quartz, 7.6 cm across, Texas orebody, South Mountain, Owyhee County; Norm and Carla Radford specimen.

Photo. 328 Spinel on ludwigite, spinel crystals up to 0.5 cm, Quartzite Canyon, Lemhi County.

Photo. 329 Spinel on diopside, spinel 2.5 mm across, Colorado claim, Lemhi Union Gulch, Lemhi County.

Photo. 330 Spinel, 1 mm across, Deep Creek, Valley County.

Photo. 331 Staurolite twin, 3 cm long, with tiny garnets on the surface, Bathtub Mountain, Shoshone County.

Photo. 333 Stibnite on quartz, B & B prospect, Big Creek District, Valley County.

Photo. 332 Stibnite with calcite, stibnite crystals to 4.2 cm long, note repaired crystal on left side, location not known, an old specimen labeled Boise County, Idaho.

are associated (Sharp, and Cavender, 1962; Trites and Tooker, 1953).

Thorium mineralization occurs at the Uranium Queen Mine 0.25 mile south of the Copper Queen Mine on Agency Creek. Thorite forms microcrystals to 0.1 mm across. They are most common in the oxidized portion of a three foot wide quartz vein with limonite and hematite. The vein cuts the Precambrian age quartzite (Sharp, and Cavender, 1962).

TITANITE

$CaTiSiO_5$, monoclinic

Commonly wedge- or envelope-shaped crystals. Gray, brown, green, yellow or black; transparent to translucent. Common as an accessory mineral in igneous rocks or in metamorphic rocks. Associated with amphibole, pyroxene, zircon, chlorite and quartz.

Adams County: Titanite is reported in some of the contact deposits of the Seven Devils District with epidote, garnet, diopside, quartz and other calc-silicate minerals (Livingston, and Laney, 1920).

Boise County: Titanite is common in the rock of the Silver Wreath Mine in the Willow Creek District (Shannon, 1926).

Camas County: The placer gravels of Bear Creek contain minute crystals of titanite. They are yellow to greenish in color and have the common envelope-shape (Shannon, 1926).

Clearwater County: Minute crystals with a yellow color occur in the placer deposits on Cow Creek near Pierce (Shannon, 1926).

Elmore County: Titanite is rare as tiny crystals in the granite of the Steel Mountain stock. The tiny crystals have a light amber color and the common wedge shape. They occur with microcline, albite, smoky quartz, epidote and chlorite in miarolitic cavities in granite (personal).

Idaho County: Wedge-shaped crystals of titanite have been found in the placer deposits of the Florence District. The crystals are up to 6 mm across, yellow or light green in color and have bright faces and sharp edges. They have been recovered from placer concentrates with gold, allanite, zircon and other heavy minerals (Reed, 1939).

Lemhi County: Small crystals occur at the Indian Creek quartz locality west of North Fork. The titanite forms small crystals with a light amber color, and have the wedge-shape habit. They occur in and on rhombic calcite crystals, lining fractures or cavities associated with quartz (personal).

Titanite is uncommon in one area near the skarn in the Spring Mountain District. It was discovered in miarolitic cavities in intrusive rock at the contact with the magnetite body at the head of Bruce Canyon. The yellow to reddish amber crystals are 2-3 mm across and are associated with epidote and quartz (Photo. 341) (personal).

Valley County: Titanite crystals, with the envelope-shape with modifying faces, occur in a coarse-grained red granitic rock on West Mountain. The crystals are up to 4 mm across and are honey-yellow or reddish yellow to black (Shannon, 1926).

Amber to light brown titanite crystals occur in the skarn 14.5 miles north of McCall. The skarn is in the roadcut, 0.25 mile south of Deep Creek. The crystals have been found up to at least 7 mm long frozen in quartz and calcite. They have the common envelope-shape and are locally abundant. Spinel, epidote, grossular and an unidentified micaceous mineral are associated. Many areas of the skarn have vugs, but most of the minerals are tiny and often not well formed; although some large well formed epidote crystals have been reported (personal).

TOPAZ

$Al_2SiO_4(F,OH)_2$, orthorhombic

In prismatic crystals or granular or crystalline masses. Colorless, straw-yellow to dark yellow, pink, bluish or greenish; transparent to translucent. Can be found in cavities in granite, pegmatites and rhyolites.

Boise, Custer and Elmore Counties: Topaz forms excellent crystals in the granite of the Sawtooth batholith in the Sawtooth Mountains (Photos. 78-82,84). Crystals are most abundant as prisms less than 2.5 cm in length, but have been found up to at least 12 cm in length. Occasionally, micro-topaz crystals coat smoky quartz or microcline. They are usually a sherry color, light yellow or colorless, rare light blue. In some areas, most of the crystals have a white cap, a coloration of the termination faces. Luster varies from brilliant to dull and etched. Most crystals are somewhat milky or fractured, but they may be transparent.

A few excellent specimens have been found on large matrix plates of microcline, albite, masutomilite and smoky quartz (Photo. 82), but due to the common collapsed nature of the cavities, matrix specimens with topaz crystals greater than about 1 cm in length are rare (personal).

Clark County: Small topaz crystals were reported from Camas Creek. These were pale yellow prisms up to 6 mm in diameter (Shannon, 1926). It is possible that these may have been gem quality andesine or labradorite from the cinder cones of the area (personal).

Clearwater County: Topaz crystals and fragments of crystals occur in a colluvial (or alluvial) deposit on the ridge 0.3 mile west of the old Fohl Picnic area at Pierce Divide. The deposit consists of rounded and angular cobbles and clay. Pieces or complete crystals of black tourmaline and smoky quartz crystals, along with fragments of muscovite, aquamarine and colored tourmaline crystals are associated. These minerals have also been reported to have been found in pegmatites in the area (personal).

Elmore County: Topaz occurs in the alluvial deposits at Dismal Swamp, 9.5 miles northwest of Rocky Bar on the headwaters of Buck Creek. Crystals are colorless to pink and up to 5 cm in length. Smoky quartz, zircon and other minerals are associated. There are miarolitic cavities in the few granitic rock outcrops around the swamp, but these are generally weathered and empty. A few of these cavities were found with smoky quartz, microcline, albite and possibly topaz crystals (personal).

Lemhi County: Topaz is uncommon in the cavities of the Crags batholith in the Yellowjacket Mountains. Only a few crystals have been found in the scarce cavities, with smoky quartz, microcline and albite. The color of these are light sherry, and they have a habit similar to the topaz of the Sawtooth batholith (personal).

Valley County: A large bluish topaz crystal was found in gold placer gravels on a tributary of Paddy Creek in the Paddy Flat area northeast of Donnelly. There are many pegmatites in the area. Although most of these are simple pegmatites, there may be a few that were more complex and contained minerals other than the simple mineralogy of most. The topaz, and the quartz crystals that also occur in the placers, probably came from rare cavities in these pegmatites (Shannon, 1926; personal).

TORBERNITE

$Cu(UO_2)_2(PO_4)_2 \cdot 8\text{-}12H_2O$, tetragonal

Tabular crystals, usually square or foliated in scaly aggregates. Several shades of green;

Photo. 334 Group of stilbite crystals, longest crystal is 2.4 cm, Lime Creek, Custer County.

Photo. 335 Small stilbite crystals on "stalactite" of quartz and blue agate; longest stalactite is 10.8 cm, Lime Creek, Custer County.

Photo. 336 Stilbite, to 3 mm long, Loon Creek Summit, Custer County.

Photo. 337 Stilbite, 2-3 mm in length, Washington Basin, Custer County.

Photo. 338 Stilbite, 7.5 cm high, Race Creek, Idaho County; Norm and Carla Radford specimen.

Photo. 340 Thomsonite, 2.6 cm across, with mesolite hairs, Pinehurst area, Adams County.

Photo. 339 Thomsonite, 1.6 mm high, with clay around base, Pinehurst area, Adams County.

Photo. 341 Titanite, 2.2 mm, contact zone of Bruce Estate deposit, Spring Mountain District, Lemhi County.

Photo. 343 Brown vanadinite crystals of an elongated habit that is uncommon at the location, Iron mask Mine, Spring Mountain District, Lemhi County.

Photo. 342 Vanadinite with descloizite, Iron Mask Mine, Spring Mountain District, Lemhi County.

transparent to translucent. A secondary mineral most common in gossans formed from the weathering of deposits containing copper sulfides and uranium. Associated with autunite.

Lemhi County: Torbernite occurs in the Garm Lamoreaux Mine 11 miles north of North Fork on Allen Creek in Sec. 31, T 26 N., R 21 E. It forms apple-green crystals to 0.1 mm with galena, pyrite, quartz and autunite. Mineralization occurs as lenses and stringers in quartzite, schist, phyllites and argillites of Precambrian age. Four adits have been driven on the mineralized zone (Trites and Tooker, 1953).

Small crystals to 0.1 mm have been found in the Moon claim in Sec. 21, T. 26 N., R 21 E. near Blosche Gulch, a tributary of the North Fork of the Salmon River, 3 miles northwest of Gibbonsville. The crystals occur with malachite on surfaces of three fractures which cut a gold-bearing quartz vein and extend into the country rock. Two of the fractures are exposed in an adit and one in an open cut. Torbernite has been found in quartz float 3,000 feet N. 70°W of the mine (Trites and Tooker, 1953).

Crystals of torbernite have been found in the Surprise Mine which is several thousand feet northwest of the Moon claim in Friedorf (Doolitle) Gulch. The torbernite occurs with autunite, both of which form crystals to 3 mm. They make conspicuous coatings on fracture surfaces. Torbernite crystals are mostly square transparent plates with a green color. Mineralization is strong 200 feet in the adit and moderate 500-600 feet. The uranium minerals are in fractured quartz and rock above a band of gouge and extend into sheared rock of the hanging wall for 30 feet (Anderson, 1958).

Torbernite has been found in the volcanic rocks of the Dot and E-Dah-How claims 6-8 miles south of Salmon along Highway 93. It occurs with autunite and uranophane on fracture surfaces (Anderson, 1958).

TREMOLITE

$Ca_2(Mg,Fe)_5Si_8O_{22}(OH)_2$, monoclinic

Forms a series with actinolite and ferro-actinolite; amphibole group. Crystals prismatic or commonly bladed or in radiating aggregates; can be coarse to fine granular. White; transparent to translucent. Occurs in impure, crystalline, dolomitic limestone, talc schist and crystalline schist.

Blaine County: Gray finely fibrous masses of tremolite were found in the Red Elephant Mine in the Wood River region. The tremolite masses contain small cubes of pyrite, and occur in a calcareous shale (Shannon, 1926).

Cassia County: Gray blades and sheaves of tremolite up to 3 mm thick and 15 mm in length occur in marble from the marble quarry at Basin. The quarry is in T. 14 S., R. 22 E. The marble is medium grained and gray in color (Shannon, 1926).

TRIDYMITE

SiO_2, monoclinic (pseudohexagonal)

Pseudohexagonal; sometimes triclinic. Polymorphous with coesite, cristobalite, quartz and stishovite. Forms minute thin tabular crystals. Colorless to white; transparent to translucent. Common in some volcanic rocks; associated with cristobalite, sanidine, hornblende and hematite.

Clark County: Small crystals of tridymite can be found in the rhyolites near Libbys Hot Springs west of Dubois. The tridymite is abundant in some of the rhyolite (Shannon, 1926).

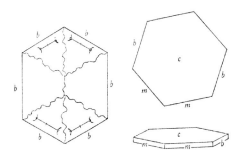

TUNGSTITE

$WO_3 \cdot H_2O$, orthorhombic

Usually massive or earthy; may form microscopic platy crystals. Bright yellow, golden yellow or yellowish green; transparent. Formed from the oxidation of wolframite and other tungsten minerals.

Lemhi County: Waxy to ocherous fillings of tungstite occur in small cavities in rusty quartz in the Blue Wing District. It is very finely crystalline and is associated with huebnerite (Shannon, 1926).

Fig. 21 Tyrolite, Liberal King claim, Pine Creek, Shoshone County; crystal drawings from Shannon, 1926).

TYROLITE

$CaCu_5(AsO_4)_2(CO_3)(OH)_4 \cdot 6H_2O$, orthorhombic

In fan-shaped or foliated aggregates, crusts and masses; rarely in lath-like crystals. Pale apple-green to verdigris-green, inclining to sky-blue; translucent. A secondary mineral erythrite, azurite, chrysocolla, cuprite and limonite.

Shoshone County: This uncommon mineral was found in the Liberal King Mine next to the Lookout Mountain Mine east of the forks of Pine Creek (Fig. 21). It was found as an oxidation product in porous quartz on the dump of the mine, forming blue-green films with a vitreous to pearly luster. The films consisted of minute, thin tabular, hexagonal crystals. It was associated with pyrite, arsenopyrite and chalcopyrite and forms on the chalcopyrite (Shannon, 1926).

Photo. 345 A "floater" matrix specimen of vanadinite, a piece of hard to powdery gossan completely coated with crystals, 4.3 cm across, Iron Mask Mine, Lemhi County.

Photo. 344 Uncommonly large vanadinite from the Iron Mask Mine, large crystal is 8 mm across, Lemhi County.

Photo. 346 Matrix specimen of vanadinite with large curved crystals in hemispherical groups, 5.2 cm across, Iron Mask Mine, Lemhi County.

Photo. 347 Yellowish tan vanadinite crystals of a spindle-shaped habit, uncommon at the location, Iron mask Mine, Spring Mountain District, Lemhi County.

Photo. 348 Octahedral variscite crystals with tabular metavariscite crystals, Two Top Creek, Fremont County.

Photo. 349 Willemite crystals in groups with goethite pseudomorphs of siderite on quartz, Keystone Mountain, Custer County.

Photo. 350 Wulfenite crystals on wulfenite, left crystal is a rare plate with sharp faces whereas the crystal on the right is a rare plate with rounded faces, crystals are 0.1-0.15 mm, the crystals sit on a varnish-like coating of wulfenite, Weimer Mine, Clark County.

Photo. 351 Wulfenite crystal with wulfenite showing few faces, crystal is 0.1 mm across, Weimer Mine Clark County.

Photo. 352 Elongated dipyramidal wulfenite associated with unknown, central crystal is 0.4 mm long, Ima Mine, Patterson, Lemhi County.

Photo. 353 Wulfenite prisms with blue-green malachite, crystals are 0.4-0.6 mm long, Ima Mine, Patterson, Lemhi County.

Photo. 354 Skeletal dipyramidal wulfenite with jarosite(?) coating, 0.5 mm, Missouri Belle Mine, Lemhi County.

UNKNOWN

Owyhee County: Two unknown silver minerals have been reported from the Flint District. One mineral forms crystals with tarnished faces as if there was a film of chalcopyrite, covellite or bornite on the surface. Under the tarnish, the crystals are iron-black. The second mineral is softer and has no tarnish. Both form microcrystals on corroded, rich silver ore (Piper and Laney, 1926).

URANOPHANE

$(H_3O)_2Ca(UO)_2(SiO_2)_2 \cdot 3H_2O$, monoclinic
Dimorphous with uranophane-beta. Crystals prismatic, radiating aggregates, massive or fibrous; yellow color. Commonly occurs in granite associated with fluorite and uraninite.

Boise, Custer and Elmore Counties: Uranophane has been identified in one small cavity and is probably the yellow fibrous microcoating in another small cavity in the Sawtooth Mountains. In the one cavity where it was identified, it formed a cluster of radiating acicular crystals to about 2 mm in length, with the specimen about 3 mm across. Individual crystals have a light yellow color and waxy luster. Quartz and microcline are associated (personal).

Lemhi County: Uranophane occurs with torbernite in the Dot claims 0.5 mile northwest of the Surprise Mine and the E-Dah-How claims 6-8 miles south of Salmon, along Highway 93, and possibly in other mines in the area. It forms pale greenish yellow fibrous or radiating needle-like crystals. Mineralization at the Dot claims is on a ridge crest exposed in bulldozer cuts in a 40 foot thick volcanic ridge cap. Crystals cover fracture surfaces. Torbernite and autunite are most common at the E-Dah-How claims, in welded tuffs where they form small crystals on fractures and in vugs (Anderson, 1958).

VALENTINITE

$Sb2O_3$, orthorhombic

Dimorphous with senarmontite. Crystals prismatic or tabular and often rounded. Commonly forms aggregates with a fan-shape or stellate group. More often in masses or druses of microcrystals. White or occasionally yellowish, reddish, brownish or gray. It is a common secondary mineral associated with stibnite, kermesite and native antimony.

Butte County: Valentinite occurs at an antimony prospect on the north branch of Lava Creek about 1.25 miles north of the Hub Mine in the Lava Creek District in Sec. 4, T. 2 N., R. 24 E. It forms olive green prismatic crystals to 1.7 cm in vugs or coatings on or pseudomorphous of stibnite. Cervantite and stibiconite are associated. Mineralization is in a brecciated limestone (Anderson, 1929).

Elmore County: Valentinite is common in the Hermada antimony mine west of Atlanta on the East Fork of Swanholm Creek. It is associated with kermesite, cervantite, stibiconite and stibnite in the oxidized surface ores, and forms a white coating on other minerals. Mineralization is in quartz veins in quartz monzonite and granodiorite (Popoff, 1953).

Shoshone County: Thin crusts or drusy coatings of valentinite occur in the Stanley antimony mine in Gorge Gulch above Burke. It is pale brown when on quartz and olive-green when on stibnite and has a waxy luster. Kermesite is associated (Shannon, 1926).

VANADINITE

$Pb_5(VO_4)_3Cl$, hexagonal

Short to long prismatic crystals, sometimes acicular to hair-like; may be hollow, rounded or skeletal. Orangish red, ruby red, brownish red, reddish brown, brown, brownish yellow or yellow; subtransparent to nearly opaque. Of secondary origin in oxidized lead deposits with mimetite, pyromorphite, wulfenite, cerussite and limonite.

Blaine County: Vanadinite was found in the Eureka Mine on Bullion Creek. Pyromorphite and wulfenite have been found with the vanadinite in the outcrop above the main adit (Umpleby et al, 1930).

Lemhi County: Only two localities for vanadinite had been reported in the various geologic literature for Idaho. One of these is the Iron Mask Mine in the Spring Mountain District (Shannon, 1926). Vanadinite occurs sparsely on the dumps of the lower mines of the Iron Mask group (Photos. 342-347). It generally occurs as tiny crystals of tabular habit with a yellow, cream or caramel color, a few are prismatic (Photo. 343). Tiny crystals of descloizite are occasionally associated (Photo. 342). The mines are caved and the

Photo. 356 Elongated dipyramidal wulfenite on quartz, long crystal is 0.8 mm, Missouri Belle Mine, Lemhi County.

Photo. 355 Transparent dipyramidal wulfenite, 0.4 mm, Missouri Belle Mine, Lemhi County.

Photo. 358 Pseudohexagonal tabular crystals of xanthoconite, group 0.7 mm across, Atlanta District, Elmore County.

Photo. 357 Translucent dipyramidal wulfenite, crystals around 0.4 mm Missouri Belle Mine, Lemhi County.

Photo. 360 Zircon-thorianite, 1.2 mm long, frozen in a small smoky quartz mass, Steel Mountain, Elmore County.

Photo. 359 Microcrystals of zalesiite forming tufts and radial groups, Monitor Mine, Shoshone County.

vanadinite is scarce on the dumps. A few crystals have found in one area of a vein exposed in some cliffs. A few specimens of goethite pseudomorphs (epimorphs) of vanadinite were also found in the vein. These have very thin hollow goethite pseudomorphs scattered on gossan. Along with these, a few specimens of similar goethite pseudomorphs of barite were found.

Although nearly all material reported from these dumps is micro crystals (<1 mm), or rarely crystals up to about 3 mm across, specimens have been found with larger crystals; the largest crystal being 8 mm, across in a group (Photo. 344).

The Iron Mask Mine is a series of small workings on the south wall of a north-facing cirque at the head of Horseshoe Gulch. Mineralization is in dolomite of the Saturday Mountain formation. The main adit of the Iron Mask mine is 650 feet long, is caved and was driven to explore small lead-silver-copper replacement deposits. Above it, there are several smaller workings. Discovery of the mineralization was in the late 1880s, but the most exploration/mining activity was in 1902-1903, 1910, 1930s and 1940s with small production of ore.

Vein material includes hard or soft brown to nearly black goethite and some hematite and a hard brown jasperoid. There are cavities and fracture surfaces coated with drusy quartz, but quartz is uncommon, although locally it is abundant. Tiny crystals of cerussite, calcite, hemimorphite, vanadinite, descloizite and patches of malachite can be seen. A small amount of rosasite was seen on one specimen and azurite on another (personal; Kuizon and Lipton, 1991).

At the Ima Mine, vanadinite is present as a small component of the prismatic crystals which are dominantly mimetite. This has been detected by analysis only, apparently no distinct vanadinite crystals are known (personal).

VARISCITE

$AlPO_4 \cdot 2H_2O$, orthorhombic
Member of the variscite group. Crystals octahedral and rare, usually massive, as crusts, veinlets or nodules. Pale green to emerald green, bluish green, white; transparent to translucent. Formed in shallow deposits from the action of phosphate-bearing meteoric waters on aluminous rocks.

Fremont County: Variscite occurs in a fault zone that runs up a ridge on the south side of Two Top Creek northeast of Mack's Inn. The variscite forms nodules and masses from a few centimeters to several centimeters across. Many of them have narrow cavities or fractures that are lined with tiny micro crystals of metavariscite and some variscite. The crystals are medium green and translucent, up to about 3 mm across (Photo. 348). Wardite is also uncommonly associated. The occurrence is claimed and being mined for gem variscite nodules (personal).

VESUVIANITE

$Ca_{10}Mg_2Al_4(SiO_4)_5(Si_2O_7)_2(OH)_4$, tetragonal
Generally prismatic crystals, may form columnar aggregates, granular or massive. Green, brown, yellow, blue or red; subtransparent or translucent. Most common in crystalline limestones formed by contact metamorphism; associated with garnet, diopside and tourmaline.

Blaine County: Deep striated crystals of vesuvianite reach a maximum length of 1.5 cm

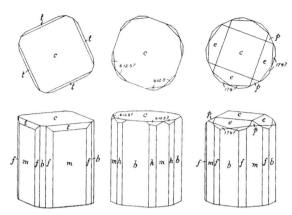

Fig. 22 Vesuvianite; left—brown crystal from Starlight Mine, Wood River District, Blaine County; center— Basin Group, Custer County; right—Mackay, Custer County; crystal drawings from Shannon (1926).

in the Starlight Mine in Elkhorn Gulch 3 miles east of Ketchum in the Warm Springs District (Fig. 22). The crystals occur as brown, long, prismatic crystals, some terminated, in wollastonite. Epidote, garnet, diopside andalusite and augite are associated. The contact metamorphic rocks have replaced beds of limestone, siliceous slate and quartzite (Shannon, 1926; Umpleby et al, 1930).

Custer County: Vesuvianite occurs in the No. 4 crosscut of the Alberta tunnel in the Mackay (Alder Creek) District (Fig. 22). It forms bunches of acicular radiating crystals replacing gray manganese-stained limestone. Bunches up to 1.5 cm have been collected. Greenish brown vesuvianite in acicular crystals occur in the Alberta No. 4 tunnel. It is apparently abundant about 100 feet into the tunnel. Small calcite-filled cavities in the vesuvianite contain terminated vesuvianite crystals (Shannon, 1926).

The Basin prospect north of the Trail Creek Divide at the head of Big Lost River, contains brown prisms of vesuvianite (Fig. 22). They occur in greenish brown garnet and are imperfectly developed, elongated crystals (Shannon, 1926).

Vesuvianite occurs in tactite zones of the Wild Horse Mine northeast of Ketchum. The mine and mill can be reached by taking the Trail Creek road from Ketchum for 23 miles, then going southeast of the East Fork of Big Lost River for 1.5 miles, then south on the Wildhorse Creek Road for 9 miles. The mine was developed for tungsten, but there was very little production.

Beryllium-bearing vesuvianite occurs at the Hard to Find open cut which is on the left fork of Wildhorse Creek about 1 mile south of the mill. The tactite is associated with alaskite and has been exposed along a 600 foot long trench. The cut has not been worked since about 1956 and the sides are slumped and caved. The tactite is poorly exposed along the walls. Most of the material is fine grained and massive, cavities are uncommon and the crystals are mostly poorly formed.

A similar occurrence is in the Beaver claims which are 0.9 mile north of the mill. Two pits expose zones of the tactite. Beryllium-bearing diopside occurs in the Pine Mouse extension which is in a cirque on the west slope of Wildhorse Creek valley about 1.4 miles north of the mill. There are several bodies of tactite in the walls of the cirque. The DMEA deposit also contained beryllium-bearing diopside. It is located about 100 feet west of the mill. This adit exposes only small zones of tactite.

The tactites are associated with alaskite dikes that formed from the metamorphism of impure marble; they occur in biotite gneiss. Calcite, garnet, actinolite, epidote, pyrite. scheelite and molybdenite occur with the vesuvianite. The deposits have not been worked in many years, and the workings are slumped and overgrown (Heungwon, 1955; Pattee et al, 1968; personal).

VIVIANITE

$Fe_3(PO_4)_2 \cdot H_2O$, monoclinic

Dimorphous with metavivianite. Prismatic crystals, may be flattened or tabular, in stellate groups, also reniform, tabular masses, crusts or earthy. Colorless and transparent when fresh and unaltered; on exposure, rapidly darkens and becomes blue or greenish blue and eventually becomes dark blue to black. A secondary mineral in oxidized ore deposits that contain phosphate, often well-crystallized; also in sediments, often associated with organic matter.

Clearwater County: Light greenish blue vivianite crystals in an unusual occurrence were found in the county. The crystals apparently coated or replaced the horn of a bison or tusk of a walrus. The crystals occur as a thin felted layer of fibrous crystals in the shape of a horn, with coarse crystals coating and projecting both inwards and outwards from a thin layer. Individual crystals reach a length of 4 cm and a thickness of 2 cm. The several fragments of the fossil were found in a gold placer (Shannon, 1926).

Idaho County: Broad blue plates of vivianite coat fractures in an altered dike in the Gold Hill property in the Dixie District (Shannon, 1926).

Latah County: Vivianite has been found in a small pegmatite on Mica Mountain near the Muscovite Mine north of Avon. It occurs as a blue alteration of the surface of tiny interlocking strengite crystals in a pegmatite. Ferriferous ankerite is associated as fine-grained veinlets with a buff color. Several pegmatites have been mined and prospected in this area, but it is not reported which one has the vivianite (Campbell, 1939).

Lemhi County: Vivianite occurs as colorless to dark blue crystals on matrix in the Blackbird District; some of the world's finest specimens have come from this locality, especially from the Blackbird Mine (Photos. 47, 48). Excellent specimens of crystals to 6 cm or more in length have been found, sometimes with ludlamite crystals. The vivianite occurs as thin to thick blades, mostly dark blue in color, often translucent. They stand upright on matrix or form tight groups of large intergrown crystals. Vivianite also occurred in the Calera Mine (personal).

Owyhee County: Colorless to deep blue crystals of vivianite occur in the Trade Dollar, Black Jack and other mines on Florida Mountain. The crystals reach a length of at least 3.5 cm. They occur in clay (Piper and Laney, 1926; Shannon, 1926).

VOLBORTHITE

$Cu_3V_2O_7(OH)_2 \cdot H_2O$, triclinic

As scales and scaly crusts, massive, compact, radiating fibers and rosette-like groups. Yellow, yellow brown to blackish brown, green to olive green; translucent. A secondary mineral in copper and vanadium-bearing deposits.

Adams County: Crystalline crusts of volborthite were found in the large pit of Can-Ida Mines north of Cuprum in the Seven Devils District. Other minerals occurring in the mine include chalcocite as disseminated grains (personal).

Lemhi County: Tiny crystals of volborthite have been reported from the Peacock Mine in the Junction District near Leadore. The tiny crystals were reported with cyanotrichite, malachite and azurite. It is not known if the identification was by analysis or visual characteristics only. See the cyanotrichite section for more information on the mineral occurrences in this district (personal).

WARDITE

$NaAl_3(PO_4)_2(OH)_4 \cdot 2H_2O$, tetragonal
Occurs as dipyramidal pseudo-octahedral crystals or as coatings. Transparent to opaque; white, colorless, pale green, blue-green, yellow-green, brown. Found in low-temperature phosphate-bearing nodules with crandallite, meta-variscite, variscite and other phosphates.

Fremont County: Wardite is uncommon in the variscite deposit on Two Top Creek, northeast of Mack's Inn. It forms a fine botryoidal coating with a blue-green color in tiny cavities in variscite nodules (personal).

WILLEMITE

Zn_2SiO_4, hexagonal
Short or elongated prismatic crystals, fibrous or granular aggregates, botryoidal and massive. Colorless to white, gray, yellow, red, green and blue; generally strongly fluorescent yellow-green in short wave ultraviolet light. A secondary mineral in zinc-bearing ore deposits in limestones.

Custer County: Tiny crystals of willemite occur with other secondary minerals in the silver mines on Keystone Mountain southwest of Challis (Photo. 349). The crystals are short to elongated prismatic and colorless. The largest seen is under 1 mm in length. To the author's knowledge, willemite has not been previously reported in Idaho (personal).

WODGINITE

$(Ta,Nb,Sn,Mn,Fe)_{16}O_{32}$, monoclinic
Sphenoidal and irregular grains, tabular grains; prismatic. Reddish brown through dark brown to black; submetallic. With albite, quartz and muscovite in granitic rocks in pegmatites.

Custer County: Wodginite was identified in one specimen from the Sawtooth batholith (Photo. 81). It occurred as two black, prismatic crystals, 1.5 mm high perched on albite. A third crystal is exposed on an apparent cleaved surface of a microcline crystal. The surfaces vary from dull, slightly pitted, to smooth and brilliant. Albite, microcline, smoky quartz, small dark green mica books (probably zinnwaldite), and tiny corroded topaz crystals are associated. The specimen is coated with a white to very light gray clay-like to micaceous material. This was the third known occurrence of wodginite in the U.S. (Cerny et al, 1985); Ream 1989a).

WOLFRAMITE

(Fe,Mn)WO$_4$, monoclinic

Intermediate in the huebnerite-ferberite series. Short prismatic to long prismatic, flattened or tabular, usually striated; groups often parallel, also massive granular or intergrowths of acicular crystals. Occurs in quartz veins and contact-metamorphic rocks with scheelite, diopside and garnet.

Blaine County: Wolframite was found on the north side at the top of Blizzard Mountain in small prospect pits. Blade-like crystals have been found frozen in the quartz vein material. There are small pits and a small trench in the area that contain the drusy quartz veins. Access is by a long hike from the road up Iron Mine Creek off Fish Creek.

Narrow, open fissures lined with a druse of quartz were prospected for tungsten. There are only a few workings and limited potential for specimens. Workings are also reported to occur on the south side of the mountain near the summit (Livingston, 1919; personal).

Boise County: Reddish to brownish black cleavable masses of wolframite were found in the Horse Fly prospect in Deadwood Basin. They are disseminated in quartz. In the same area, wolframite formed thin layers of friable material in vuggy quartz in the Merry Blue Mine (Shannon, 1926).

Butte County: Black crystals and bladed masses of wolframite were found in the Independence Mine near the summit of Granite Mountain 20 miles from Arco on the Hailey-Arco Road. The vein containing the Wolframite is at the contact of diorite and a siliceous rock. The vein consists of crystalline drusy quartz stained with iron and manganese oxides (Shannon, 1926).

Custer County: Bladed crystals of wolframite occur at the Big Fall Creek deposit at the junction of Big Fall and Summit creeks, 14 miles northeast of Ketchum. The crystals are in quartz veins in argillite, possibly in cavities (Cook, 1956).

Lemhi County: Wolframite has been found in several areas in T. 21-22 N., R. 20-21 E. It occurs in an area north and south of Baldy Mountain about 6-10 miles southeast of Leesburg, along Upper Pollard Canyon and its tributaries, in the cirque at the head of Rapps Creek and in a north-south zone along the boundary of Ranges 20 and 21 East. It forms tabular crystals to 2.5 cm across frozen in quartz veins in quartzite or on drusy quartz in vuggy quartz veins. The veins are up to two feet across and often vuggy with drusy quartz. Quartz crystals are rare up to 15 cm in length. Siderite and pyrite have been replaced by limonite pseudomorphs. Wolframite also occurs on joints in the gray quartzite which has been pyritized and bleached along the veins. The brilliant black pseudohexagonal crystals of wolframite are uncommon and have been found in only a few small areas (Shockey, 1957; personal).

WOLLASTONITE

CaSiO$_3$, triclinic or monoclinic

Polymorphous with cyclowollastonite, parawollastonite and wollastonite-7T. In tabular crystals, massive or fibrous. Colorless, white or gray; translucent. Generally in contact metamorphic crystalline limestones; calcite, diopside, grossular, tremolite and epidote are associated.

Blaine County: Wollastonite occurs in the Starlight Mine in Elkhorn Gulch near Ketchum in the Warm Springs District. It is white and fibrous and occurs in a lime-silicate contact rock with garnet and sphalerite. Dense white fibrous wollastonite occurs in the Drummond claim in the Muldoon District. It is in a contact lime-silicate rock with garnet, diopside and epidote (Shannon, 1926).

Custer County: Pink fibrous sheets of wollastonite can be found in the Basin prospect north of Trail Creek Summit on the Ketchum-Mackay Road. The sheets are up to 4 mm in thickness (Shannon, 1926).

WULFENITE

$PbMoO_4$, tetragonal

Mostly as square tabular crystals often extremely thin compared to width, octahedral, granular or massive. Orange-yellow to wax-yellow, gray, olive green, brown or red; transparent. A secondary mineral in oxidized lead-molybdenum-bearing ore deposits. Common associates are mimetite, vanadinite, pyromorphite and cerussite.

Bear Lake County: Wax-yellow crystals have been found at the Blackstone Mine in the $SE^{1/}_4$ Sec. 17 and $NE^{1/}_4$ Sec. 20, T. 15 S., R. 43 E. in the Bear River Range west of Montpelier. The mine is on the west side of St. Charles Creek, 3.5 miles west of the town of St. Charles. The tabular crystals are associated with cerussite and brown rounded crystals of sphalerite (Mansfield, 1927; Richards, 1910; Shannon, 1926).

Blaine County: Small orange-yellow wulfenite crystals were found in the Golden Bell Mine near the head of the ravine which contains the Minnie Moore Mine near Bellevue. The crystals are abundant in "siliceous skeletal masses." Some of the crystals are simple square tablets with only a single prism and basal pinacoid, but many have modifying pyramidal faces (Shannon, 1926).

Wulfenite occurs in the Eureka Mine in Bullion Creek, in the $SW^{1/}_4$ Sec. 14, T. 2 N., R. 17 E. It has been found with pyromorphite and vanadinite in the outcrop above the main adit (Umpleby, 1930).

Butte County: Wulfenite occurs in the Sentinel Mine on North Creek Canyon 1 mile above the Wilbert Camp in Sec. 33, T. 8 N., R. 29 E. in the Dome District. It occurs sparingly as tabular pale yellow plates with orange and yellow lead oxides (probably massicot or minium). Galena, sphalerite, cerussite and smithsonite are associated. The mine has been developed with an adit. There is a good zone of mineralization 145 feet in the main drift (Anderson, 1948).

Clark County: Tiny, thin orange crystals of wulfenite have been found in the Weimer Mine in Skull Canyon, in approximately Sec. 21 and 28, T. 10 N., R. 30 E. They occur in sparsely scattered bunches 30 to 150 cm across in limestone on the northeast side of the canyon and in quartzite on the southeast side. White crystals of cerussite and barite, galena, malachite, azurite, anglesite and chrysocolla are associated.

Tiny crystals are rare in limestone associated with wulfenite forming vuggy rims surrounding altered galena. Most of the wulfenite is pale yellow, but some is medium to dark yellow to yellow orange. Most of it occurs as thin coatings with the appearance of varnish and some of it shows a few crystal faces. Very rare are well formed crystals, either as dipyramids or thin platy crystals with rounded or square shape (Photos. 350, 351). These crystals are less than 0.2 mm across (Anderson and Wagner, 1944; personal; Shannon, 1926; Umpleby, 1917).

The mines are accessible via the road up Skull Canyon. Several workings can be seen on the canyon side in a northeast branch of the canyon, and a large cut is on the nose of the ridge across the canyon (personal).

The Scott Mine of the Birch Creek Mining Co., in the Birch Creek District (Sec. 31, T. 9 N., R. 31 E.), produced small crystals of wulfenite associated with cerussite, anglesite and galena. The orange crystals occurred with carbonates in the 100 foot level where they were rare but conspicuous because of their orange color. Orange crystals occur in the 150 foot level north of the shaft with cerussite on calcite and galena. They were thick tabular with modifying faces. Some pale yellow crystals occurred in the 150 foot level in pale yellow ocher. These were highly modified tabular crystals. The mine is 2 miles from the highway at the edge of the Birch Creek Valley at 6,000 feet elevation. Mineralization is in Paleozoic limestone, shale and quartzite (Anderson and Wagner, 1944; (Shannon, 1926; Trites and Tooker, 1953).

Elmore County: Wulfenite occurs with molybdenite, pyrite, chalcopyrite, sphalerite, fluorite and calcite in the Rinebold prospect in the Rocky Bar District on Roaring River. It is about 0.3 mile above the mouth of the East Fork of Roaring River at 5,500 to 6,000 feet elevation. Adits, cuts and pits have been excavated on the claims. Wulfenite occurs in two adits on the west side of the East Fork, about 60 and 110 feet above the river (Schrader, 1924).

Idaho County: The Free Gold Mine in the Dixie District contains minute orange-yellow films of wulfenite in cracks (Shannon, 1926).

Lemhi County: Pale yellow tabular crystals were found in the Lena Delta Mine in ocherous limonite (Shannon, 1926).

Small crystals of wulfenite occur in the lead-silver veins in the Little Eightmile (Junction) District. Crystals are uncommon and occur as small, thin, orange tabular crystals lining cavities in some of the masses of galena in the veins. They are known to occur in one locality in the Buckhorn Mine, 110 feet west of the main adit in the 650 foot crosscut. At the Maryland Mine, specimens with euhedral crystals to about 1.5 mm across were found. They are thin tabular crystals showing the forms (001), (110) and (100) and thin tabular truncated pyramids showing the forms (001), (111) and (101) (Thune, 1941).

Microcrystals of wulfenite are rare at the Ima Mine. It occurs with other secondary minerals including azurite, cerussite, mimetite, pyromorphite, segnitite and an unidentified mineral. The tiny crystals of wulfenite, mostly under 0.5 mm, occur in several habits, including colorless square plates, colorless to grayish square prisms and grayish elongated dipyramidal crystals (Photos. 318, 352, 353) (personal).

Wulfenite is locally common in some of the vein quartz in the oxidized zone with ferrimolybdite at the Missouri Belle Mine north of North Fork near the Montana border. The tiny wulfenite crystals are mostly octahedral in shape and are colorless to pale yellow (Photos. 354-357). Often they are elongated and skeletal; most crystals are under 1 mm across. The crystals are often stacked on each other or connected in curving groups. Clean transparent yellow crystals may be perched on top of coated crystals. It is occasionally associated with tiny barite crystals, and is often on drusy quartz which lines the walls of most of the cavities. Many have thin brown coatings of iron oxides/hydroxides or submicrocrystalline coatings of jarosite. Some cavities are clean with no coatings (Photo. 356), but in most cavities, the quartz and wulfenite are coated (personal).

Shoshone County: In the Coeur d'Alene District, tiny, reddish orange crystals have been found on pyromorphite in the Sherman Mine (Photos. 41, 42), and have been reported from other mines. In the Sherman Mine, wulfenite crystals were typically under 1 mm across and scarce to abundant on pyromorphite specimens (personal).

Wulfenite crystals are rare at the Bunker Hill Mine (Photo. 40). A few tiny yellow crystals have been found in the pyromorphite vugs of the 9 level, Jersey vein. The microscopic crystals were found on the matrix with tiny yellow pyromorphite crystals (personal).

WURTZITE

(Zn, Fe)S, hexagonal (and trigonal)

Trimorphous with matraite and sphalerite. Hemimorphic pyramidal, short prismatic to tabular, striated horizontally, also as crusts. Brownish black. The rare and unstable form for zinc sulfide; may be intergrown with sphalerite or marcasite.

Blaine County: Unusual spherical masses up to 1.5 cm across were found in the St. Louis Mine in the Era District. The masses have a spongy core of radial structure and an outer brown layer. There is no crystal outline. These masses and irregular fine-grained masses of wurtzite and sphalerite occur with galena, pyrite, chalcopyrite, proustite, tetrahedrite, acanthite, chlorargryrite, smithsonite and cerussite in quartz veins (Shannon, 1926).

Custer County: Wurtzite is reported in the mines in the Mackay area (Palache, 1944).

XANTHOCONITE

Ag_3AsS_3, monoclinic
Dimorphous with proustite. Tabular, forms flattened rhomb, may be lath-shaped or rarely pyramidal. Dark cochineal-red to orange- or clove-brown. Occurs with the ruby silver minerals.

Elmore County: Xanthoconite has been found in the mines of the Atlanta District (Photo. 358). It occurs with proustite and other silver minerals on slickensided surfaces and can be distinguished by its orange color. The tiny crystals are tabular, hexagonal and lustrous (Anderson, 1939).

Owyhee County: Xanthoconite has been reported from the Flint District. It is usually yellow to orange-red or brown in color and is associated with polybasite and stephanite (Shannon, 1926).

XENOTIME-(Y)

YPO_4, tetragonal
Mostly short to long prismatic, pyramidal or equant crystals; also as aggregates of rough crystals or rosettes. Color is yellowish brown to reddish brown, pale yellow, pale gray, reddish or greenish; luster is vitreous to resinous. Translucent to opaque. Xenotime is common in small amounts in acidic and alkalic igneous rocks, in pegmatites and also in metamorphic rocks and alpine-type veins. It also occurs as detrital minerals in alluvial deposits.

Boise County: Xenotime is commonly associated with zircon in the Boise Basin placer deposits. The small crystals are pinkish to reddish brown and have a resinous to vitreous luster (Sidler, 1957).

ZALESIITE

$(Ca,Cu)_6[(AsO_4)_2(AsO_3OH)(OH)_6] \cdot 3H_2O$, hexagonal

Member of the mixite group, green color, hexagonal crystals, fibers, tufts of acicular crystals and veinlets. Forms in the oxidation zone of copper-bearing ore deposits. A rare mineral, associated with azurite, chrysocolla, clinoclase and malachite.

Shoshone County: Zalesiite is uncommon at the Monitor Mine near the Idaho-Montana border on upper Mineral Creek. The mine was developed as a deep shaft which is caved at the collar. Oxide minerals are scarce on the dumps. This discovery of zalesiite is only the second in the United States and perhaps third in the world. The zalesiite occurs in brown oxide material with aurichalcite, azurite, chrysocolla and malachite. It forms tiny green crystals in groups and tuffs with malachite (Photo. 359). Brown micro spheres of an uncharacterized mineral occur on the zalesiite fibers. These spheres contain Cu-Mn-Fe-(Co-Ca)-Si-O; this is similar to abswurmbachite, but work has not been done to identify this mineral (personal).

ZINNWALDITE

$KLiFeAl(AlSi_3)O_{10}(F,OH)_2$, monoclinic

Member of the mica group; gray to dark brown to dark green in color. Easily mistaken for biotite. Forms scales and scaly masses or pseudohexagonal crystals. Occurs in greisens, high temperature quartz veins and granitic pegmatites.

Boise, Custer and Elmore Counties: This mica occurs with masutomilite in miarolitic cavities in the Sawtooth batholith. It forms zoned crystals that are partially masutomilite, representing changes in the iron and manganese content of the crystals. Crystals to at least 5 cm across and more than 6 cm in length occur on microcline and albite matrix.

Smoky quartz is associated along with aquamarine and topaz. Few really fine specimens of zinnwaldite have been found. The mica books are commonly altered or weathered so as to be partially rounded, cleaved, broken or covered with clays and silica coatings. Occasionally one or more zones in a complex crystal is etched away (personal).

ZIRCON

$ZrSiO_4$, tetragonal

Commonly as crystals showing the prism and dipyramid. Brown, colorless, gray, green or red; translucent or rarely transparent. A common accessory mineral in igneous rocks.

Bingham County: Sand concentrates from the Snake River near Rosa contain sharp colorless prismatic zircon crystals. Rarely, they are red-brown or brown (Shannon, 1926).

Boise, Custer and Elmore Counties: Small zircon crystals are uncommon in cavities in the granite of the Sawtooth Mountains. These have been found in only a few cavities with smoky quartz, albite, microcline and a few other minerals. Individual crystals are less than 4 mm in length and brown, reddish brown or yellowish green in color. Often they are rounded, but others are sharp and euhedral (personal).

Boise County: Small zircon crystals are associated with monzonite in the gold placers of the county. The crystals are prismatic and mostly colorless (Shannon, 1926).

Elmore County: Minute colorless crystals occur in placers on Wood Creek (Shannon, 1926).

Several minerals have been recovered as tiny crystals and waterworn crystals in the placer deposits at Dismal Swamp at the headwaters of Buck Creek. The swamp is in Sec. 34, T. 5 N., R. 9 E., about 1.5 miles down a dirt road from a point on the Rocky Bar-Middle Fork Road 6.5 miles northwest of Rocky Bar. Zircon, cassiterite and columbite have been found as well as anatase, rutile, samarskite, garnet, ilmenite, magnetite, monazite, topaz, xenotime and smoky quartz. Most of the crystals are of small size, but the topaz crystals have been up to more than 10 cm and topaz crystals to at least 7 cm (Armstrong, 1957; Idaho Bur. of Mines, 1964; personal).

In the nearby Steel Mountain stock, zircon or zircon-thorianite mixtures have been found as tiny square prismatic crystals. The occurrence is rare in the small miarolitic cavities of the stock. The few crystals seen are around 1 mm long and are cream colored (Photo. 360). Identification was by microprobe analysis (personal).

Idaho County: Small crystals are abundant in some of the placer deposits in the streams of the Warren and Florence districts. The abundance of the colorless crystals have given the placer concentrates the nickname "White Sand." In the Florence District, they are less than 3 mm in length and colorless to pale yellow. Gold, allanite, apatite and other minerals are associated (Reed, 1939; Shannon, 1926).

Latah County: Large zircon crystals, up to 2.5 cm across have been found with corundum and quartz crystals alongside a gravel road near Joel, several miles east of Moscow. The location is now reported to be overgrown with grass and vegetation (personal).

Lemhi County: Zircon is probably uncommon in the rocks of the Crags batholith. It has been found as small, elongated, euhedral crystals on albite matrix with microcline in one cavity from the eastern part of the batholith. The small crystals are light bluish color, about 1 mm across and up to about 6 mm in length and consist of the prism and dipyramid (personal).

Minidoka County: Few pink and orange-red zircon crystals have been found in the sands of the Snake River in the area around Wapi. They are long prismatic with their length 10 to 20 times their diameter (Shannon, 1926).

ZOISITE

$Ca_2Al_3(SiO_4)_3(OH)$, orthorhombic

Dimorphous with clinozoisite, which is more common. Prismatic parallel to the b axis and striated parallel to the b axis; also columnar or massive granular. White, yellowish brown, green, pink to rose-red (thulite); transparent to translucent. Most common in crystalline schists; also found in blueschist facies metamorphic rocks and in eclogites.

Adams County: Zoisite forms irregular pink masses of interlocking crystals or blades in the Red Ledge Mine in the Seven Devils District. It is common in the rock at the mine, and is formed from the alteration of the feldspars. It also occurs at the Helena and Arkansas mines as small masses and thin veins (Shannon, 1926).

Shoshone County: Zoisite crystals up to 1 cm thick by 2 cm in length occur in quartz in the metamorphic rocks southeast of Goat Peak. The prismatic crystals are poorly formed and have a dirty white color. They are found southeast of and across a branch of the Clearwater River from Goat Peak (Goat Mountain?). Biotite and garnet occur in the quartz adjacent to the zoisite-bearing vein (Shannon, 1926).

Bibliography

Abbott, A.T. and Prater, L.S., 1954, The geology of kyanite-andalusite deposits, Goat Mountain, Idaho, and preliminary beneficiation tests on the ore: Idaho Bur. of Mines and Geol., Pam. 100, 27 p.

Adams, J.W., Staatz, M.H. and Havens, R.G., 1964, Cenosite from Porthill, Idaho: Am. Min. Vol. 49, pp. 1736-1744.

Allen, R.M., Jr., 1940, Geology and ore deposits of the Volcano District, Elmore County, Idaho: M.S. Thesis, Univ. of Idaho, 41 p.

Anderson, A.L., 1929, Geology and ore deposits of the Lava Creek District, Idaho: Idaho Bur. of Mines and Geol., Pam. 32, 70 p.

_____ 1930 (1956 reprint), The geology and mineral resources of the region about Orofino, Idaho: Idaho Bur. of Mines and Geol., Pam. 34, 63 p.

_____ 1931, Geology and mineral resources of Eastern Cassia County, Idaho: Idaho Bur. of Mines and Geol., Bull. 14, 169 p.

_____ 1934, Geology of the Pearl-Horseshoe Bend gold belt, Idaho: Idaho Bur. of Mines and Geol., Pam. 41, 36 p.

_____ 1939, Geology and ore deposits of the Atlanta District, Elmore County, Idaho: Idaho Bur. of Mines and Geol., Pam. 49, 70 p.

_____ 1943a, Copper mineralization near Salmon, Lemhi County, Idaho: Idaho Bur. of Mines and Geol., Pam. 60, 15 p.

_____ 1943b, Geology of the gold-bearing lodes of the Rocky Bar District, Elmore County, Idaho: Idaho Bur. of Mines and Geol., Pam. 65, 39 p.

_____ 1943c, The antimony and fluorspar deposits near Meyers Cove, Lemhi Co., Idaho: Idaho Bur. of Mines and Geol., Pam. 62, 20 p.

_____ 1947a, Geology and ore deposits of Boise Basin, Idaho: U.S. Geol. Surv. Bull. 944-C, 319 p.

_____ 1947b, Cobalt mineralization in the Blackbird District, Lemhi County, Idaho: Econ. Geol., Vol. 42, p. 22-46.

_____ 1948a, Reconnaissance survey of the geology and ore deposits of the southwestern portion of Lemhi Range, Idaho: Idaho Bur. of Mines and Geol., Pam. 80, 18p.

_____ 1948b, Tungsten mineralization at the Ima Mine, Blue Wing District, Lemhi County, Idaho: Econ. Geol., Vol. 43, p. 181-206.

_____ 1949, Silver-gold deposits of the Yankee Fork District, Custer County, Idaho: Idaho Bur. of Mines and Geol., Pam. 83, 37 p.

_____ 1953, Gold-copper-lead deposits of the Yellowjacket District, Lemhi County, Idaho: Idaho Bur. of Mines and Geol., Pam. 94, 41 p.

_____ 1954a, A preliminary report on the fluorspar mineralization near Challis, Custer County, Idaho: Idaho Bur. of Mines and Geol., Pam. 101, 13 p.

_____ 1954b, Fluorspar deposits near Meyers Cove, Lemhi County, Idaho: Idaho Bur. of Mines and Geol., Pam. 98, 34 p.

_____ 1956, Geology and mineral resources of the Salmon Quadrangle, Lemhi County, Idaho: Idaho Bur. of Mines and Geol., Pam. 106, 102 p.

_____ 1957, Geology and mineral resources of the Baker Quadrangle, Lemhi County, Idaho: Idaho Bur. of Mines and Geol., Pam. 112, 71 p.

_____ 1958, Uranium, thorium, columbium and rare earth deposits in the Salmon Region, Lemhi County, Idaho: Idaho Bur. of Mines and Geol., Pam. 115, 81 p.

_____ 1959, Geology and mineral resources of the North Fork Quadrangle, Lemhi County, Idaho: Idaho Bur. of Mines and Geol., Pam. 118, 92 p.

Anderson, A.L. and Rasor, A.C., 1934, Silver mineralization in the Banner District, Boise County, Idaho: Econ. Geol., Vol. 29, No., 4, pp. 371-387.

Anderson, A.L. and Wagner, W.R., 1944, Lead-zinc-copper deposits of the Birch Creek District, Clark and Lemhi Counties, Idaho: Idaho Bur. of Mines and Geol., Pam. 70, 43 p.

Anderson, A.L. and Wagner, W.R., 1946, A geological reconnaissance in the Little Wood River (Muldoon) District, Blaine County, Idaho: Idaho Bur. of Mines and Geol., Pam. 75, 22 p.

Anderson, R.A., 1948, Reconnaissance survey of the geology and ore deposits of the southwestern portion of Lemhi Range, Idaho: Idaho Bur. of Mines and Geol., Pam. 80, 18 p.

Armstrong, F.C., 1957, Dismal Swamp placer deposit, Elmore county, Idaho: U.S. Geol. Surv. Bull. 1042-K, 10 p.

Asher, R.R., 1967, Geology and mineral resources of a portion of the Silver City region, Owyhee County, Idaho: Idaho Bur. of Mines and Geol., Pam. 138, 106 p.

Baker, E.D., 1979, Geology of the Phoebe Tip-Trapper Peak area, Boundary County, Idaho: M.S. Thesis, Univ. of Idaho.

Ballard, S.M., 1922, Geology and ore deposits of the Alturas Quadrangle, Blaine County, Idaho: Idaho Bur. of Mines and Geol., Bull. 5, 36 p.

_____ 1924, Geology and gold resources of Boise Basin, Boise County, Idaho: Idaho Bur. of Mines and Geol., Bull. 9, 103 p.

Beckwith, J.A., 1972, Gem minerals of Idaho: Caxton Printers, Caldwell, Idaho, 123 p.

Biddle, J.H., 1985, The geology and mineralization of part of the Bird Creek Quadrangle, Lemhi County, Idaho: M.S. Thesis, Univ. of Idaho, 119 p.

Callaghan, E. and Lemmon, D.M., 1941, Tungsten resources of the Blue Wing District, Lemhi County, Idaho: U.S. Geol. Surv., Bull. 931-A, 21 p.

Campbell, C.D., 1939, Phosphate minerals in a pegmatite near Deary, Idaho: Northwest Science, Vol. 13, pp. 19-20.

Cannon, R.S., Jr. and Grimaldi, F.S. ,1953, Lindgrenite and cuprotungstite from the Seven Devils District, Idaho: Am. Min., Vol. 38, p. 903-911.

Capps, S.R., 1939, The Dixie Placer District, Idaho, with notes on lodes by R.J. Roberts: Idaho Bur. of Mines and Geol., Pam. 48, 35 p.

Cass, H.K., 1973, Geology and alteration of the Jordan Creek area, Yankee Fork Mining

District, Custer County, Idaho: M.S. Thesis, Univ. of Idaho.

Cater, F.W., Pinckney, D.M., Hamilton, W.B., Parker, R.L., Weldin, R.D., Close, T.J. and Zilka, N.T., 1973, Mineral resources of the Idaho Primitive Area and vicinity, Idaho: U.S. Geol. Surv., Bull. 1304, 431 p.

Cerny, P., Roberts, W.L., Ercit, T.S. and Chapman, R., 1985, Wodginite and associated oxide minerals from the Peerless pegmatite, Pennington County, South Dakota: Am. Min., Vol. 70, p. 1044-1049.

Choate, R., 1962, Geology and ore deposits of the Stanley area: Idaho Bur. of Mines and Geol., Pam. 97, 122 p.

Cook, E.F., 1954, Mining geology of the Seven Devils Region: Idaho Bur. of Mines and Geol., Pam. 97, 22p.

_____ 1956, Tungsten deposits of south-central Idaho: Idaho Bur. of Mines and Geol., Pam. 108, 40 p.

Cooper, J.R., 1951, Geology of the tungsten, antimony and gold deposits near Stibnite, Idaho: U.S. Geol. Surv., Bull. 969-F, pp. 151-197.

Cox, D.C., 1954, Fluorspar deposits near Meyers Cove, Lemhi County, Idaho: U.S. Geol. Surv., Bull. 1015, p. 1-22.

Crowley, J.A. and Radford, N.A., 1982, Pyromorphite from the Coeur d'Alene district, Idaho: Min. Rec., Vol. 13, p. 273-285.

Currier, L.W., 1935, A preliminary report on the geology and ore deposits of the eastern part of the Yellow Pine District, Idaho: Idaho Bur. of Mines and Geol., Pam. 43, 27 p.

Dake, H.C., 1956, Northwest gem trails, a field guide for the gem hunter, the mineral collector and the tourist: Mineralogist Publishing Co., 80 p.

De Long, R.F., 1986, Geology of the Hall Gulch plutonic complex, Elmore and Camas Counties, Idaho: M.S. Thesis, Univ. of Idaho.

Douglas, R.M., Murphy, M.J. and Pabst, A., 1954, Geocronite: Am. Min., Vol. 39, pp. 908-928.

Dunn, P.J., 1976, Genthelvite and helvine group; Min. Mag., Vol. 40.

_____ 1982, On the chemical composition of Bunker Hill pyromorphite: Min. Rec., Vol. 13, p. 286.

Faich, J.N., 1937, Geology and ore deposits of the Gold Hill District: M.S. Thesis, Univ. of Idaho, 56 p.

Fleischer, M. 1987, Glossary of mineral species: Mineralogical Record, Inc., 227 p.

Ford, W.E., 1955, A textbook of mineralogy: John Wiley and Sons, Inc., revised from Dana, E.S. 1898

Fryklund, V.C., Jr., 1951a, A reconnaissance of some Idaho feldspar deposits with a note on the occurrence of columbite and samarskite: Idaho Bur. of Mines and Geol., Pam. 91, 30 p.

_____ 1951b, Note on the Occurrence of corundum in Idaho: Am. Min., Vol. 36, p. 776-778.

Gale, H.S., 1910, Geology of the copper deposits near Montpelier, Bear Lake County, Idaho: U.S. Geol. Surv., Bull. 430-B.

Glass, J.J. and Vhay, J.S., 1949, A new locality for ludlamite: Am. Min., Vol. 34, p. 335-336.

Glass, J.J., Jahns, R.H. and Stevens, R.E., 1944, Helvite and danalite from New Mexico and the helvite group: Am. Min., Vol. 29.

Hamilton, J.A., 1961, Geology of the Caribou Mountain Area, Bonneville and Caribou Counties, Idaho: M.S. Thesis, Univ. of Idaho.

Hamilton, W., 1963, Columbia River basalt in the Riggins Quadrangle, western Idaho:

U.S. Geol. Surv., Bull. 1141-L, pp. 1-37.

Herdlick, J.A., 1948, Be Van quartz crystal prospect, Lemhi County, Idaho: US Bureau of Mines, Rept. of Investigations 4209, 6 p.

Hess, F.L., 1917, Tungsten minerals and deposits: U.S. Geol. Surv., Bull. 652.

Heungwon, Lee, 1955, Tungsten mineralization at the Wildhorse Mine, Custer County, Idaho: M.S. Thesis, Univ. of Idaho, 45 p.

Hietanen, A., 1962, Staurolite zone near the St. Joe River, Idaho: U.S. Geol. Surv., Pro. Paper 450-C, pp. C69-C71.

_____ 1963, Anorthosite and associated rocks in the Boehls Butte Quadrangle and vicinity, Idaho: U.S. Geol. Surv., Pro. Paper 344-B, 78 p.

_____ 1968, Belt series in the region around Snow Peak and Mallard Peak, Idaho: U.S. Geol. Surv., Pro. Paper 344-E, 34 p.

Hubbard, C.R., 1956, Geology and mineral resources of Nez Perce County, Idaho: Idaho Bur. of Mines and Geol., Co. Rept. No. 1, 17 p.

Hubbard, C.R., 1957, Mineral resources of Latah County: Idaho Bur. of Mines and Geol., Co. Rept. No. 2, 29 p.

Humphreys, R.M. and Leatham, E., 1936, Geology and ore deposits of the Talache Mine: B.S. Thesis, Univ. of Idaho.

Hurlbut, C.S., Jr., 1966, Dana's manual of mineralogy: John Wiley and Sons, Inc., 609 p., revised from Dana, 1929.

Idaho Bureau of Mines and Geology, 1964, Mineral and water resources of Idaho: Idaho Bur. of Mines and Geol., Special Report No. 1, Compiled by the U.S. Geol. Surv., 335 p.

Jones, E.L., Jr., 1917, Lode mining in the Quartzburg and Grimes Pass porphyry belt, Boise Basin, Idaho: U.S. Geol. Surv., Bull. 640-E, pp. 83-111.

Kern, B.F., 1959, Geology of the uranium deposits near Stanley, Custer County, Idaho: Idaho Bur. of Mines and Geol., Pam. 117.

Kern, R.R., 1972, The geology and economic deposits of the Slate Creek area, Custer County, Idaho: M.S. Thesis, Idaho State Univ.

Kerr, P.F., 1946, Tungsten mineralization in the United States: Geol. Soc. of America, Memoir 15.

Kiilsgaard, T.H., 1949, The geology and ore deposits of the Boulder Creek Mining District, Custer County, Idaho: Idaho Bur. of Mines and Geol., Pam. 88, 28 p.

Kiilsgaard, T.H., 1983, Geologic map of the Ten Mile West Roadless Area, Boise and Elmore Counties, Idaho: U.S. Geological Survey Miscellaneous Field Studies Map MF-1500-A, scale 1:62,500

Kiilsgaard, T.H. and Bennett, E.H., 1983, Mineral Deposits in the Southern Part of the Atlanta Lobe of the Idaho Batholith and their genetic relation to Tertiary intrusive rocks and to faults: in Symposium on the Geology and mineral deposits of the Challis 1'x2' quadrangle, Idaho, U.S. Geological Survey Bulletin 1658M.

Kirkemo, H., Anderson, C.A. and Creasey, S.C., 1965, Investigations of the molybdenum deposits in the conterminous United States 1942-1960: U.S. Geol. Surv., Bull. 1182-E, 90 p.

Kirkpatrick, G.E., 1974, Geology and ore deposits of the Big Creek area, Idaho and Valley Counties, Idaho: M.S. Thesis, Univ. of Idaho.

Kuizon, Lucia and Lipton, David A., 1991, Mineral Resource Appraisal of the Diamond Peak Study Area, Butte, Clark and Lemhi Counties, Idaho: MLA-11-91, US Bur. of Mines, 222 p.

Kun, P., 1974, Geology and mineral resources of the Lakeview Mining District, Idaho:

Idaho Bur. of Mines and Geol., Pam. 156.

Lasmanis, R., Nagel, J., Sturman, B.D. and Gait, R.I., 1981, Mandarinoite from the De Lamar Silver Mine, Owyhee County, Idaho, U.S.A.: Can. Min., Vol. 19, pp. 409-410.

Le Moine, D., 1959, Thorite deposits and general geology of the Hall Mountain Area, Boundary County, Idaho: M.S. Thesis, Univ. of Idaho.

Leonard, B.F., 1963, Syenite complex older than the Idaho batholith, Big Creek Quadrangle, central Idaho: U.S. Geol. Surv., Pro. Paper 450-E, pp. 93-97.

Leonard, B. F. and Marvin, R.F., 1984, Temporal Evolution of the Thunder Mountain Caldera and Related Features, Central Idaho: in Cenozoic Geology of Idaho, pp. 23-41, Idaho Bur. of Mines and Geol., Bull. 26.

Leonard, B.F., Mead, C.W. and Conklin, N., 1968, Silver-rich disseminated sulfides from a tungsten-bearing quartz lode, Big Creek District, central Idaho: U.S. Geol. Surv., Pro. Paper 594-C, 24 p.

Leonard, B.F., Desborough, G.A. and Mead, C.W., 1978, Polhemusite, a new Hg-Zn sulfide from Idaho: Am. Min., V. 63, pp. 1153-1161.

Livingston, D.C., 1919, Tungsten, cinnabar, manganese, molybdenum and tin deposits of Idaho: Univ. of Idaho School of Mines, Vol. XIV, Bull. No. 2.

Livingston, D.C. and Laney, F.B., 1920, The copper deposits of the Seven Devils and adjacent districts, Idaho Bur. of Mines and Geol., Bull. 1, 105 p.

Mackenzie, W.O., 1949, Geology and ore deposits of a section of the Beaverhead Range east of Salmon, Idaho: M.S. Thesis, Univ. of Idaho.

Mansfield, G.R., 1927, Geography, geology and mineral resources of part of southeastern Idaho: U.S. Geol. Surv., Pro. Paper 152, 453 p.

McConnel, R.H., 1961, The Bunker Hill Mine, in Guidebook to the Geology of the Coeur d'Alene Mining District: Idaho Bur. of Mines and Geol., Bull. 16, 37 p.

McNeill, A.R., III, 1971, Geology of the Hoodoo Mining District, Latah County, Idaho: M.S. Thesis, Univ. of Idaho, 99 p.

Medrano, Marjorie D.; Evans, Howard T., Jr.; Wenk, Hans-Rudolf; and Piper, David Z.; 1998, Phosphovanadylite: A New Vanadium Phosphate Mineral with a Zeolite-Type Structure: Am. Min. 83:889-895.

Menzies, M. A. and Boggs, R. C., 1993, Minerals of the Sawtooth Batholith, Idaho: Min. Rec. Vol. 24, No. 3, pp. 185-202.

Miller, D.A., Jr., 1973, Geology of the Leonia Knob area, Boundary County, Idaho: M.S. Thesis, Univ. of Idaho.

Milner, C.E., Jr., 1950, Geology and ore deposits of the Princess Blue Ribbon Mine, Camas County, Idaho : M.S. Thesis, Univ. of Idaho.

Nash, J.J. and Hahn, G.A., 1986, Volcanogenic character of sediment-hosted Co-Cu deposits in the Blackbird Mining District, Lemhi County, Idaho — An Interior Report: U.S. Geol. Surv., OFR 86-43.

Navratil, G.J., 1958, in: World news on minerals, by King, V.T.: Rocks and Minerals, Vol. 33, p. 197.

_____, 1959, in:World news on minerals, by King, V.T.: Rocks and Minerals, Vol. 34, p. 121-122.

_____, 1961, in:World news on minerals, by King, V.T.: Rocks and Minerals, Vol. 36, p 135.

Newton, J., LeMoine, D., Adams, C.N. anderson, A.L. and Shively, J.S., 1960, Study of two Idaho thorite deposits: Idaho Bur. of Mines and Geol., Pam. 122, 58 p.

Nikischer, Tony, 2004, A "New" Discovery of Philipsbornite and Segnitite: Min. News, 20-1:1,2.

Palache, C., Berman, H. and Frondel, C., 1944, The system of mineralogy of James Dwight Dana and Edward Salisbury Dana, Yale University 1837-1892, Volume I, elements, sulfides, sulfosalts, oxides: seventh ed., John Wiley & Sons, Inc., New York, 834 p.

Palache, C., Berman, H. and Frondel, C., 1951, The system of mineralogy of James Dwight Dana and Edward Salisbury Dana, Yale University 1837-1892, Volume II, halides, nitrates, borates, carbonates, sulfates, phosphates, arsenates, tungstates, molybdates, etc.: seventh ed., John Wiley & Sons, Inc., New York, 834 p.

Pattee, E.C., Van Noy, R.M. and Weldin, R.D., 1968, Beryllium resources of Idaho, Washington, Montana and Oregon: US Bureau of Mines, Rept. of Invest. 7148, 169 p.

Perry, J. Kent, 1971, Mineralogy of Silver-Bearing Drill Core from De Lamar, Idaho: Hazen Research Inc., report for Earth Resources Co., 18 p.

Personal: information obtained by the author directly from field collecting, viewing specimens in the collections of collectors and museums, and from communications with collectors, geologists and other individuals.

Piper, A.M. and Laney, F.B., 1926, Geology and metalliferous resources of the region about Silver City, Idaho: Idaho Bur. of Mines and Geol., Bull. 11, 165 p.

Pontius, J.A., 1982, The geology of the south-central Bayhorse Mining District, Custer County, Idaho: M.S. Thesis, Univ. of Idaho, 87 p.

Popoff, C.C., 1953, Hermada antimony deposit, Elmore County, Idaho: US Bureau of Mines, Rept. of Invest. 4950, 21 p.

Purdue, G.L., 1975, Geology and ore deposits of the Blackbird District, Lemhi County, Idaho: M.S. Thesis, Univ. of New Mexico.

Radford, N. and Crowley, J.A., 1981, The Bunker Hill Mine, Kellogg, Shoshone County, Idaho: Min. Rec., Vol. 12, p. 339-347.

Ransome, F.L. and Calkins, F.C. 1908, Geology and ore deposits of the Coeur d'Alene District, Shoshone County, Idaho: U.S. Geol. Surv., Prof. Paper 62, 139 p.

Ream, L.R., 1985a, Carpholite, a new mineral for the U.S.: Mineral News, Vol. 1, No. 1, p. 1.

_____, 1985b, Carpholite, more information.: Mineral News, Vol. 1, No. 5, p. 1.

_____, 1985c, Masutomilite — a recent discovery in the Sawtooth Mountains, Idaho: Mineral News, Vol. 1, No. 5, p. 1.

_____, 1989a, Wodginite—a third U.S. locality: Mineral News, Vol. 5, No. 4, p. 9.

_____, 1989b, Carpholite—the first U.S. discovery, Sawtooth Mountains, Idaho: Mineral News, Vol. 5, No. 5, p. 9.

Reed, J.C., 1939, Geology and ore deposits of the Florence Mining District, Idaho County, Idaho: Idaho Bur. of Mines and Geol., Pam. 46, 44 p.

Reid, R.R., 1961, Guidebook to the Geology of the Coeur d'Alene Mining District:Idaho Bur. of Mines and Geol., Bull. 16, 37 p.

Reid, R.R., 1963, Reconnaissance geology of the Sawtooth Range: Idaho Bur. of Mines and Geol., Pam. 129, 19p.

Reid, R.R. and Choate, R., 1960, Prospecting for Beryllium in Idaho: Idaho Bur. of Mines and Geol., Inf. Circ. 7, 19 p.

Richards, R.W., 1910, Notes on lead and copper deposits in the Bear River Range, Idaho and Utah: U.S. Geol. Surv., Bull. 470, pp. 177-187.

Richards, R.W. and Bridges, J.H., 1910, Sulphur deposits near Soda Springs, Idaho: U.S. Geol. Surv., Bull. 470, pp. 499-503.

Roberts, W.L., Rapp, G.R., Jr. and Weber, J., 1974, Encyclopedia of Minerals: Van Nostrand Reinhold, New York, 693 p.

Ross, C.P. 1925, The copper deposits near Salmon, Idaho: U.S. Geol. Surv., Bull. 774, 44 p.

_____ 1927a, Ore deposits in Tertiary lava in the Salmon River Mountains, Idaho: Idaho Bur. of Mines and Geol., Pam. 25.

_____ 1927b, The Vienna District, Blaine County, Idaho: Idaho Bur. of Mines and Geol., Pam. 21, 17 p.

_____ 1934, Geology and ore deposits of the Casto Quadrangle, Idaho: U.S. Geol. Surv., Bull. 854, 135 p.

_____ 1956, Quicksilver deposits near Weiser, Washington County, Idaho: U.S. Geol. Surv., Bull. 1042-D, p. 79-104.

_____ 1963, Geology along US Highway 93 in Idaho: Idaho Bur. of Mines and Geol., Pam. 130, 98 p.

Ross, C.P. and Shannon, E.V., 1924, Mordenite and associated minerals from Near Challis, Custer County, Idaho: US National Museum,Proceedings, Vol. 64, Art. 10, pp. 1-19.

Salman, D.S.A., 1972, Geology of the Triangle Quadrangle area, Owyhee County, Idaho: M.S. Thesis, Univ. of Idaho, 65 p.

Sampson, E. 1928, Geology and silver ore deposits of the Pend Oreille District, Idaho: Idaho Bur. of Mines and Geol., Pam. 31, 24 p.

Savage, C.N., 1958, Geology and mineral resources of Gem and Payette Counties: Idaho Bur. of Mines and Geol., Co. Rept. No. 4, 50 p.

_____ 1967, Geology and mineral resources of Bonner County, Idaho: Idaho Bur. of Mines and Geol., Co. Rept. No. 6, 131 p.

Schipper, W.B., 1955, The Tendoy Copper Queen Mine: M.S. Thesis, Univ. of Idaho.

Schrader, F.C., 1924, Molybdenite in the Rocky Bar District, Idaho: U.S. Geol. Surv., Bull. 750-F, pp. 87-99.

Shannon, E.V., 1920, An occurrence of naumannite in Idaho: Am. Journal of Science, 4th Series, Vol. 50, pp. 390-391.

_____ 1921, Owyheeite: Am. Min., Vol. 6, pp. 82-83.

_____ 1925a, Jamesonite from Slate Creek, Custer County, Idaho: Am. Min. Vol. 10, p. 194-197.

_____ 1925b, Tetradymite from the Hailey Quadrangle, Idaho: Am. Min. Vol. 10, p. 198.

_____ 1926, The minerals of Idaho: US National Museum, Bull. 131, 483 p.

Sharp, W.N. and Cavender, W.S., 1962, Geology and thorium-bearing deposits of the Lemhi Pass Area, Lemhi County, Idaho and Beaverhead County, Montana: U.S. Geol. Surv., Bull. 1126, 76 p.

Shenon, P.J., 1938, Geology and ore deposits near Murray, Idaho: Idaho Bur. of Mines and Geol., Pam. 47., 43 p.

Shenon, P.J., and Reed, J.C., 1934, Geology and Ore Deposits of the Elk City, Orogrande, Buffalo Hump, and Tenmile Districts, Idaho County, Idaho: U.S. Geol. Surv. Cir. 9, 59 p.

Shenon, P.J. and Ross, C.P., 1936, Geology and ore deposits near Edwardsburg and Thunder Mountain, Idaho: Idaho Bur. of Mines and Geol., Pam. 44, 45 p.

Shockey, P.N., 1957, Reconnaissance geology of the Leesburg Quadrangle, Lemhi County, Idaho: Idaho Bur. of Mines and Geol., Pam. 113.

Shoup, G.E., 1953, in: World news on minerals, by King, V.T.: Rocks and Minerals, Vol. 28, p 263-264.

Sidler, A.G., 1957, The origin of heavy minerals in the Boise Basin, Idaho: M.S. Thesis,

Univ. of Idaho.

Sinkankas, J., 1959, Gemstones of North America: Van Nostrand Reinhold Co., 675 p.

_____ 1970, Prospecting for Gemstones and Minerals: Van Nostrand Reinhold, New York, 397 pp.

_____ 1976, Gemstones of North America: in Two Volumes, Vol. II: Van Nostrand Reinhold Co., 494 p.

Soregaroli, A.E., 1961, Geology of the McKim Creek area, Lemhi County, Idaho: M.S. Thesis, Univ. of Idaho.

Sorenson, R.E., 1927, The geology and ore deposits of the South Mountain Mining District, Owyhee County, Idaho: Idaho Bur. of Mines and Geol., Pam. 22, 47 p.

Stiles, C.A., 1976, Geology and alteration of the West Fork of Mayfield Creek area, Custer County, Idaho: M.S. Thesis, Univ. of Idaho.

Stinchfield, R. 1979, Collecting in Northern Idaho; Rock & Gem, July 1979, p. 16-18, 20-22.

Thune, H.W., 1941, Mineralogy of the ore deposits of the western region of the Little Eightmile District, Lemhi County, Idaho: M.S. Thesis, Univ. of Idaho, 49 p.

Trites, A.G. and Tooker, E.W., 1953, Uranium and thorium deposits in east-central Idaho and southwestern Montana: U.S. Geol. Surv., Bull. 988-H, pp. 157-209.

Tschernich, R.W. and Wise, W.S., 1982, Paulingite: variations in composition: Am. Min., V. 67, pp. 799-803.

Tuchek, E.T. and Ridenour, J., 1981, Economic appraisal of the Boulder-Pioneer Wilderness study area, Blaine and Custer Counties, Idaho: U.S. Geol, Surv., Bull. 1497-D, pp. 81-303.

Umpleby, J.B., 1913a, Geology and ore deposits of Lemhi County, Idaho: U.S. Geol. Surv., Bull. 528, 182 p.

_____ 1913b, Some ore deposits in northwestern Custer County, Idaho: U.S. Geol. Surv., Bull. 539, 104 p.

_____ 1914, Ore deposits in the Sawtooth Quadrangle, Blaine and Custer Counties, Idaho: U.S. Geol. Surv., Bull. 580-K, pp. 221-249.

_____ 1917, Geology and ore deposits of the Mackay Region, Idaho: U.S. Geol. Surv., Pro. Paper 97, 129 p.

Umpleby, J.B. and Jones, E.L., Jr., 1923, Geology and Ore Deposits of Shoshone County, Idaho: U.S. Geol. Surv., Bull. 732, 156 p.

Umpleby, J.B., Westgate, L.G. and Ross, C.P., 1930, Geology and ore deposits of the wood River region, Idaho, U.S. Geol. Surv., Bull. 814, 250 p.

van Laer, C. and Ream, L.R., 1986, Sawtooth Mountains, Boise, Custer and Elmore Counties, Idaho: Mineral News, Vol. 2, No. 1, p. 5-7, No. 2, p . 5-7, No. 3, p. 7-9, No. 4, p. 5-8.

Van Noy, Ronald M.; Ridenour, James; Zilka, Nicholas T.; Federspiel, Frank E.; Evans, Robert K.; Tuchek, Ernest T. and McMahan, Arel B., 1986, Economic appraisal of the Eastern Part of the Sawtooth National Recreation Area, Idaho, in Sawtooth National Recreation Area, US Geol. Surv., Bull. 1545, pp. 239472.

Vhay, J.S., 1948, Cobalt-copper deposits of the Blackbird District, Lemhi County, Idaho: Strategic Minerals Investigations, Prelim. Rept. 3-219.

Wagner, W.R.A., 1939, The geology and ore deposits of the Rocky Bar District, Idaho: M.S. Thesis, Univ. of Idaho.

Walker, W.P., Jr., 1965, Geology of a part of the Owyhee Mountains south of Silver City, Idaho: M.S. Thesis, Univ. of Idaho, 59 p.

Weiss, P.L. and Schmitt, L.J., Jr., 1972, Mineral resources of the Salmon River Breaks

Primitive Area, Idaho: U.S. Geol. Surv., Bull. 1353-C.

White, D.E., 1940, Antimony deposits of a part of the Yellow Pine District, Valley County, Idaho: U.S. Geol. Surv., Bull. 922-I, 279 p.

Young, E.J. and Powers, H.A., 1960, Chevkinite in volcanic ash: Am. Min., Vol. 45, pp. 875-881.

Zilka, N.T., undated, Mineral Resources of the Bruneau River drainage, Idaho: US Bureau of Mines, Report for Wild and Scenic River Study.

Index

Museum of North Idaho Publications

PO Box 812 * Coeur d'Alene, ID 83816-0812
Order by email: dd@museumni.org or phone 208-664-3448 Tues. - Sat.
See covers and read reviews at http://www.museumni.org/books/books.htm

Bayview and Lakeview: And Other Early Settlements on Southern Lake Pend Oreille
By Linda Hackbarth
Paperback $14.95 ISBN 0-9723356-2-5

The Dalton Story
   By Marvin Shadduck, 56 pages, 5 1/2" x 8 1/2"
   Paperback $10.00 no ISBN

From Hell to Heaven
   Death Related Mining Accidents in North Idaho
   by Gene Hyde, 224 pages, 8 1/2" x 11"
   Paperback $19.95 ISBN 0-9643647-9-4

Idaho Minerals 2nd Edition
Revised and Updated
   By Lanny Ream, 380 pages, 6" x 9"
   Paperback $24.95 ISBN 0-9723356-3-3

In All The West No Place Like This
A Pictorial History of the Coeur d'Alene Region
   by Dorothy Dahlgren & Simone Kincaid
   254 Pages, 8 1/2" x 11"
   Hardcover $34.95 ISBN 0-9643647-0-0
   Paperback $24.95 ISBN 0-9643647-1-9

Kootenai Chronicles
A History of Kootenai County Vol. 1
   by Robert Singletary, 52 pages, 11" x 17"
   Paperback $10.00 ISBN 0-9643647-4-3

Milwaukee Road in Idaho
A Guide to Sites and Locations Revised
   by Stanley Johnson, 360 pages, 6" x 9"
   Paperback $19.95 ISBN 0-9723356-0-9

The Milwaukee Road Olympian
A Ride to Remember
   by Stanley Johnson, 334 pages, 8 1/2" x 11"
   Hardcover $39.95 ISBN 0-9643647-7-8

North Fork of the Coeur d'Alene River
   edited by Bert Russell 440 pages, 5 1/2" x 8 1/2"
   Paperback $14.95 0-9723356-1-7

Swiftwater People
Lives of Old Timers on the Upper St. Joe & St. Maries rivers
   edited by Bert Russell, 448 pages, 5 1/2" x 8 1/2"
   Hardcover $23.95 ISBN 0-930344-05-7
   Paperback $13.95 ISBN 0-930344-02-2

Up the Swiftwater
A Pictorial History of the Colorful Upper St. Joe River Country
   by Sandra Crowell & David Asleson
   149 pages, 8 1/2" x 11"
   Hardcover $29.95 ISBN 0-9643647-2-7
   Paperback $19.95 ISBN 0-9643647-3-5

White Pine Route
The History of the Washington, Idaho and Montana Railway Company
   by Thomas E. Burg, 400 pages, , 8 1/2" x 11"
   Hardcover $49.95. ISBN 0-9643647-8-6

Wildflowers of the Inland Northwest
   Idaho, Montana, Washington, Oregon, B. C. & Alberta
   by Ralph and Peggy Faust, 156 pages, 6" x 9"
   Paperback $15.95 ISBN 0-9643647-6-X

About the Author

Lanny Ream has been interested in minerals all his life and carried an early interest in minerals, rocks and fossils with him to college, earning a Master's Degree in Economic Geology. After working for several years as a mineral exploration geologist, then as a geologist and mineral examiner for the Bureau of Land Management and US Forest Service, Lanny decided to continue working with mineral-related subjects. He founded *Mineral News*, a monthly newsletter for mineral collectors, which he published and edited for more than 18 years before selling it. He continues to explore and write about mineral localities of the Pacific Northwest with an emphasis on the mineralogy of the states of Idaho and Montana.

This second edition of *Idaho Minerals* is the result of an additional 15 years of studying the mineralogy of Idaho after publishing the first edition in 1989. This volume shows his dedication to this subject by the identification and description of several new mineral localities and the discovery of several minerals identified for the first time in Idaho due to his field work and studies.

Other books by the author include the guide to Washington minerals and lapidary materials: *Gems and Minerals of Washington* (which now after 27 of publication has been rewritten by a new author); *Northwest Volcanoes* (a guide to volcanoes in the Northwest states and British Columbia) and *Gem and Mineral Collector's Guide to Idaho*.